PSYCHOSIS IN CHILDHOOD AND ADOLESCENCE

Psychosis in Childhood and Adolescence offers an in-depth examination of the nature of psychosis, its risk factors, and its manifestations in children and adolescents who experience a continuum of emotional disorders. The chapters present a hopeful, research-based framework for treatment. They emphasize combined treatment that is based on psychodynamic and cognitive behavioral psychotherapy principles, pharmacological interventions, and supportive family approaches that reflect the vulnerabilities and resources of the individual child. This text highlights the importance of thorough assessment and the need for long-term treatment that facilitates the psychotic child's healthy maturation. Readers will benefit from the case examples that illustrate the complexity of psychosis and the discussions of diagnostic and treatment issues as presented by experienced clinicians and researchers.

James B. McCarthy, PhD, ABPP, is Director of Field Training and Associate Professor of Psychology, Pace University PsyD program in School-Clinical Child Psychology, and Clinical Professor of Psychology, Adelphi University Postgraduate Program in Child, Adolescent, and Family Psychotherapy. Formerly the Director of Psychology at Queens Children's Psychiatric Center in New York, he has published extensively in professional journals. His previous books include *Death Anxiety: The Loss of the Self; Adolescence and Character Disturbance;* and *Adolescent Development and Psychopathology.*

"Although the signs and symptoms of psychosis in childhood allow the clinician to appreciate the breadth and range of these conditions, the underlying causes remain elusive. McCarthy and his colleagues summarize the current understanding of these issues in an informative and useful fashion. Through reading this volume, mental health professionals can provide more effective treatments to this high risk population of youth. This often overlooked and important topic is clearly described in this volume."

—Victor M. Fornari, MD, Director, Division of Child & Adolescent Psychiatry, The Zucker Hillside Hospital; Professor of Psychiatry & Pediatrics, Hofstra North Shore LIJ School of Medicine

"With the increased frequency of mass murders due to poorly diagnosed and treated psychosis in youth, McCarthy's timely book calls for quality mental health care for these youth. The book's clinical examples highlight that comprehensive assessment of evidence-based biological factors, as well as psychosocial/environmental factors impact the inner life and development of psychosis. Most importantly, in contrast to currently employed superficial revolving door, symptom-based psychopharmacological treatment, the book argues for sensitive, thoughtful, individually designed, and multifaceted long-term treatment that includes psychotherapy for psychotic youth. This book is essential for mental health professionals looking for quality care approaches for adolescents with psychosis."

—Rochelle Caplan, MD, Emeritus Professor, Semel Institute for Neuroscience and Human Behavior, Department of Psychiatry, UCLA

"This is a gracefully written book authored by child psychiatrists who see the child patient with psychosis as an individual situated in a family context, who has patterns of looking at the world (cognitive schemas) and patterns of relating with others (patterns of attachment), which are disturbed by their symptoms. McCarthy and his colleagues build upon knowledge about brain circuits and genes, and move beyond nosology, to consider the lived experience of these children and their families, and how that should inform thoughtful and personalized care."

—Cheryl M Corcoran, MD, Assistant Professor of Psychiatry, Columbia University; Research Scientist, New York State Psychiatric Institute

"In this comprehensive volume, Dr. McCarthy has provided mental health professionals with an invaluable and highly practical resource that bring clarity and focus to the diagnosis and treatment of psychosis in children and adolescents. I highly recommend this book for therapists, educators, and graduate students who work with this challenging population."

—David Pelcovitz, PhD, Straus Chair in Psychology and Education, Azrieli Graduate School, Yeshiva University

"McCarthy presents an impressive and important comprehensive review of diagnostic conceptualizations and treatment of psychosis in children with particular attention to controversial and complex issues encountered by clinicians. The integration of clearly presented theoretical underpinnings with an examination of current research advances the reader's understanding and treatment of psychosis. This book is an invaluable text and resource for students and seasoned practitioners alike."

—Francine Conway, PhD, Professor and Chair, Derner Institute for Advanced Psychological Studies, Adelphi University

PSYCHOSIS IN CHILDHOOD AND ADOLESCENCE

Edited by James B. McCarthy

NEW YORK AND LONDON

First published 2015
by Routledge
711 Third Avenue, New York, NY 10017

and by Routledge
27 Church Road, Hove, East Sussex BN3 2FA

Routledge is an imprint of the Taylor & Francis Group, an informa business

Library of Congress Cataloging-in-Publication Data
A catalog record for this title has been requested

ISBN: 978-0-415-82105-6 (hbk)
ISBN: 978-0-415-82106-3 (pbk)
ISBN: 978-0-203-56920-7 (ebk)

Typeset in Bembo
by Apex CoVantage, LLC

Printed and bound in the United States of America
by Edwards Brothers Malloy

CONTENTS

CONTRIBUTORS

Jimmy Choi, PhD
Columbia University Medical Center

Zana Dobroshi, MD, PhD
New York City Children's Center, Queens Campus

Allan M. Eisenberg, PhD
Brooklyn College, City University of New York

Andrew J. Gerber, MD, PhD
Columbia University College of Physicians & Surgeons

Gladys Branly Guarton, PhD
Adelphi University Postgraduate Program in Psychoanalysis & Psychotherapy

Endra K. Henry, PhD
New York City Children's Center, Queens Campus

Shelby Inouye, BS
University of Southern California

Emily Kline, MA
University of Maryland, Baltimore Campus

Aaron Krasner, MD
Yale University School of Medicine

Christiana Laitner, PhD
New York University Child Studies Center

Maria G. Master, MD, JD
New York City Children's Center, Bronx Campus

James B. McCarthy, PhD
Pace University

Littal Melnik, MD
New York City Children's Center, Bronx Campus

Jon Rogove, PhD
New York City Children's Center, Bronx Campus

Jason Schiffman, PhD
University of Maryland, Baltimore Campus

K. Mark Sossin, PhD
Pace University

Meritxell Fortea Vila, MD
Universitat de Valencia, Fundacion Alicia Koplowitz, Spain

Dirk Winter, MD, PhD
Columbia University College of Physicians & Surgeons

PREFACE

The suffering of emotionally disturbed children and adolescents with severe mental health disorders rarely garners a great deal of public attention. Their parents and caretakers frequently struggle with anxiety while trying to summon up sufficient hope for the future to allow them to persevere. It can be particularly devastating for family members to interact with children whose disorganized behavior and deteriorating thought processes begin to indicate that they are experiencing a psychotic mental state. Through collaborative partnerships with parents and other family members, professionals who work with psychotic children and adolescents strive to offer sensitive, age-appropriate treatment in spite of continuing questions about mental illness and the limitations of present-day clinical practice.

There has been controversy in the scientific literature about the origins of psychotic disorders in childhood and the relative importance of psychological stressors and biologically influenced problems with affect and cognition. Investigations of the developmental trajectories of psychosis from childhood to adulthood have produced variable results. While classifications of core symptom patterns, particularly in schizophrenia, have been clearly delineated, the underlying causal mechanisms for psychotic reactions and syndromes in childhood have not been thoroughly defined. Successful treatment with psychotic children and adolescents entails multidisciplinary efforts and a continuum of care that needs to include careful assessment, ongoing psychotherapy, and support for the child and the family. Optimal psychotherapeutic approaches incorporate multiple modalities, coordinated with interventions that address the social and behavioral problems that can be associated with psychotic disorders. Child and family clinicians face wide-ranging challenges in trying to accomplish these goals, including the limits of scientific knowledge about psychotic disorders in children and the serious shortcomings of the mental health care system.

This work provides the chapter authors with an opportunity to build a conceptual framework for understanding historically changing perspectives of psychosis and to synthesize significant research studies about its manifestations in children. As experienced clinicians who have had an in-depth exposure to youth with very severe psychiatric illness, the authors summarize the current understanding of childhood psychosis. They offer their reflections on diagnostic schema and practice parameters and caution about the danger of ignoring individual differences and the subjectivity of children's fluctuating psychotic states. They suggest that creative engagement in psychotherapy requires attunement with the ways in which psychotic symptoms and disorders become intertwined with the child's emotional conflicts and developmental processes. On the whole, the authors argue for applying integrated psychodynamic and cognitive behavioral psychotherapy principles and the judicious use of pharmacological interventions with coordinated services. Even though clinical work with psychotic children and adolescents can be very rewarding, the complexity of psychotic phenomena, the limited extent of contemporary knowledge about early onset psychotic disorders, and the inadequacies of the health care system all present particular challenges for practicing clinicians.

The following chapters are organized so that readers will first be presented with an introduction to developmental psychopathology concepts and a general overview of the lack of certainty about etiology. Uncertainties about psychotic phenomenology persist in light of the multiple pathways that influence psychotic symptoms and disorders in children and the lack of research about treating complex disorders that co-occur with psychosis. Changing diagnostic concepts are presented in a historical context and re-evaluated in terms of the recent research literature. As the construct of "vulnerability to psychosis" is introduced, increasing emphasis is placed on the numerous risk factors and early precursors of psychotic disorders. The chapters on psychotic disorders include careful syntheses of etiological factors, clinical features, diagnostic controversies, and contemporary treatment approaches. The chapters endorse the importance of medication, integrative approaches to psychotherapy, and the need to exceed a narrow focus on symptom remission in favor of trying to restore psychotic youth to healthy maturation in all spheres of functioning.

ACKNOWLEDGEMENTS

What causes psychosis in children? How does the interaction of psychological stressors and biological factors stimulate the onset of psychotic symptoms? Can effective treatment restore psychotic children to healthy maturation and age-appropriate functioning? The chapter authors have worked diligently to address these challenging questions. Their work reflects a careful synthesis of research findings, a clear conceptualization of diagnostic controversies, and an analysis of the current treatment methods in their areas of study. I'm grateful to the authors for their efforts and their insightful observations about this volume's evolution.

Many individuals have contributed to my thinking about the nature of psychosis in children, including the emotionally disturbed children and adolescents I've gotten to know in the course of my clinical responsibilities. Many other people have helped greatly with the development of this work. I'd like to thank the following colleagues for their longstanding support: Drs. Leon Anisfeld, Allan Eisenberg, Janet Fisher, Gladys Guarton, Spyros Orfanos, John Ozehosky, Sophia Richman, and David Rube, and I'm very grateful to my sister, Loreen McCarthy, for her valuable suggestions. I also owe a great deal to the clinical staff at Queens Children's Psychiatric Center, currently known as New York City Children's Center, Queens Campus, in Bellerose, New York; the clinicians at Sagamore Children's Psychiatric Center in Dix Hills, New York; and my colleagues on the faculty of the Pace University Psychology Department, Manhattan Campus; the Columbia University College of Physicians and Surgeons, Division of Child Psychiatry; and the Adelphi University Postgraduate Program in Child, Adolescent, and Family Therapy.

Following general chapters in Part I that outline changing concepts of psychosis and the precursors of psychosis, specific disorders are considered in-depth in Part II. Well-informed insights about the course of psychotic illness in children are balanced by the recognition that, despite treatment advances, universally effective treatment for the continuum of psychotic disorders has yet to be developed. Part III includes representative examples of the difficult dilemmas mental health clinicians face in providing care for children and adolescents with psychotic features. I appreciate that the authors have chosen different approaches to accomplish these aims as they juxtapose historically important treatment methods with scrutiny of recent research findings about early onset psychosis.

The editorial staff at Routledge, Taylor & Francis have steadily maintained their interest in childhood-onset psychosis while offering their support. I particularly appreciate Elizabeth Lotto's help with the development of the manuscript and George Zimmar's guidance about bringing it to completion.

INTRODUCTION

The Complexity of Psychosis

James B. McCarthy

Psychosis represents a fluctuating state of anxiety-laden psychological experience and poor reality testing that is frequently accompanied by symptomatic behavior. For several hundred years, scientists have tried to demystify psychosis and to differentiate the characteristics of brief periods of psychotic symptoms from those of acute illness and long-lasting psychotic disorders. Only in the last few decades has there been significant progress in identifying multiform neurobiological and environmental influences on psychosis and the importance of early assessment and treatment. At this point, the onset of psychotic symptoms and the emergence of psychotic disorders in children and adolescents are still largely unexplained. In some cases, both childhood-onset or adolescent-onset schizophrenia and mood disorders with psychosis reflect relatively stable, severe patterns of illness, which can impede the child's maturational processes. Providing compassionate, effective psychotherapy and appropriate medication for psychotic youth requires the willingness to apply evolving scientific knowledge with an acceptance of considerable uncertainty and the recognition that the stigma associated with mental illness has far from disappeared. Effective treatment planning entails reconciling the need for research-informed treatment guidelines with the realization that the individual vulnerabilities of psychotic children and adolescents can never be completely illuminated simply by symptom clusters and diagnostic categories. By delineating the complexity of psychosis through an examination of empirical research findings and integrative treatment principles, this work aims to acknowledge both the dedicated family members who raise chronically mentally ill children, and the mental health professionals who contribute to their care.

Various scientific and applied disciplines advance knowledge about biological and environmental influences on psychopathology. Research concerning the genesis of psychiatric problems has entailed a continuum of insights into basic science and innovative technologies that allow for more comprehensive explanations about etiology. Cognitive neuroscience studies are gradually making it possible to correlate specific brain mechanisms with a spectrum of mental states that become activated in severe psychological disturbance. Increasing evidence about early exposure to excessive levels of stress hormones corroborates that adverse childhood environments can have very deleterious effects on brain and personality development, intensifying the overall risk of susceptibility to mental illness. Rather than uncovering singular configurations of genetic predispositions for psychosis, research is steadily pointing to heterogeneous etiologies and complex interactions between environmental factors and genetic vulnerabilities. Increasingly sophisticated technology continues to discern variable genetic mutations underlying the vulnerability for childhood-onset and adult-onset psychosis as well as associated links to multiple disorders.

Among biological influences on psychosis, genetic factors account for some of the overall variance in childhood- or adolescent-onset schizophrenia, bipolar illness, and depression with psychosis. At least 11 different gene combinations have been specifically associated with schizophrenia (Crespi, Stead, and Elliot, 2010), and rare mutations seem to be present in a substantial number of individuals who develop schizophrenia (McClellan and King, 2010). The results from family genetic mapping studies similarly suggest that the permutations of genetic influences on mental illness don't necessarily correlate with some of the present categories of psychiatric diagnoses. Diathesis-stress models further denote that poorly understood interactions between genetic aberrations, functional and structural changes in brain mechanisms, and environmental risk factors that induce psychological stress can easily stimulate the onset of symptoms associated with more than one disorder. Recent evidence is demonstrating that abuse and neglect suffered in childhood has neurobiological consequences that might include increased vulnerability for schizophrenia and bipolar disorder in adulthood. However, in contrast to the advances in defining biological and genetic influences on psychosis in adulthood, few studies have thoroughly examined negative life events, severe trauma, and chronic family stressors as factors that might contribute to the onset of psychotic disorders in children. Treatment guidelines need to take into consideration the widespread heterogeneity of psychotic disorders in children and adolescents, their ties to co-occurring disorders, and the crucial importance of listening to the individual patient's experience of psychosis. Increased understanding of the course of symptom patterns in psychotic children and adolescents has been accompanied by questions about how to help them transcend the manifestations of their illness without compromised functioning.

Risk Factors and Vulnerability to Psychosis

In recent decades, there has been increasing curiosity about the risk factors for psychosis and the outcome of psychotic disorders in children and adolescents with different types of emotional disturbance. The relative significance of the biological factors that contribute to the etiology of psychosis continues to be the subject of controversy, along with the criteria for distinguishing correlational from causal variables. Purely psychogenic theories about the onset of psychotic syndromes in children and adolescents are lacking in evidence. However, a great deal is unknown about the origins of psychosis, especially in relationship to the aftereffects of cumulative trauma and chronic anxiety. Converging lines of evidence suggest a "vulnerability to psychosis" hypothesis and value of assessing not only intrinsic risk factors such as genetic background, but also social and environmental risk factors like marijuana use and social adversity, particularly exposure to stress, violence, and prolonged maltreatment by close family members. In addition, some studies of youth with schizophrenia suggest that developmental stressors and anxiety related to conflictual family communication might contribute to the onset of psychotic symptoms. With adolescents, stressful life events and heightened sensitivity to negative emotions due to early trauma can likewise contribute to the severity of mood disorders and their association with episodes of psychosis.

For adolescents and young adults, substance abuse frequently co-occurs with psychosis, increasing the risk of experiencing repeated psychotic episodes. Research has established that if adolescent marijuana users are genetically vulnerable to psychosis, they will tend to have their first psychotic episodes at earlier ages and there will be a relationship between the persistence of their use and the frequency of their psychotic episodes. For these unfortunately vulnerable youth, marijuana use constitutes a serious risk factor for the continuum of psychotic symptoms and disorders (Semple, McIntosh, and Lawrie, 2005). In fact, studies suggest that marijuana use can impede frontal lobe maturation, increasing the likelihood of schizophrenia among high-risk adolescents. Substance abuse also generally adds to the risk of recurrent episodes of mania among youth with bipolar disorder. Although not all of the key underlying biological mechanisms are certain, marijuana-related dopamine dysregulation seems to give rise to some of the psychotic symptoms in schizophrenia (Kuepper, Morrison, van Os, Murray, Kenis, and Henquet, 2011). With the exception of a number of studies about trauma variables, there have been few investigations of the interaction between psychological stressors and social factors that contribute to the onset of psychotic symptoms in children and adolescents. Outcome studies of the effectiveness of combining medication with multiple forms of psychotherapy for psychotic children are also lacking in number and scientific rigor.

In the early 20th century, Emil Kraepelin (1915) made the twofold observation that *dementia praecox* could begin in childhood and that the prevalence rates of both *dementia praecox* and manic depression increase significantly following puberty. In 1911, Bleuler speculated that numerous psychotic illnesses in children involve a gradually deteriorating course. In keeping with the views of other researchers in child psychopathology in the 1930s and 1940s, Lauretta Bender argued for a developmental explanation of schizophrenia as the genetically influenced result of abnormal brain maturation. In her theory, a variety of aberrant neurobiological patterns beginning in the prenatal stages foreshadowed the initial signs of schizophrenia in childhood, based on the assumption that the symptoms of schizophrenia would be expressed differently during later maturational stages (Bender and Grugett, 1956). Bender's longitudinal research studies and her emphasis on the importance of anxiety in psychotic disorganization in children and adolescents, and its interplay with biologically based vulnerabilities, was consistent with her recommendation for combining different forms of psychotherapy with psychopharmacology.

Despite Bender's prescience in anticipating some aspects of the currently accepted neurodevelopmental theory of schizophrenia (Weinberger, 1987), her hypotheses are no longer endorsed. Like Kanner's (1949) views of infantile autism, her constructs of childhood psychosis were criticized for being overly inclusive and for lacking an empirically sound foundation because of their failure to use narrowly defined diagnostic criteria.

In the 1970s, studies of psychosis in children and adults, especially schizophrenia, were criticized for their heavy reliance on clinical descriptions that lacked operational definitions (Fish and Ritvo, 1979). Kolvin (1971) and Rutter (1972) were among the first to demonstrate convincingly that childhood schizophrenia and autism are distinct disorders. Other studies in the 1970s and 1980s established that there is a much greater continuity between childhood-onset and adulthood-onset schizophrenia than had previously been found. Around the same period, the possibility of children experiencing severe mood disorders as well as mood disorders with psychotic features was also established. Contemporary hypotheses about the etiology of psychotic disorders point to partially unknown gene-environment interactions, structural and functional brain abnormalities, such as atypical changes in cortical volume and hippocampal system vulnerability (Mittai and Walker, 2011), and biologically based continuities between developing signs of schizophrenia or mood disturbance with psychosis in childhood and adolescence and the symptoms experienced by those with adult-onset psychotic illnesses (Doyle, Wilens, Kwon, Seidman, Faraone, Fried, Swezey, Snyder, and Biederman, 2005). Current etiological models of psychosis stress the importance of multiple risk factors, comorbid features, and the viability of diathesis-stress models that emphasize the complexity and mutuality of interacting developmental pathways.

Developmental Pathways and Psychosis

In the history of the study of psychopathology, clinical descriptions of hallucinations, delusions, thought disorder, and disorganized behavior were replaced by the use of more carefully defined diagnostic criteria for psychosis. Reliance on standardized diagnostic criteria has facilitated research on the biological and psychological factors that might contribute to the onset and continuance of psychotic disturbance. As evidence about the etiology of psychotic disorders has gradually accumulated, there has been a heightened awareness of the need for multifactorial developmental models that take into account the social and cognitive domains impacted by psychotic processes. Longitudinal research and empirical studies of neurobiological models of psychosis in childhood and adolescence indicate that looking for a one-dimensional explanation about the etiology of psychotic disorders will remain an illusory goal. For example, when prospective cohort study data in the United Kingdom were analyzed to assess whether autism spectrum disorder traits could predict core positive symptoms of psychosis in adolescence, even though the results suggested that there might be shared neurodevelopmental origins for autism and psychosis, the youth with psychotic features were much more likely to be from families with greater social disadvantage and more adverse life events (Sullivan, Raj, Golding, Zammit, and Steer, 2013). In addition, as the links between childhood trauma and first episodes of psychosis have been carefully examined, a multifactorial relationship has been hypothesized. Adults with psychosis have significantly greater histories of childhood trauma than others, and there seems to be a clear association between trauma exposure in childhood; cognitive weaknesses in attention, concentration, language ability, processing speed; and changes in brain structure, especially amygdala volume in first-episode psychosis (Aas, Navari, Gibbs, Mondelli, Fisher, Morgan, Morgan, MacCabe, Reichenberg, Zanelli, Fearon, Jones, Murray, Pariante, and Dazan, 2012). Among adults with severe bipolar illness, including those with psychosis, there is also a prevalence of histories of childhood trauma. As these studies illustrate, achievements in discerning neurobiological influences on the etiology of psychotic symptoms and disorders can't be fully separated from the assessment of environmental and cognitive factors and the psychological impact of negative life experiences. In recent decades, the developmental psychopathology perspective has become ascendant as a multidisciplinary effort to integrate the scientific fields that assess psychopathology. From its shared focus on etiology to its emphasis on the evolution of symptom trends from childhood and adolescence to adulthood, developmental psychopathology research highlights multidetermined atypical developmental patterns that are characterized by maladaptation and impairment (Cicchetti, 1984; Hinshaw, 2013).

Across cultures, the incidence of primary psychotic disorders in children and adolescents is low, with much higher prevalence rates for mood disorders with psychosis than for schizophrenia. Studies suggest that the prevalence of schizophrenia prior to age 12 may be less than 1 in 10,000, but discrete psychotic symptoms are fairly common in many emotional and behavioral disorders. Psychotic disorders in children and adolescents are frequently associated with premorbid signs of the disorder and difficulties in social and academic functioning, even though multidisciplinary, early intervention efforts can have very positive effects on later outcomes. When a cross-sectional study of prevalence rates was done with adolescents in central Scotland over a three-year period, 5.9 out of 100,000 at-risk youth were identified as having a psychotic disorder, with more than half of the adolescents having severe impairments in global functioning. Many also had significant side effects from treatment with antipsychotic medications (Boeing, Murray, Pelosi, MacCabe, Blackwood, and Wrate, 2007). In general, longitudinal studies about the vulnerability for psychosis and its continuity over time yield fairly modest results, except for children who clearly have childhood-onset schizophrenia spectrum disorders.

In Meehl's (1962; 1990) influential model of personality disorder traits that reflect a proneness to schizophrenia, only 10% of the individuals who develop schizotypy—a type of personality organization that represents a strong latent liability for schizophrenia—will eventually experience schizophrenia later in life. In more recent studies of schizotypal personality disorder in childhood and childhood-onset schizophrenia, 78% to 89% of the children continued to demonstrate schizophrenia spectrum disorders over the course of a three year follow-up (Asarnow, 2005). A number of longitudinal investigators of adolescents with an onset of schizophrenia before age 18 have shown that neurocognitive weaknesses, especially in attention, verbal memory, and working memory, remain stable over time and are associated with worse outcomes in functioning (Cervellione, Burdick, Cottone, Rhinewine, and Kumra, 2007).

About a quarter of adults with borderline personality disorder experience symptoms of psychosis, but follow-up studies of children with borderline personality disorder features indicate that even if they are subject to brief psychotic decompensations as a result of severe stress and trauma (Zelkowitz, Paris, Gudzer, Feldman, Roy, and Rosaval, 2004), very few of them will develop psychotic disorders during adulthood. Although mood lability is extremely common in most children and adolescents with borderline pathology, and long-term hypomanic mood dysregulation is associated with psychotic features in adults with borderline personality (Benvenuti, Rucci, Ravani, Gonnelli, Frank, Balestrieri, Sbrana, Dell'Osso, and Cassano, 2005), not all borderline children and adolescents demonstrate severe mood dysregulation problems as adults. Unfortunately, high levels of borderline symptoms in early adolescence have been associated with lower academic and occupational outcome and the attainment of fewer developmental milestones of adulthood over a 20-year period (Winograd, Cohen, and Chen, 2008). Much has been learned about the risk factors for psychosis in general and the similarities and differences between its onset in childhood and its onset in adulthood, but the relationship between coexisting personality disorders with psychotic features in childhood and those in adulthood has yet to be clearly illuminated. In contrast to the research on schizophrenia, the continuities between childhood trauma, mood disorder–related psychosis, and their manifestations in adulthood are even less well established (Jacobsen and Rapoport, 1998). Fully comprehensive explanations about the course of childhood psychosis and completely satisfactory treatments for psychotic children and adolescents have yet to be developed.

The diagnosis of a psychotic disorder in a child or an adolescent can easily be the result of insufficient attention being paid to the co-occurrence of severe emotional disturbance and trauma and the boundaries of our knowledge about psychosis. Current nosological categories of primary psychotic disorders generally include those within the schizophrenia spectrum; brief or schizophreniform disorders; depression or bipolar illness–related psychotic disorders; and those related to the experience of delusions. The recent publication of the latest, revised *Diagnostic and Statistical Manual of Mental Disorders* (DSM 5) has done little to erode serious concerns about what constitutes mental illness and dissatisfaction with the validity of a purely symptom-based classification system without reference to the neurobiological underpinnings of emotional disorders and the social contexts in which they evolve. In addition, the early precursors of a number of severe disorders, such as schizophrenia and bipolar illness with psychosis, often include nonspecific signs during childhood that can overlap with many forms of disturbance. Longitudinal investigations and literature reviews point to the need for avoiding both overdiagnoses and underdiagnoses of psychotic disorders as well as assiduously taking into account the complexity of psychotic phenomena that can co-exist with many psychiatric disorders in children and adolescents.

Difficulties differentiating psychotic symptoms from comorbid disorders and the prevalence of comorbidity with psychosis further complicate the need for accurate, reliable assessment. The co-occurrence of two or three disorders with psychotic symptoms is routine in clinical treatment settings, and about 68% of youth with early onset schizophrenia have at least one comorbid disorder (Russell, Bott, and Sammons, 1989). In a study of over sixty 16- to 28-year-old individuals in Australia who were treated for a first episode of psychosis, 69% had at least one Axis I psychiatric disorder prior to or during their first episode of psychosis with a predominance of anxiety and mood disorders and substance abuse (Bendall, Allott, Johnson, Jackson, Killackey, Harrigan, and McGorry, 2008). Appropriate treatment for psychotic youth rests on integrating developmental theory, the vast array of pertinent research findings about diagnosis and comorbidity, and the range of psychotherapy, supportive, and pharmacological interventions that might be suitable for a particular child. However, as research insights burgeon, translating findings into individually tailored treatment strategies doesn't occur automatically. In the midst of the efforts to apply relevant research findings and to expand nosological classifications to include dimensional features in diagnosis, contemporary clinicians have to steadfastly fight with the ethos of cost containment in order to sustain necessary assessment and intensive long-term treatment with chronically, severely disturbed patients. Both positive and negative symptoms of psychosis can be associated with disruptions in development and impaired functioning in children and teenagers, while innovative psychotherapy and pharmacological treatment interventions with psychotic disorders are slow to develop.

From developmental psychopathology and diagnostic perspectives, it is essential for child practitioners to refute reductionist thinking about psychotic mental states by recognizing the interaction of diverse developmental processes that could possibly contribute to the overt expression of psychiatric disorders. Maintaining a developmental perspective about the origins and the progression of psychotic disorders in children is in keeping with the evolution of clinical studies from purely observational to more scientifically designed investigations that have been guided by a range of etiological models (Cicchetti, 1990; Cicchetti and Cohen, 2006). As models of etiology that derive from brain research and the study of psychosis in adulthood are being evaluated, contemporary views of psychosis in childhood and adolescence emphasize the mutuality of interrelated antecedents that seem to stimulate the emergence and the continuance of psychotic features. In spite of considerable research having been done on the structural and biochemical changes and the brain connectivity alterations that are correlated with psychotic disorders, much is still unknown about their unfolding during childhood and adolescence. Furthermore, risk factors for psychosis, such as having a strong family history of schizophrenia or severe mood disorders with psychosis, can contribute to etiology independently or through myriad interactive combinations. Study findings regularly imply that risk factors for early onset psychosis involve multiple developmental pathways that might very well have different degrees of relevance at poorly defined periods during childhood. Investigators of psychosis try to pinpoint major variables and periods of sensitivity for the overt expression of psychotic disorders without having entrenched assumptions about how or when the risk factors might aggregate.

With psychotic children and youth, thorough treatment planning has to entail careful history taking and sustained, comprehensive assessment. It requires giving a great deal of thought to the interplay between neurobiological, developmental, and cognitive variables; the child or adolescent's symptoms; inner emotional experience and psychological vulnerabilities; and the cultural, social, and interpersonal environment of the child and the family. From an integrative perspective, attempts to understand clinical data in psychotherapy with psychotic youth similarly incorporate cognitive behavioral, psychoanalytic, and family therapy principles along with an effort to identify ameliorative factors and supportive psychosocial interventions that might contribute to the child's overall better functioning and improved quality of life. In contrast to young adults who experience a first episode of psychosis, adolescents between 15 and 18 years old who present a first episode of frankly psychotic behavior with diagnostic certainty experience longer delays in receiving appropriate, sustained mental health treatment. If their first episode is associated with schizophrenia rather than a mood disorder with psychosis, they are also more likely to have a more guarded prognosis than individuals with an onset of psychosis in young adulthood, and they have a greater need for early intervention and treatment (Ballageer, Malla, Manchanda, Takhar, and Haricharan, 2005).

The Continuum of Research and Multimodal Treatment

Since scientific disciplines intersect at points of integration in clinical practice, throughout this volume the chapter authors synthesize critical insights from many fields of investigation. In accordance with the foundational principle that psychopathology reflects the interplay of interacting developmental pathways, the authors present well-formulated, eclectic perspectives about psychosis in childhood and adolescence. They examine extant models of pathogenesis, identify early precursors of psychotic disorders, and try to integrate findings about treatment from the psychiatry, psychology, psychoanalysis, and cognitive neuroscience literature. They depict some of the strengths and weaknesses of psychotherapy and refer to the shortcomings of currently available antipsychotic medications, which are generally not specific to particular disorders. Scrupulous reviews of the efficacy and safety of antipsychotic medication with children point to the need for more randomized controlled trials and comparisons of antipsychotic medications that take into account their long-terms effects on children's health, academic and interpersonal functioning, and their development throughout the life cycle. The literature about combinations of antipsychotic medications and augmentation strategies with treatment-resistant psychotic adults is much more robust than comparable research studies with children and adolescents (Kranzler and Cohen, 2013). Although some children with psychotic symptoms benefit from brief psychiatric hospitalizations with a limited use of antipsychotic medications, brief treatment without the benefit of psychotherapy and supportive interventions is often insufficient to maximize the chances that the child will have the most optimal long-term outcome. Having a dedicated, supportive family and long-term treatment adherence substantially improve outcomes for children and adolescents with psychotic disorders.

The following chapters point to the significant value of comprehensive, multimodal, long-term treatment for psychotic children and adolescents as they address controversies about the similarities and differences between psychosis in childhood and adulthood. The authors highlight psychotic features and treatment approaches in early childhood and adolescence, as well as clinical issues associated with developmental disorders, severe mood disorders, schizophrenia, trauma, and posttraumatic stress disorder. For example, in a recent study about the prevalence of visual hallucinations in childhood-onset schizophrenia, 80% of the children reported having had visual hallucinations and those with visual hallucinations had an earlier age of onset and a greater severity of illness than those who did not (David, Greenstein, Clasen, Gochman, Miller, Tossell, and Rapoport, 2011). In an attempt to summarize far-reaching fields of data, the chapters on psychotic disorders present common themes. They encompass the characteristics of psychotic symptoms and disorders in childhood with the associated risk factors and developmental precursors. Also examined are the possible course of psychotic disorders, the significance of comorbidity as well as findings from longitudinal studies about the long-term outcome of psychosis in children and adolescents. The chapters incorporate clinical vignettes and hopeful data, which signify that, despite studies pointing to a generally worse outcome for early-onset psychosis than later-onset psychosis, not all very high-risk children develop long-lasting psychotic disorders. A number of studies have indicated that a little more than one-third of high-risk children and adolescents develop psychotic disorders, and not all children and adolescents with psychotic disorders become chronically ill. For youth with early-onset schizophrenia with impairment, negative symptoms and neuropsychological deficits tend to be associated with a worse long-term outcome, but psychotic disorders early in life don't necessarily predict disabling psychoses during adulthood. Based on a large 10-year follow-up study of children and youth diagnosed with schizophrenia, 20% had a very good outcome but 42% had a poor outcome associated with impaired functioning (Fleischhaker, Schulz, Tepper, Martin, Hennighausen, and Remschmidt, 2005).

Based on contemporary elaborations of historical concepts and current research findings, the authors address essential issues about psychosis in childhood and adolescence, while acknowledging that there are unanswered questions that could refine future research and treatment. They offer informed insights about psychosis that occurs during the first two decades of the lifespan by answering the following questions. First, how frequently do the childhood precursors of psychosis evolve into true psychotic disorders and are the risk factors for psychotic disorders continuous throughout development? Second, do the signs of psychosis in children and adolescents differ from those associated with psychotic disorders in adults? Third, how do early trauma and attachment problems influence severe disorders in children and adolescents, and how can trauma-related psychotic symptoms be best treated in psychotherapy? The authors elucidate the characteristics of psychoses that are associated with the course of pediatric depression and bipolar illness, early-onset schizophrenia, posttraumatic stress disorder, and autism spectrum disorders, and discuss the issue of what accounts for dangerously violent behavior in a small proportion of psychotic youth. In addition, the authors explore how research studies on play therapy, cognitive behavior therapy, and the applications of psychoanalytic therapy principles inform effective psychotherapy with psychotic children and adolescents. Long-term interdisciplinary investigations will be necessary in order to provide more definitive answers to these questions and to identify the best combined treatments for co-occurring disorders with psychosis.

In spite of enormous advances in understanding neurobiological influences on psychotic illness, many questions remain about the development of psychosis and its treatment in children that can have a significant bearing on the direction of future research. Clinicians are generally poor at predicting which at-risk youth will develop psychotic disorders and what the outcome of treatment will entail. There are very few studies about either cognitive behavior therapy approaches or attachment theory–based approaches with psychotic children, and only a few about how the treatment of depression and anxiety disorders in children might serve a protective function against the later occurrence of psychotic disorders. In one very recent longitudinal study of the linkage of a specific pattern of genetic vulnerability to psychosis, the 22q11.2 Deletion Syndrome, 9 out of 10 individuals who developed a psychotic disorder over a four-year period suffered from an earlier anxiety disorder (Gothelf, Schneider, Green, Debbane, Frisch, Glasser, Zilka, Schaer, Weizman, and Elizer, 2013). There are also only a small number of investigations of the characteristics of thought disorder in youth who are at risk for psychosis that might help identify those who are the most likely to later experience psychotic disorders. Brearden, Wu, Caplan, and Cannon (2011) reviewed the speech samples of over 100 adolescents at high risk for developing schizophrenia and found that those who had the highest rates of illogical thinking and poverty of content of speech were most likely to develop psychosis.

Investigators have assembled considerable findings about the tremendous value of psychosocial and family interventions, such as supportive services and case management. Even though family history variables and confusing communication patterns that inhibit a sustained focus of attention have been correlated with elevated risks of vulnerable youth developing psychosis, there is a need for much more research about combining family therapy approaches, stress management, and supportive interventions in the treatment of psychotic children and adolescents. In contrast to youth who have attention deficit disorder, adolescents with bipolar disorder have a greater likelihood of experiencing stressful life events (Tillman, Geller, Nickelsburg, Bolhofner, Craney, Del Bello, and Wigh, 2003). In contrast to young- and middle-aged adults who first experience a mood disorder–related psychosis, children and adolescents who have an early onset of a mood disorder–related psychosis are also more likely to have a family history of mood disorders and substance abuse (Sax, Strakowski, Keck, McElroy, West, Bourne, and Larson, 1997).

Studies of early attachment problems and difficulties with self-regulation have increasingly guided treatment in clinical practice, especially psychotherapeutic engagement with children and adults who are limited in mood regulation and flexible modes of attachment. Like investigations of cognitive behavioral treatment, these studies can be expanded with children and adolescents who are at risk for psychosis and those who have episodes of psychosis. Furthermore, in a recent review of several major studies about childhood psychosis in clinical populations, McClellan (2011) recommended that future research about the development of psychosis should place more stress on ascertaining causal factors in both individuals and families, since unique genetic events may interfere with shared processes that can be the subject of prevention and treatment efforts.

Some children who are exposed to trauma suffer from a variety of adjustment problems and numerous expressions of psychopathology that can include psychotic-like symptoms, such as brief hallucinations. Although these psychotic-like phenomena typically represent dissociative symptoms that have to be differentiated from a true psychotic disorder, histories of trauma aren't unusual in the life histories of youth who are genuinely psychotic. In recent years, investigators have also convincingly argued that substance abuse in adolescence influences the genetic expression of vulnerability for psychosis. Nevertheless, given the interrelationship between genetic vulnerability, environmental adversity, and early developmental delays in many spheres of functioning, additional studies are needed in order to clarify which factors account for the greatest degree of variance in the emergence of psychosis in a child. Uncertainties persist about which combinations of psychotherapy and regimens of medication offer the best prospect for remedying the lingering social and cognitive impairments that are sometimes connected with psychotic disturbance in childhood and adolescence. Currently, there is insufficient knowledge to offer fully satisfactory answers to all of these questions. Nevertheless, the chapter authors refer to promising areas for research and successful therapeutic strategies that stem from the contemporary neuroscience, psychodynamic, cognitive psychology, and psychiatry literature. Further research investigations are similarly needed in order to better grasp the impact of trauma on developmental processes when there is a persistence of intermittent, trauma-related brief psychotic reactions in children and adolescents. Epidemiological studies indicate that up to a quarter to a third of the adolescents in the United States have experienced some type of noteworthy childhood adversity. The occurrence of traumatic adversity, such as the early death of a parent, is extremely widespread among adolescents who are later subject to anxiety and mood disorders, but relatively few traumatized youth develop signs of psychosis or psychotic disorders. After removal from the traumatic situation, trauma-related psychotic symptoms in children are frequently transitory and improve readily with psychotherapy and at times with the brief use of medication. However, adults' narratives about the course of auditory hallucinations that represent psychotic symptoms often attribute their onset to traumatic events during childhood, such as being the victim of physical assaults and bullying or the death of a parent (Romme and Escher, 1993). The relationship between prolonged exposure to trauma such as neglect or physical and sexual abuse, decreased cortical limbic functioning, and stress-related elevations in blood cortisol levels has been well established along with the importance of these factors in children and adolescents who suffer from severe anxiety and mood disorders.

In a two-year longitudinal study that compared youth with brief psychotic symptoms, youth with schizophrenia, and those with bipolar disorder with psychotic features, none of the adolescents with brief or atypical psychotic symptoms developed a psychotic illness after a two-year period. The youth with brief psychotic symptoms had significantly more dissociative symptoms, histories of abuse, and diagnoses of posttraumatic stress disorder or depressive disorder than those with bipolar illness or schizophrenia (Hlastala and McClellan, 2005). In a study of the diagnostic and symptomatic outcome of adolescents at high risk for schizophrenia who also had brief psychotic disorder or psychosis not otherwise specified (NOS), the remission of the psychotic symptoms was predicted by the use of antidepressant medication and a diagnosis of brief psychotic disorder. The results suggest that cognitive executive functioning deficits are a major risk factor for the progression of the psychotic symptoms to schizophrenia, while the presence of an anxiety disorder is associated with a greater risk of developing bipolar disorder (Correll, Smith, Auther, McLaughlin, Shah, Foley, Olsen, Lencz, Kane, and Cornblatt, 2008). Less is known about the cumulative effect of prolonged trauma on children and adolescents who experience recurrent, transitory psychotic symptoms as part of their having mood disorders, schizophrenia, or a substance abuse disorder. Since psychotic disorders are rare in children, little is known about the manifestations of psychosis associated with extreme violence by children and adolescents.

Limitations of Current Treatment Research

Even though factors that contribute to the onset and progression of psychotic disorders have been identified, the treatment of psychotic children remains largely symptom-focused without underlying curative mechanisms for either the more frequently occurring mood disorder–related psychoses, or childhood schizophrenia. Studies of psychotic psychopathology and its treatment frequently fail to take into account significant variables. Among the variables, cultural and racial differences, the chronicity of the psychotic disorders, comorbidity, and levels of cognitive functioning are often overlooked. A great many research studies automatically exclude subjects with psychosis who have full-scale IQs under 70 or 75, based on the assumption that the results might be more reflective of intellectual disability than psychotic functioning. This rationale excludes the large number of children and youth whose levels of cognitive deterioration, in concert with psychosis, may not reflect their true levels of intellectual functioning. Additionally, there are very significant challenges to developing innovative, appropriate treatment strategies. Carrying out treatment studies with severely disturbed youth, in general, often involves overcoming methodological limitations that diminish the possibility of making generalizations based on the data. Some of these limitations are briefly sketched below.

Differences in clinical characteristics among subjects in research populations can make it very difficult to compare samples based on diagnoses, since categorical and dimensional diagnostic systems both have limitations. As noted above, research about psychotic disorders in children is similarly curbed by the difficulty of including cognitive variables, cultural, ethnic, and racial differences, and the importance of comorbidity and chronicity. Study conclusions can be easily compromised by the need to limit the number of variables under consideration and by the inevitability of having small sample sizes in research on early onset psychotic disorders. For example, many of the studies about children and adolescents with brief psychotic disorders and psychosis NOS have relied on a very small number of subjects, thereby yielding results with limited statistical power. As a result, the NOS diagnoses are considered fairly unstable and unreliable as predictors of future psychotic disturbance unless comorbid disorders and patterns of cognitive weaknesses are taken into account (McClellan, McCurry, Snell, and DuBose, 1999; Pillmann, Haring, Balzuweit, and Marneros, 2002).

There are further, major methodological challenges associated with conducting research on psychotherapy with psychotic children and adolescents. It would be very difficult to conduct randomized controlled trials comparing the effect of psychodynamic and cognitive behavior therapy with psychotic youth. It would also be very valuable to assess whether combining several forms of psychotherapy with antipsychotic medication might reduce symptom chronicity. In addition, many youngsters who are being treated for psychotic symptoms and disorders have, along with their parents, understandable concerns about providing informed consent and assent for participation in research. Since patient care, rather than the accumulation of research data, is always the main priority in any treatment study involving children who have symptoms of psychiatric disorders, the completion of treatment research protocols may not always be possible.

Investigators who conduct research in clinical settings likewise recognize that the necessary use of narrow inclusion—and exclusion—criteria can potentially erode meaning, since common domains of psychopathology occur across diagnoses, and multiple disorders often contribute to symptoms and behavior in chronically and severely disturbed youth. In fact, having multiple risk factors and comorbid disorders is usually the norm in most clinical populations, while treatment outcome and longitudinal studies that include comorbidity are generally rare. Finally, in a substantial number of clinical settings, psychotic children and adolescents are not treatment-naïve, having previously had partially successful combined treatment that included psychotherapy and a number of trials of antipsychotic medication. As a result of the vast range of psychotic phenomena and the limitations inherent in conducting research with severely disturbed children, knowledge about the treatment of psychotic children and adolescents evolves at a modest pace.

Summary and Therapeutic Objectives

There is an increasing consensus about the need for multidimensional models of the development of childhood psychosis. As researchers delineate the complexity of psychotic disorders, clinicians grapple with the need for appropriate, multimodal treatment for psychotic children and adolescents. The coalescence of several important scientific trends has elevated the level of inquiry about childhood-onset psychosis in the last three decades. There have been significantly more treatment studies of high-risk populations and more research about the nascent indications of personality disorders during childhood and early adolescence. Increasing numbers of longitudinal studies of youth who are at high risk for psychosis have also been completed. In addition, a greater awareness of the interaction between genetic influences and biological and environmental factors has helped to animate the overall exploration of psychotic reactions and disorders in childhood. Yet, in contrast to the genetic research studies and investigations of first-episode psychosis, the research studies about childhood psychosis and co-occurring disorders, and the studies of psychotherapy with psychotic children and adolescents, have been characterized by their narrow scope.

Almost fifty years ago, Rudolph Ekstein (1966) observed that psychotic youth very rarely respond to the content of therapists' interpretative language. Psychotic children's frequently compromised ability to understand others and to communicate without being encumbered by disturbed thinking frustrates therapeutic agenda, which are guided by cost-driven needs to demonstrate very measurable progress in a time-limited number of sessions. The psychotic child's difficulties with symbolic language and reality-based communication reflect early Freudian delineations of the deleterious role of unconscious conflicts that aren't filtered by organized ego-defensive processes. Effective psychotherapy with psychotic children and adolescents thus inevitably relies on the therapist's ability to listen, observe, and adapt strategies and techniques to the patient's unique experience of psychosis within a comprehensive, multimodal treatment framework. The exercise of these abilities rests on the premise elaborated by Freud, Sullivan, Anna Freud, Winnicott, and other psychoanalytic theorists—which is endorsed by cognitive behavior theorists—that the psychotherapeutic relationship constitutes the essential curative framework underlying the specific treatment strategies and techniques. Although some brief psychotherapy models and many pharmacological regimens with psychosis have strong research support, short-term psychotherapy with psychotic children can't take as much advantage of the therapeutic relationship as a potentially transformative experience. The chapters thus present key insights about both sustained psychotherapy based on psychoanalytic theory and principles, and cognitive behavioral techniques as part of combined, comprehensive treatment approaches for psychosis.

Chapter 1 synthesizes the pertinent literature about psychotic disorders in childhood and the current understanding of psychotic symptoms that accompany many forms of emotional disturbance in children and adolescents. In Chapter 2, Dr. Vila and Dr. Gerber emphasize the importance of early attachment and the evolution of cognitive schemas and their influence on the unfolding of patterns of vulnerability for severe psychic disturbance such as childhood psychosis. In Chapter 3, Dr. Sossin thoroughly discusses neurobiological, attachment, and other risk factors that predispose infants and toddlers to developmental weaknesses that are within the autistic spectrum and those that may be very early precursors of psychotic disturbance. In Chapter 4, Dr. Krasner and Dr. Winter's review of the literature about schizophrenia in children and adolescents and its treatment is enhanced by richly drawn illustrative case examples. The literature on mood disorders and psychotic features is summarized in Chapter 5, which emphasizes the clinical phenomenology of major depressive disorder and bipolar disorder in children in contrast to their manifestations in adults. This chapter especially clarifies the significant relationship between severe mood disorder–symptoms and emergent signs of psychosis.

Dr. Henry's comprehensive analysis of the relationship between trauma and psychosis in Chapter 6 similarly provides rich clinical examples of patients whose successful treatment relied on a positive therapeutic alliance and the considerable flexibility of the therapist. Their treatment illustrates the clearly effective integration of trauma-focused cognitive behavior therapy and psychodynamic psychotherapy with highly traumatized children who have psychotic symptoms and disorders. In Chapter 7, Dr. Guarton's case summary notes offer a sensitive example of the creative use of play therapy techniques as essential to the curative relationship with a very developmentally delayed, intermittently psychotic young child. The chapter articulates how the developmental ramifications of play therapy approaches can be defined with clarity in spite of the infinite possible permutations of children's play.

Dr. Eisenberg's thoughtful case discussions in Chapter 8 elaborate the significant role of the therapeutic relationship in psychodynamic work and the textured unfolding of the therapeutic process with severely disturbed children. In support of Dr. Eisenberg's thesis, the increasing availability of objective measures of treatment variables has allowed for accumulating empirical evidence about the quintessential influence of the therapeutic alliance and its impact on treatment outcome with children and adolescents. Ms. Kline and Drs. Schiffman, Choi, Laitner, and Rogove provide a solid theoretical foundation for evidence-based treatment in Chapter 9, as they assimilate the continuum of the non-pharmacological interventions for youth with psychosis and they describe the use of cognitive remediation and cognitive behavior therapy with psychotic disorders. They offer moving illustrations of how the functional impairments of children and adolescents with early onset psychotic disorders can be enormously improved through a combination of psychosocial interventions, recovery-oriented approaches, and community treatment efforts in conjunction with pharmacological, behavioral, and cognitive behavior therapy techniques. In Chapter 10, Dr. Master, Dr. Melnik, and Ms. Inouye elucidate important forensic questions about psychotic behavior in children and adolescents who commit grave acts of violence. They trace the weakness of the mental health system with violent youth and the crucial need for intervention strategies for these very high-risk youth.

Case Example

Christopher, an 11-year-old boy whose parents had immigrated to the United States from Eastern Europe prior to his birth, suffered from longstanding psychotic symptoms with mood disturbance, a history of trauma, and unrelenting behavior problems in spite of having had multiple hospitalizations over a two-year period that included treatment with psychotherapy, antipsychotic and mood-stabilizer medications, and residential treatment. He was re-hospitalized for the fifth time after punching his sixth-grade teacher and stating that he was going to kill himself. He reported being frightened by hearing the devil's voice, which told him that he was evil and should die.

Christopher's father had deserted the family when he was an infant, and Christopher and his mother lived in a homeless shelter for the first few years of his life. He had early delays in receptive and expressive language and was described as being very impulsive and hyperactive at home and at school. There was no known history of psychiatric disorders on either side of the family, except for learning problems. At age 2, Christopher began to throw and break objects and to bang his head in the midst of violent temper outbursts that continued throughout his childhood. At age 4, he was physically abused by a relative's boyfriend.

Christopher was generally socially isolated with few friends, a mediocre student in spite of average intelligence, and was very hypersensitive to perceived slights and criticisms from peers at school who were usually tolerant of him. When he was 5 years old, Christopher was diagnosed with attention deficit hyperactivity disorder, oppositional defiant disorder, and posttraumatic stress disorder. His more recent diagnoses alternated between schizoaffective disorder and psychosis, NOS with posttraumatic stress disorder, attention deficit hyperactivity disorder, and mood disorder, NOS. He was treated with Olanzapine, Risperidone, Lithium, and stimulant medication with little effect, and efforts to engage him in cognitive behavior therapy were relatively unsuccessful in deceasing his delusional thinking or improving his limited frustration-tolerance and social skills.

After six months of inpatient care that included the combined use of two antipsychotic medications and a mood stabilizer, consistent psychotherapy, and an additional year of psychiatric day treatment with twice-weekly psychotherapy sessions in a structured milieu, Christopher was able to remain free from psychotic symptoms and to retain therapeutic improvement. Even though attempts to help him through verbal psychotherapy and cognitive behavioral techniques weren't initially productive, Christopher was able to maintain a positive relationship with his psychotherapist and to participate in the sessions for over a year of therapy. By creating drawings of frightening monsters and responding to encouragement to use them in trauma-focused play therapy sessions, he became better able to recognize and articulate his fears, develop better anxiety tolerance, and to gradually ask adults for help when he was feeling frustrated or threatened by his peers.

Conclusion

An appreciation of the complexity of psychotic phenomena and recognition of the modest extent of present-day knowledge about psychosis are consistent themes woven throughout the chapters' discussions of the research and the case reports.

Their conceptual landscape yields a full panorama of hopeful possibilities for treatment interventions, even if the current scope of research investigations seems somewhat limited. The chapter authors' elucidation of therapeutic objectives for psychotic children and adolescents can be succinctly summarized. Rapid stabilization and short-term treatment, only, represent inadequate care for children and adolescents with psychosis. Gains in reducing the frequency and severity of psychotic symptoms must be considered insufficient if the improvement isn't inextricably linked to establishing a medium for the child or adolescent's return to a continuum of healthy developmental processes.

As an integration of scholarly essays, this book isn't intended to provide a fully exhaustive examination of all of the voluminous current research on psychotic illness that occurs prior to adulthood. By synthesizing the research and the clinical literature, we aim to underscore the theme of the complexity of psychosis in developmental, assessment, and treatment studies. Our dual goals are to highlight efforts to enhance knowledge about psychosis and to honor the guardians of very mentally ill youth, whose attempts to fathom their behavior and use of language without discourse can be profoundly disconcerting. The leitmotif of sustained, integrative, research-informed care for psychotic children and adolescents is sounded consistently in the following chapters. It is beyond the scope of these essays to unravel in-depth analyses of health care systems or the obvious shortcomings of current mental health services. It remains to be seen whether a consciousness of the complexity of psychosis will become mired in the cost-driven reduction of mental health services for severely and chronically mentally ill children and adolescents or help to galvanize their thoughtful treatment.

References

Aas, M., Navari, S., Gibbs, A., Mondelli, V., Fisher, H. L., Morgan, C., Morgan, K., MacCabe, J., Reichenberg, A., Zanelli,J., Fearon, P., Jones, P. B., Murray, R. M., Pariante, C. M., & Dazan, P. (2012). Is there a link between childhood trauma, cognition, and amygdala and hippocampus volume in first-episode psychosis? *Schizophrenia Research,* 137(1), 73–79.

Asarnow, J. R. (2005). Childhood-onset schizotypal disorder: A follow-up study and comparison with childhood-onset schizophrenia. *Journal of Child and Adolescent Psychopharmacology,* 15(3), 395–402.

Ballageer, T., Malla, A., Manchanda, R., Takhar, J., & Haricharan, R. (2005). Is adolescent-onset first-episode psychosis different from adult-onset? *Journal of the American Academy of Child and Adolescent Psychiatry,* 44(8), 782–789.

Bendall, S., Allott, K., Johnson, T., Jackson, H. J., Killackey, E., Harrigan, S. & McGorry, P. D. (2008). Pattern of lifetime axis I morbidity among treated sample of first-episode psychosis patients. *Psychopathology,* 41(2), 90–95.

Bender, L., & Grugett, A. E. (1956). A study of certain epidemiological factors in a group of children with childhood schizophrenia. *American Journal of Orthopscychiatry,* 26(1), 131–145.

Benvenuti, A., Rucci, P., Ravani, L., Gonnelli, C., Frank, E., Balestrieri, M., Sbrana, A., Dell'Osso, L., & Cassano, G. B., (2005). Psychotic features in borderline patients: Is there a connection to mood dysregulation? *Bipolar Disorders,* 7(4), 338–343.

Bleuler, E. (1950). *Dementia praecox or the group of schizophrenias.* New York, NY: International Universities Press.

Boeing, L., Murray, V., Pelosi, A, MacCabe, R., Blackwood, D., & Wrate, R. (2007). Adolescent-onset psychosis: Prevalence, needs and service provision. *British Journal of Psychiatry,* 190(1), 18–26.

Brearden, C. E., Wu, K. N., Caplan, R., & Cannon, T. D. (2011). Thought disorder and communication deviance as predictors of outcome in youth at clinical high risk for psychosis. *Journal of the American Academy of Child & Adolescent Psychiatry,* 50(7), 669–680.

Cervellione, K. L., Burdick, K. E., Cottone, J. G., Rhinewine, J. P., & Kumra, S. (2007). Neurocognitive deficits in adolescents with schizophrenia: Longitudinal stability and predictive utility for short-term functional outcome. *Journal of the American Academy of Child and Adolescent Psychiatry*, 46(7), 867–878.

Cicchetti, D. (1984). The emergence of developmental psychopathology. *Child Development,* 55(1), 1–7.

Cicchetti, D. (1990). A historical perspective on the discipline of developmental psychopathology. In J. Rolf, A. Mastern, D. Cicchetti, K. Neuchterlein, & S. Weintraub (Eds.), *Risk and protective factors in the development of psychopathology* (pp. 2–28). New York, NY: Cambridge University Press.

Cicchetti, D., & Cohen, D. J. (Eds.), (2006). *Developmental psychopathology: Risk, disorder, and adaptation.* New York, NY: Wiley.

Correll, C. U., Smith, C. W., Auther, A. A., McLaughlin, D., Shah, M., Foley, C., Olsen, R., Lencz, T., Kane, J. M., & Cornblatt, B. (2008). Predictors of remission, schizophrenia, and bipolar disorder in adolescents with brief psychotic disorder or psychotic disorder not otherwise specified considered at very high risk for schizophrenia. *Journal of Child and Adolescent Psychopharmacology,* 18(5), 475–490.

Crespi, B., Stead, P., & Elliot, M. (2010). Comparative genomics of autism and schizophrenia. *Proceedings of the National Academy of Sciences,* 107, 1736–1741.

David, C., Greenstein, D., Clasen, L., Gochman, P., Miller, R., Tossell, J. W., & Rapoport, J. L. (2011). Childhood onset schizophrenia: High rate of visual hallucinations. *Journal of American Academy of Child and Adolescent Psychiatry,* 50(7), 681–686.

Doyle, A. E., Wilens, T. E., Kwon, A., Seidman, L. J., Faraone, S. V., Fried, R., Swezey, A., Snyder, L., & Biederman, J. (2005). Neuropsychological functioning in youth with bipolar disorder. *Biological Psychiatry,* 58(7), 540–548.

Ekstein, R. (1966). *Children of time and space, of action, and impulse.* New York, NY: Appleton-Century Crofts.

Fish, B., & Ritvo, E. R. (1979). Psychosis of childhood. In J. D. Noshpitz (Ed.), *Basic handbook of child psychiatry* (pp. 249–304). New York, NY: Basic Books.

Fleischhaker, C., Schulz, E., Tepper, K., Martin, M., Hennighausen, K., & Remschmidt, H. (2005). Long-term course of adolescent schizophrenia. *Schizophrenia Bulletin,* 31(3), 769–780.

Gothelf, D., Schneider, M., Green, T., Debbane, M, Frisch, A., Glasser, B., Zilka, H., Schaer, M., Weizman, A., & Elizer, S. (2013). Risk factors and the evolution of psychosis in 22q11.2 deletion syndrome. *Journal of the American Academy of Child and Adolescent Psychiatry,* 52(11), 1192–1203.

Hinshaw, S. P. (2013). Developmental psychopathology as a scientific discipline. In T. D. Beauchaine & S. P. Hinshaw (Eds.), *Child and adolescent psychopathology* (pp. 3–27). Hoboken, NJ: Wiley.

Hlastala, S. A., & McClellan, J. (2005). Phenomenology and diagnostic stability with atypical psychotic symptoms. *Journal of Child and Adolescent Psychopharmacology,* 15(3), 497–509.

Jacobsen, L. K., & Rapoport, J. L. (1998). Research update. Childhood-onset schizophrenia: Implications of clinical and neurobiological research. *Journal of Child Psychology and Psychiatry,* 39(1). 101–113.

Kanner, L. (1949). Problems of nosology and psychodynamics of early infantile autism. *American Journal of Orthopsychiatry,* 19(3), 416–426.

Kolvin, I. (1971). Studies in childhood psychosis: I. diagnostic criteria and classification. *British Journal of Psychiatry,* 118, 381–384.

Kraepelin, E. (1915). *Psychiatrie.* Leipzig, Germany: Verlag Von Johann Ambrosius Barth.

Kuepper, R., Morrison, P. D., van Os, J., Murray, R. M., Kenis, G., & Henquet, C. (2011). Does dopamine mediate the psychosis-inducing effects of cannabis? A review and integration of findings across disciplines. *Schizophrenia Research,* 121(1–3), 107–117.

McClellan, J., McCurry, C., Snell, J., & DuBose, A. (1999). Early-onset psychotic disorders: Course and outcome over a 2-year period. *Journal of the American Academy of Child and Adolescent Psychiatry,* 38(11), 1380–1388.

McClellan, J., & King M. C. (2010). Genomic analysis of mental illness: A changing landscape. *Journal of the American Medical Association,* 303(24), 2523–2524.

McClellan, J. (2011). Clinically relevant phenomenology: The nature of psychosis. *Journal of the American Academy of Child and Adolescent Psychiatry,* 50(7), 642–644.

Meehl, P. E. (1962). Schizotaxia, schizotypy, schizophrenia. *American Psychologist,* 17(12), 827–838.

Meehl, P. E. (1990). Toward an integrated theory of schizotaxia, schizotypy, and schizophrenia. *Journal of Personality Disorders,* 4, 1–99.

Mittai, V. A., & Walker, E. F., (2011). Minor physical anomalies and vulnerability in prodromal youth. *Schizophrenia Research,* 129(2), 116–121.

Pillmann, F., Haring, A., Balzuweit, S., & Marneros, A. (2002). A comparison of DSM-IV brief psychotic disorder with "positive" schizophrenia and healthy controls. *Comprehensive Psychiatry,* 43(5), 385–392.

Romme, M., & Escher, S. (1993). *Accepting voices.* London, UK: MIND.

Russell, A. T., Bott, L., & Sammons, C. (1989). The phenomenology of schizophrenia occurring in childhood. *Journal of the American Academy of Child and Adolescent Psychiatry,* 28(3), 399–407.

Rutter, M. (1972). Childhood schizophrenia reconsidered. *Journal of Autism and Childhood Schizophrenia,* 2(4), 315–337.

Sax, K. W., Strakowski, S. M., Keck, P. E., McElroy, S. L., West, S. A., Bourne, M. L., & Larson, E. R. (1997). Comparison of patients with early-, typical, and late-onset affective psychosis. *American Journal of Psychiatry,* 154(1), 1299–1301.

Semple, D. M., McIntosh, A. M., & Lawrie, S. M. (2005). Cannabis as a risk factor for psychosis: Systematic review. *Journal of Psychopharmacology,* 19(2), 187–194.

Sullivan, S., Raj, D., Golding, J., Zammit, S., & Steer, C. (2013). The association between autism spectrum disorder and psychotic experiences in the Avon Longitudinal Study of Parents and Children (ALSPAC) birth cohort. *Journal of the American Academy of Child & Adolescent Psychiatry,* 52(8), 806–814.

Tillman, R., Geller, B., Nickeslburg, M. J., Bolhofner, K., Craney, J. L., Del Bello, M. P., & Wigh, W. (2003). Life events in prepubertal and early adolescent bipolar disorder phenotype compared to attention deficit hyperactive and normal controls. *Journal of the Child and Adolescent Psychopharmacology,* 13(3), 243–251.
Weinberger, D. R., (1987). Implications of normal brain development for the pathogenesis of schizophrenia. *Archives of General Psychiatry,* 44(7), 660–669.
Winograd, G., Cohen, P., & Chen, H. (2008). Adolescent borderline symptoms in the community: Prognosis for functioning over 20 years. *Journal of Child Psychology and Psychiatry,* 49(9), 933–941.
Zelkowitz, P., Paris, J., Gudzer, J., Feldman, R., Roy, C., & Rosaval, L. (2007). A five-year follow-up of patients with borderline pathology of childhood. *Journal of Personality Disorders,* 21(6), 664–674.

PART I

The Development of Psychosis

1

CONTEMPORARY VIEWS OF PSYCHOTIC DISORDERS

James B. McCarthy

More than twenty-five years ago, a violent, very mentally ill 10-year-old boy told me that his having been hospitalized as a result of trying to jump out of the window of his family's 12th-floor apartment had been a misunderstanding. He said that he never had any intention of hurting himself. When I asked him what was in his mind when he tried to open the window, he explained that he had been bored and just wanted to fly. He added that he knew that he could fly because he was Superman. It became apparent that entrenched delusions had governed his dangerous actions during transient psychotic episodes. Around the same time, a highly anxious 13-year-old girl who had frightening visual hallucinations told me about a repetitive, intrusive memory. When she was 5, she had seen her acutely psychotic father put her infant brother into the oven as he turned to her and said that the baby was a witch who needed to be cooked so that the whole family would be saved from evil. The first child who suffered from repetitive psychotic states of disorganization in the course of unfolding schizophrenia improved significantly after one year of hospitalization with two to three times a week psychotherapy, antipsychotic medication, and the involvement of an interdisciplinary team of mental health professionals. The second child whose adjustment problems and disturbing symptoms largely reflected posttraumatic phenomena was able to remain free from crippling anxiety and psychotic features after a year and a half of outpatient psychoanalytic psychotherapy with a great deal of family support. The assumption that rapid diagnosis and short-term symptom alleviation offers the best hope for restoring disturbed children and adolescents' mental health is increasingly used as the rationale for limiting the possibility that sustained treatment can occur in the contemporary climate of health insurance and industry-managed mental health care. Understanding the intricacies of providing accurate assessment and effective treatment for disturbed children and adolescents and their families requires questioning this naïve assumption.

Introduction

With children who are vulnerable to psychosis, a careful examination of appropriate treatment options rests on understanding the child as an evolving individual whose behavior needs to be scrutinized in neurobiological, developmental, intrapsychic, cognitive, family, and social contexts. Troubled adolescents' symptomatic behavior typically conveys multiple meanings, depending on where it rests on a continuum of psychopathology and how it manifests the individual's internal psychological world and interpersonal environment. In contrast to short-term, exclusively symptom-stabilization treatment, both cognitive behavior therapy and psychodynamic psychotherapy can allow for flexible, long-term treatment approaches. Cognitive behavioral approaches to severe psychopathology in children elucidate underlying schemas and patterns of cognition that frequently fuel the child's distress and anxiety. Psychoanalytic perspectives entail openness to the possibility that the disturbed child's temporary ego regressions and difficulty with modulating anxiety and depressed moods will become manifest in the therapeutic relationship. The transformations of the psychotic patient's internal world and their ties to psychopathology are integral to integrative psychoanalytic psychotherapy conceptualizations. Both of the young patients I described profited from thorough, collaborative treatment including in-depth, long-term psychotherapy which incorporated psychoanalytic principles in order to become sufficiently psychologically minded to create boundaries between internal and external, to develop adequate reality testing, and to slowly grasp the defensive connections between their symptoms and the projection of their inner experience. Evidence is lacking for the argument that research supports time-limited, purely symptom-reduction treatments for psychotic children and adolescents and many others with severe psychiatric disorders. Nevertheless, financial pressures for rapid solutions and authorization for sustaining assessment and therapy in mental health treatment settings threatens to render comprehensive assessment and thoughtful treatment obsolete.

In order to illustrate the shortcomings of the reductionist thinking that permeates behavioral health care limitations on inpatient and outpatient treatment of psychotic youth and to highlight the need for adequate assessment and long-term child and family therapy, I will try to accomplish several aims. In addition to introducing the need for combing psychodynamic and cognitive models of psychotherapy with the appropriate use of medication, I will draw further attention to the multiplicity of diagnostic and treatment issues with children and adolescents who have symptoms of psychosis and psychotic disorders. Their treatment planning relies on extensive assessment and an appreciation of the multidimensional factors that contribute to the severely ill child's symptoms and impairments. Comprehensive planning for the needs of psychotic youth requires consideration of neurobiological and social/environmental factors, the possibility of prodromal phases and comorbidity, and the evidence for mood disorder and trauma-related psychotic features. I will also elaborate on the contributions of several psychoanalytic papers about psychotic anxiety and ego regressions that occur in psychotherapy with disturbed children and adolescents. The complexity of caring for psychotic children leaves little room for doubt about the compelling need for flexible, long-term, multimodal treatments, including cognitive behavioral strategies and psychoanalytically informed psychotherapy interventions that stress the crucial organizing role of the therapeutic relationship.

Schizophrenia and Prodromal Psychosis

Like other disorders that can encompass periods of psychosis, childhood-onset schizophrenia is a heterogeneous, highly complex disorder that can seriously interfere with social and cognitive development. At times, its early signs appear to reflect several disorders and a variety of developmental delays, while some at-risk youth experience partial symptoms in formation. Other children who demonstrate risk factors and schizophrenia-like symptoms never develop the disorder during adulthood. Studies of high-risk children and adolescents who develop schizophrenia in adulthood have revealed that they tend to show early delays in talking and motor development, as well as poor social and academic abilities in childhood (Niemai, Suvisaari, Tuulio-Hendriksson, and Lonnqvist, 2003). Prodromal symptoms of an illness reflect deteriorations in functioning and less severe symptoms of the illness for a period prior to the full or syndromal signs of the disorder. Longitudinal research studies have established that up to three-quarters of the people who suffer from schizophrenia first have a prodromal phase, but no more than about a third of those who have elevated risk factors for schizophrenia will eventually develop the disorder. Many adolescents with early onset bipolar disorder also exhibit prodromal signs of the disorder prior to first having mania or mania with psychosis (Correll, Penzer, Kafantaris, Nakayma, Auther, Lencz, Malhotra, Kane, and Cornblatt, 2005). In the months preceding a first episode of mania, mood lability, increased irritability, and sleep disturbance all may be present. However, in some individuals these signs can be lacking in specificity and overlap with the prodromal symptoms of schizophrenia, suggesting that there is a phenotypic similarity between the schizophrenia prodrome and vulnerability for bipolar illness.

In a multisite longitudinal North American study of 291 adolescents who were at high risk for schizophrenia, 35% of the adolescents transitioned to psychosis, with a declining rate of conversion over two and a half years (Cannon, Cadenhead, Cornblatt, Woods, Addington, Walker, Seidman, Perkins, Tsuang, McGlashan, and Heinssen, 2008). A high genetic risk for schizophrenia and recent decrements in functioning were the two characteristics that contributed the most significantly to the prediction of schizophrenia. A recent set of data analyses from this investigation of the outcome of late adolescents who were prodromal for schizophrenia revealed encouraging findings. In spite of some continuing impairment, 71% of those at high risk did not make the transition to psychosis at a two-and–a-half-year follow up, although 41% of the sample continued to experience at least one attenuated positive symptom after two years (Addington, Cornblatt, Cadenhead, Cannon, McGlashan, Perkins, Seidman, Tsuang, Walker, Woods, and Heinssen, 2011). Except for the severity of the original psychotic-like symptoms at the baseline, there was little difference between the adolescents and the young adults whose symptoms converted to psychosis and those whose symptoms did not. In a smaller study of high-risk adolescents who were assessed after two years, 51% continued to have prodromal or positive signs of psychosis, but there were no differences in clinical characteristics between the adolescents who had psychotic symptoms and those who were symptom free (Ziemans, Schothors, Sprong, van Engeland, 2011). Among diagnostically heterogeneous groups of adolescents and young adults who experience a recent onset of psychosis, over half of them have serious deficits in their overall functioning, especially in social and emotional functioning (Boeing, Murray, Pelosi, McCabe, Blackwood, and Wrate, 2007). Probably at least half of the adolescents and young adults who present signs of a definable prodromal stage also display brief positive symptoms of psychosis.

Psychosis, Comorbidity, and Personality Disorders

Comorbidity—the simultaneous occurrence of a number of psychiatric disorders—is a notable factor that complicates treatment with children and adolescents who have psychotic disorders. Research studies suggest that comorbidity is generally the norm in most clinical populations. For example, about 70% of adults with schizophrenia have multiple disorders, about 50% have co-occurring schizophrenia and substance abuse, and approximately 40% to 45% have anxiety disorders. Comorbidity rates in children and adolescents with psychotic disorders are quite high, but not as well-established, with greater uncertainty about the reliability and validity of some of the diagnostic criteria, especially with adolescents who have coexisting psychosis, substance abuse, and posttraumatic stress disorder (Thompson, Kelly, Kimhy, Harkavy-Friedman, Khan, Messinger, Schobel, Goetz, Malaspina, and Corcoran, 2009). When over 2,500 adolescents and young adults who had an early experience of trauma were interviewed prospectively, self-reported psychological trauma slightly increased the magnitude of the risk of their developing a psychotic disorder particularly when the trauma was associated with feelings of helplessness, intense fear, and horror (Spauwen, Krabbendam, Lieb, Wittechn, and van Os, 2006). The cumulative effect of multiple daily stressors on chronic anxiety and depression needs to be much better delineated in adolescents who have psychotic-like experiences and those who are at high risk for psychotic disorders. In addition, the limited research on comorbidity rates with childhood-onset psychosis suggests that the targeted pharmacological treatment of the comorbid disorders is fairly infrequent. In one study of eighty-three 4- to 15-year-old children who were carefully diagnosed with schizophrenia or schizoaffective disorder, 99% had at least one comorbid disorder, 84% had attention deficit hyperactivity disorder (ADHD), 43% had oppositional defiant disorder, 30% had depression, and 25% had separation anxiety disorder, while the absolute rate of medication use for the comorbid conditions was below 25%, except for the addition of mood stabilizers to treat the ongoing mood disturbance (Ross, Heinlein, and Tregellas, 2006).

There have only been a few investigations of the similarities and differences in comorbidity between children, adolescents, and adults who undergo a first episode of psychosis (Ballageer, Malla, Manchanda, Takhar, and Haricharan, 2005), and a number that have substantiated the comorbidity between anxiety disorders, mood disorders, developmental disorders, and psychosis. One examination of the frequency of psychotic symptoms in children and adolescents enrolled in anxiety and mood disorders clinics suggests that about 5% have psychotic symptoms with auditory hallucinations as the most frequent symptom (Ulloa, Birmaher, Axelson, Williamson, Brent, Ryan, Bridge, and Baugher, 2000). Self-report studies of adults in community mental health programs reveal that psychotic symptoms are much more common, leading investigators to hypothesize that psychotic features vary in quantity across numerous diagnostic categories. In comparison with children and adolescents who have unipolar depression, psychotic features are very prominent in children and adolescents who have bipolar disorder, although recovery from the illness and symptomatic improvements are often less compromised in youth with bipolar illness than in those with schizophrenia (Borchardt and Bernstein, 1995). Multiple comorbidities, including psychotic symptoms, are not rare in children and adolescents who have mood disorders along with severe conduct disturbance. Such comorbidity is also present in a minority of children and adolescents with autism. Comorbidities in children and adolescents with autistic features are also increasingly being explored, chiefly the underlying genetically based continuities and connections between developmental disorders and psychotic symptoms. In a longitudinal investigation of over 6,400 children, early speech problems and very odd ritualistic habits were associated with an increased likelihood of psychotic symptoms during adolescence (Bevan, Thapar, Lewis, and Zammit, 2012).

The overlap between emerging personality disorder features and psychosis in children and adolescents is a very significant but understudied area of investigation. Until recently, there has been a lack of prospective studies about personality disorder features in children, in spite of the importance of identifying developmental precursors of psychopathology in adulthood. One exception is the increasing number studies of schizotypal personality disorder in adolescence and its relationship to schizophrenia. In the previously mentioned study by Asarnow

(2005), childhood-onset schizotypal personality disorders were found to be relatively stable for a two- to three-year follow up in adolescence, but the results were based on a small number of subjects. In community samples, 10% to 20% of children and adolescents show signs of personality disorders, but in clinical samples youth with borderline personality disorder constitute a very significant subgroup of most patient populations. At least 20% of adolescent psychiatric inpatients suffer from borderline personality disorder, often with major depression and self-injurious or suicidal behavior (Bernstein, Cohen, Valez, Schwab-Stone, Siever, and Shinsato, 1993; Crick, Murray-Close, and Woods, 2005).

Beginning in the 1990s, a constitutional predisposition to irritability, impulsivity, and negative affect has been identified as central to the unfolding of borderline personality disorder (Siever and Davis, 1991), and there has been increasing recognition of the negative impact of biological factors on emotional and cognitive development (Bleiberg, 2001). Studies estimate that between 3% to 6% of adults have borderline personality disorder, but it is unclear how many first had signs of psychosis in childhood. Borderline personality disorder characteristics in latency children and young adolescents often co-occur with signs of depression, anxiety, and conduct disturbance, as well as transient psychosis, and are more pronounced if there has been physical abuse, a harsh family environment, or a biological family history of marked psychiatric illness (Belsky, Caspi, Arseneault, Bleidorn, Fonagy, Goodman, Houts, and Moffitt, 2012). In addition, within the last two years, developmental pathways have been identified from early ADHD, oppositional defiant disorder, and conduct disorder in childhood to the emergence of borderline personality disorder in adolescent girls and boys (Burke and Stepp, 2012; Stepp, Burke, Hipwell, and Loeber, 2012). Psychoanalytic pioneers who first described the concept and coined the term "borderline children" referred to fluctuating symptoms and impairments stemming from ego disturbance at the mild end of a continuum of psychosis in children who don't actually become psychotic (Mahler, Ross, and De Fries, 1949; Ekstein and Wallerstein, 1954). They emphasized borderline children's vulnerability to regression and associated limitations in many aspects of their social and emotional functioning. In some children and adolescents with borderline personality disorder characteristics, stress and intense anxiety can precipitate temporary symptoms of hallucinations, thought disorder, and delusional thinking, even though borderline personality features in childhood and adolescence much more frequently lead to a longitudinal course of mood disorders and personality disorders rather than psychotic disorders during adulthood. Similarly, for adolescents with schizotypal personality features, the frequency of daily stressors predicts an increase in positive prodromal symptoms of schizophrenia over a period of years (Tessner, Mittal, and Walker, 2011). Although borderline personality disorder features in children tend to reflect vulnerability to a variety of personality disorders in adulthood, the associated cognitive features of paranoid thinking, psychotic thought content, and dissociation are relatively stable characteristics in adults with borderline personality disorder (Zanarini, Gunderson, and Frankenberg, 1990). These trends point to the important need for more prospective studies of psychotic features, anxiety symptoms, and cognitive disturbances in children and adolescents with borderline personality disorder features in order to better understand the developmental antecedents of similar symptoms and impairments in adults with borderline personality disorders. The lack of sufficient, reliable information about the full extent of comorbidity and the potential impact of comorbid disorders on the continuity of psychotic disorders in children and adolescents compounds the challenge of understanding their diagnostic dilemmas and offering the most appropriate treatments. Subclinical symptoms of psychosis during adolescence most likely represent an underlying general vulnerability for a range of psychopathology that could become evident later in life. The need for carefully considered, dimensional psychological and psychiatric assessments, effective psychotherapy approaches, and metabolically safe antipsychotic medications with psychotic youth continues to be paramount.

Brief Psychotic Reactions and Trauma

In the last twenty years, there has been a heightened appreciation of the impact of trauma, especially physical and sexual abuse, on children's reality testing and their problems with affect regulation. Severely maltreated children are also very often compromised in their ability to organize their thoughts and communicate them logically. Some children experience transitory, psychotic-like phenomena, while others may be susceptible to short periods of true psychotic symptoms and thought disturbance during extreme stress. Disagreement continues about whether trauma in childhood can cause the development of psychotic disorders (Bendall, Jackson, Hulbert, and McCorry, 2008). However, one explanation for the greater frequency of psychotic symptoms in children whose abuse has been chronic is the negative effect of trauma on the developing brain, particularly the resulting changes in the dopaminergic and serotonergic neurotransmitter systems (Read, Perry, Moskowitz, and Connolly, 2001). In a recent investigation of the association between childhood trauma, cognitive deficits, and brain volume in first episode psychosis, childhood trauma was associated with smaller amygdala volume and worse cognitive functioning (Aas, Navari, Gibbs, Mondelli, Fisher, Morgan, Morgan, MacCabe, Reichenberg, Zanelli, Fearon, Jones, Murray, Pariante, and Dazan, 2012). These studies point to the unclear pathophysiological associations between trauma and brain changes and their impact on later psychosis during childhood and adolescence. The links between trauma, psychotic symptoms, and the dimensions of trauma-induced psychotic reactions in children and adolescents require much further empirical examination (Morrison, Frame, and Larkin, 2003).

The dominant prevalence of the history of serious trauma among youth who report transient psychotic symptoms for brief periods, usually characterized as psychosis not otherwise specified (psychosis NOS) or psychosis not elsewhere specified (psychosis NES) in DSM 5 terms, suggests that for many, these symptoms might be trauma and mood related. Yet, other adolescents with psychosis NOS who remain more treatment refractory have cognitive deficits in memory and verbal learning problems which are similar to those found in schizophrenic youth and adults, implying that a small percentage of those with psychosis NOS might later develop schizophrenia spectrum disorders. Cognitive deficits frequently associated with negative symptoms are present in many of the adolescents and adults who have schizophrenia usually prior to, or at the onset of the psychosis (Cullen, Dickson, West, Morris, Mould, Hodgins, Murray, and Laurens, 2010). Some patterns of cognitive weaknesses, such as social cognition deficits in the theory of mind, also appear to be widespread in adolescents and young adults who are experiencing a first episode of psychosis (Thompson, Papas, Bartholomeusz, Allot, Amminger, Nelson, Wood, and Yung, 2012).

Several wide-ranging attempts have been made to compare and contrast groups of youth with psychosis NOS with other clinical groups who have early-onset psychotic disorders. In one noteworthy study, when pre-morbid characteristics were assessed in adolescents who have early-onset psychotic disorders, distinctive findings emerged. The adolescents with schizophrenia typically enjoyed fewer friendships, had much greater social isolation, and much worse general impairment than youth with either bipolar disorder with psychotic features, or those with psychosis NOS (McClellan, Brieger, McCurry, and Hlastala, 2003). Increased clarity about the reliable indications of thought disorder in childhood has contributed to greater accuracy in the diagnosis of schizophrenia in children (Caplan, 1994). Nevertheless, temporary psychotic reactions in children and adolescents and those which don't meet the full diagnostic criteria for psychotic disorders are not always well understood.

Mood Disorders and Psychosis

Neuroimaging, neuropsychological, and other research reports have considerably advanced knowledge about the continuum of mood disorders in adults. Although there has only been a limited amount of research about psychosis in children and adolescents with mood disorders, and their co-occurrence may be infrequent, a number of important findings have been identified. Several investigators have demonstrated a strong correlation between very severe mood symptoms and psychosis in adolescents. In fact, among many adolescent inpatients, those with psychotic features are much more likely to be severely depressed, to have histories of sexual abuse, and to have mild indications of bipolar disorder (Haley, Fine, and Marriage, 1988). In a large community study of psychotic-like experience in depressed adolescents, a strong positive correlation was found between the depressive symptoms and positive signs of psychosis, including persecutory ideation, hallucinatory experience, as well as some negative symptoms, such as social withdrawal and avolition (Barragan, Laurens, Navarro, and Oboils, 2011). A substantial number of adolescents who have severe depression are subject to a panoply of self-esteem problems, self-critical thinking, ruminative tendencies, and weaknesses in social abilities, which compound their tendency to become self-isolative. In addition, many depressed adolescents who are at high risk for psychosis tend to suffer from a significant difficulty identifying and verbalizing their emotions, regardless of their level of intellectual functioning.

Adults and adolescents with unipolar major depression and bipolar illness most likely share similar brain-based weaknesses in emotional sensitivity and emotional regulation. In a two-year-long prospective study of adolescent inpatients with major depression, the two-year probability of recovery was 90%, but the adolescents with psychotic features tended to have more social impairment for longer periods and were more likely to have symptoms of mania (Strober, Lambert, Schmidt, and Morell, 1993). Lewinsohn, Seeley, Buckley, and Klein, (2002) reported that only a narrowly defined group of adolescents with bipolar illness who had symptoms of mania continued to show signs of the disorder in adulthood. However, an ongoing longitudinal investigation has found that 64% of a group of adolescents with bipolar illness experienced mania at a four-year follow up (Geller, Tillman, Craney, and Bolhofner, 2004).

Individuals who are at high risk for developing mood and psychotic disorders simultaneously reveal weaknesses in emotional processing that contribute to their decreased sense of social competence (van Rijn, Schothorst, van't Wout, Sprong, Ziemans, van Engeland, Aleman, and Swaab, 2011). Various current studies suggest that bipolarity and depression co-inhabit a neurobiologically based spectrum of mood disorders. However, it remains to be seen how often juvenile bipolar disorder is continuous with bipolar disorder in adulthood, and if there are aspects of bipolar disorder in childhood that might predict psychotic episodes in adulthood.

Two-thirds of adults with bipolar disorder have a full onset of the disorder by age 18, but most epidemiological studies conclude that its syndromal occurrence in children is infrequent. The enormous increase in the diagnosis of pediatric bipolar disorder in recent years has led to concern about its validity and to the emergence of the DSM 5 diagnosis of disruptive mood dysregulation disorder. A common misunderstanding about the nature of lability in children and adolescents with mood dysregulation problems and a lack of clarity about what constitutes mania in highly irritable children and youth have contributed to the overdiagnosis of bipolarity. In an effort to differentiate the criteria for mania in pediatric bipolar disorder from the symptoms of ADHD, Geller, Zimmerman, Williams, Del Bello, Bolhofner, Craney, Frazier, Beringer, and Nickelsburg (2002) determined that only five symptoms (elation, grandiosity, flight of ideas or racing thoughts, decreased need for sleep, and hypersexuality) successfully discriminated prepubertal and early adolescent bipolar disorder from the symptoms of ADHD. Persistent irritability is very common in children with ADHD, and the symptoms of irritability, hyperactivity, inattentiveness, and aggressive behavior did not reliably and validly differentiate between the two disorders. Nevertheless, the frequent co-existence of bipolar illness and ADHD has been well documented in the scientific literature. Meta-analytic genetic studies have substantiated that this frequently clinically observed comorbidity between bipolar illness and ADHD isn't simply the result of misdiagnosis. Elevated rates of bipolar disorder have been found in youths (Faraone, Biederman, Wozniak, Mundy, Mennin, and O'Donnell, 1997) and adults with ADHD (Sachs, Baldassano, Truman, and Guille, 2000), and their biological relatives (Faraone, Biederman, and Wozniak, 2012). In addition, the co-occurrence of these two disorders in children and adolescents is commonly associated with much more impaired functioning than if there is only one disorder.

In spite of the controversy and the increasing use of the diagnosis of bipolar disorder with emotionally dysregulated youth, there has been significantly less research about psychosis in children and adolescents who have bipolar disorder than in adults with bipolar disorder. When a well-standardized, structured interview was used in a study of over two hundred and fifty 6- to 16-year-old children and adolescents with bipolar disorder, psychotic phenomena—either hallucinations or delusions—were present in 76% of the subjects. The psychotic symptoms were equally prevalent in the 6- to 9-year-old children and the 10- to 16-year-olds (Tillman, Geller, Klages, Corrigan, Bolhofner, and Zimmerman, 2008). More-recent explorations of pediatric bipolar illness have also reported a 70% prevalence rate of psychotic symptoms, but these estimates are considered to be quite high by some investigators. Systematic reviews of psychosis in children and youth with bipolar disorder designate mood-congruent delusions, in particular delusions of grandiosity, as the most frequent psychotic symptom and the appearance of the psychotic features in the context of mood symptoms as the characteristic that distinguishes pediatric bipolar disorder from childhood schizophrenia (Pavuluri, Herbener, and Sweeney, 2004). Geller et al.'s (2004) longitudinal study of children and adolescents with bipolar disorder has demonstrated the frequently long duration of mania in these children and also that the presence of psychosis predicts a substantially longer period of mania or hypomania. The very high prevalence of psychotic symptoms in children and adolescents who genuinely have bipolar disorder reinforces the urgent need for the development of better treatment interventions, and is consonant with the evidence of the severity of childhood-onset bipolar disorder when it has been validly and reliably diagnosed. There has been very little research on protective factors that might prevent adolescents with severe major depression or bipolar illness from developing psychosis.

Cognitive Behavior Therapy and Combined Treatment

There have been several promising empirical investigations of cognitive behavior therapy and its combination with medication trials in adolescents who have psychotic symptoms and disorders. In fact, when a trial of cognitive behavior therapy was randomly compared with supportive therapy in the treatment of a group of individuals who were at very high risk for developing psychosis, conversions to psychosis occurred only with those who received supportive therapy. Even though both groups improved in positive symptoms, depression, and anxiety, neither group improved in negative symptoms or social functioning (Addington, Epstein, Liu, French, Boydell, and Zipursky, 2011). In a similar study of auditory hallucinations in adults with schizophrenia, group cognitive behavior therapy was more successful than supportive therapy in generally lowering overall psychotic symptoms, while supportive therapy was more beneficial in reducing the impact of the auditory hallucinations (Penn, Meyer, Evans, Wirth, Cai, and Burchinal, 2009). With adults who have psychotic disorders, mindfulness training has proven to be effective in lowering anxiety and impaired functioning associated with auditory hallucinations and delusional thinking (Abba, Chadwick, and Stevenson, 2008). However, one study with children and adolescents suggests that, based on current research, there may only be limited efficacy differences in psychotherapy modalities among youth with psychoses (Miller, Wampold, and Varhely, 2008).

The emphasis on the development of skills for gaining self-acceptance, tolerating feelings of anxiety, and challenging delusions and hallucinations represents a foremost strength of cognitive behavior therapy interventions with psychotic and high-risk children and adolescents. Given the increasing evidence that childhood trauma involving the intent to harm the child, such as being the victim of chronic parental abuse or bullying, greatly increases the possibility of the child experiencing psychotic symptoms, expanding the scope of trauma-focused cognitive behavior therapy might be helpful with children and adolescents who have psychotic symptoms and impairments associated with histories of complex trauma that contribute to severe problems with emotional regulation (Cohen, Mannarino, and Berliner, 2000). Even though dialectical behavior therapy was not designed for the treatment of psychotic youth, it has been shown to have effectiveness as an evidence-supported treatment for adolescents who have major depression, bipolar disorder, and disabling problems with affect regulation (Goldstein, Axelson, Birmaher, and Brent, 2007). There is accumulating evidence for its value with self-injurious and suicidal behavior, and it is beginning to be successfully applied with school-aged children (Perletchikova, Axelrod, Kaufman, Rousaville, Douglas-Palumberi, and Miller, 2011). The pressing need for research about cognitive behavioral treatments with psychotic children and youth was made apparent when 750 treatment protocols were analyzed for indicators of efficacy and effectiveness in the most recent comprehensive review of evidence-based treatments, and none were included for psychotic disorders in children and adolescents (Chorpita, Daleiden, Ebesutani, Young, Becker, Nakamura, Phillips, Ward, Lynch, Trent, Smith, Okamura, and Starace, 2011).

Longitudinal studies of adolescents who are at risk for psychosis and those who exhibit early signs of psychotic disorders have led to important preventative efforts with combined treatment and long-term follow up, especially with those who may be susceptible to developing schizophrenia and severe mood disorders with psychosis (Cornblatt, Lenz, Smith, Correll, Auther, and Nakayama, 2003). Partially successful attempts have been made to combine atypical antipsychotic medication with family interventions and supportive therapy in order to try to prevent the full-blown manifestations of psychosis in high-risk youth (Cannon, et al., 2008; Liu, Parker, Hetrick, Callahan, de Silva, and Purcell, 2010)

Despite the evolution of current knowledge about youth with psychotic disorders, for those whose evanescent psychotic symptoms stem from trauma and mood problems, two further cautionary notes should be considered in order to appreciate the complexity of combining treatments with psychotic children and adolescents. First, the differentiation of definitively psychotic symptoms from subjective mental phenomena can become extremely difficult with children and adolescents who have limited cognitive ability, as it is with those who have pervasive developmental disorder features (Dossetor, 2007). Future studies that explore the most effective psychiatric medication strategies for psychosis, such as those that were done by Blader and Kafantaris (2007), and those that summarize the advantages of cognitive behavior therapy approaches for psychotic disorders (Ford, 2005), need to take into account the range of the neuropsychological deficits in psychotic children and their impairments in functioning. Severely traumatized children with histories of cumulative trauma may have serious neuropsychological deficits that interfere with their ability to use either cognitive or psychodynamic interventions. Second, the frequency of comorbidity in youth with psychosis magnifies the difficulty of conducting valid psychotherapy research. Within an evidence-supported treatment framework, divergence from empirically based guidelines about psychotherapy is essential when there is a serious misalliance between the guidelines and the patient's deficits and clinical characteristics (Shapiro, 2009).

Research Summary

Diathesis-stress models have incorporated genetic findings with brain imaging data and other kinds of research in order to better account for the onset of mental illness. Investigators have been able to distinguish attenuated or psychotic-like symptoms and discrete trauma-related psychotic reactions from the indications of psychotic disorders and comorbid disorders that occur with psychosis. They've elaborated the central themes of early identification and intervention and highlighted the great value of multi-faceted treatment, which address psychotic youngsters' social skills weaknesses, their self-regulation problems, their cognitive deficits in memory and attention, and the enormous demands that are often placed on their family members. Based on the extant research, clinicians have begun to report the results of efforts at prevention and early intervention (Liu, Parker, Hetrick, Callahan, de Silva, and Purcell, 2010) and the advantages and limitations of psychotherapeutic and pharmacological treatments for individuals who have started to exhibit the signs of psychotic disorders in childhood or adolescence.

In spite of the advances in knowledge about atypical antipsychotic and other medications with psychotic youth, efficacious medications still need to be developed that are without the potential risks of damaging metabolic side effects. There have also been an insufficient number of investigations of combining short-term cognitive therapy with medication. In Target and Fonagy's (1994) seminal examination of psychoanalytic treatment with emotionally disturbed children, the length of the treatment was one of the predictors of clinical improvement, but as far as I know, there have been few controlled studies comparing psychoanalytic therapy with cognitive behavior therapy in psychotic youth. Furthermore, research about factors that might influence the onset of psychosis in at-risk children and adolescents need to be balanced by investigations of whether innovative combinations of therapy might serve a protective function or help to reduce the frequency and acuity of psychotic symptoms.

Two conceptual models that have been delineated throughout the literature are important for practicing psychotherapists. First, research findings provide a basis for combining psychotherapies with medication in order to address the truly psychotic child's maladjustment and deficits. Second, features of comorbid disorders have to be explored in light of their impact on the psychotic child or adolescent's impairments in functioning. Similarities and differences also have to be distinguished between mental phenomena associated with divergent disorders and psychosis (Kaur, Dobroshi, McCarthy, and Coffey, 2010). For example, there appears to be considerable overlap in cognitive weaknesses in executive functioning ability, verbal memory, and attention ability found in youth with early-onset schizophrenia and those with bipolar illness, which implies that the disorders might share some as-yet poorly identified biological continuity (Nieto and Castellanos, 2011). McClellan, Prezbindowski, Breiger, and McCurry (2004) reported that attention and memory deficits are fairly widespread in youth with psychosis, regardless of whether they have been diagnosed with schizophrenia, bipolar disorder with psychosis, or psychosis, NOS.

In contrast to the profusion of recent research findings about the brain and the basic science underlying the genetics and the neurodevelopmental anomalies of serious psychiatric disorders, there has been a disappointing gap between the advances in science and the lack of innovative psychotherapy techniques and risk-free medication treatment strategies. Multi-disciplinary prospective investigations might better help to identify variables that could be associated with more-positive outcomes for children and adolescents who are suffering from intermittent psychotic symptoms, as well as those with chronic psychoses. An integrative, research-informed frame of reference for combining appropriate medication with multiple psychotherapeutic modalities, including psychoanalytic conceptualizations, is designed to minimize the potentially damaging effects of psychotic disorders on children and adolescents' development.

The Therapeutic Relationship

Evidence has accumulated that the therapeutic relationship makes as much of a contribution to the positive outcome of psychotherapy as the specific techniques that are employed (Norcross, 2011). The paramount importance of the therapeutic relationship as the basis for treating children and adolescents underlies the integrative thinking I have described, but considerable research needs to be done on which moderating variables might contribute to successful therapeutic outcomes with specific patient populations. For example, with young adults who have abuse-related posttraumatic stress disorder, the strength of the therapeutic relationship actually predicts the extent of the symptomatic improvement (Cloitre, Stovall-McClough, and Chemtob, 2004). There have been more studies about therapeutic relationship variables and outcome effects with psychotic adults than studies with children and adolescents who have psychotic disorders. The maintenance of a therapeutic alliance is a hallmark of a successful treatment outcome with adults and adolescents who have psychotic disorders. Symptomatic improvement and encouragement of developmentally appropriate growth opportunities constitute essential therapeutic goals for children, whether the psychotherapy interventions rely more heavily on cognitive behavioral techniques or the application of psychoanalytic principles about the dyadic nature of patient–therapist interactions.

Considerable research supports the legitimacy and efficacy of psychodynamic psychotherapy and attachment theory–based approaches. The therapeutic relationship has a more encompassing significance in psychodynamic/relational psychotherapy, with its greater emphasis on attunement to emotional engagement and the mutative influence of unconscious transference–countertransference communication. Early investigators of the therapeutic relationship in psychoanalytic therapy with psychotic children and adolescents recognized that even the experienced psychotherapist can easily become overwhelmed by the child's emotional lability and occasionally bizarre patterns of communication. The process of establishing and deepening the therapeutic relationship with the severely disturbed patient, one that is sensitive to the unconscious meaning and persistent influences of trauma, offers opportunities for resolving the psychotic elements of the child's anxieties through their recreation with the therapist (Settlage, 1989; Guarton and McCarthy, 2008).

Psychoanalytic Formulations

Psychoanalytic conceptualizations about psychotic youth have been shaped by general principles that were first established by psychoanalytic pioneers beginning with the work of Freud, Anna Freud, Melanie Klein, Harry Stack Sullivan, and Frieda Fromm-Reichmann. The following concepts were later re-affirmed by a number of authors in subsequent decades:

First, each patient is a singular combination of strengths, deficits, and emotional disturbance. The average child's specific ego function weaknesses and overall levels of psychological functioning are characterized by unevenness and gaps in age-appropriate development in at least some areas. Expected patterns of immaturity partially account for the child's compromised capacities for responding to threatening anxiety, and they influence the therapist's evolving role as the patient's temporary auxiliary ego.

Second, the expressions of a child or adolescent's psychopathology can't simply be reduced to a diagnostic category. Understanding the psychotic aspects of personality development is impossible without exploring the child's internal object world, self and object representations, and emotional experience in the family environment.

Third, each family represents a unique constellation. The parents' communication, the family process, and the social and cultural milieu all either facilitate, or impede the maturation of the child's healthy ego functioning.

These organizing principles have been widely discussed in the psychoanalytic literature, quite apart from controversial, early dynamic theories about the etiology of psychosis, and they are very compatible with attachment theory views of psychopathology that will be described in Chapter 2 and Chapter 3. These principles sway strategies and techniques with disturbed children and adolescents, techniques that must be balanced by efforts to strengthen the therapeutic alliance and to facilitate unfettered emotional communication between patient and therapist. Rather than summarizing the literature and its reports of the extensive ego deficits in psychotic children and adolescents, I will mention two early papers about the treatment of disturbed youth that are rarely referenced.

From a Freudian and ego-psychology perspective, Ekstein and Wallerstein (1956) described psychotic decompensations during play therapy with intermittently psychotic children as regressions to primary process functioning that require the therapist to use a range of interpretative strategies, including making metaphoric interpretations about the play. This initial statement in the literature about interpreting "within the metaphor" became a cornerstone of dynamic psychotherapy with seriously ill children and adolescents. This kind of interpretative approach encourages the child to express disorganizing anxieties through symbolic displacement and play and to decrease the likelihood of impulsive enactments of psychotic mental states. Rosenfeld and Sprince (1965) emphasized monitoring the ways in which anxiety molds the child or adolescent patient's fluctuating ego regressions and trying to identify how the failure of signal anxiety might evoke fears of disintegration. They further advocated the importance of the therapist temporarily entering the psychotic components of the child or adolescent's internal world and refraining from making conflict interpretations when they are likely to be experienced as annihilating attacks. These authors stressed the prominent role of the points of emergence in the therapeutic interaction of the patient's more or less psychotic experience of anxiety, a concept that is synchronous with Freudian, interpersonal, object-relations theories, and self-psychology psychoanalytic orientations. From the perspective of each of these psychoanalytic orientations, the development of the therapeutic relationship and the permutations of the therapeutic interaction are cardinal areas for having an impact on the patient's changing level of anxiety and personality organization. Transference–countertransference exchanges point to themes in the child or adolescent patient's internalized object relations as their shifts in mental functioning help to identify their greatest vulnerabilities as they are expressed in relationship to the therapist.

For example, a deeply psychotic 13-year-old girl became withdrawn and sullen during her therapy sessions for no apparent reason. She eventually reported to her female therapist that she was being increasingly bothered by two-inch-long exact replicas of the therapist that were crawling on her neck and becoming lodged in her hair. The patient noted that even though these miniature versions of the therapist, which were called "Marys," had long been present on her skin, they had never before been unpleasant. This revelation prompted the therapist—who was named Mary—to inquire if she might have seemed untrustworthy when she raised questions about the self-defeating aspects of the patient's aggressive outbursts.

A schizophrenic 16-year-old girl became highly preoccupied with God and the devil whenever she expressed any spontaneous feelings during sessions. At the moment when she realized that she had volunteered a comment or conveyed an inner experience, this assertion had to be immediately undone by repetitiously reciting prayers, which she delivered as tangential sermons. Any effort by the therapist to get the patient to reflect on either her own mental state or their interaction was experienced as an attack that could only be thwarted by additional sermons. Greater clarity about this girl's anxious preoccupations emerged when the therapist started to inquire about the detailed nuances of dogma that the sermons conveyed.

With both of these adolescent girls, their therapists first tried to help them observe their transient feelings in order to be better able to identify them and to enhance their sense of subjectivity. The therapists' interests in the details about the "Marys" and the sermons created a foundation for representation and the beginning of a dialogue that couldn't be hastened by refocusing the patients on practicing nascent psychological skills. After they began to tolerate having their feelings reflected by another, both girls were encouraged to try to start writing about them and to tell them to the therapist, who recorded them in a notebook. Writing together can gradually became a collaborative process that strengthens the therapeutic relationship while establishing a relatively accessible narrative of patients' lives and some of the major changes in their family environments. The creation of a biographical notebook containing children's positive and negative memories and their observations is designed to facilitate increasing their sense of inner continuity and developing their emotional vocabulary about stress, anxiety-laden interpersonal experience, and disturbances of the self. For both patients, their brief statements in the sessions signaled sufficient trust to acknowledge feeling recognized and persecuted, which implied that there had been a subtle reorganization of their internal worlds. This shift might have been much less likely to occur without the therapists' attentiveness to the nature of the interaction and the patients' transitions between regressed functioning and slightly greater ego integration. This kind of transformative therapeutic interaction requires an unhurried openness to ambiguity and the complexity of unconscious communication. Its objectives can't be fully expressed in measurable, behavioral terms or reduced to strategies that can be completely focused on stabilization and immediate symptom reduction.

Conclusion

Psychotic-like symptoms are relatively common. Their fleeting occurrence in children and adolescents needs to be distinguished from the genuinely psychotic manifestations of psychiatric disorders that emerge from diverse developmental pathways as a result of heritable characteristics and a variety of adverse influences. Uncertainties continue about the interplay of complex genetic interactions and unknown environmental factors in the origin of psychotic features and disorders that first occur during childhood and adolescence. Psychotic disorders in older adolescents and adults can be understood as developmental disorders, in that about half originate during childhood. Rapidly increasing knowledge about the genetic contributions and the underlying brain abnormalities in childhood-onset and adolescent-onset psychotic disorders has not been accompanied by corresponding revolutionary advances in how to intervene psychotherapeutically with psychotic patients. Further research is necessary in order to know how to reverse the premorbid declines in social and academic functioning that can be associated with childhood and adolescent-onset psychotic disorders. As industry-driven behavioral health objectives compel justifying treatment even in community- and hospital-based programs designed to treat chronically disturbed children and adolescents, the dangers of reductionist reasoning about serious emotional disturbance and psychotherapy intensify. Formulaic, artificially imposed lengths of stay for the inpatient and outpatient treatment of severely disturbed children and adolescents heighten the risks of misdiagnosis and superficial psychotherapy that overlooks the individual patient's idiosyncratic characteristics.

With all of the patients I've discussed, the manifestations of their psychotic features were irreducibly multidimensional in their etiology and their behavioral implications. Extensive data gathering was necessary in order to understand their psychotic thinking and behavior. Comprehensive treatment planning has to include an investigation of multiple risk factors, developmental stresses, trauma variables, and comorbid disorders, in addition to the psychological impact of the child's family environment and internal object world. Integrative treatment for disturbed children and adolescents with psychosis emphasizes the value of the therapeutic relationship and the willingness to examine how the stimuli for psychotic decompensations might stem, in part, from anxiety-laden unconscious conflicts, as well as biological, developmental, and social influences. In contrast to short-term treatment, psychoanalytically informed psychotherapy endorses complexity by investigating the partially unconscious nature of the psychotic child or adolescent's mental functioning. As Freud predicted, the validity of the unconscious aspects of mental functioning is increasingly being demonstrated by neuroscience research. Brief, purely symptom-focused treatment and integrative, intensive psychotherapy approaches that include psychoanalytic formulations about the nuances of the therapeutic interaction represent disparate sensibilities.

References

Aas, M., Navari, S., Gibbs, A., Mondelli, V., Fisher, H. L., Morgan, C., Morgan, K., MacCabe, J., Reichenberg, A., Zanelli, J., Fearon, P., Jones, P., Murray, R., Pariante, C., & Dazan, P. (2012). Is there a link between childhood trauma, cognition, and amygdala and hippocampus volume in first-episode psychosis? *Schizophrenia Research,* 137(1), 73–79.

Asarnow, J. R. (2005). Childhood-onset schizotypal disorder: A follow-up study and comparison with childhood-onset schizophrenia. *Journal of Child and Adolescent Psychopharmacology,* 15(3), 395–402.

Abba, N., Chadwick, P., & Stevenson, C. (2008). Responding mindfully to distressing psychosis: A grounded theory analysis. *Psychotherapy Research,* 18(1), 77–87.

Addington, J., Cornblatt, B., Cadenhead, K. S., Cannon, T. D., McGlashan, T. H., Perkins, D. O., Seidman, L. J., Tsuang, M. T., Walker, E. F., Woods, S. W., & Heinssen, R. (2011). At clinical high risk for psychosis: Outcome for nonconverters. *American Journal of Psychiatry,* 168(8), 800–805.

Addington, J., Epstein, I., Liu, L., French, P., Boydell, K. B., & Zipursky, R. B. (2011). A randomized controlled trial of cognitive behavior therapy for individuals at clinical risk for psychosis. *Schizophrenia Research,* 125(1), 54–61.

Ballageer, T., Malla, A., Manchanda, R., Takhar, J., & Haricharan, R. (2005). Is adolescent-onset first-episode psychosis different from adult onset? *Journal of the American Academy of Child & Adolescent Psychiatry,* 44(8), 782–789.

Barragan, M., Laurens, K. R., Navarro, J. B., & Obiols, J. E. (2011). Psychotic-like experience and depressive symptoms in a community sample of adolescents. *European Psychiatry,* 26(6), 396–401.

Belsky, D. W., Caspi, A., Arseneault, L., Bleidorn, W., Fonagy, P., Goodman, M., Houts, R., & Moffitt, T. E. (2012). Etiological features of borderline personality related characteristics in a birth cohort of 12-year-old children. *Development and Psychopathology,* 24, 251–265.

Bendall, S., Jackson, H. J., Hulbert, C. A., & McCorry, P. D. (2008). Childhood trauma and psychotic disorders: A systematic, critical review of the evidence. *Schizophrenia Bulletin,* 34(3), 568–579.

Bernstein, D. P., Cohen, P., Valez, C. N., Schwab-Stone, M., Siever, L. J., & Shinsato, L. (1993). Prevalence and stability of the DSM-III-R personality disorders in a community-based survey of adolescents. *American Journal of Psychiatry,* 150, 1237–1243.

Bevan, J. R., Thapar, A., Lewis, G., & Zammit, S. (2012). The association between early autistic traits and psychotic experience in adolescence. *Schizophrenia Research, 135*(1–3), 164–169.

Blader, J. C., & Kafantaris, V. (2007). Pharmacological treatment of bipolar disorder among children and adolescents. *Expert Reviews in Neurotherapeutics, 7*(3), 259–270.

Bleiberg, E. (2001). *Treating personality disorders in children and adolescents: A relational approach.* New York, NY: Guilford Press.

Boeing, L., Murray, V., Pelosi, A., McCabe, R., Blackwood, D., & Wrate, R. (2007). Adolescent-onset psychosis: Prevalence, needs, and service provision. *British Journal of Psychiatry, 190*, 18–26.

Borchardt, C. M., & Bernstein, G. A. (1995). Comorbid disorders in hospitalized bipolar adolescents compared with unipolar depressed adolescents. *Child Psychiatry & Human Development, 26*(1), 11–18.

Burke, J. D., & Stepp, S. D. (2012). Adolescent disruptive behavior and borderline personality disorder symptoms in young adult men. *Journal of Abnormal Child Psychology, 40*(1), 35–44.

Cannon, T. D., Cadenhead, K., Cornblatt, B. A., Woods, S. W., Addington, J., Walker, E., Seidman, L. J., Perkins, D., Tsuang, M., McGlashan, T., & Heinssen, R. (2008). Prediction of psychosis in youth at high clinical risk youth: A multisite longitudinal study in North America. *Archives of General Psychiatry, 65*(1), 28–37.

Caplan, R. (1994). Thought disorder in childhood. *Journal of the American Academy of Child & Adolescent Psychiatry*, 33(5), 605–615.

Chorpita, B. F., Daleiden, E. L., Ebesutani, C., Young, J., Becker, K. D., Nakamura, B. J., Phillips, L., Ward, A., Lynch, R., Trent, L., Smith, R. L., Okamura, K., & Starace, N. (2011). Evidence-based treatments for children and adolescents: An updated review of indicators of efficacy and effectiveness. *Clinical Psychology: Science and Practice, 18*(2), 154–172.

Cloitre, M., Stovall-McClough, K. C., & Chemtob, C. M. (2004). Therapeutic alliance, negative mood regulation, and treatment outcome in child abuse-related posttraumatic stress disorder. *Journal of Consulting and Clinical Psychology, 72*(3), 411–416.

Cohen, J. A., Mannarino, A. P., & Berliner, L. (2000). Trauma focused-CBT for children and adolescents: An empirical update. *Journal of Interpersonal Violence, 15*(11), 1202–1223.

Cornblatt, B. A., Lenz, T., Smith, C. W., Correll, C. U., Auther, A. M., & Nakayama, E. (2003). The schizophrenia prodrome revisited: A neurodevelopmental perspective. *Schizophrenia Bulletin, 29*(4), 633–651.

Correll, C. U., Penzer, J., Kafantaris, V., Nakayma, E., Auther, A., Lencz, T., Malhotra, A., Kane, J. M., & Cornblatt, B. A., (2005). The prodrome in early-onset bipolar disorder: Onset pattern and symptom constellation. *Biological Psychiatry, 57*, (Suppl.8), 35.

Crick, N. R., Murray-Close, D., & Woods, W. (2005). Borderline personality features in childhood: A short-term longitudinal study. *Development and Psychopathology, 17*(4), 1051–1070.

Cullen, A. E., Dickson, H., West, S. A., Morris, R. G., Mould, M. L., Hodgins, S., Murray, R. M., & Laurens, K. R. (2010). Neurocognitive performance in children aged 9–12 years who present putative antecedents of schizophrenia. *Schizophrenia Research, 121*(1), 15–23.

Dossetor, D. R., (2007). 'All that glitters is not gold': Misdiagnosis of psychosis in pervasive developmental disorders—A case series. *Clinical Child Psychology and Psychiatry, 12*(4), 537–548.

Ekstein, R., & Wallerstein, J. (1956). Observations on the psychotherapy of borderline and psychotic children. *Psychoanalytic study of the Child,* 11, 303–311.

Faraone, S. V., Biederman, J., & Wozniak, J. (2012). Examining the comorbidity between attention deficit hyperactivity disorder and bipolar I disorder: A meta-analysis of family genetic studies. *American Journal of Psychiatry,* 169(12), 1256–1266.

Faraone, S. V., Biederman, J., Wozniak, J., Mundy, E., Mennin, D. S., & O'Donnell, D. (1997). Is comorbidity with ADHD a marker for juvenile-onset mania? *Journal of the American Academy of Child & Adolescent Psychiatry,* 36(8), 1046–1055.

Ford, J. D. (2005). On finding a mind that has lost itself: Implications of neurobiology and information processing research for cognitive behavior therapy with psychotic disorders. *Clinical Psychology: Science and Practice,* 12(1), 57–64.

Geller, B., Tillman, R., Craney, J. L., & Bolhofner, K. (2004). Four year prospective outcome and natural history of mania in children with prepubertal and early adolescent onset bipolar disorder phenotype. *Archives of General Psychiatry,* 61(5), 459–467.

Geller, B., Zimmerman, B., Williams, M., Del Bello, M. P., Bolhofner, K., Craney, J. L., Frazier, J., Beringer, L., & Nickelsburg, M. J. (2002). DSM-IV mania symptoms in a prepubertal and early adolescent bipolar disorder phenotype compared to attention deficit hyperactive and normal controls. *Journal of Child and Adolescent Psychopharmacology,* 12(1), 11–25.

Goldstein, T. R., Axelson, D. A., Birmaher, B., & Brent, D. A., (2007). Dialectical behavior therapy: A 1-year open trial. *Journal of the American Academy of Child & Adolescent Psychiatry,* 46(7), 820–830.

Guarton, G., & McCarthy, J., (2008). Treatment of a borderline child with developmental delays: A play therapy case revisited after thirty years. *Journal of Infant, Child, and Adolescent Psychotherapy,* 7(1), 1–13.

Haley, G. M., Fine, S., & Marriage, K. (1988). Psychotic features in adolescents with major depression. *Journal of the American Academy of Child and Adolescent Psychiatry,* 27(4), 489–493.

Kaur, T., Dobroshi, Z., McCarthy, J., & Coffey, B. J., (2010). New onset of psychotic symptoms in an adolescent with pervasive developmental disorder, not otherwise specified. *Journal of Child and Adolescent Psychopharmacology,* 21(1), 87–90.

Lewinsohn, P. M., Seeley, J. R, Buckley, M. E., & Klein, D. N. (2002). Bipolar disorder in adolescence and young adulthood. *Child and Adolescent Psychiatric Clinics of North America,* 11(3), 461–475.

Liu, P., Parker, A. G., Hetrick, S. E., Callahan, P., de Silva, S., & Purcell, R. (2010). An evidence map of interventions across premorbid, ultra-high risk and first episode phases of psychosis. *Schizophrenia Research,* 123(1), 37–44.

Mahler, M. S., Ross, J. R., & De Fries, Z. (1949). Clinical studies in benign and malignant cases of childhood psychosis (schizophrenia-like). *American Journal of Orthopsychiatry,* 19(2), 295- 305.

McClellan, J., Brieger, D., McCurry, C., & Hlastala, S. A. (2003). Premorbid functioning in early-onset psychotic disorders. *Journal of the American Academy of Child & Adolescent Psychiatry,* 42(6), 666–672.

McClellan, J., Prezbindowski, A., Brieger, D., & McCurry, C., (2004). Neuropsychological functioning in early onset psychotic disorders. *Schizophrenia Research,* 68(1), 21–26.

Miller, S., Wampold, B., & Varhely, K. (2008). Direct comparisons of treatment modalities for youth disorders: A meta-analysis. *Psychotherapy Research,* 18(1), 5–14.

Morrison, A. P, Frame, L., & Larkin, W. (2003). Relationships between trauma and psychosis: A review and integration. *British Journal of Child Psychology,* 42, 331–353.

Niemai, L. T., Suvisaari, J. M., Tuulio-Hendriksson, A., & Lonnqvist, J. (2003). Childhood developmental abnormalities in schizophrenia: Evidence from high-risk studies. *Schizophrenia Research,* 60(2–3), 239–258.

Nieto, R. G., & Castellanos, F. X. (2011). A meta-analysis of neuropsychological functioning in patients with early onset schizophrenia and pediatric bipolar disorder. *Journal of Clinical Child Clinical & Adolescent Psychology,* 40(2), 266–280.

Norcross, J. (2011). *Psychotherapy relationships that work: Evidence-based responsiveness.* London, UK: Oxford University Press.

Pavuluri, M. N., Herbener, E. S., & Sweeney, J. A. (2004). Psychotic symptoms in pediatric bipolar disorder. *Journal of Affective Disorders,* 80(1), 19–28.

Penn, D. L., Meyer, P. S., Evans, E., Wirth, R. J., Cai, K., & Burchinal, M. (2009). A randomized controlled trial of group cognitive–behavioral therapy vbs. Enhanced supportive therapy for auditory hallucinations. *Schizophrenia Research,* 109(1–3), 52–59.

Perletchikova, F., Axelrod, S. R., Kaufman, J., Rousaville, B. J., Douglas-Palumberi, H., & Miller, A. L. (2011). Adapting dialectical behavior therapy for children: Towards a research agenda for paediatric suicidal and non-suicidal self-injurious behaviors. *Child & Adolescent Mental Health,* 16(2), 116–121.

Read, J., Perry, B. D., Moskowitz, A., & Connolly, J. (2001). The contribution of early traumatic events to schizophrenia in some patients. A traumagenic neurodevelopmental model. *Psychiatry,* 64(4), 319–345.

Rosenfeld, S. K., & Sprince, M. P. (1965). Some thoughts on the technical handling of borderline children. *Psychoanalytic Study of the Child,* 20, 495–517.

Ross, R. G., Heinlein, S., & Tregellas, H. (2006). High rates of comorbidity are found in childhood-onset schizophrenia. *Schizophrenia Research,* 88(1–3), 90–95.

Sachs, G. S., Baldassano, C. F., Truman, C. J., & Guille, C. (2000). Comorbidity of attention deficit hyperactivity disorder with early-onset and late-onset bipolar disorder. *American Journal of Psychiatry,* 157(3), 466–468.

Settlage, C. F., (1989). The interplay of therapeutic and developmental process in the treatment of children: An application of contemporary object relations theory. *Psychoanalytic Inquiry,* 9(3), 375–396.

Shapiro, J. P. (2009). Integrating outcome research and clinical reasoning in psychotherapy planning. *Professional Psychology: Research and Practice,* 40(1), 46–53.

Siever, L. J., & Davis, K. L., (1991). A psychobiological perspective on the personality disorders. *American Journal of Psychiatry,* 148(12), 1647–1658.

Spauwen, J., Krabbendam, L., Lieb, R., Wittchen, H. U., & van Os, J. (2006). Impact of psychological trauma on the development of psychotic symptoms: Relationship with psychosis proneness. *British Journal of Psychiatry,* 188, 527–533.

Stepp, S. D., Burke, J. D., Hipwell, A. E., & Loeber, R. (2012). Trajectories of attention deficit hyperactivity disorder and oppositional defiant disorder symptoms as precursors of borderline personality disorder symptoms in adolescent girls. *Journal of the American Academy of Child & Adolescent Psychiatry,* 50, 563–573.

Strober, M., Lambert, C., Schmidt, S., & Morell, W. (1993). The course of major depressive disorder in adolescents: I. Recovery and risk of manic switching in a follow up of psychotic and nonpsychotic subtypes. *Journal of the American Academy of Child & Adolescent Psychiatry,* 32(1), 34–42.

Target, M., & Fonagy, P. (1994). Efficacy of psychoanalysis for children with emotional disorders. *Journal of the American Academy of Child & Adolescent Psychiatry,* 33(3), 361–371.

Tessner, K. D., Mittal, V., & Walker, E. F. (2011). Longitudinal study of stressful life events and daily stressors among adolescents at high risk for psychotic disorders. *Schizophrenia Bulletin,* 37(2), 432–441.

Thompson, A., Papas, A., Bartholomeusz, C., Allot, K., Amminger, G. P., Nelson, B., Wood, S., & Yung, A. (2012). Social cognition in clinical "at risk" for psychosis and first episode psychosis populations. *Schizophrenia Research,* 141(2), 204–209.

Thompson, J. L., Kelly, M., Kimhy, D., Harkavy-Friedman, J. M., Khan, S., Messinger, J. W., Schobel, S., Goetz, R., Malaspina, D., & Corcoran, C. M. (2009). Childhood trauma and prodromal symptoms among individuals at clinical risk for psychosis. *Schizophrenia Research,* 108(1–3), 176–181.

Tillman, R., Geller, B., Klages, T., Corrigan, M., Bolhofner, K., & Zimmerman, B. (2008). Psychotic phenomena in 257 young children and adolescents with bipolar 1 disorder: Delusions and hallucinations (benign and pathological). *Bipolar Disorders,* 10(1), 45–55.

Ulloa, R. E., Birmaher, B., Axelson, D., Williamson, D. E., Brent, D. A., Ryan, N. D., Bridge, J., & Baugher, M. (2000). Psychosis in pediatric mood and anxiety disorders clinic: Phenomenology and correlates. *Journal of the American Academy of Child & Adolescent Psychiatry,* 39(3), 337–345.

van Rijn, S., Schothorst, P. van't Wout, M., Sprong, M., Ziemans, T. B., van Engeland, H., Aleman, A., & Swaab, H. (2011), Affective dysfunctions in adolescents at risk for psychosis: Emotion awareness and social functioning. *Psychiatry Research,* 187(1–2), 100–105.

Zanarini, M. C., Gunderson, J., & Frankenberg, F. (1990), Cognitive features of borderline personality disorder. *American Journal of Psychiatry,* 147(1), 57–63.

Ziemans, T. B., Schothorst, P. F., Sprong, M., & van Engeland, H. (2011). Transition and remission in adolescents at ultra-high risk for psychosis. *Schizophrenia Research,* 126(1), 58–64.

2

COGNITIVE SCHEMAS AND THE ROLE OF ATTACHMENT IN PSYCHOSIS

Meritxell Fortea Vila and Andrew J. Gerber

Psychosis as a phenomenon is one of the most widely studied in the scientific community and yet one of the least understood. Its complexity lies in the variety of its expressions affecting multiple mental capacities and dimensions. But the essential feature in all of its expressions is the loss of a sense of reality. It has therefore been a primary task for researchers to explore the psychological and brain structures that govern reality, but despite all of the advances in this regard, many questions remain unresolved. Foremost among these are questions about the development of psychosis and the onset of psychotic disorders.

It is essential, as the author points out in Chapter 1, to distinguish the occurrence of psychotic phenomena in childhood and adolescence from the early onset of a truly psychotic disorder, since a better understanding of their different underlying processes might have implications in many areas, for example, the improvement of treatment.

The aim of this section is to focus on psychosis as a disorder and the characteristics of its early development and onset. Psychosis represents an established disturbance in reality testing, a deficiency in ego functioning, and impairments in social relationships.

A lot remains unclear about the development of psychotic disorders. Nevertheless, there has been increasing evidence in the research literature about the essential role that adverse early life experiences play during childhood in addition to the genetic components. Adverse early life experiences modulate and influence the development of a vulnerability to psychosis on one hand, and on the other hand, they also influence the coping skills that are challenged by the disorder itself.

Childhood experiences, such as trauma, sexual or physical abuse, and neglect, are considered risk factors for neurodevelopmental deficiencies and psychosis.

But a deeper exploration of the significance of early life experience must highlight the relational dimensions of the concept of trauma. An individual's early life experiences are always mediated by the main caregivers or the lack of them, so that the core domains of study and research on the development of a psychotic disorder should necessarily include the subject, his or her main attachment figures, and their interaction.

How life experiences are incorporated into the mind is a process that has been addressed extensively from many theoretical perspectives. In the last few decades, attachment theory has been increasingly emphasized due its comprehensive and integrative framework. According to Bowlby (1969), infants organize their experiences with their closest caregivers in what is called an "internal working model" at a very early stage. These internal working models become critical to the child's formation of future relations and form the basis for their future view of everything that happens in life. Some authors have been able to successfully integrate psychoanalytical theory, attachment models, and knowledge about neuroaffective development with the attachment theory and cognitive neuroscience literature (Stern, 1985).

Attachment theory offers a very suitable theoretical framework for exploring and understanding how early childhood conditions determine adult attachment styles and relational cognitive affective schema. There is also beginning evidence about how attachment styles influence adults' ways of coping with psychosis.

The nature of internal working models of experience has been given careful scrutiny in cognitive science research. The concept of cognitive schemas has become very useful in describing how early life experiences are internalized in ways that become regular mental patterns that impact future experiences (Rumelhart, 1980). Young children internalize their relations with significant others as patterns of mind that influence their subsequent relationships as well as their sense of self (Fonagy, 2004). The establishment of these cognitive schemas can be influenced by the genetic substrate and background of the individual, but the genetic influences represent latent vulnerabilities as starting points from which interpersonal patterns and cognitive schemas emerge (Bretherton and Munholland, 1999).

Cognitive schemas have been extensively used in research to evaluate the role of self and other schema in several psychiatric symptoms and syndromes, mainly depression and personality disorders. It has also been postulated that cognitive schema represent underlying substrates that trigger mental symptomatology.

Cognitive schemas (and related conceptual constructs) have also been the focus for developing several types of psychotherapies, based on the recognition that engagement in a new, long-term relationship can significantly modify well-established relational templates.

One of the purposes of this chapter is to explore the nature of the developmental process that leads to a psychotic mind, within the framework of attachment theory and cognitive schemas. The other purpose is to relate this process to the ameliorative, healing aspects of psychotherapy and to highlight the importance of the long-term psychotherapy treatments in facilitating effective change.

Psychosis

Psychosis is a complex phenomenon of losing connection with reality that can present many symptomatic expressions. Distinctive hallucinations and delusions are the more striking features, and deficits in cognitive capacities may frequently appear. But the subtle impairments in the individual's relational capacities may represent signs of psychotic experience in terms of deficiencies in the self–other boundary. In many cases of psychosis, such relational weaknesses precede the full unfolding of the symptoms. How a psychotic state of mind develops and whether it constitutes a mental disorder, or not, is still a central issue in scientific research.

Psychosis has been typically described categorically for clinical purposes, but current lines of investigation consider the incidence of sub-threshold psychotic characteristics in clinical populations as well as in the general population (van Os et al., 2009). These studies reflect a renewed emphasis on understanding the prevalence and the epidemiology of mild psychotic symptoms and psychotic-like experience. Authors like van Os and others have conducted clinical trials on this issue, contributing data that demonstrate a continuity of psychotic experiences in clinical samples and also in the general population (van Nierop and van Os, 2012). The existence of such lesser states of psychosis on a continuum of disturbance in the population may, perhaps, instead of being considered a *forme fruste* of disease, be better thought of as a risk factor for what clinicians would call psychotic disorders (Johns and van Os, 2001).

Since the late 1960s, there has also been speculation that the major categories of the symptoms of schizophrenia could reflect divergent neurobiological underpinnings with different forms of pathophysiology. The etiology of positive symptoms, negative symptoms, and disorders of relatedness and cognition have all been investigated separately as well as in concert, and their prevalence rates have been studied in clinical samples and the general population. Psychotic symptoms and psychotic-like symptoms have been increasingly studied along a continuum that includes sub-threshold phenomena that may be associated with schizotypal traits and schizotypal personality disorder features. Thus, there has been an increasing overlap in the literature as psychosis is investigated dimensionally. The continuum of psychotic-like experiences, schizotypal personality traits, the characteristics of the prodromal phase of schizophrenia, and the first episodes of psychosis are all relevant areas for scientific inquiry.

Current diagnosis classifications, like DSM 5, recognize that several psychiatric disorders typically present with psychotic phenomena in different manifestations. But even in schizophrenia, the most representative psychotic disorder, combinations of symptoms vary significantly so that expressions of the disorder and patterns of dysfunction are very different from one patient to another.

This heterogeneity of symptom expression has been a major issue for researchers who have tried to reliably address questions about etiology. Questions remain about whether there are unitary or multiple underlying neurodevelopmental processes because of the complex clinical phenotype of the schizophrenia syndrome.

For example, although many structural and functional abnormalities have been related to schizophrenia, until now, no single biological marker has been of diagnostic clinical utility. As a result, some scientists have decided to focus more on specific symptoms, such as auditory hallucinations, rather than on diagnostic categories.

Following this line of research that considers individual differences and psychotic experiences on a continuum that includes non-clinical populations, several investigators have systematically explored the course of hallucinatory experiences in childhood and adolescence. There has been a consensus in the findings that hallucinatory experiences are fairly common in children and adolescents and that most of their hallucinations spontaneously discontinue in a short period of time. A subset of these cases, in which the symptoms don't discontinue, represent those who are at-risk for a transition to psychosis, probably related to indications of the severity of the hallucinations (Rubio, Sanjuán, Florez-Salamanca, and Cuesta, 2012). These study conclusions reinforce the importance of differentiating a truly psychotic disorder from transient psychotic experiences during childhood.

There has also been a shift in the genetic research since it has been demonstrated that non-genetic abnormalities are contributory to the occurrence of psychotic disorders. Genetic research on psychosis has recently focused more on epigenetics, the mechanisms regulating gene functions and gene expression, which is providing new insights into heritable and non-heritable components of complex psychiatric diseases (Labrie, Pai, and Petronis, 2012). In a 1991 paper, Jones and Murray pointed out how we should not expect to find a gene that codes directly for first-rank or negative symptoms of schizophrenia. Instead, investigators have explored genetic defects that influence neurodevelopment with the end result that structural changes occur which predispose the individual to the later unfolding of schizophrenia. Thus, the study of the genetics of schizophrenia has shifted to examinations of the genetics of neurodevelopment.

This shift of focus in research on neurodevelopment has stressed the importance of critical developments in early brain and mind development. It also supports the "vulnerability to psychosis" model considered the most acceptable hypothesis on the bio-psychosocial paradigm of the etiology of psychosis.

This vulnerability to psychosis model considers the heterogeneous etiology of psychotic disorders, including as risk factors not only genetic background, but also environmental factors that might be involved in the onset of psychosis. All of the available evidence about the environmental factors point to social adversities, childhood trauma, early exposure to violence in close family members, and drug-marijuana abuse, showing how genetically vulnerable individuals with strong social adversities will be more likely to develop a psychotic disorder. Nevertheless, it is still not completely understood how these risk factors interact with each other. It is postulated that particular early social and relational environments constitute a vulnerability to psychosis, itself, that can predispose the individual to later psychotic disorders, including schizophrenia, in the course of exposure to continuing strong social adversities.

In an attempt to build a bridge between the experiences of delusions and hallucinations and the biological changes in the brain seen in psychotic patients, Kapur (2003) elaborated the concept of motivational "salience" as a way to better understand the pathophysiological mechanisms that lead to delusions and hallucinations. Based on this concept, a psychotic state would be considered a state of aberrant salience. The normal attribution of salience and the structures and functions responsible are mediated by stimulus-linked releases of dopamine. But in psychosis, it is proposed that there is a dysregulated dopamine transmission that leads to stimulus-independent releases of dopamine. "This neurochemical aberration usurps the normal process of contextually driven salience attribution and leads to aberrant assignment of salience to external objects and internal representations. Thus, dopamine, which under normal conditions is a mediator of contextually relevant saliences, in the psychotic state becomes a creator of saliences, aberrant ones" (Kapur, 2003, p. 15).

Among the many important implications of this useful framework is the important status that the biological research confers on cognitive schemas in psychosis. For the psychotic patient, the experience of psychosis and its associated new beliefs are incorporated into larger cognitive schemas. As a result, "blocking the neurochemical abnormality will only take away the driving force but will not demolish the schemas already constructed. Improvement, assisted with drugs, finally involves psychological strategies that have timelines of weeks and months" (Kapur, 2003, p. 17).

Development of Cognitive Schemas

Cognitive scientists have argued that the mechanisms by which social adversities constitute a vulnerability to psychosis in susceptible individuals is through the incorporation of particular cognitive schemas, namely, one's beliefs about the world, the self, and others. Since evidence has established that environmental factors are involved in the development of psychotic disorders and schizophrenia, considerable research has been done in the last few decades on the thought process and cognitive styles underlying psychosis. These cognitive patterns include making external events internal, personalizing and attributing personal responsibility for negative events, jumping to conclusions on the basis of limited data, and misinterpreting internal thoughts or memories as external events, which is common in instances of poor reality testing. Cognitive affective schema can also be considered as integral to the link between childhood trauma and psychosis (Larkin and Morrison, 2006). For example, the mental schema developed by abused children influence how they interpret anomalous experiences later in life. Based on these negative schemas, the distress that is associated with their faulty interpretations has a significant influence on which traumatized children will be most vulnerable to becoming psychotic.

Thus, the current emphasis in biological research on developmental pathways and neurodevelopmental processes has already been stressed in psychology and cognitive science research. Theorists in each of these fields have increasingly paid attention to the central role of relationships in the developmental pathways in psychosis, with major heuristic value.

In the psychoanalytic literature, seminal articles by Blatt have integrated a number of these ideas about cognitive schemas. In Blatt's (1995, 1996) exposition of representational structures in psychopathology, he summarized the similarity between this concept in psychoanalysis and the concepts of cognitive affective schemas in cognitive developmental psychology and internal representational models in attachment theory. The research that stems from these theories has identified particular nodal points in the development of representational structures while explaining how disruptions of the developmental process are inherent in many forms of adult psychopathology (Behrends and Blatt, 1985; Blatt, 1991). The study findings suggest that cognitive affective schemas, thus, develop from intimate relationships throughout life, based on the template of the crucial early relationships established with caregivers. Blatt suggests that there are several milestones in early psychological development that will constitute important points for the later occurrence of psychopathology as a consequence of serious disruptions of the relationship between the child and the caregivers.

According to Blatt, cognitive schemas therefore constitute long-term, enduring psychological structures. They constitute modes of processing and organizing information, including affects, that provide templates that guide and direct the individual's interactions in the interpersonal and impersonal world (Blatt and Blass, 1990; Blatt and Wild, 1976; Blatt, Wild, and Ritzler, 1975). Cognitive-affective schemas emerge first and foremost in the caring relationship and are then stabilized as generalized cognitive structures. A number of developmental investigators and theorists have described essentially the same developmental sequence for the emergence of cognitive-affective schemas, and their findings can be integrated into a consistent theoretical model. Based on a synthesis of concepts from cognitive developmental psychology, developmental psychoanalytic theory, and attachment theory and research, one can specify several major nodal points in the development of cognitive-affective schemas from infancy through adulthood.

The following table presents Blatt's overview of the various levels in the development of cognitive schema with the associated developmental theorists.

Levels of Cognitive Schema: Developmental Levels and Behavioral Indications

I. ***Developmental Level:*** *Boundary Constancy (2–3 months).* ***Behavioral Indication:*** *Smiling response, initiates engagement with others.*

II. ***Developmental Level:*** *Recognition (libidinal) Constancy (6–8 months).* ***Behavioral Indication:*** *Stranger anxiety, differentiation among people, libidinal attachment to a specific individual.*

III. ***Developmental Level:*** *Evocative Constancy (16–18 months).* ***Behavioral Indication:*** *Sense of the object not immediately present in perceptual field. Anticipation of invisible displacement (Piaget), initiation of separation from the caring agent (Mahler).*

IV. ***Developmental Level:*** *Self and Object Constancy (30–36 months).* ***Behavioral Indication:*** *Stable concepts of self and other, as expressed in use of terms such as "mine," "me," and "I."*

V. ***Developmental Level:*** *Concrete Operational Thought (5 years).* ***Behavioral Indication:*** *Capacity for coordinating several dimensions simultaneously. Capacity for anticipation, transformation, conservation, and reversibility of external manifest features. Triadic configurations and the emergence of a concept of "we."*

VI. ***Developmental Level:*** *Formal Operational Thought (11–12 years).* ***Behavioral Indication:*** *Transformation, reversibility and conservation of abstract, inner features, dimensions, and processes such as values and principles. Recognition that one constructs meaning and a sense of reality. Appreciation of personal and cultural relativism.*

VII. ***Developmental Level:*** *Self Identity (late adolescence–young adulthood).* ***Behavioral Indication:*** *Synthesis and integration of mature expressions of both individuality, and relatedness in a capacity to be intimate with another and to contribute to a collective without losing one's individuality. Emergence of a fuller sense of "we" (e.g., "self-in-relation" or "ensembled individualism ...")*

VIII. ***Developmental Level:*** *Integrity (mature adulthood).* (Blatt, 1996)

It is a fundamental premise of Blatt's work that a wide range of psychopathology that occurs in adults can be understood more fully as expressions of disruptions in the development of these various levels of cognitive-affective schema. Disruptions of caring relationships, at particular times in the life cycle, can lead to distortions in the development of significant cognitive schema.

Based on these ideas, psychosis is understood as a disturbance in the earliest and most fundamental cognitive-affective schema boundary constancy that involves a disturbance in the ability to experience, perceive, and represent a separation and differentiation between independent events and objects (Blatt and Wild, 1976; Blatt, Wild, and Ritzler, 1975). This inclusive formulation provides a framework for integrating a large segment of the vast research literature on the disruptions of cognitive, perceptual, and interpersonal processes that take place with schizophrenic patients (Blatt and Wild, 1976). This integrative construct helps to explain how a psychotic state of mind develops and how it may be expressed differently according to the individual's context, significant-other relationships, social environment, and maturity, and whether or not there are temporary expressions or the full establishment of a psychotic disorder.

Can Attachment Theory Help to Explain How Cognitive Schemas Develop in Psychosis?

In recent decades, the increasing study of the interpersonal relationships of infants, children, adolescents, and adults has been remarkably influenced by attachment theory. Attachment theory was articulated by Bowlby in his study of the dynamics of attachment and separation (1969, 1973) which was later enriched by the work of Ainsworth (1969) and Main (1991, 1995). Attachment theory evolved from Bowlby's observations of the disruptive consequences of maternal deprivation in institutionalized children separated from their primary caregiver, usually their mothers. His observations led him to argue that, "the young child's hunger for his mother's love and presence is as great as his hunger for food," and that her absence inevitably generates "a powerful sense of loss and anger" (Bowlby, 1969). Bowlby concluded that the infant–caregiver attachment bond is a complex, instinctually guided behavioral system that has functioned throughout human evolution to protect the infant from danger. Secure attachment in infancy is thus based on the mother's reliable and sensitive provision of safety and love, as well as food and warmth.

By studying behavioral patterns of attachment and separation between mothers and their infants in the first 18 months of life, Bowlby, Ainsworth, Main, and others distinguished secure attachment from several types of insecure attachment, and demonstrated the impact of these attachment styles on subsequent behavior during later childhood years.

Three main patterns of early organized attachment emerged from their investigations: secure, avoidant, and resistant (or ambivalent) attachment. However, a minority, around 15%, failed to develop a recognizable, organized, and coherent attachment pattern (van Ijzendoorn, Schuengel, and Bakermans-Kranenburg, 1999). In these cases, the infant's attachments are said to be disorganized (Main, 1991). Secure attachment in the infant is predicted by autonomous states of mind in the caregiver. Ambivalent (resistant) infant attachment is paralleled by the caregiver's preoccupied/enmeshed states of mind. Avoidant infant attachment is associated with an adult stance that is avoidant/dismissing of attachment (Main, 1995).

Disorganization of infant attachment behavior is statistically linked to unresolved traumas or losses in the caregiver (Main and Hesse, 1990; van Ijzendoorn, Schuengel, and Bakermans-Kranenburg, 1999), or to a caregiver's state of mind characterized by non-integrated hostile and helpless representations of the self and the attachment figures. The caregiver's attitudes that mediate between their unresolved/disaggregated states of mind and the disorganization of the infant attachment behavior have been hypothesized to be frightening to the infant, either because these attitudes involve abrupt emotional and physical aggression, or because they express fear, helplessness, and dissociative absorption in painful memories (Main and Hesse, 1990).

Attachment theory further hypothesizes two interrelated dimensions of attachment. The first, *interactional or behavioral dimension* (Bowlby, 1969), which is based on ethological theory, is concerned with the development and maintenance of specific patterns of behavior that are established in infant–parent interactions. The second, *representational or cognitive dimension,* is based on cognitive developmental and psychoanalytic theories (Bowlby, 1973, 1980; Cassidy and Mohr, 2001). It is concerned with how intimate interpersonal interactions are established (internalized or interiorized) in the mind as "internal working models" of caring experiences and how these schemas influence later emotional states and the capacity to develop and maintain intimate relations with others.

According to Blatt and Blass (1990), the concept of the internal working model in attachment theory is similar to the psychoanalytic concept of mental representations. A number of psychoanalytic authors have described mental representations as the essence of the internal drama in which the individual establishes representations of self and others in multiple roles. Kernberg (1990) described mental representations as units of self-object-affect that provide the basis for the formation of self and object representations. A number of psychoanalytic theorists have similarly stressed the internalization of early interactions with caregivers and how this process results in the formation of representations of self and others, and of their actual and potential relationships (Blatt, Wild, and Ritzler, 1975).

Blatt also considers the internal working model as similar to cognitive-affective schema, since he highlights internal working models' affective valence. However, Berry, Barrowclough, and Wearden (2007) point out that working internal models, which are based on psychoanalytic theories, differ from traditional considerations of cognitive schemas. Psychoanalytic conceptualizations of working models reflect more motivated and affectively charged constructs, constructs that refer to emotional states associated with interpersonal relationships as well as beliefs.

Hence, as Read and Gumley (2008) stress in an important paper, the concept of internal working models potentially integrates the various psychological approaches to making sense of madness. While retaining a focus on cognition, this concept incorporates the crucial domains of affect and relationships. In so doing, the notion of internal working models is particularly well placed to help us understand the processes by which childhood abuse or neglect—interpersonal events with potentially dire affective consequences—can lead to psychosis later in life. Therefore, at least some instances of attachment disorganization are the outcome of subtle relational trauma, not of other adverse influences, such as evident abuse or primary neurobiological anomalies (Schore, 2003). Even when early attachment disorganization is not causally linked to maltreatment suffered at the hand of an attachment figure, it yields a vulnerability to respond to later traumas with a fragmentation of self-experience, and is therefore of great relevance for the understanding of trauma-related disorders (Liotti and Gumley, 2008).

There is some evidence that attachment representations tend to be stable throughout the life span. The child who has been securely attached is likely to become an adult with an autonomous state of mind, while children who have been ambivalent, avoidant, and disorganized in their early attachment are likely to develop preoccupied, dismissing, and unresolved or hostile/helpless states of mind (Benoit and Parker, 1994; Waters, Merrick, Treboux, Crowell, and Albersheim, 2000). Recent meta-analytic evidence shows that disorganized infant attachment does not arise from temperamental (van Ijzendoorn, Schuengel, and Bakermans-Kranenburg, 1999) or genetic variables (Bokhorst, Bakermans-Kranenburg, Fearon, van Ijzendoorn, Fonagy, and Schuengel, 2003).

An increasing number of studies have investigated the link between insecure attachment and psychosis. Although some methodological and conceptual issues have arisen from some of the assessment measures, psychosis has been demonstrated to be associated with childhood trauma, loss, neglect, sub-optimal parenting styles, and insecure attachment.

More recently, some researchers are developing theories about the processes involved in this association (Gumley and MacBeth, 2006; Gumley, White, and Power, 1999; Larkin and Morrison, 2006; Berry, Barrowclough, and Wearden, 2007; Liotti and Gumley, 2008). Berry, Barrowclough, and Wearden (2007) argued that attachment theory offers a suitable framework for understanding the mutual interaction and influence of social cognition, interpersonal factors, and emotional factors on the development and the longitudinal course of psychotic disorders. From this perspective, attachment theory models integrate and enhance psychological models of psychosis.

Gumley and Schwannauer suggest, "It may be that early adverse experiences contribute to the development of core predictors associated with the development of psychosis and the emergence of a negative trajectory of psychosis. This is characterized by problematic emotional and interpersonal adaptation, heightened sensitivity to interpersonal stress (e.g. criticism and emotional over-involvement), poor pro-social coping and help-seeking, social withdrawal and avoidant and/or conflicted coping styles, and impoverished reflective function and affect regulation" (Gumley and Schwannauer, 2006, p. 46).

In a recent systematic review of studies that investigated attachment among individuals with psychosis, Gumley and MacBeth (2006) found small to moderate associations between greater attachment insecurity (as reflected in anxiety and avoidance) and poorer engagement with services, more interpersonal problems, more avoidant coping strategies, more negative appraisals of parenting experiences, and more severe trauma. They also found small to modest associations between attachment insecurity and more positive and negative symptoms of psychosis and greater affective symptom problems.

It is clear at this point that attachment theory seems ideal for furthering our understanding of precisely how abuse, neglect, and loss in childhood can lead to psychosis later in life. But many questions remain unresolved. Further research is needed to clarify how specific attachment patterns are associated with psychotic processes, in order to better understand how disturbances in attachment lead to a psychotic mind in some instances and not to other mental disorders.

More attention as well should be paid in research to marked changes that occur in the developmental process in adolescence since it is in late adolescence and early adulthood that psychosis usually begins. In spite of the importance of this period, little attention has been paid to the interpersonal and developmental tasks of this stage in life. Attachment theory is hugely relevant to these tasks.

Conclusion

It has become increasingly important to highlight both the role of early attachment in the vulnerability for psychosis and the enormous potential value of attachment theory in future approaches to the treatment of psychosis (Brisch, 2002). There is no longer any doubt about how intense, long-term therapies and therapeutic relationships are paramount for a recovery beyond pharmacological improvement. As Bowlby (1973, 1988) already discussed, though early caring experiences are quite significant and have considerable impact in determining developmental pathways, subsequent life experiences and interpersonal relationships can compound initial vulnerabilities. But if these experiences occur within a secure psychotherapeutic relationship, they may serve to ameliorate or compensate for earlier disruptions. Thus, these compromised developmental pathways and impaired cognitive-affective or representational schemas are not necessarily fixed and immutable, but can be altered by subsequent experiences.

References

Ainsworth, M. D. (1969). Object relations, dependency, and attachment: A theoretical review of the mother-infant relationship. *Child Development,* 40, 969–1025.

American Psychiatric Association. (2013). *Diagnostic and Statistical Manual of Mental Disorders* (5th ed.). Arlington, VA: Author.

Behrends, R. S., & Blatt, S. J. (1985). Internalization and psychological development throughout the life cycle. *Psychoanalytic Study of the Child,* 40, 11–39.

Benoit, D., & Parker, K. (1994). Stability and transmission of attachment across three generations. *Child Development,* 65, 1444–1456.

Berry, K., Barrowclough, C., & Wearden, A. (2007). A review of the role of attachment style in psychosis: Unexplored issues and questions for further research. *Clinical Psychology Review,* 27, 458–475.

Bokhorst, C., Bakermans-Kranenburg, M., Fearon, P., van Ijzendoorn, M., Fonagy, P., & Schuengel, C. (2003). The importance of shared environment in mother–infant attachment security: A behavioural-genetic study. *Child Development,* 74, 1769–1782.

Blatt, S. J. (1991). A cognitive morphology of psychopathology. *Journal of Nervous and Mental Disease,* 179, 449–458.

Blatt, S. J. (1995). Representational structures in psychopathology. In: D. Cicchetti & S. Toth (Eds.), *Emotion, Cognition, and Representation: Rochester Symposium on Developmental Psychopathology VI* (pp. 1–33). Rochester, NY: University of Rochester.

Blatt, S. J. (1996). *Representational Structures in Psychopathology.* Retrieved from http://www.psychomedia.it/rapaport-klein.

Blatt, S. J., & Blass, R. B. (1990). Attachment and separateness: A dialectic model of the products and processes of psychological development. *Psychoanalytic Study of the Child,* 45, 107–127.

Blatt, S. J., & Wild, C. M. (1976). *Schizophrenia: A Developmental Analysis.* New York, NY: Academic Press.

Blatt, S. J., Wild, C. M., & Ritzler, B. A. (1975). Disturbances of object representations in schizophrenia. *Psychoanalysis and Contemporary Science,* 4, 235–288.

Bowlby, J. (1969a). *Attachment.* New York, NY: Basic Books

Bowlby, J. (1969b). *Attachment and Loss, Vol. 1: Attachment.* New York, NY: Basic Books

Bowlby, J. (1973). *Attachment and Loss, Vol. 2: Separation, Anxiety, and Anger.* New York, NY: Basic Books.

Bowlby, J. (1980). *Attachment and Loss, Vol. 3: Loss, Separation and Depression.* New York, NY: Basic Books.

Bowlby, J. (1988). Developmental psychiatry comes of age. *American Journal of Psychiatry,* 145, 1–10.

Bretherton, I., & Munholland, K. A. (1999). Internal working models in attachment relationships: A construct revisited. In: J. Cassidy and P. R. Shaver (Eds.), *Handbook of Attachment: Theory, Research and Clinical Applications* (pp. 89–114). New York, NY: Guilford Press.

Brisch, K. (2002). *Treating Attachment Disorders; From Theory to Therapy.* London, UK: Guilford.

Cassidy, J., & Mohr, J. (2001). Unsolvable fear, trauma and psychopathology: Theory, research and clinical considerations related to disorganized attachment across the life cycle. *Clinical Psychology: Science and Practice,* 8, 275–278.

Fonagy, P. (2004). *Affect Regulation, Mentalization, and the Development of the Self.* London, UK: Karnac.

Gumley, A., & MacBeth, A. (2006). A trauma-based model of relapse in psychosis. In: W. Larkin & A. Morrison (Eds.), *Trauma and Psychosis* (pp. 283–304). London, UK: Routledge.

Gumley, A., & Schwannauer, M. (2006*). Staying Well after Psychosis: A Cognitive Integration Approach to Recovery and Relapse Prevention.* Cambridge, UK: Cambridge University.

Gumley, A., White, C. A., & Power, K. (1999*).* An interacting cognitive subsystems model of relapse and the course of psychosis. *Clinical Psychology and Psychotherapy,* 6, 261–279.

Johns, L., & van Os, J. (2001). The continuity of psychotic experiences in the general population. *Clinical Psychology Review,* 21(8), 1125–1141.

Jones, P., & Murray, R. M. (1991). The genetics of schizophrenia is the genetics of neurodevelopment. *British Journal of Psychiatry* 158(5), 615–623.

Kapur, S. (2003). Psychosis as a state of aberrant salience: a framework linking biology, phenomenology, and pharmacology in schizophrenia. *American Journal of Psychiatry* 160(1), 13–23.
Kernberg, O.F. (1990). New perspectives in psychoanalytic affect theory. *Emotion: Theory, Research and Experience,* 5, 115–131.
Labrie, V., Pai, S., & Petronis, A. (2012). Epigenetics of major psychosis: Progress, problems and perspectives. *Trends in Genetics: TIG.* 28(9), 427–35.
Larkin, W., & Morrison, A. (Eds.) (2006). *Trauma and Psychosis: New Directions for Theory and Therapy.* London, UK: Routledge.
Liotti G., & Gumley, A. (2008). An attachment perspective on schizophrenia: Disorganized attachment, dissociative processes, and compromised mentalisation. In: A. Moskowitz, I. Schäfer, M. J. Dorahy & J. Martin (Eds.), *Psychosis, Trauma and Dissociation.* New York, NY: Wiley.
Main, M. (1991). Metacognitive knowledge, metacognitive monitoring, and singular (coherent) versus multiple (incoherent) models of attachment. In: C. Parkes, J. Stevenson-Hinde, & P. Marris (Eds.), *Attachment Across the Life Cycle* (pp. 127–160). London, UK: Routledge.
Main, M. (1995). Recent studies in attachment: Overview, with selected implications for clinical work. In: S. Goldberg, R. Muir, & J. Kerr (Eds.), *Attachment Theory: Social, Developmental and Clinical Perspectives* (pp. 407–474). Hillsdale, NJ: Analytic Press.
Main, M., & Hesse, E. (1990). Parents' unresolved traumatic experiences are related to infant disorganized attachment status: Is frightened and/or frightening parental behavior the linking mechanism? In: M. Greenberg, D. Cicchetti, & E. Cummings (Eds.), *Attachment in the Preschool Years* (pp. 161–182). New York, NY: Plenum.
Read, J., & Gumley, A. (2008). Can attachment theory help explain the relationship between childhood adversity and psychosis? *Attachment: New directions in Psychotherapy and Relational Psychoanalysis,* 2(1), 1–35.
Rubio, J. M., Sanjuán J., Florez-Salamanca, L., & Cuesta, M. J. (2012). Examining the course of hallucinatory experiences in children and adolescents: A systematic review. *Schizophrenia Research,* 138(2), 248–254.
Rumelhart, D. E. (1980). Schemas: The building blocks of cognition. In: R. Spiro, B. Bracc, & W. Brewer (Eds.), *Theoretical Issues in Reading Comprehension* (pp. 35–58). Hillsdale, NJ: Erlbaum.
Schore, A. (2003). *Affect Dysregulation and the Disorders of the Self.* New York, NY: Norton.
Stern, D. N. (1985). *The Interpersonal World of the Infant.* New York, NY: Basic Books.
van Ijzendoorn, M., Schuengel, C., & Bakermans-Kranenburg, M. (1999). Disorganized attachment in early childhood: Meta-analysis of precursors, concomitants and sequelae. *Development and Psychopathology,* 11, 225–250.
van Nierop, M., & van Os, J. (2012) Phenotypically continuous with clinical psychosis, discontinuous in need for care: Evidence for an extended psychosis phenotype. *Schizophrenia Bulletin,* 38(2), 231–238.
van Os, J., Linscott, R. J., Myin-Germeys, I., Delespaul, P., & Krabbendam, L. (2009). A systematic review and meta-analysis of the psychosis continuum: Evidence for a psychosis proneness–persistence–impairment model of psychotic disorder. *Psychological Medicine,* 39(2), 179–195.
Waters, E., Merrick, S., Treboux, D., Crowell, J., & Albersheim, L. (2000). Attachment security in infancy and early adulthood: A 20-year longitudinal study. *Child Development,* 71, 684–689.

3

EARLY CHILDHOOD RISK FACTORS FOR AUTISM AND PSYCHOSIS

K. Mark Sossin

The Infant Mental Health Perspective and Early Childhood Diagnosis

Considering the young child, birth to 3, brought for assessment or intervention, the attention of the early childhood consulting or treating clinician is multiply focused. Sensory processes, self- and interactive-regulation, attachment-related behaviors, temperament, and affect are in need of appraisal, as are cognitive, motor, and social-emotional competencies. All the while, attention is equally focused on the "goodness of fit" between this child and the caregiving environment. Observational and conceptual anchors shape the methods, constructs, and adopted nosologies the clinician is likely to apply in both assessment and intervention planning. The challenge of integrating impressions of constitutional (e.g., genetic, neurobiological) vulnerabilities, parental functioning, and experiential risk (e.g., traumatic stress, relationship difficulties) generally involves substantial consideration and observation. When significant disturbance is emergent, the clinician appraising the system within which the child experiences and learns reality may find the task of locating the primary source of the disturbance perplexing.

In integrative early childhood assessment, the clinician's awareness of genetic factors (Sanders et al., 2012; Murdoch & State, 2013) and pre- and perinatal (Suren et al., 2013; Nosarti et al., 2012) risk factors for disorders such as psychosis and autism are necessarily balanced with understandings of the effects of the "ghosts in the nursery" (Fraiberg & Adelson, 1976), potential sequelae of disorganized attachment (O'Connor, Bureau, McCartney, & Lyons-Ruth, 2011; Beebe, Lachmann, Markese, & Barhrick, 2012; Beebe, Lachmann, Markese, Buck et al., 2012; Claussen, Mundy, Mallik, & Willoughby, 2002; Hesse & Main, 2000), and trauma (Osofsky, 2009, 2011). Standardized tools available for early childhood assessment need to be interwoven with thorough history, direct observation, and interactive assessment (Zaccario, Sossin, & DeGroat, 2009). Ideally, assessment is not only "disorder-focused," but is also resilience-focused and strength-based (Papousek, 2011), attentive to the infant's regulatory competencies and assets in the parent–infant relationship. The ghosts certainly pertain, but so do the "angels in the nursery" (Lieberman, Padrón, van Horn, & Harris, 2005). Both developmental psychopathology (Cicchetti, 1987) and current psychodynamic approaches (Barrows, 2000; Moskowitz, Reiswig, & Demby, 2014) attend to relational processes and difficulties. Developmentally, the parent's capacity to reflect, mentalize, or treat the child as a psychological agent (Sharp & Fonagy, 2008; Rutherford, Goldberg, Luyten, Bridgett, & Mayes, 2013) relates to the parent's additional capacity to tolerate infant distress, and also influences the child's own emotion regulation and social perception.

The traditional "medical model," which has driven most psychodiagnostic thinking, asks: is this infant, toddler, or young preschooler, "typical" or "atypical": and if the latter, in what way? What symptom cluster is apparent, and to what defined criteria do the symptoms conform? The so-labeled de-contextualized young child involves some classificatory artifice, however, and efforts to assess the contextualized child have grown within the infant mental health field. Classification systems, such as the multiaxial DC:0–3R (Zero to Three, 2005), designed with the complexity of early childhood mental health in mind, capture some of the intricacies involved in identifying significant early disturbance. Integrated models have grown within infant mental health (Foley & Hochman, 2006), often calling upon the functional emotional developmental levels described by Greenspan (2007a, b) and Greenspan and Wieder (2006; Wieder & Greenspan, 2006) in their employment of the Developmental, Individual-Difference, Relationship-Based (DIR) model. Within DIR, individual differences are viewed *vis a vis* child–parent interaction patterns.

The diagnosis of childhood psychosis, particularly with reference to the DSM-IV/5 diagnosis of schizophrenia, is currently hardly ever made in childhood before age 6 (Volkmar, 1996; Werry, 1996). Schizophrenic spectrum disorders remain rarely labeled before adolescence. Historically (until the transition from DSM-III to -IV), descriptors of childhood psychosis, childhood-onset schizophrenia, and infantile autism overlapped (Kolvin, 1971; R. G. Asarnow & Asarnow, 1994; Russell, 1994). The presentation of clear psychotic symptoms such as hallucinations, delusions, and/or thought disorder generally lacked developmental specificity and elaboration earlier in life, making such identification difficult. Childhood schizophrenia, while meeting the same diagnostic criteria as adult schizophrenia, is considered of more insidious onset than its manner of presentation in adulthood, but is not identified in the early childhood period. In the 1980s, a powerful research methodology for the study of early risk factors for psychosis was introduced with the gathering of retrospective films of diagnosed children, allowing observational study of younger years (birth to 4), particularly parent–infant interaction, examining patterns antecedent to the later diagnosis.

Past labeling of "infantile psychosis," as in "autistic psychosis" or "symbiotic psychosis" (Mahler & Furer, 1960) followed from psychodynamic impressions that some young children never developed beyond the earliest phase of development, and others regressed out of terror upon the experience of separation. Ideas pertaining to psychogenic autism in relation to unbearable stress upon bodily separateness are still discussed (Tustin, 1992), as are early defensively mobilized dissociations in infancy (Alvarez, 2006), but such psychoanalytic lines of discourse have largely remained separate from those paths of scientific investigation viewing both early appearing autism spectrum disorders and later-appearing schizophrenic spectrum disorders as rooted in biogenic etiology (e.g. "diseases of the synapse").

Determining age of onset of bipolar disorder in children, its phenomenology, and, more particularly, age of first manic episode (Carlson, 2005; Carlson & Meyer, 2006) also presents a diagnostic conundrum, as here, too, adult criteria are applied to children, and rarely to the youngest. Children showing attention deficit hyperactivity disorder (ADHD) symptoms and/or anxiety symptoms may later be found to have bipolar disorder, raising questions about premorbid or comorbid manifestations.

Autism Spectrum Disorder/Neurodevelopmental Disorders

Diagnostically, DSM 5 (American Psychiatric Association, 2013), denotes autism spectrum disorder (ASD) as "characterized by persistent deficits in social communication and social interaction across multiple contexts, including deficits in social reciprocity, nonverbal communicative behaviors used for social interaction, and skills in developing, maintaining, and understanding relationships. In addition to the social communication deficits, the diagnosis of autism spectrum disorder requires the presence of restricted, repetitive patterns of behavior, interests, or activities." Considerable controversy has followed the manual's dropping of the diagnosis of Asperger's disorder (Volkmar, State, & Klin, 2009)

Young children demonstrating autism spectrum disorder show social and communication deficits that go beyond language delays. Infants later diagnosed with ASD do not do what typical children do, such as following another's shift in gaze, reciprocally smile, or vocalize "back" to an interacting person (Baraneck, 1999). Children with ASD also show restricted and repetitive behaviors and interests (with objects or in hand/finger mannerisms), insistence on sameness, and circumscribed interests (as in intense "attachment" to specific objects, or preoccupation with specific topics, Kim and Lord, 2010). ASD diagnostic instruments have been reviewed by Worley and Matson (2011). DSM 5 (American Psychiatric Association, 2013) introduces criteria for three severity levels for ASD, essentially corresponding to the level of support the child needs, which may be less clear in early childhood than later. Atypical sensory behaviors are frequently apparent in children with ASD, as with hyperacusis or extreme tactile sensitivity. Motor impairments have also been reported to be frequent among ASD individuals. Generally, motor functioning is gauged by skill acquisition or demonstration (Mayes & Calhoun, 2003). It may be that more underlying problems of postural control (Minshew, Sung, Jones, & Furman, 2004) or more qualitative kinesic patterns (Loman & Sossin, 2009) are more central than skill acquisition. This subject is returned to below.

Standardized measures, specific to the identification of ASD, have added to the diagnostic toolbox. This is especially true of the Autism Diagnostic Interview-Revised (ADI-R), with algorithms keyed to those 12–47 months of age (Kim & Lord, 2011), and the toddler version of the Autism Diagnostic Observation Schedule-Toddler (ADOS-T) (Luyster et al., 2009), extending the scorable semi-structured measure to children 12–30 months of age.

One strand of the literature holds that the Autism Diagnostic Interview-Revised (ADI-R) in combination with the ADOS (in the case of this chapter, the Toddler-Module) provides a "gold standard" for diagnostic evaluation (Luyster et al., 2009; Oosterling, 2009; T. Falkmer, Anderson, Falkmer, & Horlin, 2013). Empirical studies find that, particularly in combination, they provide the highest sensitivity and specificity across published diagnostic tools. However, there is clearly another strand of literature that still considers clinical observation and interview by a skilled expert (or expert team) to be the "gold standard" to which such tools are compared, and this is especially true with infants and toddlers (Volkmar, Chawarska, & Klin, 2008).

Early concerns of parents are prospectively relevant. Delays in speech and language development are among the first issues reported by parents, and atypical social responsivity, as well as a host of attention, sleeping, and eating problems are often manifest upon initial referral. Other factors raising parental concern include sensory deficits, a late social smile, and delays in gross motor skills. Some studies have pointed to concerns that (as per DSM-IV, at least) led later to labeling a child with language or social engagement weaknesses as having autism or pervasive developmental disorder-not otherwise specified (PDD-NOS). The non-specific issues pertaining to toddlers more likely led to a PDD-NOS diagnosis (Chawarska et al., 2007; Volkmar, Chwarska, & Klin, 2008). It has been noted that parents of young children report regression in as many as a third of cases. There remains uncertainty as to how common such regressions truly are. They clearly occur (Werner & Dawson, 2005), but probably occur at lower percentages (such as 11%) than previously reported, and in some cases careful interviewing reframes findings in terms of the child reaching a plateau more than an actual regression. Recent studies, such as that of Barbaro and Dissanayake (2013), who looked at social attention and communication in children at 12, 18, and 24 months, note the importance of screening for other behavioral markers of ASD, such as deficits in eye contact and pointing, and also (at 18 and 24 months) deficits in showing and pretend-play.

The prevalence of autism, or ASD, has continued to show notable increases. Reports showed equivalence of 1 child in 70–90 children (French, Bertone, Hyde, & Fombonne, 2013), and, across 14 Autism and Developmental Disability Monitoring (ADDM) Network sites across the United States, an 11.3% prevalence was demonstrated, or 1 in 88 children (at age 8, as of 2008, Centers for Disease Control, 2012). The even more up-to-date Centers for Disease Control follow-up study, reported in 2014 (reflecting data across 11 ADDM sites through 2010), showed an alarming increase to 14.7%, or 1 child in 68 (1 in 42 boys and 1 in 189 girls). The average age of the child upon initial diagnosis was 53 months. Symptom substitution and varying availability of professional supports leave open the question of the changing incidence even in the face of such increasing prevalence.

Current epidemiology studies find variation across locale, sex, race/ethnicity, and intellectual ability. Estimates have thus far been derived using DSM-IV criteria, inclusive of autistic disorder, PDD-NOS, and Asperger's disorder. It remains unclear how a shift to DSM 5 will influence prevalence findings (American Psychiatric Association, 2013). Among controversies related to changes in ASD diagnosis in DSM 5 (Hazen, McDougle, & Volkmar, 2013), one pertains to whether such prevalence estimates will be lowered, following from the negation of the Asperger's syndrome diagnosis (which had previously been included as an ASD), and the addition of a distinct social (pragmatic) communication disorder (which is not included as an ASD). It is agreed that ASDs appear in the first three years, and are often diagnosable by 2 years old, though initial diagnoses are often made later. Later diagnoses leave a significant number of children with impairments in social and communicative functioning, alongside restricted and stereotyped patterns of behavior, without early therapies and interventions that could potentially be more helpful if applied earlier.

The early-childhood clinician is informed by concurrent models of ASD that are inherently linked to models of early affect and relational development. Examples include the role of contingency perception in Gergely and Watson's (2011) Social-Biofeedback model. Infants are generally aware of contingencies between their behavior and events around them. Such work builds upon key parent–infant interactive-regulatory research demonstrating how important facial and vocal behaviors are in the mutual regulation system (Beebe et al., 2007; Stern et al., 1998), and adds attention to the benefits of "marked: affect reflection." ASDs essentially reflect the result of "specific faults in the contingency-seeking module" (Gergely & Watson, 2014, p. 130). Moreover, when children with ASD are aware of contingencies, they may seek remarkably high contingencies (they are much more likely to satisfy this need from the inanimate world rather than within relationships).

The theory of mind (Baron-Cohen, 1993) evolves, with notable precursors in the first year of life, as beliefs, desires, affects, perceptions, and intentions come to be understood and attributed to both self and others as mental states. Between the ages of 3 and 5, neurotypical children grow in their capacity to manage "false-beliefs," demonstrating understanding of another's perspective, as well as their emotions. Young children with ASDs show less joint attention, less pretend/symbolic play, less social referencing, and impediments in reading emotions and intentions in others through implicit nonverbal communication. Such "mind-blindness" came to be one way to describe a core deficit. Baron-Cohen (1997) extended his ideas by suggesting that individuals with autism have "extreme male brains," and hence, are high systemizers, inclined toward repetitive actions. Quite different are those with notably "female" brains, who could more naturally attend (with developing empathy) to the feelings of others.

Whereas strong central coherence might underlie one's challenges with a disembedded-figures task, weak central coherence (Frith, 2003; Happe & Booth, 2008) might make such a task, or a challenging puzzle, easy. As many ASD individuals do quite well on Block Design subtests of intelligence tests, puzzles, and rote memory tasks, while showing cognitive deficits on tasks requiring "connection" or meaning-making, weak central coherence has evolved as partially explanatory about cognition in autism. Within the early childhood period, weak central coherence may also be demonstrated by a lack of integration between thought and feeling (Capps & Sigman, 1996). A detachment appears—an "autistic aloneness."

Thoughtful research on mirror-neurons (e.g., Rizzolatti, Fadiga, Fogassi, & Gallese, 1996; Iacoboni, 2008; Levin & Trevarthen, 2000; Rizzolatti & Sinigaglia, 2010; Hickok & Sinigaglia, 2013; Sinigaglia, 2013) has increasingly implicated deficits in mirror-neuron functioning as related to a young child's deficits in the acquisition of the ability to satisfactorily attribute/decipher another's intentions, beliefs, desires, or feelings. Research to date supports the postulations that deficits in motor simulation and motor representation of another's actions greatly impede the accurate attribution of intention, and hence greatly decrease the predictability of the other. The discovery that some primates, including humans, experience motor-specific brain activation upon observing another move has opened considerable enthusiasm for considerations of empathy and the reading of intentions. Gallese and Sinigaglia (2010) suggest that the very experience of oneself as a bodily self is anchored in mirror neuron functioning. Hickock and Sinigaglia (2013) further contend that "motor processes and representations are a basis of action understanding" (p. 65). Hence, early impairment in the mirror neuron system may contribute to deficits in theory of mind and the related social impairments exemplified by individuals with ASD (Dapretto et al, 2006).

Additional research regarding individuals with ASD, using structural and functional MRIs (Stigler, Erickson, & McDougle, 2013), further identify corresponding brain differences. Young children with autism consistently show a total brain volume (TBV) such that, by 2 to 4 years of age, it is larger than their neurotypical peers. The trajectory seems to be that those children who will demonstrate autism have reduced or normal TBV at birth, then show very rapid brain grown in early childhood, and then plateau. By adolescence, their TBV seems to be comparable to controls (Redcay & Courchesne, 2005). Whereas typical individuals process faces relying on the other's eyes with a holistic approach, individuals with ASD seem to focus more on the mouth, and use a feature-focused approach (Klin, Jones, Schultza, Volkmar, & Cohen, 2002). Overall, young individuals with autism seem to pay preferential attention to inanimate stimuli rather than to other people (Klin, 2009). A recent study finds that infants who later demonstrate autism spend less time looking at the eyes of others between 2 and 6 months of age, followed by waning involvement in eye-to-eye gaze, whereas neurotypical infants continue to increase eye-gaze through 9 months of age, and sustain a high level of such gaze (Jones & Klin, 2013).

Psychobiology and Genetics: Overlap between Autism Risk and Schizophrenia Risk

Very high concordance for identical twins showing autism spectrum disorders, alongside far more modest concordance for fraternal twins, is indicative of a strong genetic component (Geschwind & Levitt, 2007). Genetic and gene-mapping/sequencing studies have made significant advances in identifying ASD risk loci (Mudoch & State, 2013; State & Sestan, 2012; Morrow et al, 2008), implicating several regions, often involving multiple genes. Recent genetic research also points to pathways and molecular differences related to neuronal function that have long-lasting behavioral consequences. Remarkable heterogeneity has been reported regarding de novo variants (i.e. there are a great many "ASD" genes), and several candidate-genes are being actively investigated. Gene specificity corresponds to cellular localization bearing upon specific proteins, synaptic functions, and higher male vulnerability. By increasing de novo mutation frequency, greater paternal age at conception has been clearly implicated in elevating the risk of both autism and of schizophrenia among the children (Kong, Bachmann, Thomann, Essig, & Schröder, 2012; Sanders et al, 2012). Epigenetic factors are relevant. Studies of autism families involving more than one identified member found that females are more severely affected than males, and that second ASD children within a family to show lower functioning than first children (Martin & Horriat, 2012).

It has been noted that relevant environmental risk factors identified to date fall within the categories of drugs, environmental chemicals, infectious agents, dietary factors, and other physical/psychological stressors, (R.R. Dietert, Dietert, & DeWitt, 2010). However, research attempting to narrow these broad categories has not yet pinpointed specific causes. Some have postulated that factors affecting underlying processes such as synthesis of monoamine neurotransmitters, implicating excess multivitamin exposure in infancy (Zhou, Zhou, Li, & Ma, 2013) could be risk factors, but such hypotheses greatly outdistance current research findings.

Disorders of Movement and Their Possible Relevance to ASD

Viewing autism as "a developmental disorder in intentional movement and affective engagement," Trevarthen & Delafield-Butt (2013) articulate an integrative neuropsychological set of propositions. They suggest that motor sequencing, attention (selective or exploratory), expression of affects, and intersubjective engagement with parents are all compromised in autism, dating to prenatal failure of timing, coordination, and prospective control of movements. In the wake of such failure, affects cannot be well regulated. Trevarthen and Delafield-Butt suggest that the original deficits pertain to brain stem and cerebellar activity, but that these deficits interfere with neocortical elaborations in early childhood. This model, with some evidence behind it, supports the idea that creative art therapies (e.g., music, dance, art therapies) can be effective because of the integrative motor actions they incorporate (Trevarthen, Aitken, Papoudi, & Robarts, 1998; St. Clair, Danon-Boileau, & Trevarthen, 2007).

Within the Trevarthen and Delafield-Butt model, the social, emotional, language, and cognitive delays and disruptions are secondary to more primary errors in "early growth of intrinsic motive and motor systems of the brainstem during prenatal ontogenesis" (p. 2). Vitality affects (Stern, 2010; Koppe, Harder, & Vaever, 2008) do not develop fully, neither does an "integrated self," as anchored in basic deficits at a sensory-motor level. In fact, an essential element of the Trevarthen and Delafield-Butt model is that a great deal of early emotional regulation develops without neocortical involvement. The orbito-frontal cortex and temporal lobe lay structural basis for parental care and for repair of emotional difficulties (Schore, 2003). A neurotypical child encodes and decodes social communication in the sounds made as well as eyes and overall facial features. When these are not functioning, self- and interactive-regulation goes awry.

Coinciding ideas are emerging regarding autism, from cognitive, behavioral, emotional, and neuroscientific perspectives, identifying the child as unable to know, read, or engage with another person's intentions or emotions (Hobson & Hobson, 2011; Greenspan, 2007a; Gallese & Rochat, 2013; Rochat et al., 2013; Rizzolatti & Sinigaglia, 2013; Trevarthen & Delafield-Butt, 2013). The evolutionary and ontogenetic unfolding of mindreading (Gergely & Unoka, 2008) bears upon the young child's ability to surmise, and represent both the intentional mental state of other minds and of one's own mind as well. The child with autism can't pay the type of internal attention to self-monitor affectively charged processes, or the external attention to mentalize, compromising self- and relational-development. Trevarthen and Delafield-Butt (2013), focusing on autism's anchor in prenatal abnormalities of the brain stem, suggest that "autism results from disorders of imaginative and sociable playfulness itself, for which the motives and emotions are apparent from birth" (p. 3). The "intrinsic motive formation" (IMF) that has been proposed as a central component of sensory-motor communicative processes

(Trevarthen & Aitken, 1994) has gone awry. Vitality affects (Stern, 2010; Vaever & Harder, 2008) available to neurotypical newborns and infants are impeded, and the "synrhythmic" communication (Malloch & Trevarthen, 2009) that would be elemental for affiliative, relational processes is inaccessible. This perspective has supported the enlivening and body-attuning approaches of music therapy (Malloch & Trevarthen, 2009; Trevarthen, 1998; Hardy & LaGasse, 2013), and movement-informed therapies (Loman & Sossin, 2009).

It would seem that an ASD interrupts the action of what Kestenberg (1978) long ago called "transsensus," referring to an affective, multi-sensory, and pre-ideational movement toward others (involving muscle spindles, stretch and incorporation—perhaps analogous to embodied intersubjectivity). Kestenberg's model of transsensus is integral to feelings of confidence, trust, and contribute to body-image formation. This may also be linked to the Polyvagal theory proposed by Porges (2003), with roots in Maclean's (1985) triune brain theory. Porges focuses on the vagus nerve as a key component of the autonomic nervous system, and goes further in separating it into two evolutionary parts. The ASD individual may be getting erroneous messages about safety and danger, and may need particular help engaging the part of the vagus that can be employed in calming and relating.

Prenatal and Early Experience as Risk Factors

Nature and nurture are partnered in development. Humans seem to share genetic and neuro-preparedness for experience-expectant information. Nonetheless, experience-dependent synaptogenesis is very specific to the individual. Synaptic connections are formed and/or pruned notably on the basis of idiosyncratic experience (Greenough, Black, & Wallace, 1987). Hence, in considering an infant or toddler manifesting atypical development, it is essential to consider genetics, neurodevelopment, and the child's experiences across a wide range of sensory, affective, cognitive, motor, and relational involvements. Ideally, such knowledge is integrated with theory and research pertaining to a young child's mind, subjectivity, and intersubjectivity.

Maternal stress during pregnancy has been recognized as a risk factor for the well-being of the fetus. For instance, pregnant women exposed to the World Trade Center attacks, through glucocorticoids and other neuroendocrine functions, were affected in such ways that could have led to intergenerational transmission of stress, influencing fetal brain development, such that babies were born at increased risk for stress-related difficulties (Yehuda et al., 2005; Yehuda & Bierer, 2008; Feldman & Eidelman, 2009). As denoted in a review chapter by Lange (2012), prenatal stress, as evidenced in non-human research, bears influence on major neural structures such as the amygdala and hippocampus, as well as on synaptogenesis, HPA-axis reactivity, and levels of proteins and neurotransmitters, impacting postnatal mood regulation, behavioral organization, and stress-response.

The presumption that prenatal stress exposure will lead to later serious psychopathology is unwarranted, however. A population-based cohort study in Sweden (Abel et al., 2014) found that bereavement stress occurring preconception or prenatally (in any trimester) did not correspond to higher risks of psychotic illness in the children. Nonetheless, such risks did increase if a child or adolescent experienced a family death, especially more so if the death was within the nuclear family. The risk of a later-appearing psychosis (especially affective psychosis) was especially apparent if the death in the family was by suicide. While this study implies caution against extrapolating too generally regarding fetal stress sequelae, it underscores the susceptibility of children to serious psychopathology triggered, or set along a pathway, by earlier traumatic loss.

Notably, large prospective data studies explored whether the risk of offspring with ASD would follow from high life-stress during pregnancy. Rai et al. (2012) found no evidence of an association between the prenatal events and the risk of offspring with ASD. Prenatal and postnatal stress may affect relational patterns, as gauged, perhaps, by emotional availability (Biringen & Easterbrooks, 2012), but it is unwarranted to link autism and prenatal stress.

Longitudinal studies of individuals suffering perinatal obstetric complications have been linked to an increased risk of later-diagnosed schizophrenia up to age 22 (Clarke, Harley, & Cannon, 2006; Nicodemus et al., 2008). It has been suggested that obstetric complications interact with genetic vulnerability to increase the risk of psychosis (Preti et al., 2012). Very premature infants (less than 32 weeks gestation) are approximately three times more likely to suffer psychiatric illness serious enough to warrant hospitalization than are full-term infants. Such findings suggest that the gene–environment relationship potentiates genes for expression because of hypoxia, an underdeveloped nervous system, or some other medical phenomenon. However, it has also been found that mothers seeing their very low birth-weight infants within three hours after birth, establishing close contact, heighten the likelihood of establishing a secure attachment with their infants (Mehler, Wendrich, Kissgen, Roth, Oberthuer et al., 2011), underscoring variations in the social-emotional course that follows at-risk births, and lending itself to further discussion of "sensitive periods" after birth. Perhaps this is an example of early cognitive and social-emotional facets of development being affected by early relational processes (Hofer, 1996; Field, 1994, 2012), in which, epigenetically, relationships operate as regulators.

The neurobehavioral and neurophysiological dysfunction that often follows children beginning life in the Neonatal Intensive Care Unit (NICU) for severe prematurity, or even intrauterine growth restriction, can be significantly ameliorated by the type of care children get in the NICU. For instance, application of the Newborn Individualized Developmental Care and Assessment Program (NIDCAP) has been shown to improve executive function, neurostructure (e.g., cerebellar volumes), and spectral coherence among occipital, frontal, and parietal regions of the brain (McAnulty et al., 2013; Als et al., 2012).

A number of empirical studies have linked greater prevalence of childhood trauma with psychotic disorders (Wurr & Partridge, 1966). In a literature review, Bendall, Jackson, and Hulbert (2010), found relatively convincing linkage between childhood trauma and some manifestations of psychosis in either childhood or adulthood. Some hallucinations are themselves trauma-linked. The early childhood clinician may not be able to diagnose psychosis using current nosologies during the earliest years, but the clinician can look for signs of dissociative and other precursors to severe thought and affective disturbance in cases of maltreatment and neglect (Zeanah, Boris, & Lieberman, 2000).

Bipolar Patterns in Early Childhood

The diagnosis of bipolar disorder in preadolescent children has risen greatly (Biederman et al., 2005). Diagnostic muddles persist regarding early childhood diagnosis, however. For instance, questions about whether grandiosity and elation are key symptoms (Geller et al., 2002), or whether episodes of mania are required, remain unclear. Concerted research has sought a prodrome of bipolar disorder in early childhood, but the exact clinical markers remain debated. Offspring of bipolar parents seem to carry heritability as a statistical marker of risk (Birmaher et al., 2009). Specifically, preschool children of parents with bipolar disorder showed a notably greater prevalence of ADHD, but as children were under the age of higher risk for bipolar and/or major depressive disorders, it was not clear what proportion would demonstrate bipolar disorder. Notably, toward the goal of decreasing risk, Birmaher et al. recommended psychosocial interventions directed toward enhancing mood-regulation in children with subthreshold mood disorders alongside treatment of parental psychopathology.

Reviewing 54 relevant research studies of childhood bipolar disorder, Luby and Navsaria (2010) considered the evidence for prodromal markers and non-prodrome risk factors. They noted many features that related to higher risk of developing bipolar disorder, including mood lability, anxiety, excitement, somatization, stubbornness, high energy, decreased sleep, problems with thinking and concentrating, and loud speech (cf. Shaw et al., 2005). A deficit in emotional labeling based on facial expression has been linked as an endophenotype (heritable biological traits marking risk) for bipolar disorder. Children at 21 months of age who showed behavioral disinhibition also showed notably higher rates of mood and disruptive behavior disorders at age 6 (Hirshfeld-Becker et al., 2006). By extrapolation, they might demonstrate more bipolar disorder, but further research would be needed to test such an expectation. As per studies reviewed and cited by Luby and Navsaria (2010), approximately one-third of young children diagnosed with major depressive disorder later showed evidence of ("switching to") bipolar disorder.

Developmental psychopathology differentiates prodromes, in which early forms of symptomatology are already evidenced, from markers that indicate higher levels of risk. When high levels of risk are combined with very adverse life experiences, there is an increased likelihood that the combination might lead to a manifestation of symptoms. Clear-cut early childhood prodromes of bipolar disorder have not been reliably described, however a significant body of research suggests markers that identify risk. Faced with a family history of bipolar disorder, the clinician may heighten attention to these signs of risk. Temperamental features are often conceived as biologically based features, heightening vulnerability to experiential-psychosocial stressors that combine to manifest a later bipolar condition. Such temperamental features identified in research reviewed by Luby and Navsaria (2010) include behavioral disinhibition, "cyclothymic" temperament, and impaired emotion regulation (as manifest in more intense and longer lasting emotions). In addition, there is relatively new interest in identifying mania manifestations in very young (preschool) children (Luby & Belden, 2006; Luby, Tandon, & Nicol, 2007; Luby, Tandon, & Belden, 2009).

Regarding prevention and early intervention, one research line would appear to be the identification of prodromes for pharmacologic intervention. Another would be for a psychotherapeutic approach to improving emotion regulation. As Miklowitz, Biuckians, and Richards (2006) describe a developmental psychopathology model underscoring the risk factors of high family conflict and mood exacerbation, they underscore the utility of family-focused treatment (FFT). In their identification of early-onset adolescent bipolar patients, Miklowitz and Chang (2008) describe such an approach when at least one first-degree relative shows bipolar disorder alongside subsyndromal signs in the child. Adapting a directive form of FFT, they apply considerable family education (e.g., about triggers, signs of mood episodes) in conjunction with communication enhancement training attending to the expression of positive feelings, active listening, making positive requests for change, and expressing negative feelings. This model was not designed with the youngest of children in mind, and would need to be further adapted to parent-training and active therapeutic facilitation of emotion sharing if it were to be implemented in early childhood.

Greenspan and Glovinsky (2002; cf. Glovinsky, 2002) argue that bipolar patterns can be identified in early childhood, if not the more DSM-IV or DSM 5 delineated "disorder" more likely to be diagnosed in adolescence and adulthood. Less empirical, but more theoretically grounded, than the studies reviewed by Luby and Navsaria (2010), the Greenspan and Glovinsky approach is anchored clinically, and wedded to the specific developmental scheme intrinsic to the DIR approach (Greenspan & Wieder, 2006). This developmental model is woven in some measure into the diagnostic manuals of DC:03R (Zero-to-Three, 2005), the *Diagnostic Manual for Infancy and Early Childhood* (Interdisciplinary Council on Developmental and learning Disorders, 2005) and the *Psychodynamic Diagnostic Manual* (PDM; American Psychoanalytic Association / Alliance of Psychoanalytic Organizations, 2006). The model describes six capacities that emerge sequentially and are referred to as levels of development, each involving new levels of adaptive, sensory, and affective organization. The model is an integrated one, knitting together psychodynamic, cognitive, emotional, and relational facets that frame approaches to assessment and developmental therapy. In the presentation of bipolar patterns, severe emotional dysregulation alongside difficulties in executive functioning appear, with differences in sensory reactivity and processing as well as in affective and motor functioning. Greenspan and Glovinsky (2002) describe a "developmental signature" for bipolar patterns marked by (1) sensory craving (leading to impulsivity, aggression, over-agitation); (2) difficulties with long co-regulated affective reciprocity (especially marked by trouble reading emotional signals related to aggression, sadness, loss or vulnerability); and (3) a lack of mastery of the fifth (creating representations) and sixth (building bridges between ideas) functional emotional levels within the developmental model. Hence, the emotions of a young child demonstrating bipolar patterns are more organized on a behavioral or somatic level than at a symbolic level. Emotions remain relatively unintegrated in that they are "represented as global, polarized affect states" (Greenspan & Wieder, 2006, p. 145). This "signature" further includes a deficit representing intense feelings communicatively. The child's emotional range is limited even when imagination seems far-reaching. In that thinking and feeling are more polarized, their lack of integration leads to compromised reflective awareness, and more modulated thinking patterns are less available.

Note that within this model, the "hypersensitivity" to sensory input (e.g., sound, touch) is not followed by avoidance (as in some presentations of ASD) or fear but by the seeking of more stimulation, which can appear frenzied. Children evidencing bipolar patterns are noted to "crave movement." They are described as "underreactive to vestibular patterns, and . . . crave vestibular stimulation" (Greenspan, 2007b, p. 219). The portrait is of an overloaded child getting even more overloaded via the sensory input sought. Co-regulation with caregivers appears incomplete and unsuccessful. Emotions are not represented as much as acted out. Bipolar patterns often complicate relationships with caregivers as such children elicit greater punitiveness, less consistency, and less empathy. Within this model, such children lack the ability to participate in what Greenspan dubs as "long communicative chains of reciprocal gestures." Linked to modulation and soothing, children engaged in such interactive gestures are not readily calmed from upset. Greenspan (2007a) suggests that the "back-and-forth set of affective exchanges" (p. 197) are crucial to acquisition of a working sense of causality and, hence, of initiation, purposefulness, and will, all contributing to a pre-representational sense of self. The coherence of this pre-symbolic self is a function of both self- and interactive-regulation. A child's hypersensitivity or a parent's lack of responsiveness or emotional availability may heighten the risk to the coherence of that sense of self. Many factors pertain, including the child's ability to decipher expression and gesture in another. In Greenspan's model, highlighting the centrality of relationships (Balamuth, 2007), without adequate reciprocal signaling in infancy and early toddlerhood, the hypersensitive child might experience greater intensity of emotion, or withdrawal and self-absorption.

Regarding early intervention, Greenspan and Glovinsky's (2002) contention is that interactive regulation patterns between parent and child, incorporating improved affective signaling, as well as more differentiated identification of feelings, need to be framed within the home in addition to any specific psychotherapy. The child's self-soothing is a goal. Aware of movement and rhythm, Greenspan focuses on slowing down (downregulating) the child's affective rhythm through interactive regulation, as in creating slow-motion games (Greenspan, 2007b). With self-calming achieved, therapeutic intervention aims at enhancing the symbolic level (the representational level being built upon the pre-representational level) aiding the child in the capacity to reformulate experience, away from polarized all-or-none emotions and symbols to more nuanced and mixed-experienced states.

Considering early psychopathological development, including attachment problems, Greenspan (2007a) underscores the risk of trauma and loss. Imitation, for instance, is cited for its importance in regulatory and internalizing processes, expanding a sense of self. However, influenced by trauma, imitation becomes more about holding on to something lost than about experimenting with something new. Imitation becomes about desperately attaining a compensatory "security." Developmentally appropriate internalizations are substituted for by isolated, external, and split-off experiences. Flexibility becomes less available, and rigidity and repetition remain. In a manner that interweaves the child's biological dispositions and his or her experience in interaction with caregivers at nodal points, defined by Greenspan (2007b) and Balamuth (2007), models of specific psychopathological pathways arise. Affect-diatheses complicate development as core-deficits arise from biological challenges that interfere with the infant making connections between sensations, affects, and motor responses.

Nonverbal Behavior and What Does a Prodrome of Autism Look Like in the First Year of Life?

Motor impairments in infancy of those who later show ASD include a "primary deficit in the capacity to perceive and move the body in a planned way, which limits the capacity to control the timing of actions of the body and their perceptual consequences, and thence impairs the communication of intentions and ideas" (Trevarthen & Delafield-Butt, 2013, p. 10). Trevarthen and Daniel (2005) found disorganized rhythm and synchrony in play behavior between a father and an 11-month-old child who later demonstrated autism. F. Muratori, Apicella, Muratori, and Maestro (2011) also analyzed retrospective home videos of children with autism, filmed during the first six months, finding that children with ASD lacked social engagement and did not attend to or read the affect states of others. Between the ages of 6 and 12 months, the authors describe further "intersubjective abnormalities." A common observation among infant mental health therapists is that in response to the under-responsive infant, many parents become hyperarousing. Recent research articulating the complex "dance" of reciprocities, synchronicities, and contingencies in interpersonal nonverbal communication (e.g. Beebe et al., 2010; Tronick, 2002; Tronick & Reck, 2009; Feldman, 2007; Trevarthen, 2011) lays ground for future studies of children with ASD, or possibly prodromes of autism, to study up close features compromising the building blocks of intersubjective experiences.

It has been noted that early motor development and proficiency have largely been under-investigated regarding the early identification of ASD (Samango-Sprouse et al., 2014). Flanagan, Landa, Bhat, and Bowman (2012) have reported low muscle tonus and persistent head lag evident in infants who later show ASD when only 6 months old. Following this lead and that of Teitelbaum et al. (2004), who described atypical head tilt reflex (HTR) as atypical by the ASD child's first birthday, Samango-Sprouse et al. (2014) reported on the development of screening tools in a study of over 1,000 infants. It was demonstrated that autism spectrum disorder, developmental learning delay, and neurotypical development could all be differentiated based upon the biomarkers of head circumference (larger or accelerated head growth), and atypical HTR, administered by 9 months. The single biomarker of head circumference growth was not specific to ASD children, but in combination with the HTR findings, a notable number of infants at risk for ASD were identified by 9 months of age. It was also found in the Samango-Sprouse et al. study that early markers of receptive language dysfunction are evident before 12 months of age, though more difficult to assess. Notably, early identification studies find a more even distribution of males and females than are generally found in epidemiological studies.

Increased focus on motor development, a confluence of observations and constructs about movement patterns and qualities, and diagnostic and therapeutic approaches to infants in the first year (Teitelbaum et al., 2004; Frank & La Barre, 2011; Kestenberg Amighi, Loman, Lewis, & Sossin, 1999) sharpen focus on both neuro-atypical indices and qualitative patterns involved in both self- and interactive-regulation (Beebe, Lachmann, Markese, & Barhrick, 2012; Beebe, Lachmann, Markese, Buck et al., 2012; Greenspan 2007b).

A complex picture of interacting genetic, neurobiological and experiential factors influencing the early pathway to autism spectrum disorder is emerging (Yirmiya & Charman, 2010; Yirmaya & Ozonoff, 2007; Trevarthen & Delafield-Butt, 2013), albeit with many unanswered questions remaining. Yet the idea of early identification of ASD, or a prodrome of ASD, or of high-risk factors, corresponds to questions regarding what methods are available for amelioration (or rerouting). Voran (2013) describes a six-month-old brought for consultation, with a proclivity for distress responses, a lack of responsivity to parental soothing, who lacked a smile response for her mother, and was prone to hitting herself in the head with toys when upset. Her description is psychoanalytically framed, informed by Tustin (1991), and richly descriptive of the parents' complex and often negative feelings about their child. Motoric patterns such as withdrawing, freezing, staring-blankly, keying-in on visual sensations, locking her knees while rhythmically moving her legs, "looking vacuous," and breath-holding were observed in the young girl, alongside patterns that Voran linked to early dissociative types of emotion regulation. The parental patterns ranged from high stimulation, to exasperation, and reactive spurning. Voran framed the girl's behaviors as defenses early in their development—coping mechanisms that could be rerouted in informed parent-infant psychotherapy. Therapeutic progress was attributed to emotional containment for the parents, leading to an increase in reflectivity, empathy, and a greater awareness of the linkage between their states and the child's. Voran's thoughtful discussion about the positive outcome incorporated essential questions about early diagnosis, the convergence of bio- and psychogenic factors, and about the potential responsivity to psychodynamically framed infant–parent psychotherapy methods (as she employed).

Anolim (2007, 2013), who had written of a parallel case of a five-month-old at high risk, prefers the term "pre-autism" to the term "prodrome." Anolim argues that while not all attachment disorders develop toward an ASD, "most autistic disorders involve an attachment disorder and infants that later develop autistic disorders show a lack of attachment at the very early stages of their life" (2013, p. 160). The idea that there is any overlap between autism and attachment disorders is highly controversial, and does not readily fit with current biogenic findings. Anolim reports that, at the Mifne Center, she reviewed hundreds of retrospective video recordings of infants who were later diagnosed with autism when they were between 2 and 3 years of age. Her conclusion was that pre-autism youngsters often do show early signs of attachment disorders. Such a view is theoretically consistent with Tustin (1992) and Alvarez (2012) in the manner in which each frames autism. The attachment formulations of Voran (2013) and Anolim (2013) are also consistent with Schore's (1994; 2013) interpersonal-neurobiological perspective of a critical period of high sensitivity-yet-plasticity of brain development, but Schore, as many others, would not view Voran's case as forecasting autism. Schore attributes Voran's success less to heightened reflectivity and more to improved interactive regulation of affect, and thus to better emotional communication and an improved attachment system.

So is there meaning in such symptoms as stereotypic/repetitive movement, echolalia, and seeming-withdrawal? The analyst, unlike therapists from other traditions, may see the movement as protective, and as warding off unendurable states. While a behaviorist may look upon wheel spinning of a toy car as a maladaptive behavior having no intrinsic meaning, Tustin and others have looked upon this and related behaviors as sensation-creating, and hence of experience-creating, as in the experience of constancy or immutability. Autistic shapes belong to the child alone, upon the skin, or inside the body, from this perspective. Such "safety" comes at the high price of vitality, or even animateness. Bodily rhythms, which have been elaborated by others (Kestenberg, 1975; Loman & Sossin, 2009), are notably central in forming relationships, and therapeutic empathy and attunement allows the sensory and rhythmic facets of the child's patterns to be shared and reciprocated.

Epigenetics, Risk, and Infant–Parent Psychotherapy

Developmental neuroscience and infant mental health fields are generating increasing clarity regarding early autism. The literature varies in suggesting that autism shows a general onset at between 6 and 12 months of age (Hazlett et al., 2005), with some studies pointing to prenatal origins (Trevarthen & Delafield Butt, 2013). Building on concepts resonant with experience-dependent synaptogenesis, Yirmaya and Charman (2010) open the door to consideration of interactive relational experiences influencing brain development in pregnancy and in the earliest months of life, creating epigenetic changes that may heighten risk for ASD. Amygdala abnormalities, and impaired limbic circuitry, have been reported in 2-year-olds with ASD (Nordahl et al., 2012), and these have been related to a particular hyperarousal leading to diminished attention to faces (Schumann, Barnes, Lord, & Courchesne, 2009).

Schore (2013) draws upon neurobiological studies of autism, (e.g. showing abnormal development of Von Economo neurons, right insula dysfunction, and his own prior work on the anterior cingulate in the right hemisphere to explain very early developmental influences on autism. He hypothesizes that during a critical period of early infancy, some children disposed toward autism may experience such stress levels that neurons of the developing anterior cingulate are destroyed, leading to "regressive" patterns shown by some young children with autism. Psychodynamically informed infant–parent psychotherapies, as well as movement-specific therapies (Tortora, 2006; Sossin, 1999), and music therapy (Kim, Wigram, & Gold, 2009) for families with very young children showing the earliest signs of ASD, offer approaches that correspond to "regulation theory." They have linked the neuroscientific approach of Schore and Newton (2012) in enhancing efforts to improve the communication of affects between the right brains of parent and infant.

Disorganized Attachment and Therapeutic Implications

In addition to the traditional three organized attachment categories, a fourth category was noted, in which the child appears far less organized (Main & Hesse, 1990), and is far more vulnerable to unfavorable outcomes, including dissociative disorders, anxiety, and heightened aggressiveness (Main & Morgan, 1996). An adult with unresolved/disorganized attachment status shows "marked lapses in reasoning and discourse surrounding the discussion of loss or abuse" (Hess & Main, 2000, p. 1097). When this adult is a parent, such status predicts that the child will show the types of interruptions and deficits in organization corresponding to disorganized-attachment when observed in Ainsworth's strange situation between 12 and 18 months of age. It appears that the parent's behavior is frequently perceived as frightening.

The intergenerational relationship between parent state and toddler state, and the developmental risk represented, suggests that consideration of attachment status, and the identification of disorganized attachment processes is an important facet of early childhood consultation. The D-status child does not enter or sustain joint-attention (Claussen et al., 2002) and shared affect, leading to poorer mentalization. D-status has, thus, been discussed as a forerunner of borderline personality organization by interrupting the development of mentalization, symbolization, reflectivity, and self-other representations. It is not suggested that disorganized attachment is causal to psychosis or to autism. Nonetheless, a diathesis-stress model pertains to the overall risks for difficulty particularly fragile or burdened children face when struggling with compromises of disorganized attachment.

The early childhood clinician brings several tools to parent-guidance, infant–parent psychotherapy, or direct work with the young child. The manner of play in session (Sossin & Cohen, 2012) involves meaning making, and therapeutic facilitation of the parent's comprehending engagement with the child. Video-feedback is a potent technique that can heighten awareness, and possibly empathy, in the parent/caregiver for the child (Beebe, 2003; Cohen & Beebe, 2002; Sossin, Cohen, & Beebe, 2014). Video-feedback and therapeutic parent-child collaborative play can enhance reflective functioning (Fonagy, Steele, Steele, Moran, & Higgit, 1991; Slade, 2005). The child who feels "known," and the parent who feels "knowing," has tools to redirect the relationship and the developmental trajectory of the child more positively (Beebe, Lachmann, Markese, Buck et al., 2012). Collaborative dialogues are promoted and contradictory dialogues are diminished (Beebe and Steele, 2014). Psychoanalytically oriented parent-child therapy, as demonstrated with the Watch, Wait, and Wonder (WWW) program (Cohen, Muir, et al., 1999), has shown efficacy in helping to shift to more organized and secure attachment.

In a series of papers, Beebe and colleagues (Beebe et al., 2010; Beebe, Lachmann, Markese, & Bahrick, 2012) developed a research approach with four month old babies and their mothers to delineate micro-processes of disorganized attachment and its precursors. Key is the knowledge that infants can and do perceive contingent relations so as to develop anticipations intrapersonally and interactively. The infant/parent interaction and regulation involve "patterns of infant procedural forms of self-and object representations" (Beebe, Lachmann, Markese, & Barhrick, 2012, p. 261). The therapy potentiates rupture-repair sequences (Tronick, 1989). Research informs therapy such that the therapist needs to attend to modalities of communication (gaze, touch, engagement, vocalization, etc.), and helps the parent employ them in greater coordination with the child. The therapist's "knowing" the dyad (in not just a verbal/conceptual way, but also a nonverbal, procedural way) will help parent and child "know" each other.

Conclusions: Addressing Risk Factors for Serious Psychopathology in the First Three Years of Life

Significant research progress is being made regarding the genetic and neurobiological substrates of serious child psychopathology. Though Schore (2003), Panksepp, (2002), and others are notable exceptions, there is a tendency to disconnect biological and psychological considerations of ASD and childhood psychosis that will, hopefully, give way to more integration and synergy. Considering the frequency with which young children with ASD, its prodrome, or markers will present themselves with concerned families to the early childhood clinician, there is some urgency that diagnostic and therapeutic methods be refined. While biological markers may come to identify young children at risk for later expressions of psychosis, it may also be that behavioral and psychological precursors will become more recognized and more epigenetic factors will be identified and processes clarified.

Across multiple sources identifying early risk and associated interventions, there is some confluence of understanding about developmental vulnerability and treatment approaches in infancy, toddlerhood and the earliest preschool years. As Greenspan (2007a, b) outlined, assessment of functional emotional levels informs the therapist regarding the level of communication that can be reciprocated (e.g., in floor time) with both the therapist and in the parent-child dyad. Infant–parent psychotherapies, whether employing video feedback or facilitating joint attention and shared-affect experiences, similarly need to keep in mind the process of meaning making about the potentially communicative gestures employed by the child. The fundamental framework for dyadic therapy outlined by Stern (1995), in which the therapist conceives of entering alternatively through the parent's representations, the dyadic interaction, the child's representation, or the therapist's reflective awareness (the varied ports of entry) to bring mutative factors into the therapeutic experience, gives shape to the therapist's choices of action. The literature and clinical experience support the offering of in-depth, attentive clinical services that can potentiate change in the face of impediments brought by the child's biology, the parent's personality or behavior, or an amalgam of bidirectional influences. As reviewed, the embodied nature of the young child's experience encourages clinicians to attend closely to the components of self- and interactive-regulatory processes, which so often call upon varying degrees of harmonious or clashing nonverbal patterns. Languages for such patterns (Kestenberg Amighi et al., 1999; Frank & La Barre, 2011; Tortora, 2009; Beebe, Lachmann, Markese, & Barhick, 2012) enhance the perceptivity and tools of the therapist.

References

Abel, K. M., Heuvelman, H. P., Jorgensen, L. Magnusson, C., Wicks, S., Susser, E., Hallkvist, J., & Dalman, C. (2014). Severe bereavement stress during the prenatal and childhood periods and risk of psychosis in later life: Population based cohort study. *BMJ, 348,* 76–79.

Albertsson-Karlgren, U., Graff, M., & Nettelbladt, P. (2001). Mental disease postpartum and parent-infant interaction—Evaluation of videotaped sessions. *Child Abuse Review, 10,* 5–17.

Als, H., Duffy, F. H., McAnulty, G., Butler, S. C., Lightbody, L., Kosta, S., Weisenfeld, N. I., Robertson, R., Parad, R. B., Ringer, S. A., Blickman, J. G., Zurakowski, D., Warfield, S. K., & Alvarez, A. (2012). NIDCAP improves brain function and structure in preterm infants with severe intrauterine growth restriction. *Journal of Perinatology, 32,* 797–803.

American Psychiatric Association. (2013). *Diagnostic and statistical manual of mental disorders* (5th ed., *DSM 5*). Arlington, VA: Author.

American Psychoanalytic Association/Alliance of Psychoanalytic Organizations (2006). *Psychodynamic diagnostic manual—PDM.* Bethesda, MD: The Interdisciplinary Council on Development and Learning (ICDL).

Alonim, H. A. (2007). Infants at risk—early signs of autism—diagnosis and treatment. In S. Acquarone (Ed.), *Signs of autism in infants: Recognition and early intervention.* London, UK: Karnac.

Alonim, H. A. (2013). Commentary on "The protest of a 6-month-old girl: Is this a prodome of autism." *Journal of Infant, Child, and Adolescent Psychotherapy, 12,* 156–163.

Asarnow, R. G., & Asarnow, J. R. (1994).Childhood onset schizophrenia: Editors' introduction. *Schizophrenia Bulletin, 20,* 591–597.

Balamuth, R. (2007). An introduction to Stanley Greenspan's clinical thinking: Autism as an intention deficit disorder. *Journal of Infant, Child, and Adolescent Psychotherapy, 6,* 163–173.

Baranek, G. T. (1999). Autism during infancy: A retrospective video analysis of sensory-motor and social behaviors at 9–12 months of age. *Journal of Autism and Developmental Disorders, 29,* 213–224.

Barbaro, J., & Dissanayake, C. (2013). Early markers of autism spectrum disorders in infants and toddlers prospectively identified in the Social Attention and Communication Study. *Autism, 17,* 64–86.

Baron-Cohen, S. (1993). From attention-goal psychology to belief-desire psychology: The development of a theory of mind and its dysfunction. In S. Baron-Cohen, H. Tager-Flusberg, & D. J. Cohen, (Eds.), *Understanding other minds: perspectives from autism.* Oxford, UK: Oxford University Press.

Baron-Cohen, S. (1997). The child with autism: First lessons in mind-reading. *Psychology Review, 3,* 30–33.

Barrows, P. (2000). Making the case for dedicated Infant Mental Health Services. *Psychoanalytic Psychotherapy, 14,* 111–128.

Beebe, B. (2003). Brief mother-infant treatment: Psychoanalytically informed video-feedback. *Infant Mental Health Journal, 24,* 24–52.

Beebe, B., Jaffe, J., Buck, K., Chen, H., Cohen, P., Blatt, S., Kaminer, T., Feldstein, S., & Andrews, H. (2007). Six-week postpartum maternal self-criticism and dependency and 4-month mother-infant self- and interactive contingencies. *Developmental Psychology, 43,* 1360–1376.

Beebe, B., Jaffe, J., Markese, S., Buck, K., Chen, H., Cohen, P., & Feldstein, S. (2010). The origins of 12-month attachment: A microanalysis of 4-month mother–infant interaction. *Attachment and Human Development, 12,* 3–141.

Beebe, B. Lachmann, F., Markese, S., & Barhrick, L. (2012). On the origins of disorganized attachment. Paper I. A dyadic systems approach. *Psychoanalytic Dialogues, 22,* 253–272.

Beebe, B., Lachmann, F. M., Markese, S., Buck, K. A., Bahrick, L. E., & Chen, H. (2012). On the origins of disorganized attachment and internal working models: Paper II. An empirical microanalysis of 4-month mother-infant interaction. *Psychoanalytic Dialogues, 22,* 352–374.

Beebe, B., & Steele, M. (2014). How does microanalysis of mother-infant communication inform maternal sensitivity and infant attachment? *Attachment and Human Development, 15,* 583–602.

Bendall, S., Jackson, H., & Hulbert, C. A. (2010). Childhood trauma and psychosis: Review of the evidence and directions for psychological interventions. *Australian Psychologist, 45*(4), 299–306

Biederman, J., Faraone, S. V., Wozniak, J., Mick, E., Kwon, A., Cayton, G. A., & Clark, S. V. Clinical correlates of bipolar disorder in a large, referred sample of children and adolescents. *Journal of Psychiatric Research, 39,* 611–622.

Biringen, Z. & Easterbrooks, M. A. (2012). Emotional availability: Concept, research, and window on developmental psychopathology. *Development and Psychopathology, 24*(1), 1–8.

Birmaher, B., Axelson, D., Goldstein, B., Monk, K., Kalas, C., Obreja, M., Hickey, M. B., Iyengar, S., Brent, D., Shamseddeen, W., Diler, R., & Kupfer, D. (2009). Psychiatric disorders in preschool offspring of parents with bipolar disorder: The Pittsburgh Bipolar Offspring Study (BIOS). *American Journal of Psychiatry, 167,* 321–330.

Capps, L., & Sigman, M. (1996). Autistic aloneness. In R. D. Kavanaugh, B. Zimmerberg, & S. Fein (Eds.), *Emotion: Interdisciplinary perspectives* (pp. 273–296). Hillsdale, NJ: Lawrence Erlbaum Associates.

Carlson, G. A. (2005). Early onset bipolar disorder: Clinical and research considerations. *Journal of Clinical Child and Adolescent Psychology, 34*(2), 333–343.

Carlson, G. A., & Meyer, S. E. (2006). Phenomenology and diagnosis of bipolar disorder in children, adolescents, and adults: complexities and developmental issues. *Developmental Psychopathology, 18,* 939–969.

Center for Disease Control and Prevention (2012). Prevalence of Autism Spectrum Disorders—Autism and Developmental Disabilities Monitory Network, 14 sites, United States, 2008. *MMWR: Morbidity and mortality Weekly Report, Surveillance Summaries, 61,* 1–19.

Center for Disease Control and Prevention (2014). Prevalence of Autism Spectrum Disorder Among Children Aged 8 Years—Autism and Developmental Disabilities Monitoring Network, 11 Sites, United States, 2010. *MMWR: Morbidity and Mortality Weekly Report, Surveillance Summaries 63*(SS02), 1–21.

Chawarska, K., Paul, R., Klin, A., Hannigan, S., Dichtel, L., & Volkmar, F. (2007). Parental recognition of developmental problems in toddlers with autism spectrum disorders. *Journal of Autism and Developmental Disorders, 37*(1), 62–72.

Cicchetti, D. (1987). Developmental psychopathology in infancy: Illustration from the study of maltreated youngsters. *Journal of Consulting and clinical Psychology, 55,* 837–845.
Clarke, M. C., Harley, M., & Cannon, M. (2006). The role of obstetric events in schizophrenia. *Schizophrenia Bulletin, 32*(1), 3–8.
Claussen, A. H., Mundy, P. C., Mallik, S. A., & Willoughby, J. C. (2002). Joint attention and disorganized attachment status in infants at risk. *Development and Psychopathology, 14*(2), 279–291.
Cohen, N. J., Muir, E., Lojkasek, M., Muir, R., Parker, C. J., Barwick, M., & Brown, M. (1999). Watch, Wait, and Wonder: Testing the effectiveness of a new approach to mother-infant psychotherapy. *Infant Mental Health Journal, 20,* 429–451.
Cohen, P., & Beebe, B. (2002). Video feedback with a depressed mother and her infant: A collaborative psychoanalytic and mother-infant treatment. *Journal of Infant, Child & Adolescent Psychotherapy, 2,* 1–55.
Dapretto, M., Davies, M. S., Pfeifer, J. H., Scott, A. A., Sigman, M., Bookheimer, S. Y., & Iacoboni, M. (2006). Understanding emotions in others: Mirror neuron dysfunction in children with autism spectrum disorders. *Nature Neuroscience, 9*(1), 28–30.
Dietert, R. R., Dietert, J. M., & DeWitt, J. C. (2011). Environmental risk factors for autism. *Emerging Health Threats, 4.* doi:10.3402/ehtj.v4i0.7111.
Falkmer, T., Anderson, K., Falkmer, M., & Horlin, C., (2013) Diagnostic procedures in autism spectrum disorders: A systematic literature review. *European Child & Adolescent Psychiatry, 22,* 329–340.
Feldman, R. (2007). Parent-infant synchrony: Biological foundations and developmental outcomes. *Current Directions in Psychological Science, 16,* 340–345.
Feldman, R., & Eidelman, A. (2009). Biological and environmental initial conditions shape the trajectories of cognitive and social-emotional development across the first years of life. *Developmental Science, 12,* 194–2000.
Field, T. (1994). The effects of mother's physical and emotional unavailability on emotion regulation. *Monographs of the Society for Research in Child Development, 59,* 208–227.
Field, T. (2012). Relationships as regulators. *Psychology, 3,* 467–479.
Flanagan, J. E., Landa, R., Bhat, A., & Bauman, M. (2012). Head lag in infants at risk for autism: A preliminary study. *American Journal of Occupational Therapy, 66,* 577–585.
Foley, G. M., & Hochman, J. D. (2006). Moving toward an integrated model of infant mental health and early intervention. In G. M. Foley & J. D. Hochman (Eds.), *Mental health in early intervention: Achieving unity in principles and practice* (pp. 3–32). Baltimore, MD: Paul H. Brookes.
Fonagy, P., Steele, M., Steele, H., Moran, G., & Higgitt, A. (1991). The capacity for understanding mental states: The reflective self in parent and child and its significance for security of attachment. *Infant Mental Health Journal, 13,* 200–217.
Fraiberg, S., & Adelson, E. (1976). Infant-parent psychotherapy on behalf of a child in a critical nutritional state. *Psychoanalytic Study of the Child, 31,* 461–491.
Frank, R., & La Barre, F. (2011). *The first year and the rest of your life: Movement, development, and psychotherapeutic change.* New York, NY: Routledge.
French, L., Bertone, A., Hyde, K. L., & Fombonne, E. (2013). Epidemiology of autism spectrum disorders. In J. D. Buxbaum & P. R. Hof (Eds.), *The neuroscience of autism spectrum disorders* (pp. 3–24). Boston, MA: Academic Press.
Frith, U. (2003). *Autism: Explaining the enigma, Second edition.* Oxford, UK: Blackwell.
Gallese, V., & Sinigaglia, C. (2010). The bodily self as power for action. *Neuropsychologia, 48,* 746–755.

Geller, B., Zimmerman, B., Williams, M., Del Bello, M. P., Bohofner, K., Craney, J. L. Frazier, J., Beringer, L., & Nickelsburg, M. (2002). DSM-IV mania symptoms in a prepubertal and early adolescent bipolar disorder phenotype compared to attention-deficit hyperactive and normal controls. *Journal of Child and Adolescent Psychopharmacology, 12,* 11–25.

Gergely, G., & Unoka, Z. (2008). Attachment, affect-regulation, and mentalization: The developmental origins of the representational affective self. In C. Sharp, P. Fonagy, & I. Goodyer (Eds.), *Social cognition and developmental psychopathology* (pp. 305–342). New York, NY: Oxford University Press.

Gergely, G., & Watson, J. S. (2011). The social biofeedback theory of parental affect-mirroring: The development of emotional self-awareness and self-control in infancy. *The International Journal of Psychoanalysis, 77,* 1181–1212.

Gergely, G., & Watson, J. S. (2014). Early socio-emotional development: Contingency perception and the social-biofeedback model. In P. Rochat (Ed.). *Early social cognition: Understanding others in the first months of life* (pp. 101–136). Mahwah, NJ: Lawrence Erlbaum.

Geschwind, D. H., & Levitt, P. (2007). Autism spectrum disorders: Developmental disconnection syndromes. *Current Opinion in Neurobiology, 17,* 103–111.

Glovinsky, I. (2002). A brief history of childhood-onset bipolar disorder through 1980. *Child and Adolescent Psychiatric Clinical of North America, 11,* 443–460.

Greenough, W. T., Black, J. E., & Wallace, C. (1987). Experience and brain development. *Child Development, 58,* 539–559.

Greenspan, S. I. (2007a). Levels of infant-caregiver interactions and the DIR model: Implications for the development of signal affects, the regulation of mood and behavior, the formation of a sense of self, the creation of internal representation, and the construction of defenses. *Journal of Infant, Child, and Adolescent Psychotherapy, 6,* 174–210.

Greenspan, S. I. (2007b). Infant-caregiver interactions and the developmental, individual-difference, relationship-based (DIR) model: Implications for psychopathology and the psychotherapeutic process. *Journal of Infant, Child & Adolescent Psychotherapy, 6,* 211–244.

Greenspan, S. I., & Glovinsky, I. (2002). *Bipolar patterns in children: New perspectives on developmental pathways and a comprehensive approach to prevention and treatment.* Bethesda, MD: The Interdisciplinary Council on Developmental and Learning Disorders.

Greenpan, S. I., & Wieder, S. (2006). *Infant and early childhood mental health: A comprehensive developmental approach to assessment and intervention.* Washington, DC: American Psychiatric Press.

Happe, F.G.E., & Booth, R.D.L. (2008). The power of the positive: Revisiting weak coherence in autism spectrum disorders. *The Quarterly Journal of Experimental Psychology, 61,* 50–63.

Hardy, M. W., & LaGasse, A. B. (2013). Rhythm, movement, and autism: Using rhythmic rehabilitation research as a model for autism. *Frontiers in Integrative Neuroscience,* 7 (19). doi:0.3389/fnint.2013.00019.

Hazen, E. P., McDougle, C., & Volkmar, J. (2013). Changes in the diagnostic criteria for autism in DSM-5: Controversies and concerns. *Journal of Clinical Psychiatry, 74,* 739–740.

Hazlett, H. C., Poe, M., Guido, G., Smith, R. G., Rovenzale, J., Ross, A., Gilmore, J., & Piven, J. (2005). Magnetic resonance imaging and head circumference study of brain size in autism. *Archives of General Psychiatry, 62,* 1366–1376.

Hesse, E., & Main, M. (2000). Disorganized infant, child, and adult attachment: Collapse in behavioral and attentional strategies. *Journal of the American Psychoanalytic Association, 48,* 1097–1127.

Hickok, S., & Sinigaglia, C. (2013). Clarifying the role of the mirror system. *Neuroscience Letters, 540,* 62–66. doi:10.1016/j.neulet.2012.11.029.

Hirshfeld-Becker, D. R., Biederman, J., Henin, A., Faraone, S. V., De Petrillo, L. A., Markowitz, S. M., & Rosenbaum, J. F. (2006). Psychopathology in the young offspring of parents with bipolar disorder: A controlled pilot study. *Psychiatry Research, 145,* 155–167.

Hobson, P., & Hobson, J. (2011). Joint attention or joint engagement? Insights from autism. In A. Seemann (Ed.), *Joint attention: New developments in psychology, philosophy of mind, and social neuroscience* (115–135). Cambridge, MA: MIT Press.

Hofer, M. (1996). On the nature and consequences of early loss. *Psychosomatic Medicine, 58,* 570–581.

Iacoboni, M. (2008). *Mirroring people: The new science of how we connect with others.* New York, NY: Picador.

Interdisciplinary Council on Developmental and Learning Disorders (ICDL) (2005). *Diagnostic manual for infancy and early childhood.* Bethesda, MD: Author.

Jones, W., & Klin, A. (2013). Attention to eyes is present but in decline in 2–6-month-old infants later diagnosed with autism. *Nature, 504,* 427–431.

Kestenberg, J. S. (1975). *Children and parents.* Northvale, NJ: Jason Aronson.

Kestenberg, J. S. (1978). Transsensus-outgoingess and Winnicott's intermediate zone. In S. A. Grolnick, L. Barkin, & W. Muensterberger (Eds.), *Between fantasy and reality: Winnicott's concepts of transitional objects and phenomena* (pp. 61–74). Northvale, NJ: Jason Aronson.

Kestenberg Amighi, J., Loman, S., Lewis, P., & Sossin, K. M. (1999). *The meaning of movement: Developmental and clinical perspectives of the Kestenberg Movement Profile.* New York, NY: Brunner-Routledge.

Kim, S. H., & Lord, C. (2010). Restricted and repetitive behaviors in toddlers and preschoolers with autism spectrum disorders based on the Autism Diagnostic Observation Schedule (ADOS). *Autism Research, 3*(4), 162–173.

Kim, S. H., & Lord, C. (2011). New autism diagnostic interview-revised algorithms for toddlers and young preschoolers from 12 to 47 months of age. *Journal of Autism and Developmental Disorders, 42,* 82–93.

Kim, J., Wigram, T., & Gold, C. (2009). Emotional, motivational and interpersonal responsiveness of autism in improvisational music therapy. *Autism, 13,* 389–409.

Klin, A. (2009). Subtyping the autism spectrum disorders: Theoretical, research, and clinical considerations. In S. Goldstein, J. A. Naglieri, & S. Ozonoff (Eds.), *Assessment of autism spectrum disorders.* New York, NY: Guilford.

Klin, A., Jones, W., Schultza, R., Volkmar, F., & Cohen, D. (2002). Defining and quantifying the social phenotype in autism. *The American Journal of Psychiatry, 159,* 909–916.

Kolvin, I. (1971). Studies in the childhood psychoses: I. Diagnostic criteria and classification. *British Journal of Psychiatry, 118,* 381–384.

Kong, L., Bachmann, S., Thomann, P. A., Essig, M., & Schröder, J. (2012). Neurological soft signs and gray matter changes: A longitudinal analysis in first-episode schizophrenia. Schizophrenia Research, *134,* 27–32.

Koppe, S., Harder, S., & Vaever, M. (2008). Vitality affects. *International Forum of Psychoanalysis, 17,* 169–179.

Lange, A. (2012). Prenatal maternal stress and the developing fetus and infant: A review of animal models as related to human research. In B. Beebe, P. Cohen, K. M. Sossin, &

S. Markese. (Eds.), *Mothers, infants and young children of September 11, 2001* (pp. 175–189). New York, NY: Routledge.

Levin, F. M., & Trevarthen, C. (2000). Subtle is the Lord: The relationship between consciousness, the unconscious, and the executive control network (ECN) of the brain. *The Annual of Psychoanalysis, 28,* 105–125.

Levy, K. N., Beeney, J. E., & Temes, C. M. (2011). Attachment and its vicissitudes in borderline personality disorder. *Current Psychiatry Reports, 13*(1), 50–59.

Lieberman, A. F., Padrón, E., Van Horn, P., and Harris, W. W. (2005).Angels in the nursery: Intergenerational transmission of benevolent parental influences. *Infant Mental Health Journal, 26*(6), 504–520.

Loman, S., & Sossin, K. M. (2009). Current clinical applications of the Kestenberg Movement Profile. In S. Chaiklin & H. Wengrower (Eds.), *Life is dance: The art and science of DMT* (pp. 237–264). New York, NY: Routledge.

Luby, J., & Belden, A. (2006). Defining and validating bipolar disorder in the preschool period. *Development and Psychopathology, 18,* 971–988.

Luby, J., & Navsaria, N. (2010) Pediatric bipolar disorder: Evidence of prodromal states and early markers. *Journal of Child Psychology and Psychiatry, 51,* 459–471.

Luby, J., Tandon, M., & Belden, A. (2009). Preschool bipolar disorder. *Child and Adolescent Psychiatric Clinics of North America, 18,* 391–403.

Luby, J., Tandon, M., & Nicol, G. (2007). Three-clinical case of DSM-IV mania symptoms in preschoolers. *Journal of Child and Adolescent Psychopharmacology, 17,* 237–243.

Luyster, R., Gotham, K., Guthrie, W., Coffing, M., Petrak, R., Pierce, K., Bishop, S., Esler, A., Hus, V., Oti, R., Richler, J., Risi, S., & Lord, C. (2009). The Autism Diagnostic Observation Schedule—Toddler Module: A new module of a standardized diagnostic measure for autism spectrum disorders. *Journal of Autism and Developmental Disorders, 39,* 1305–1320.

Maclean, P. (1985). Brain evolution relating to family, play, and the separation call. *Archives of General Psychiatry, 42,* 405–417.

Mahler, M., & Furer, M. (1960). Observations on research regarding the "symbiotic syndrome" of infantile psychosis. *Psychoanalytic Quarterly, 29,* 317–327.

Main, M., & Hesse, E. (1990). Parents' unresolved traumatic experiences are related to infant disorganized attachment status: Is frightened and/or frightening parental behavior the linking mechanism? In M. T. Greenberg, D. Cicchetti, & E. M. Cummings (Eds.), *Attachment in the preschool years: Theory, research, and intervention* (pp. 161–182). Chicago, IL: University of Chicago Press.

Main, M. & Morgan, H. (1996). Disorganization and disorientation in infant strange situation behavior: Phenotypic resemblance to dissociative states. In L. K. Michelson & W. J. Ray (Eds.), *Handbook of dissociation: Theoretical, empirical, and clinical perspectives* (pp. 107–138). New York, NY: Plenum.

Malloch, S., & Trevarthen, C. (2009). Musicality: Communicating the vitality and interests of life. In S. Malloch & C. Trevarthen (Eds.), *Communicative musicality: Exploring the basis of human companionship* (pp. 1–11). New York, NY: Oxford University Press.

Martin, L. A., & Horriat, N. I. (2012). The effects of birth order and birth interval on the phenotypic expression of autism spectrum disorder. *PLoS ONE* 7(11), e51049. doi:10.1371/journal.pone.0051049.

Mayes, S. D., & Calhoun, S. L. (2003). Ability profiles in children with autism: Influence of age and IQ. *Autism, 7,* 65–80.

McAnulty, G., Duffy, F. H., Kosta, S., Weisenfeld, N. I., Warfield, S. K., Butler S. C., Alidoost, M., Bernstein, J. H., Robertson, R., Zurakowski, D., & Als, H. (2013). School-age effects of the newborn individualized developmental care and assessment program for preterm infants with intrauterine growth restriction: preliminary findings. *BMC Pediatrics, 19,* 13–25.

Mehler, K., Wendrich, D., Kissgen, R., Roth, B., Oberthuer, A. et al. (2011). Mothers seeing their VLBW infants within 3h after birth are more likely to establish a secure attachment behavior: Evidence of a sensitive period with preterm infants? *Journal of Perinatology,31*(6), 404–410.

Miklowitz, D. J., Biuckians, A., & Richards, J. A. (2006). Early-onset bipolar disorder: A family treatment perspective. Development and Psychopathology,18(4), 1247–1265.

Miklowitz, D. J., & Chang, K. D. (2008). Prevention of bipolar disorder in at-risk children: Theoretical assumptions and empirical foundations. *Development and Psychopathology, 20,* 881–897.

Minshew, N., Sung, K, Jones, B. L., & Furman, J. M. (2004). Underdevelopment of the postural control system in autism. *Neurology, 63,* 2056–2061.

Morrow, E. M., Yoo, S. Y., Flavell, S. W., Kim, T. K., Lin, Y., Hill, R. S., . . . Walsh, C. A. (2008). Identifying autism loci and genes by tracing recent shared ancestry. *Science, 321,* 218–223.

Moskowitz, S., Reiswig, R., & Demby, G. (2014). From infant observation to parent-infant treatment: The Anni Bergman Parent-Infant Psychotherapy Training Program. *Journal of Infant, Child, and Adolescent Psychotherapy, 13,* 1–8.

Murdoch, J. D., & State, M. W. (2013). Recent developments in the genetics of autism spectrum disorders. *Current Opinion in Genetics and Development, 23,* 310–315.

Muratori, F., Apicella, F., Muratori, P., & Maestro, S., (2011) Intersubjective disruptions and caregiver–infant interaction in early autistic disorder. *Research in Autism Spectrum Disorders, 5,* 408–417.

Nicodemus, K. K., Marenco, S., Batten, A. J., Vakkalanka, R., Egan, M. F., Straub, R. E., & Weinberger, D. R. (2008). Serious obstetric complications interact with hypoxia-regulated/vascular-expression genes to influence schizophrenia risk. *Molecular Psychiatry, 13,* 873–877.

Nordahl, C. W., Scholz, R., Yang, X., Buonocore, M. H., Simon, T., Rogers, S., & Amarai, D. G. (2012). Increased rate of amygdala growth in children aged 2 to 4 years with autism spectrum disorders: A longitudinal study. *Archives of General Psychiatry, 69,* 53–61.

Nosarti, C., Reichenberg, A., Murray, R. M., Cnattingius, S., Lambe, M. P., Yin, L., MacCabe, J., Rifkin, L., Hultman, C. M. (2012). Preterm birth and psychiatric disorders in young adult life. *JAMA Psychiatry, 69,* E1–E8.

O'Connor, E., Bureau, J-F., McCartney, K., & Lyons-Ruth, K. (2011). Risks and outcomes associated with disorganized/controlling patterns of attachment at age three years in the national institute of child health & human development study of early child care and youth development. *Infant Mental Health Journal, 32,* 450–472.

Oosterling, I. J., Swinkels, S. H., van der Gaag, R. J., Visser, J. C., Dietz, C., Bultclaar, J. K. (2009). Comparative analysis of three screening instruments for autism spectrum disorder in toddlers at high risk. *Journal of Autism and Developmental Disorders, 39,* 897–909.

Osofsky, J. D. (2009). Perspectives on helping traumatized infants, young children, and their families. *Infant Mental Health Journal, 30,* 673–677.

Osofsky, J. D. (2011). Introduction: Trauma through the eyes of a young child. In J. D. Osofsky (Ed.), *Clinical work with traumatized young children.* New York, NY: Guilford.

Panksepp, J. (2002). On the animalian values of the human spirit: The foundational role of affect in psychotherapy and the evolution of consciousness. *European Journal of Psychotherapy, counseling & Health, 5,* 225–245.

Papousek, M. (2011). Resilience, strengths, and regulatory capacities: Hidden resources in developmental disorders of infant mental health. *Infant Mental health Journal, 32,* 29–46.

Porges, S. W. (2003). The Polyvagal Theory: Phylogenetic contributions to social behavior. *Physiology & Behavior, 79,* 503–513.

Preti, A., Pisano, A., Cascio, M. T., Monzani, E., Meneghelli, A., & Cocchi, A. (2012). Obstetric complications in early psychosis: Relation with family history of psychosis. *Psychiatry Research, 200*(2–3), 708–714.

Rai, D., Golding, J., Magnusson, C., Steer, C., Lewis, G., & Dalman, C. (2012) Prenatal and early life exposure to stressful life events and risk of autism spectrum disorders: Population-based studies in Sweden and England. *PLoS ONE, 7,* e38893. doi:10.1371/journal.pone.0038893.

Redcay, E., & Courchesne, E. (2005). When is the brain enlarged in autism? A meta-analysis of all brain size reports. *Biological Psychiatry, 58,* 1–9.

Rizzolatti, G., & Sinigaglia, C. (2010) The functional role of the parieto-frontal mirror circuit: Interpretations and misinterpretations. *Nature Reviews Neuroscience, 11,* 264–274.

Rizzolatti, G., & Sinigaglia, C. (2013). Understanding action from the inside. In W. Prinz, M. Beisert, & A. Herwig (Eds.), *Action Science: Foundations of an emerging discipline* (pp. 201–227). Cambridge, MA: MIT Press.

Rizzolatti, G., Fadiga, L., Fogassi, L., & Gallese, V. (1996). Premotor cortex and the recognition of motor actions. *Cognition and Brain Research, 3,* 131–41.

Rochat, M. J., Veroni, V., Bruschweiler-Stern, N., Pieraccini, C., Bonnet-Brilhault, F., Barthélémy, C., Maly, J., Sinigaglia, C., Stern, D. N., & Rizzolatti, G. (2013) Impaired vitality form recognition in autism. *Neuropsychologia, 51,* 1918–1924.

Russell, A. T. (1994). The clinical presentation of childhood-onset schizophrenia. *Schizophrenia Bulletin, 20,* 631–646.

Rutherford, H.J.V., Goldberg, B., Luyten, P., Bridgett, D. J., & Mayes, L. C. (2013). *Infant Behavior & Development, 36,* 635–641.

Samango-Sprouse, C. A., Stapleton, E. J., Aliabadi, F., Graw, R., Vickers, R., Haskell, K., Sadegin, T., Jameson, R., Parmele, C. L., & Gropman, A. L. (2014). Identification of infants at risk for autism spectrum disorder and developmental language delay prior to 12 months. *Autism. Advance online publication.* doi:10.1177/1362361314521329.

Sanders, S. J., Murtha, M. T., Gupta, A. R., Murdoch, J. D., Raubeson, M. J., Willsey, A. J., Ercan-Sencicek, A. G., DiLullo, N. M., Parikshak, N. N, Stein, J. L. et al. (2012). De novo mutations revealed by whole-exome sequencing are strongly associated with autism. *Nature, 485,* 237–241.

Schore, A. (1994). *Affect regulation and the origin of the self: The neurobiology of emotional development.* Hillsdale, NJ: Erlbaum.

Schore, A. N. (2003). *Affect dysregulation and disorders of the self.* New York, NY: W. W. Norton.

Schore, A. N. (2013). Regulation theory and the early assessment of attachment and autistic spectrum disorders: A response to Voran's clinical case. *Journal of Infant, Child, and Adolescent Psychotherapy, 12,* 164–189.

Schumann, C. M., Barnes, C. C., Lord, C., & Courchesne, E. (2009). Amygdala enlargement in toddlers with autism related to severity of social and communication impairments. *Biological Psychiatry, 66,* 942–949.

Sharp, C., & Fonagy, P. (2008). The parent's capacity to treat the child as a psychological agent: Constructs, measures and implications for developmental psychopathology. *Social Development, 17*(3), 737–754.

Shaw, J. A. Egeland, J. A., Endicott, J., Allen, C. R., Hostetter, A. M. (2005). A 10-year prospective study of prodromal patterns for bipolar disorder among Amish youth. *Journal of the American Academy of Child & Adolescent Psychiatry, 44,* 1104–1111.

Sinigaglia, C. (2013). What type of action understanding is subserved by mirror neurons? *Neuroscience Letters, 54* 62–66. doi:10.1016/j.neulet.2012.10.016.

Slade, A. (2005). Parental reflective functioning: An introduction. *Attachment and Human Development, 7,* 269–281.

Sossin, K. M. (1999). The KMP and infant-parent psychotherapy. In J. K. Amighi, S. Loman, P. Lewis, & K. M. Sossin (Eds.), *The Meaning of Movement: Developmental and Clinical Perspectives of the Kestenberg Movement Profile.* New York, NY: Brunner-Routledge.

Sossin, K. M., & Cohen, P. (2012). Children's play in the wake of loss and trauma. In B. Beebe, P. Cohen, K. M. Sossin, & S. Markese (Eds.), *Mothers, infants and young children of September 11,* 2001 (pp. 110–127). New York, NY: Routledge.

Sossin, K. M., Cohen, P., & Beebe, B. (2014). Death of a father on September 11, 2001: Video informed consultations with widowed mothers. In P. Cohen, K. M. Sossin, & R. Ruth (Eds.), *Healing after parent loss in childhood and adolescence.* Lanham, MD: Rowman & Littlefield.

St. Clair, C., Danon-Boileau, L., & Trevarthen, C. (2007). Signs of autism in infancy: sensitivity for rhythms of expression in communication. In S. Acquarone (Ed.), *Signs of autism In infants: Recognition and Early intervention (pp. 21–45).* London, UK: Karnac.

State, M. W., & Sestan, N. (2012). The emerging biology of autism spectrum disorders. *Science, 337,* 1301–1303.

Stern, D. (2010). *Forms of vitality: Exploring dynamic experience in psychology, the arts, psychotherapy, and development.* New York, NY: Oxford University Press.

Stern, D. N. (1995). *The motherhood constellation: A unified view of parent-infant psychotherapy.* New York, NY: Basic Books.

Stern, D. N., Sander, L. W., Nahum, J. P., Harrison, A. M., Lyons-Ruth, K., Morgan, A. C., Bruschweiler-Stern, N., & Tronick, E. Z. (1998). Non-interpretive mechanisms in psychoanalytic therapy: The 'something more' than interpretation. *International Journal of Psychoanalysis, 79,* 903–921.

Stigler, K. A., Erickson, C. A., & McDougle, C. J. (2013). Autism and other pervasive developmental disorders. Clinical manual of child and adolescent psychopharmacology (2nd edition). In M. McVoy & R. L. Findling (Eds.), *Clinical manual of child and adolescent psychopharmcology* (pp. 269–309). Arlington, VA: American Psychiatric Publishing.

Suren, P., Roth, C., Bresnahan, M., Haugen, M., Hornig, M., Hirtz, D., Lie, K. K., Lipkin, W. I., Magnus, P., Reichborn-Kjennerud, T., Scholberg, S., Oyen, A-S., Susser, E., Stoltenberg, C. (2013). Association between maternal use of folic acid supplements and risk of autism spectrum disorders in children. *Journal of the American Medical Association, 309,* 570–577.

Teitelbaum, O., Benton, T., Shah, P. K., Prince, A., Kelly, J. L., & Teitelbaum, P. (2004), Eshkol–Wachman movement notation in diagnosis: The early detection of Asperger's syndrome. *Proceedings of the National Academy of Sciences of the United States of America, 101,* 11909–11914.

Tortora, S. (2006). *The dancing dialogue: Using the communicative power of movement with young children.* Baltimore, MD: Paul H. Brookes.

Tortora, S. (2009). The "Ways of Seeing" program—Dance-movement psychotherapy in early childhood treatment. In S. Caiklin & H. Wengrower (Eds.), *The art and science of dance/movement therapy.* New York, NY: Routledge.

Trevarthen, C. (1998). The concept and foundations of infant inter-subjectivity. In S. Braten (Ed.), *Intersubjective communication and emotion in early ontogeny* (pp. 15–46). Cambridge, UK: Cambridge University Press.

Trevarthen, C. (2011). What is it like to be a person who knows nothing? *Infant and Child Development, 20,* 119–135.

Trevarthen, C., & Aitken, K. J. (1994) Brain development, infant communication, and empathy disorders: Intrinsic factors in child mental health. *Developmental Psychopathology, 6,* 599–635. doi:10.1017/S0954579400004703.

Trevarthen, C., Aitken, K., Papoudi, D., & Robarts, J. (1998). *Children with autism: Diagnosis and interventions to meet their needs, second edition.* London, UK: Jessica Kingsley.

Trevarthen, C., & Daniel, S. (2005).Rhythm and synchrony in early development, and signs of autism and Rett syndrome in infancy. *Brain Development, 27,* (Suppl.1), S25–S34. doi:10.1016/j.braindev.2005.03.016.

Trevarthen, C., & Delafield-Butt, J. T. (2013). Autism as a developmental disorder in intentional movement and affective engagement. *Frontiers in integrative neuroscience, 7* (49), 1–16.

Tronick, E. (1989). Emotions and emotional communication in infants. *American Psychologist, 42,* 192–189.

Tronick, E., & Reck, C. (2009). Infants of depressed mothers. *Harvard Review of Psychiatry, 17,* 147–156.

Tronick, E. Z. (1998). Dyadically expanded states of consciousness and the process of therapeutic change. *Infant Mental Health Journal, 19,* 290–299.

Tronick, E. Z. (2002). A model of infant mood states and Sanderian affective waves. *Psychoanalytic Dialogues, 12,* 73–79.

Tustin, F. (1991). Revised understandings of psychogenic autism. *The International Journal of Psychoanalysis, 72,* 585–591.

Tustin, F. (1992). *Autistic states in children, second edition.* London, UK: Routledge.

Volkmar, F. R. (1996). Childhood and adolescent psychosis: A review of the past 10 years. *Journal of the American Academy of Child & Adolescent Psychiatry 35,* 843–851.

Volkmar, F. R., Chawarska, K., & Klin, A. (2008). Autism spectrum disorders in infants and toddlers: An introduction. In K. Chawarska, A. Klin, & F. R. Volkmar (Eds.), *Autism spectrum disorders in infants and toddlers: Diagnosis, assessment, and treatment* (pp. 1–22). New York, NY: Guilford.

Volkmar, F., State, M., & Klin, A. (2009). Autism and autism spectrum disorders: Diagnostic issues for the coming decade. *Journal of Child Psychology and Psychiatry, 50,* 108–115.

Voran, M. (2013). The protest of a 6-month-old girl: Is this a prodrome of autism? *Journal of Infant Child Adolescent Psychotherapy, 12,* 139–155.

Werner, E., & Dawson, G. (2005). Validation of the phenomenon of autistic regression using home videotapes. *Archives of General Psychiatry, 62,* 889–895.

Werry, J. S. (1996). Childhood schizophrenia. In J. Vokmar (Ed.), *Psychoses and developmental disorders in childhood and adolescence* (pp. 1–56). Washington, DC: American Psychiatric Press.

Wieder, S., & Greenspan, S. I. (2006). Infant and early childhood mental health: The DIR model. In G. M. Foley, & J. D. Hochman (Eds). *Mental health in early intervention: Achieving unity in principles and practice* (pp. 175–189). Baltimore, MD: Paul H. Brookes Publishing.

Worley, J. A., & Matson, J. L. (2011). Psychiatric symptoms in children diagnosed with autism spectrum disorder: An examination of gender differences. *Research in Autism Spectrum Disorders, 5,* 1086–1091.

Yehuda, R., & Bierer, L. M. (2008). Transgenerational transmission of cortisol and PTSD risk. *Progress in Brain Research, 167,* 121–135.

Yehuda, R., Engel., S. M., Brand, S. R., Seckl, J., Marcus, S. M., & Berkowitz, G. S. (2005). Transgenerational effects of posttraumatic stress disorder in babies of mothers exposed to the World Trade Center attacks during pregnancy. *Journal of Clinical Endocrinology & Metabolism, 90*(2005) 4115–4118.

Yirmiya, N., & Charman, T. (2010). The prodrome of autism: Early behavioral and biological signs, regression, peri- and post-natal development and genetics. *Journal of Child Psychology and Psychiatry, 51,* 432–458.

Yirmiya, N., & Ozonoff, S. (2007). The very early autism phenotype. *Journal of Autism and Developmental Disorders, 37,* 1–11.

Zaccario, M., Sossin, K. M., & DeGroat, J. (2009). Assessment of infants and toddlers. In B. Mowder, F. Rubinson, & A. Yasik (Eds.), *Evidence-based practice in infant and early childhood psychology* (pp. 93–128). Hoboken, NJ: Wiley.

Zeanah, C. H., Boris, N. W., & Lieberman, A. F. (2000). Attachment disorders in infancy. In A. Sameroff, M. Lewis, & S. M. Miller (Eds.), *Handbook of developmental psychopathology,* 2nd edition (293–307). Dordrecht, Netherlands: Kluwer Academic Publishers.

Zero to Three (2005). DC:0–3R. *Diagnostic classification of mental health and developmental disorders of infancy and early childhood: Revised edition.* Washington, DC: Author.

Zhou, S. S., Zhou, Y. M., Li, D., & Ma, Q. (2013). Early infant exposure to excess multivitamin: A risk factor for autism? *Autism Research and Treatment, 2013,* Article ID 963697. Retrieved from http://dx.dboi.org/10.1155/2013/963697.

PART II

Psychosis and Co-occurring Disorders

4

CHILDHOOD ONSET SCHIZOPHRENIA

Aaron Krasner and Dirk Winter

Introduction

Childhood onset schizophrenia is among the more perplexing psychiatric disorders for patients, families, and allied mental health professionals because of the bizarre, intractable, and persistent nature of the symptoms and its poor prognosis. Though recent advances in the study of childhood onset schizophrenia point toward possible causes and identifiable risk factors and neurobehavioral correlates, we continue to await answers to critical questions. Why do certain patients develop this neuropsychiatric illness so early? Are there biomarkers that may predict the illness, define its endophenotypes, and ultimately guide its treatment? These and other essential questions remain the focus of ongoing research and some of the newer developments will be reviewed in this chapter. While updating readers on new scientific developments, the authors advocate for a flexible approach to the diagnosis, management, and framework for understanding childhood onset schizophrenia that will be useful to clinicians.

As we appreciate the advances that genomics and evolving imaging technologies bring to psychiatry and neuroscience, we remain mindful of two key facts. First, despite advances in drug medication tolerability and efficacy, current research findings do not substantively alter the procedures for diagnosing and treating childhood onset schizophrenia. Second, because of the nosological ambiguities of neuropsychiatric illnesses and the lack of a complete understanding of their pathophysiology, resistances to accepting treatment are typically encountered among patients and families. In addition, neuropsychiatric illnesses are often challenging to detect, adequately treat, and monitor. Thus, the authors advocate a broad, psychodynamic understanding of the child, family, and system of care as a theoretical umbrella for incorporating multiple types of interventions across the spectrum of patients' needs. A working understanding of the basic psychodynamic principles enables child psychiatrists to be effective with these most vulnerable patients. Principles of psychic determinism, such as the repetition of the past in the present, the role of defenses in the course of psychological development, maturational and relational influences on the development of the self, and the importance of maintaining a developmental understanding of children and families are all very relevant to formulations about seriously ill children. Multiple authors have advocated a similar approach to child psychiatry, medication management (Mallo and Mintz, 2013), and adult psychiatry.

To illustrate this perspective, consider the following brief example. Peter, a boy of 9, is diagnosed with childhood onset schizophrenia. However, his mother, who herself struggles with bipolar disorder, declines to seek ongoing psychiatric treatment for Peter because of her previous negative experiences with the mental health system. Her marriage suffers as Peter's illness advances, and a divorce ensues. The child's symptoms deteriorate and his mother, accused of medical neglect, loses custody and attempts suicide, resulting in her psychiatric rehospitalization. A psychodynamic framework that considers Peter's and his mother's unconscious fears and worries would be flexible enough to allow the practitioner to anticipate the roadblocks in the treatment, to deliver biologically active interventions successfully, and to enable access to care that would address Peter's fundamental brain-based illness. In contrast to an emphasis on psychoanalytic interpretive interventions, this psychodynamic framework incorporates a broader appreciation of the biopsychosocial and family influences on the exacerbations of the child's illness. Furthermore, such a framework allows child psychiatrists to assist families in addressing challenging questions that families like Peter's must face. Should Peter attend college nearby or far away? Should he be entrusted with administering his own medications? What level of control can patients expect to assume regarding dating, experimentation with drugs and alcohol, and engagement with peers? Children and youth with schizophrenia frequently need very consistent support as they negotiate the developmental tasks of late adolescence and early adulthood.

In the case of childhood onset schizophrenia, there can also be a sense of loss due to persistent disappointment and dashed expectations that parents have for their children. This phenomenon has been referred to as ambiguous loss (Boss and Carnes, 2012), in that the child is physically present but mentally absent, and resolution for the perceived loss is challenging to achieve. Psychodynamic psychiatrists can empathically appreciate the enormity of the perceived parental loss and the uphill battle that the families must face in providing the kind of care and structure that is not typically available in educational and medical settings. This chapter, therefore, should serve not only as an update on the science of childhood onset schizophrenia but also a reminder about treatment principles for these vulnerable patients and their families.

Overview of Childhood Onset Schizophrenia

In order to understand the current state of knowledge about childhood onset schizophrenia, it is helpful to keep in mind the challenges in developing meaningful psychiatric diagnoses in general and how the diagnosis of childhood onset schizophrenia came to exist. Unlike some medical diagnoses, such as cancer or infectious diseases, psychiatric diagnoses have been developed without a known link to underlying pathophysiology. Instead, the field has been forced to rely on descriptive phenomenology and then work backward toward the underlying mechanisms. A major advance occurred with the publication of DSM-III, which advocated and proposed uniform sets of criteria required to diagnose individual psychiatric disorders. In 1980, the DSM-III for the first time created a separate diagnosis for childhood onset schizophrenia. This diagnosis was based on similar criteria as adult onset schizophrenia, except that the onset occurs prior to age 13. Before this time, children who would now be diagnosed with autism spectrum disorders would have been diagnosed with schizophrenia.

The development of diagnostic symptom clusters has been useful in defining relatively homogenous populations. It has facilitated, working backward so to speak, the elucidation of underlying pathophysiology, and, also going forward toward understanding prognosis and developing and improving evidence-based treatments. However, because an understanding of the pathophysiology of the illnesses is incomplete, it should also not be surprising that illnesses that share overlapping criteria, such as childhood onset schizophrenia and autism, frequently co-occur and also share predisposing genes and risk factors. Large studies have found that pervasive developmental disorder (PDD, now reclassified in DSM 5 as autism spectrum diagnosis) and autism have 30% to 50% comorbidity, share a period of early accelerated brain development, and also a growing number of similar genetic anomalies. Neuroimaging studies are making it increasingly easier to identify differences in rates of brain development and structural and functional differences associated with each of these separate disorders in spite of their degree of comorbidity (Rapoport, Chavez, Greenstein, Addington, and Gogtay, 2009; Cochran, Dvir, and Frazier, 2013). Schizophrenia is a complex and debilitating neuropsychiatric illness that typically emerges in late adolescence and early adulthood. It is characterized by hallucinations and delusions (known as positive symptoms), social withdrawal, alogia, flat affect (negative symptoms), and cognitive disabilities (DSM 5). The negative symptoms herald decrements in adaptive function characterized by inability to care for oneself, maintain a job, or nurture important social relationships, and an inexorable decrement in academic and intellectual function. Underlying these global deficiencies is a myriad of neuropsychological aberrancies that have been carefully studied over time (White, Shmidt, and Karatekin, 2010) and correlated in some cases with possible biological vulnerabilities. Social cognition, the encoding, storage, retrieval, and processing of information in the brain which relates to members of the same species, is impaired in schizophrenia (Korkmaz, 2011). Retrospectively, patients with schizophrenia perform differently on a host of neurobehavioral assessments, but no single neuropsychological finding currently bears sufficient statistical or clinical significance to render a schizophrenia diagnosis (Gurovich, Shmukler, and Zaitseva, 2012).

Diagnostic Issues and Epidemiology

In childhood onset schizophrenia, the onset is earlier (the average age of diagnosis is 12). The illness is less common, the prognosis more guarded, and the premorbid level of functioning is lower (Rapoport and Gogtay, 2011). Psychosis is a non-specific symptom that cuts across psychiatric diagnoses and is defined as impaired reality testing. Among adults, common psychotic delusions include paranoid, persecutory worries, either about other people or about aliens; bizarre conspiratorial worries; and blurred boundaries between religious preoccupation and non-reality-based attributions of power to religious practices. Children with schizophrenia endorse these, among other symptoms. However, it has become recognized that psychotic children report higher rates of visual hallucinations than their adult counterparts (Rapoport and Gogtay, 2011). It is important to highlight here the perils of diagnosing psychosis among children. Is a 4-year-old whose imaginary friend told him to steal the cookie from the cookie jar psychotic? Of course not, but paradigmatically the accurate assessment and positive predictive value of psychotic symptoms as predictive of lifelong psychotic illness is not simple (Fisher et al., 2013). Developmental changes complicate the diagnosis of pediatric psychosis. Core obfuscating factors in the pediatric population include comorbid or atypical presentations of different psychiatric illnesses, including anxiety and mood disorders (so-called affective psychoses); undetected neurodevelopmental disorders and intellectual disabilities; and personality pathology, all of which can masquerade as psychosis but may remit with appropriate treatment. Cultural factors and culturally bound symptom clusters are an additional consideration that any competent evaluating physician considers in evaluating the significance of psychotic symptoms. To highlight the diagnostic complexity among seemingly psychotic children, the Rapoport group at the National Institute of Mental Health (NIMH: the premier group for the study of childhood psychosis) regularly redefines referred probands as non-psychotic, despite multiple community clinicians' impression to the contrary (Shaw, Rapoport, and Hamilton, 2006).

The epidemiology of childhood onset schizophrenia suggests that the illness is quite rare. If adult onset schizophrenia occurs in 0.3% to 0.7% of the population around the world, then childhood onset schizophrenia is much rarer, but there are few epidemiologic estimates for the illness at all (Rapoport and Gogtay, 2011). Yet, childhood onset schizophrenics are an interesting and challenging group of patients to treat and study. They typically have more severe premorbid neurodevelopmental abnormalities, more cytogenetic anomalies, and family histories of schizophrenia and associated disorders. Whether childhood onset schizophrenia represents a prodrome for adult onset schizophrenia or is its own a distinct illness remains a topic of some controversy (Nicolson and Rapoport, 1999). Regardless, it is generally accepted in medicine that the study of early onset illness (i.e., more severe illness) proffers the hope of greater insight into the etiopathogenesis of the condition and, as such, this clinically complex sample is deserving of study and intensive treatment.

Clinical Presentation and Treatment

Children with childhood onset schizophrenia overwhelmingly have a family history of schizophrenia. In what may be related to the genetic phenomenon of anticipation,[1] it has been postulated that earlier schizophrenia presentations represent a more virulent, debilitating form of the illness whose early onset heralds a treatment refractory course characterized by intransigent psychosis, social withdrawal, and intellectual disability (DSM 5, 2013). The differential diagnosis for early onset schizophrenia is broad and relatively unstable (Rapoport and Gogtay, 2011). Anxiety disorders, such as post-traumatic stress disorder (PTSD) and obsessive-compulsive disorder (OCD), can be confused with primary psychotic disorders. Mood disorders, such as major depression and bipolar disorder, can present with psychotic symptoms.

Neurodevelopmental disorders, disruptive behavioral disorders, intellectual disabilities, and reactive attachment syndromes, seen among severely deprived and neglected children, are the most commonly misdiagnosed etiologies for positive psychotic symptoms in the pediatric population (Rapoport and Gogtay, 2011). When these diagnoses co-occur, which is not uncommon, the ensuing mélange of diagnoses and symptoms may not be reduced to a schizophrenia. The Rapoport group has published widely about multidimensionally impaired children (MDI)—children whose pleotropic symptoms do not cohere in accordance with the most sophisticated diagnostic procedures to a diagnosis of schizophrenia.

The standard of care suggests that all cases of suspected childhood onset schizophrenia go through a rigorous diagnostic evaluation, including a thorough neurological assessment to rule out reversible causes of psychosis, including neoplasia, metabolic, infectious or endocrinologic perturbation, or seizures. Once these illnesses are ruled out, psychotic children ought to undergo thorough neuropsychological assessments, including projective assessments. A complete neuropsychological evaluation serves as a baseline that helps chart the neurodegenerative descent to intellectual disability. There seems to be a difference in neuropsychological profiles between men and women in the premorbid phase of the illness, which merits further study. The early treatment of psychotic symptoms in children has been systematically examined in the TEOSS (Findling et al., 2010), whose inconclusive results suggest that treatment decisions be determined clinically. In our experience, helping patients and families accept a multidimensional psychiatric treatment for childhood onset schizophrenia and its symptoms helps inform appropriate treatment throughout the lifespan.

The first goal, as is the first goal in all effective psychological treatments, is the establishment of a working therapeutic alliance (Gerber, Fonagy, Bateman, and Higgitt, 2004). This is particularly challenging when the patient's (and possibly the parents') capacity for basic trust may have been abrogated by mental illness. Therefore, helping families engage treatment for themselves, as well as their children, is crucial. This has been well established in other fields, and conventional wisdom has suggested that the community mental health setting in which families, not just individual patients, may be treated ought to form the backbone for the treatment of severe and persistently mentally ill children. Therefore, the heart of the mission for early intervention is psycho-education delivered in a humanistic and mindful way, and with the family system in mind. This is particularly important as the exigencies of mentally ill children change with development. That is, psychotic 7-year-olds differ from psychotic 12-year-olds and 18-year-olds in accordance with their respective developmental trajectories, and appropriate developmentally pitched care is indicated.

In keeping with the adult literature, antipsychotic medication tends to help with positive symptoms more effectively compared to the negative, insidious symptoms that dominate the later phases of the illness. If there are co-occurring illnesses, it is crucial to address them. Recent work on the impact of anxiety on severe and persistent mental illness parameters and outcomes (Ballageer, Malla, Manchanda, Takhar, and Haricharan, 2005) clearly reflects that comorbidity, often the rule in cases of childhood onset schizophrenia, modulates prognosis and, thus, necessitates treatment.

Without appropriate treatment, which often involves not just outpatient but inpatient evaluation, treatment, and support, the prognosis for a child with childhood onset schizophrenia is questionable. Early intervention with medication—in our experience, clozapine is superior—and a multimodal psychiatric, therapeutic, and educational approach offers the most support for patients and families struggling with this illness. Even under the best circumstances as outlined here, the illness is intransigent and offers lifelong struggles for patients and families. These struggles transcend symptom management and include financial burdens, vocational ambiguities, the concern for self-injury and suicide, and the development of substance abuse disorders, which compound the underlying psychotic vulnerabilities and may undermine treatment efforts by complicating adherence (Whiteford et al., 2010). It is noteworthy that the relationship between cannabis and psychosis is well established and merits clinical observation (Husted et al., 2012). Patients with genetic vulnerability to schizophrenia should be strongly discouraged from experimenting with cannabis, especially at early ages as it has been shown to hasten and complicate psychosis among future schizophrenia populations.

There is an unfortunate risk of suicide among psychotic children. Suicide is a rare act in prepubertal children (Pfeffer, Normandin, and Kakuma, 1998);

however, psychotic males tend to complete suicide with greater success than matched controls. This may have to do with the fixed nature of their delusions and the paucity of auxiliary coping skills and the kind of intellectual rigidity inherent among young children, especially those with cognitive deficits typically seen in childhood onset schizophrenia. Adults who experience command auditory hallucinations may give pause, recalling previous episodes, and have the wherewithal to report such symptoms to their physician or caretakers. Children, on the other hand, either under-supervised or perhaps impulsive because of the normative maturational processes of brain development, may simply enact a psychotic behavior. Psychotic children whose parents suffer with a related syndrome are at greater risk for completing suicide and as previously underscored this has should be addressed as part of any comprehensive treatment plan.

Behavioral Genetics

The longstanding conflict among psychoanalysts and general psychiatrists regarding the relative significance of environment and heredity has evolved into a new science called epigenetics, the study of heritable changes in gene activity that are not thought to be "predetermined" by mutations in the DNA sequence (Mahgoub, 2013). Unlike simple genetics based on changes to the DNA sequence (the genotype), in complex diseases changes in gene expression have environmental causes, and these complex interactions have been the target of behavioral molecular psychiatric genetics for more than 20 years. In addition, the basic science underlying the study of psychiatric genetics has included linkage analyses studies (linking genes to disease states in given populations), and most recently Genome-Wide Association studies—a technique informed by advances in bioinformatics allowing big data to cross-reference symptoms and disease states with genetic anomalies.

A compelling example of the study of epigenetics within the field of behavioral genetics is the study of the serotonin transporter gene. Twenty years ago, Caspi, Hariri, Holmes, Uher, and Moffitt (2012) discovered that variable allelic manifestations predicted late-life depression when moderated by early childhood adversity. In short, Caspi argued that particularly women who possessed the short allele for the serotonin transporter gene, when exposed to early traumatic stressors, tended to manifest symptoms of major depression later in life. Such a model was also used in studying the relationship between the MAO gene and callous, unemotional traits in adolescent victims of early childhood abuse and deprivation. These findings have been variably reproduced but hold allure for those of us who aspire to a biopsychosocial interactive model for the etiopathogenesis of psychiatric illnesses. Some challenges for the field of psychiatric genetics include sample heterogeneity (genomic variability across different populations), polygenic modes of inheritance (the relatively small effect size of genes implicated in psychiatric diseases), and stigma (challenges in funding large-scale psychiatric studies compared to other branches of medicine). The result has been slow but steady progress, but without clear answers. This is shocking and troublesome given the highly heritable nature of psychiatric illnesses, which are more heritable, in fact, than other major medical problems for which we often have a more nuanced understanding of the biological underpinnings of the illness). It is particularly frustrating because in the absence of a biological understanding of major mental illness, opportunities for charlatans and naysayers to negatively impact treatments and public opinion abound.

Some of the more studied genetic lesions in samples of adult onset schizophrenia include COMT (*catechol-o-methyltransferase*), DISC1 (*disrupted in schizophrenia*), and NRG1 (*neuregulin*), among others (Allen et al., 2008). COMT, specifically the *val 158met* polymorphism, has been implicated in a number of psychiatric illnesses given the gene's prominent role in the degradation of catecholamines, a neurotransmitter family that is regulated by a number of classes of psychotropic medications. While it may play a role in the etiology of major mental illness, it alone cannot explain the morphological changes seen typically in schizophrenia or other major mental illnesses. The same is true for the other genes noted above. A compelling finding that derives from a very large Genome-Wide Association study of more than 30,000 cases showed that specific SNPs (single nucleotide polymorphisms) are associated with a range of psychiatric disorders of childhood-onset or adult-onset. In particular, variation in calcium-channel activity genes seems to have pleotropic effects on psychopathology, which points toward the goal of moving beyond descriptive syndromes in psychiatry and towards a nosology informed by disease cause (Smoller, 2012). New hopes for the study of behavioral genetics include the discovery of copy number variants (CNV), alterations of the DNA of a genome that results in the cell having an abnormal or, for certain genes, a normal variation in the number of copies of one or more sections of the DNA. Larger, homogenous samples have been assembled to study psychiatric genetics and its funding has expanded despite recent budget cuts to NIMH. Integration of this basic science with other state-of-the-art modalities including neuroimaging may offer longitudinal insights into the illness onset and trajectory. If the aforementioned variables—heterogeneity, polygenic risk factor profiles, and stigma—negatively impact current understanding of adult onset psychiatric illness, then the issues of development, research attitudes among parents of mentally ill children, and the challenges of diagnosing mental illness in pediatric populations make the genetic study of childhood onset schizophrenia even more challenging. One success story, however, is the development of commercially available assays for the liver metabolism of common psychotropic medications. This tool allows psychiatrists to predict with some certainty how a patient will metabolize a given medication and, thus, may inform the sequence of medication recommendations, dosing, and anticipation of debilitating side effects that negatively impact adherence (Xu et al., 2013).

Neuro-Imaging of Childhood Onset Schizophrenia

With the development of increasingly sophisticated neuro-imaging techniques, investigators have made inroads into better understanding the cerebral neurophysiologic correlates of childhood onset schizophrenia. Statistically significant alterations in the structure and function of the brain are detected in all psychiatric disorders and these perturbations are often detectable during childhood and adolescence. Gathering the samples, funding their longitudinal study, and generalizing the findings, however, have posed challenges to the integration of neuroimaging findings with behavioral genetics in the study of longitudinal pediatric psychiatric illnesses, including childhood onset schizophrenia. There are two main classes of neuro-imaging studies: *structural imaging studies,* which compare variables such as brain volume and morphology, and *functional imaging studies,* which measure blood flow and glucose metabolism, primarily either in a resting state or when subjects are asked to perform a task under observation. The technology behind imaging studies changes rapidly but remains the primary obstacle for scientific achievement. For example, the x-ray, or its successor the CT scan, offers comparatively little data about the finer nuances of brain morphology, but is cheap and readily available. On the other hand, functional and structural Magnetic Resonance Imaging (MRI), which in variable iterations uses magnetized fields to study the chemical composition of tissue, offers a nuanced and sophisticated window into brain function. But MRI studies are expensive, unwieldy, and relatively new. With some skeptical reflection, one can imagine readily the host of problems posed by linking brain-based findings to disease or even symptoms states. What is the extent of normal variation in structural studies? How much significance can be attributed to changes in regional blood flow when a subject views a given image—i.e., how do we generalize the neurobiological finding to the disease state? If multiple cognitive processes are activated by a prompt like, "Think of your mother," how can the various processes be identified, studied, and linked to genetic vulnerabilities or performance on neuropsychological testing? Regardless of the methodological challenges, neuroimaging offers insight into the brain functions that underlie mental illness and thus will be the focus of this section. A more nuanced discussion of the neuroscience that underlies schizophrenia—from neural circuitry to relevant neurotransmitter systems—goes beyond the scope of this chapter.

According to the neurodevelopmental theory of schizophrenia proposed by Weinberger (1987), early brain insults affect prenatal brain development and resultant pathophysiological mechanisms, causing dysfunction of the mature brain and predisposing to schizophrenia. Current evidence suggests that insults at all stages of development are relevant, which may explain the heterogeneity of brain structural abnormalities in schizophrenia. Below, we will summarize a few of the more significant findings in the field of structural imaging for childhood onset schizophrenia. In studies of childhood onset schizophrenia that compare anatomical MRI findings of children with schizophrenia and healthy controls, there are variable findings about the extent to which the childhood onset schizophrenia patients differ from the controls and from their own siblings in brain volume and the developmental trajectory of the corpus collosum and other brain regions (Gerber, Peterson, Gogtay, and Rapoport, 2008). Much has been written about aberrant neuronal migration and alleged neurodevelopmental abnormalities in schizophrenia, which may well underlie the dynamic accrual of deficits that ultimately presents as schizophrenia (Cornblatt et al., 2003). In addition, the relationship between neurons and their support cells, glia, has been postulated as playing a role in the etiology of the illness (Bernstein, Steiner, and Bogerts, 2009) and imaging findings have supported this theory. Classic morphological findings—postmortem and in vivo—in adult schizophrenia patients include enlarged ventricles (Nesvåg et al., 2012), diffuse white matter changes, and gray matter volume and thickness changes, and have been elucidated in particular with the development of diffusion tensor imaging (a kind of MRI technique) which has enabled investigators greater resolution in studying these morphological aberrancies. Notwithstanding, none of these findings are both necessary and sufficient to render a diagnosis of schizophrenia or at this point sophisticated enough to lend diagnostic clarity in an ambiguous clinical presentation, despite the claims of some private clinics and practitioners.

In terms of functional imaging, a methodological evolution in recent years reflects an increased interest not just in task-oriented experimental paradigms, but an interest in resting state and the so-called default mode network (DMN). Specifically, a newer hypothesis for the symptoms detected in schizophrenia called the "dysconnectivity hypothesis" posits that schizophrenia relates to abnormal resting-state connectivity within the default mode network and this aberrant connectivity is considered as contributory to difficulties in self-referential and introspective processing (Khadka et al., 2013). The default mode network is essentially the brain as it idles. Neuroscientists increasingly demonstrate an interest in unconscious, implicit functions that were originally described by Freud as relevant for all forms of psychopathology. Despite these ambiguities, a theme elaborated throughout the literature about the search for the pathophysiology of childhood onset schizophrenia resounds: subtle, regionally specific, and genetically influenced alterations during developmental age windows influence the course of psychosis and resultant brain phenotype. Characterizing this process longitudinally with imaging techniques may offer an exciting opportunity to chronicle the brain changes that epistatically determine symptoms and outcome.

Clinical Vignette

The clinical portrayal of a psychotic child and her family may illustrate aspects of the principles outlined above. M., a 6-year-old child referred for manic behavior, had not met her milestones normally and demonstrated signs of early developmental deviation that had been previously conceptualized as autistic. Speech, fine motor, and social interaction were all impaired and/or delayed and a treatment plan centered on early intervention was elaborated by a consulting physician but discounted by the family, specifically M.'s mother, Charlotte, who imagined she might manage the situation on her own. Reading books and occasionally consulting professionals, she developed an ersatz intervention for M. with elements of occupational, physical, and academic therapies. Charlotte's mother had committed suicide when Charlotte was 19, with a presumed diagnosis of schizophrenia and her husband, a successful physician, reported that his father had been intermittently psychotic throughout his life and had died of early-onset Alzheimer's. Both parents perceived M.'s vulnerabilities as threatening and acknowledged during our consultation that their wishful thinking in regards to her developmental aberrancies had countermanded advice from professionals and peers. Quite simply, the prospect of reliving their early childhood adversity, now as parents, was so aversive to this otherwise-sophisticated couple that their judgment floundered and the child's illness progressed. This story exemplifies the prominent family history and genetic predisposition inherent in cases of childhood onset schizophrenia, the complexities posed by the illness for parents, and the vulnerability of family systems to antecedent traumata.

M. herself was disheveled, declining to attend to her activities of daily living. She appeared mildly dysmorphic with not only an odd countenance but also a guarded, paranoid regard of her psychiatrist. She seemed, for want of a better description, lost in her own frightening world. Distractedly, she entered the consulting suite, commenting tangentially on the toys in the bin while looking intently at the window, shifting her gaze suspiciously around the room. Quickly, she alluded to a "they"—a coterie of characters in her mind who reminded her to sit in the corner and check in with them throughout the interview. She paused pensively throughout the hour, interrupting our efforts at play, to attend to internal stimuli. She was as interested in the psychiatrist as she was any other object in the room, and she approached her mother, who nervously sat looking at her cell phone, to inform her of one or another hallucination. There was nothing fun or pretend about her regard of her inner voices—rather, they were a confusing and relentless maelstrom of commands and commentaries that derailed the child's thought process and disabled her capacity to engage her surroundings. Her distracted confusion elicited a vague and menacing feeling within the treating clinician, a clear sense that all was indeed not OK—and that it never would be. In comparison with other young children, the reassuring incipient rapport elicited with comedy or light play was supplanted by a foreboding sense of dread and impending doom. It would not have been difficult to lose one's footing in this treacherous world and equally daunting to convey this countertransferentially informed impression to her mother, whose wish for normalcy could only be matched by the intensity of the presenting symptoms of the child. A neurologic examination and workup was normal. There were no inborn errors of metabolism and no Lyme titers to follow up. The child's affect was flat and, despite her odd behavior, symptoms of frank autism were not present in the current psychiatric examination. Anxiety, though free floating, could not explain her bizarre internal experience and the diagnosis of childhood onset schizophrenia was rendered. She was treated with clozapine and some of her positive symptoms, but not all, abated and with substantial psycho-education, the family began to adjust to the child's psychiatric needs and the disheartening prognosis of early onset schizophrenia. The concept of the ambiguous loss was addressed with the parents. Though M. would be physically present in their lives, normative hopes and expectations for separation and individuation would inevitably be challenged by the realities of persistent psychosis.

Concluding Remarks

There are areas of study that will offer greater insights into the etiopathogenesis of this costly illness. Greater cooperation across disciplines (psychiatry, neurology, psychology, and immunology), funding opportunities, and the integration of behavioral, genetic, and imaging data will ultimately advance the study of childhood and adult onset schizophrenia, yielding a biomarker. Like the electrocardiogram, this will not only substantiate and reify the illness, but it will also give treating physicians tools beyond clinical impressions. Biomarkers—genetic, imaging, or integrated—will assist in diagnostic quandaries, guide further research, and offer hope for the development of novel treatments. But nothing will replace the human role in the management of the illness. Cardiologists use advanced imaging techniques to guide effective interventions, but they nonetheless contend with low compliance rates, resistant patients, and the tragedy of advanced disease. Psychiatrists, especially child psychiatrists who are the stewards of hope for ailing patients and families, will one day have additional tools and more effective medications, but that cannot take the place of their relational expertise in helping families in need. Imagining the experience of psychosis, tolerating intense affect, and empathically listening and guiding severely impaired patients and families will remain key goals for the future training of successful child and adolescent psychiatrists, irrespective of the exciting discoveries that await our field.

Note

1 In genetics, anticipation is a phenomenon whereby the symptoms of a genetic disorder become apparent at an earlier age as it is passed on to the next generation.

References

Allen, N. C., Bagade, S., McQueen, M. B, Ioannidis, J. P., Kavvoura, F. K., Khoury, M. J., Tansi, R. E., & Betram, L. (2008). Systematic meta-analysis and field synopsis of genetic association studies in schizophrenia the SZGene database. *Nature Genetics,* 40 (7), 827–834.

Ballageer, T., Malla, A., Manchanda, R., Takhar, J., & Haricharan, R. (2005). Is adolescent-onset first-episode psychosis different from adult onset? *Journal of the American Academy of Child & Adolescent Psychiatry,* 44 (8), 782–789.

Bernstein. H. G., Steiner, J., & Bogerts, B. (2009). Glial cells in schizophrenia pathophysiological significance and possible consequences for therapy. *Expert Review of Neurotherapeutics,* 9 (7), 1059–1071.

Boss, P., & Carnes, D. (2012). The myth of closure. *Family Process,* 51 (4), 456–469.

Caspi, A. Hariri, A. R., Holmes, A., Uher, R., & Moffitt, T. E. (2010). Genetic sensitivity to the environment the case of the serotonin transporter gene and its implications for studying complex diseases and traits. *The American Journal of Psychiatry,* 167 (5), 509–527.

Cochran, D., Dvir, Y., & Frazier, J. A. (2013). "Autism-plus" spectrum disorders: Intersection with psychosis and the schizophrenia spectrum. *Child & Adolescent Psychiatric Clinics of North America,* 22 (4), 609–627.

Cornblatt, B., Lencz, T., Smith, C. W., Correll, C. U., Auther, A. M., & Nakayama, E. (2003). The schizophrenia prodrome revisited: A neurodevelopmental perspective. *Schizophrenia Bulletin,* 29 (4), 633–651.

Findling, R. L., Johnson, J. L., McClellan, J., Frazier, J. A., Vitiello, B., Hamer, R. M., Lieberman, J. A., Ritz, L., McNamara, N. K., Lingler, J., Hlastala, S., Pierson, L., Puglia, M., Maloney, A. E., Kaufman, E. M., Noyes, N., & Sikich, L. (2010). Double blind maintenance safety and effectiveness findings from the treatment of early onset schizophrenia spectrum (TEOSS) study. *Journal of the American Academy of Child and Adolescent Psychiatry,* 49 (6), 583–594.

Fisher, H. L., Caspi, A., Poulton, R., Meier, M. H., Houts, R., Harrington, H., Arseneault, T. L., & Moffitt, E. E. (2013). Specificity of childhood psychotic symptoms for predicting schizophrenia by 38 years of age: A birth cohort study. *Psychological Medicine,* 8 (2), 1–10.

Gerber, A. J., Fonagy, P., Bateman, A., & Higgitt, A. (2004). Structural and symptomatic change in psychoanalysis and psychodynamic psychotherapy: a quantitative study of process, outcome, and attachment. *Journal of the American Psychoanalytic Association,* 52 (4), 1235–1236.

Gerber, A. J., Peterson, B. S., Gogtay, N., & Rapoport, J. L. (2008). Childhood-onset schizophrenia: Insights from neuroimaging studies. *Journal of the American Academy of Child & Adolescent Psychiatry,* 47 (10), 1120–1124.

Gurovich, I. I., Shmukler, A. B., & Zaitseva, I. S. (2012). Dynamics of neurocognitive functioning in patients in early stages of schizophrenia and schizophrenia spectrum disorders. *Zhurnal nevrologii i psikhiatrii imeni S. S. Korsakova Ministerstvo zdravookhraneniia i meditsinskoi promyshlennosti Rossiiskoi Federatsii Vserossiiskoe obshchestuvo nevrologov [i] vserossiiskoe obshchestvo psikhiatrov,* 112 (8). 7–14.

Husted, J. A., Ahmed, R., Chow, E. W., Brzustowicz, L. M., & Bassett, A. S. (2012). Early environmental exposures influence schizophrenia expression even in the presence of strong genetic predisposition. *Schizophrenia Research,* 137 (1–3), 166–168.

Khadka, S., Meda, S. A., Stevens, M. C., Glahn, D. C., Calhoun, V. D., Sweeney, J. A., Tamminga, C. A., Keshavan, M. S., O'Neil, K., Schretlen, D., & Pearlson, G. D. (2013). Is aberrant functional connectivity a psychosis enophenotype? A resting state functional magnetic resonance imaging study. *Biological Psychiatry,* 74 (6), 458–466.

Korkmaz, B. (2011). Theory of mind and neurodevelopmental disorders of childhood. *Pediatric Research,* 69 (5), 101R-108R.

Mallo, C. J., & Mintz, D. L. (2013). Teaching all the evidence bases: Reintegrating psychodynamic aspects of prescribing into psychopharmacology training. *Psychodynamic Psychiatry,* 41 (1), 13–37.

Nesvåg, R., Bergmann, Ø., Rimol, L. M., Lange, E. H., Haukvik, U. K., Hartberg, C. B., Fagerberg, T., Söderman. E., Jönsson, E. G., & Agartz, I. (2012). A 5-year follow-up study of brain cortical and subcortical abnormalities in a schizophrenia cohort. *Schizophrenia Research,* 142 (1–3), 209–216.

Nicolson, R., & Rapoport, J. L. (1999). Childhood-onset schizophrenia rare but worth studying. *Biological Psychiatry,* 46 (10), 1418–1428.

Pfeffer, C. R., Normandin, L., & Kakuma, T. (1998). Suicidal children grow up: Relations between family psychopathology and adolescents' lifetime suicidal behavior. *The Journal of Nervous and Mental Disease,* 186 (5), 269–275.

Rapoport, J., Chavez, A., Greenstein, D., Addington, A., & Gogtay, N. (2009). Autism spectrum disorders and childhood-onset schizophrenia: Clinical and biological contributions to a relation revisited. *Journal of the American Academy of Child & Adolescent Psychiatry,* 48 (1), 10–18.

Rapoport J. L., & Gogtay, N. (2011). Childhood onset schizophrenia support for a progressive neurodevelopmental disorder. *International Journal of Developmental Neuroscience,* 29 (3), 251–258.

Shaw, P., Rapoport, J. L., & Hamilton, J. D. (2006). Decision making about children with psychotic symptoms: Using the best evidence in choosing a treatment. *Journal of the American Academy of Child & Adolescent Psychiatry,* 45 (11), 1381–1386.

Weinberger, D. R. (1987). Implications of normal brain development for the pathogenesis of schizophrenia. *Archives of General Psychiatry,* 44 (7), 660–669.

White, T., Shmidt, M., & Karatekin, C. (2010). Verbal and visuospatial working memory development and deficits in children and adolescents with schizophrenia. *Early Intervention in Psychiatry,* 4 (4), 305–313

Whiteford, H. A., Degenhardt, L., Rehm, J., Baxter, A., Ferrari, A. J., Erskine, H. E., Charlson, F. J., Norman, R. E., Flaxman, A. D., Johns, N., Burstein, R., Murray, C., J., & Vos, T. (2010). Global burden of disease attributable to mental and substance use disorders: findings from the global Burden of Disease Study 2010. *Lancet,* 382 (9904), 1575–1586.

Xu, Q., Wu, X., Xiong, Y., Xing, Q., He, L., & Qin, S. (2013). Pharmacogenomics can improve antipsychotic treatment in schizophrenia. *Frontiers of Medicine,* 7 (2), 180–190.

5

MOOD DISORDERS AND PSYCHOSIS

James B. McCarthy and Zana Dobroshi

Mood disorder-related psychotic features are significantly more common among children and adolescents than are non-affective psychoses, such as acute schizophrenia. In the current psychiatric nosology, primary mood disorders include major depressive disorder, otherwise known as major depression, dysthymia, and bipolar disorder. All three disorders constitute very heterogeneous forms of psychopathology, and their origins are only partially explained. Like many psychiatric disorders, major depressive disorder and bipolar disorder must be considered expressions of complex, interacting, multifactorial developmental pathways. Both disorders can be associated with psychotic features, and they each have a poorly understood etiology that reflects the interaction of genetic vulnerabilities with environmental factors and sensitivities to adverse life experience.

With adolescents in particular, the severity of mood disorders is often related to a propensity for psychotic features. Although there is a diversity of opinion about the overall incidence of mood disorders and psychosis in youth, some studies indicate that up to 60% of adolescents with bipolar illness eventually develop psychosis as part of the disorder. Because of the heterogeneity and the complexity of mood disorders, single etiological models can't account for either the etiology or the co-occurrence of mood disorders and psychotic symptoms. In addition, the co-occurrence of major depressive disorder and bipolar disorder with psychotic features in children and adolescents must be evaluated in terms of the similarities and differences in developmental trajectories.

Introduction

According to Campbell's *Psychiatric Dictionary* (1989), the term "mood" refers to both prolonged emotional states that characterize one's personality and inner life, and to one's dominant emotional state at any particular time. In contrast to mood, the term "affect" refers to the feelings that accompany one's ideas and mental representations. In psychodynamic theory, affects are understood as psychic derivatives of the drive-based instincts. Affects represent the bodily manifestations of drive derivatives, which regularly become attached to ideas and mental representations of inner experience. As a result of this unconscious process, the underlying origin and symbolic meaning of affects often remain relatively hidden from consciousness. If the drive derivatives of affective experience have been completely repressed, they may appear not as emotions, but rather as a series of physical manifestations, such as perspiration, tachycardia, or paresthesia. In other cases, especially in states of catatonia or manic excitement, affects can appear overtly without disguise, such as the excitement and euphoria that sometimes accompanies grandiose preoccupations in mania. In addition to defining general aspects of emotional experience, mood and affect therefore represent abstractions that refer to specific tendencies to react emotionally in idiosyncratic ways. Inferences about mood largely stem from observations in the present and from the exploration of past events. Inferences about affect usually stem from present observations only. Thus, what can be said about affect also generally applies to mood. However, what can be said about mood doesn't always apply to affect (Burgin and Meng, 2004). Although these distinctions are very relevant to discussions of mood disorders in general, we aim to offer an overview of mood disturbance and psychosis in childhood and adolescence with a focus on differentiating developmental differences.

Diagnostic Issues and Developmental Differences

The terms "mood disorders" and "affective disorders" have often been used interchangeably. The third American Psychiatric Association *Diagnostic and Statistical Manual of Mental Disorders* (DSM-III) listed under affective disorders those conditions that are referred to as mood disorders in the fourth and fifth editions (DSM-IV) and (DSM 5). The diagnosis of mood disorders in children and adolescents has mainly relied on the same diagnostic criteria used for adults, except for the shorter duration of some of the symptom patterns and an increased emphasis on irritability as a mood symptom in children. However, the steadily evolving emotional, cognitive, and psychological development of children results in wide-ranging variations in their ability to describe their subjective experience. Since diagnosis rests on the assessment of manifest and reported symptoms, the importance of careful observation, a thorough developmental history, and the use of multiple informants and rating scales can serve as useful aides to diagnostic assessment. The difficulty of ascertaining a child's inner emotional experience creates considerable challenges in diagnosing mood disorders. Since children rarely report psychotic symptoms spontaneously, the evaluation of possible psychotic phenomena similarly requires clinical expertise and an unhurried effort to put the child at ease. In the course of clinical assessments, it is very important to distinguish true psychotic features from odd beliefs, transitory hallucinations, and other attenuated or psychotic-like symptoms. The assessment of the presence of delusions in children with mania or hypomania can be especially challenging because of children's individual rates of cognitive maturation and their age-appropriate difficulties distinguishing fantasy from reality. The use of structured or semi-structured interviews like the Structured Interview for Psychosis-Risk Syndromes (SIPS) and the child version of the Schedule for Affective Disorders and Schizophrenia (K-SADS) can yield extremely useful clinical data.

Although the existence and prevalence of mood disorders in children and adolescents is no longer questioned as it was prior to the late 1970s, there is an insufficient number of studies about the differential diagnosis of psychosis that occurs during major depression, mania, and acutely fluctuating mood states (Campbell, 1989). When psychotic symptoms are present in school-aged children and adolescents with mood disorders, they have frequently been misdiagnosed as having schizophrenia. Despite the use of fairly uniform criteria for diagnosing children and adults with mood disorders, it is generally true that the developmental trajectory of psychiatric disorders appears in subtly different ways with the transition from childhood to adolescence to adulthood (Caldieraro, Baeza, Pinheiro, Ribeiro, Parker, and Fleck, 2013; Duffy, 2010).

Since infants and very young children lack the capacity to be articulate, reliable reporters, diagnostic evaluations require more time and experience by the examiner. Depression and anxiety may be recognized by the configuration of facial expressions in infants and their lack of emotional responsiveness, which can easily be confused with reactive attachment disorder. Depressed infants have reduced activity, appear withdrawn with a sad facial expression, and may refuse feeding or regurgitate their food (Spitz, 1965). In both Spitz's and Bowlby's (2010) classic reports, emotionally neglected and maternally deprived infants were described as being depressed. According to Strober and Carlson (1982), infants and very young children can be diagnosed with depression if they regularly demonstrate depressed or irritable mood and they show little interest and pleasure in developmentally suitable activities. They reveal a pattern of excessive whining, a diminished repertoire of affective and social interactions, little initiative, and a lack of interest in interactive play. These signs must be present for at least two weeks, and they may also be accompanied by sleeping and eating problems. The nature of mood disorders in infants and toddlers are described in greater detail by Strober and Carlson (1982) in their classification of mood symptoms and developmental disorders in children from birth to age 3.

Even when reliable DSM diagnostic criteria are utilized, the diagnosis of mood disorders with psychotic symptoms can be more difficult with children and adolescents than it is with adults. Some noteworthy developmental differences in symptom patterns have been clearly established. Major depressive disorder is typically uncommon in preschool-aged children. Young children with mood disorders and psychotic features have, at times, been mistakenly diagnosed with schizophrenia. Major depression in children frequently doesn't involve the feelings of hopelessness and the marked sleep and appetite disturbance that is often present with major depression in adulthood. The prevalence rates of depression in children reflect insignificant gender differences until puberty, when there is a substantial increase and a greater frequency of depression in girls throughout adolescence. The prevalence rates of major depression increase steadily during adolescence. In adolescents, especially older adolescents, the signs and symptoms of major depression increasingly resemble the clinical presentation seen in adulthood. Nevertheless, the full extent of the developmental differences between children, adolescents, and adults hasn't been completely resolved for either major depression, or bipolar illness (Birmaher, Arbelaez, and Brent, 2002).

As part of an effort to resolve the controversy about the apparent overuse of the diagnosis of bipolar disorder in excessively volatile, aggressive children, the diagnosis of disruptive mood dysregulation disorder was established in DSM 5. This new diagnosis has been formulated in order to capture recurrent, very severe temper outbursts that are inconsistent with the developmental level of the child, are out of proportion to the situation, and are present along with consistent irritability in the child for most of the day, nearly every day. These symptoms need to be present for 12 months or longer, and the diagnosis can only be made if the symptoms are present at age 6 or above, and not after age 18. The diagnosis also needs to take into account and to rule out that the behaviors are an expression of major depression, autism spectrum disorder, posttraumatic stress disorder, separation anxiety disorder, and dysthymia. Even though this addition to the diagnostic nomenclature has been initiated as a result of a recognition of the overdiagnosis of mood disorders in children in general and especially the overdiagnosis of bipolar disorder in prepubertal children, it will require additional research in order to corroborate its validity and reliability (Carson, 2013).

At this point, it seems clear that symptoms of either major depressive disorder or bipolar disorder in childhood constitute a risk factor for the emergence of bipolar disorder in adulthood. A number of longitudinal studies have shown that only a small proportion of children diagnosed with bipolar disorder continue to meet the criteria for this diagnosis as adults. Nevertheless, it has also been established that a great many adolescents who demonstrate significant mood symptoms will continue to experience recurrent mood episodes during adulthood (Findling, Gracious, McNamara, Youngstrom, Demeter, Branicky, and Calabrese, 2008; Duffy, 2012).

Major Depressive Disorder with Psychotic Features

Major depressive disorder in school-age children has a prevalence rate of about 2.8%, but its occurrence increases to about 6% of the population in adolescents (Costello, Erkanli, and Angold, 2006). Another important consideration in assessment and treatment of children and adolescents with major depression is that psychiatric comorbidities are very common; there are especially high rates of anxiety disorders, attention deficit hyperactivity disorder (ADHD), and conduct disorder (Angold, Costello, and Erkanli, 1999). A genetic predisposition for depression, environmental factors, and early stressors can all impact the developing child's brain structure and functioning, with a resulting vulnerability for mood symptoms that is correlated with abnormalities in the amygdala, the cingulate gyrus, and other brain regions involved with emotional processing and regulation. The impact of early traumatic experiences and the child's temperament can likewise influence the emergence and the course of major depression and bipolar disorder. The severity of major depression in children and adolescents appears to be highly correlated with an increased risk of psychotic features, but individuals can have severe major depression without any signs of psychosis (Campbell, 1989). There is also a greater possibility that depressed youth with psychotic features will eventually manifest symptoms of bipolar disorder (Geller, Zimmerman, Williams, Bolhofner, and Craney, 2001). This conclusion has similarly been reached by DelBello, Carlson, Tohen, Bromet, Schwiers, and Strakowski (2003).

In DSM 5, major depression is diagnosed by having depressed mood or loss of interest or pleasure with a minimum of 5 symptoms out of total 9 accounting for the range of the disorder's manifestations. In spite of the developmental differences between children and adolescents, these symptoms typically remain the same with the transition from childhood to adolescence. The diagnosis of major depressive disorder also requires the presence of a depressed mood and/or irritability most of the day, nearly every day. Depressed adolescents frequently report feeling sad, empty, hopeless, or bored, and not being interested in or not enjoying things as they did in the past. As noted above, one significant difference in major depression between children and adults is in the area of appetite and weight. Children with major depression often fail to make age-expected weight gains, while adolescents and adults either lose or gain weight. Additional vegetative signs of major depression in adolescence include the presence of insomnia or hypersomnia. Psychomotor agitation or retardation can occur with signs of fatigue or the loss of energy.

Feelings of worthlessness and inappropriate guilt are common in major depressive disorder, as is a diminished ability to think about challenging topics and to concentrate and be decisive. The child or adolescent with major depression may also have recurrent thoughts of death or suicide. In the current DSM 5, severity ratings and specifiers are provided to try to make the diagnosis truly reflective of the individual's mental state at the time of the assessment. Depressive disorders include specifiers with codes for the severity and course of the disorder that delineate ratings of mild, moderate, and severe, as well as major depression with psychotic features; with partial remission; with full remission or unspecified; and with a single episode or recurrent episodes. Major depression has also specifiers that apply to the current episode, such as: with anxious distress, with mixed features, with melancholic features, with atypical features, with mood congruent psychotic features or mood incongruent psychotic features, with catatonia, with a peripartum onset, and with seasonal patterns.

There are only a limited number of studies that identify the incidence of psychotic features in children and adolescents with major depressive disorder or bipolar disorder, with significant variations in the findings across the studies. In Pavuluri, Herbener, and Sweeney's (2004) review of the published studies on pediatric bipolar disorder and psychotic symptoms, the prevalence rates of psychosis varied from 16.5% to 87.5%, based on the ages of the subjects and the study methodologies. In a significant naturalistic study of psychotic versus non-psychotic youth with major depressive disorder, the patients with psychotic symptoms presented a more severe course of illness, longer hospitalizations, and lower rates of remission (Caldierero, Baeza, and Pinheiro, Ribeiro, Parker, and Fleck, 2013). The patients with psychotic features also presented greater levels of cognitive weaknesses and a higher incidence of suicidal risk. Other studies have found that major depressive disorders in youth with melancholic features frequently include psychotic symptoms (Carlson, 2013). Major depressive disorder with melancholic features involves having a distinct quality of depressed mood that is characterized by a profound feeling of despondency, despair, and emptiness, with worse periods of depression in the morning. These morning periods of mood disturbance usually include early awakening and significant anorexia or weight loss. Taken as a whole, these studies add support to the dual hypotheses that episodes of major depression with psychotic features at times share a continuum with bipolar disorder, and that there is a spectrum of mood disorders with underlying neurobiological commonalities.

Case Example 1

Adam, a 15-year-old boy with good premorbid functioning, presented with severe feelings of depression, emptiness, worthlessness, hopelessness, helplessness, and a sense of doom about the future. He felt that he was "just taking up space in the world" and that his parents and his siblings would be better off if he had succeeded with a suicide attempt he had made one month prior to his evaluation for re-hospitalization. He reported having had no appetite and that he had lost around 20 pounds in very short period of time. Adam observed that he thought of himself as being an ugly, worthless blob. He had a difficult time doing anything well in school, and he did not enjoy reading or hobbies as he had in the past. He said, "I can't enjoy a simple movie." He felt that since his life consisted of nothing but suffering, it would be better if it ended. As a result of the severity of his major depressive disorder, his suicidal ideation, and several suicidal attempts, Adam had been previously hospitalized several times.

In his most recent hospitalization, Adam continued to wake up very early in the morning, complaining of feeling chronically tired and troubled by hearing voices. He heard both men's and women's voices commenting about him in a derogatory way and making statements about his being bad and a disappointment to his family. The voices Adam heard continued throughout the day with their disparaging comments. He reported that when he heard the voices he had sometimes contemplated hanging himself with his jacket even while he was in the hospital.

Adam's overall symptoms became severe very soon after the start of his first episode of depression at age 13. At that time, he experienced some symptoms of generalized anxiety and incipient sleeping difficulties. Although there was no specific stimulus for the onset of Adam's depressive symptoms, the precipitating factors seemed to be his perception of pressure from his parents and the academic demands he faced in high school. Adam also had one episode of reckless, impulsive behavior, but there was no other sign that might suggest the latent possibility of mania or hypomania. During Adam's previous hospitalizations, his depression had remained relatively treatment resistant, with a lack of response to multiple antidepressants. During his most recent hospitalization, the combination of one-to-one observation with the use of antidepressant and antipsychotic medication, intensive psychotherapy, and the support of his involved family all helped Adam to achieve a slight improvement, but he continued to be severely depressed.

In terms of psychodynamic formulations, Adam experienced the internalized guilt and the hatred directed against the self, as first described by Freud. The concept of depression-inducing cognitive distortions proposed by Beck (Newman and Beck, 1990) and the concept of learned helplessness suggested by Seligman (1975) were both relevant to Adam's depressogenic thinking. In the beginning of his treatment, Adam could not make sense out of the voices he heard criticizing him throughout the day. With an increased awareness of his highly self-critical and self-defeating thought patterns as a result of the psychotherapy, he began to recognize that the men and women's voices he heard were projected elaborations of his self-persecutory thoughts. He eventually recognized that the voices felt like "having Mom and Dad tell me how bad I am all day long." These realizations allowed Adam to begin to address his negative feelings about his parents in therapy and to feel less like he "was going crazy."

During Adam's most recent inpatient hospitalization, the addition of Lithium and later Quetiapine to the antidepressant medication, both in therapeutic doses, produced only slight improvement in his depressive symptoms. His treatment also included consideration of further changes in the antidepressant medication and the eventual possibility of the use of electroconvulsive therapy. Adam didn't have a family history of psychiatric illness and there were no indications of manic symptoms in his developmental history. Even though he was most likely suffering from only major depressive disorder that was recurrent, severe with psychotic and melancholic features, it was also possible that his illness could later evolve into bipolar disorder or schizoaffective disorder.

In children and adolescents like Adam, the longitudinal trajectory of the symptoms and the course of the episodes become the key to understanding the true nature of the illness. In many children and adolescents with severe mood disorders, the mood episodes are frequently recurrent, whereas the mood-related psychotic symptoms can be present in only one episode or in many episodes (Campbell, 1989). The essential diagnostic consideration in understanding mood disorders with psychotic features in both children and adults is that the psychotic symptoms occur only during periods of the mood symptoms. Mood-congruent delusions of grandiosity frequently occur during states of mania, and mood-congruent delusions of criticism or persecution often occur during episodes of severe major depression. If psychotic symptoms remain after the mood symptoms have been ameliorated, then the diagnostic impression must include consideration of schizophrenia or schizoaffective disorder. Despite an accurate diagnostic assessment, medication algorithms for the treatment of major depressive disorder with psychotic features in adults frequently don't work with children and adolescents, not only because of physiologic differences, but also because of the evolving nature of the disorder (Duffy, 2012).

Trauma, Developmental Delays, and Mood-Related Psychotic Features

Young children with significant mood symptoms who also have speech and cognitive delays and distractibility may be more vulnerable to experiencing anxiety disorders, ADHD, and learning disorders, as well as sleeping problems in later childhood. For some of these vulnerable children, the severity of major depressive disorder symptoms can escalate, contributing to the onset of psychotic symptoms during adolescence. Such at-risk children are much more vulnerable to developing psychotic spectrum disorders than are children who do not present with mood, cognitive, speech, ADHD, and learning disorder symptoms in early childhood. Although it's a rare occurrence, signs of extreme depression and bipolar disorder can be apparent in children who are under 2 years of age. Furthermore, like all psychotic symptoms in early childhood, transient, mood-related brief psychotic symptoms can be induced by trauma and can be very difficult to distinguish from fantasies in very early childhood. Research reports corroborate that early traumatic life events can induce and exacerbate severe depression in children and adolescents (Cole, Nolen-Hoeksema, Girgus, and Paul, 2006).

Case Example 2

Brian, a 2-year-old boy, became anorectic, didn't sleep, appeared apathetic, and cried very easily. He had been hospitalized in a pediatric intensive care unit after an accident in which his mother was killed when she was pushing him in a stroller in the street and was hit by a passing car. Brian had no medical injuries and no physical aftereffects of the accident. His father tried to console Brian and to feed him, but he would not take any food from his father or from the nurses in the hospital and he began to lose weight. As a result of considerable effort, his maternal grandmother was then able to come to the United States temporarily to try to provide help and care. While in his grandmother's care, Brian gradually began to eat and to slowly recover his normal weight. At age 3, he was still a very thin child who appeared to be generally sad and had difficulty focusing his attention and engaging in play. His sleep was often poor, and he was frightened of the dark. He regularly woke up in a state of apparent anxiety in the middle of the night and searched his room for monsters. Even though Brian's father had difficulty understanding all of his son's symptoms and the process of child psychotherapy, he was deeply committed to Brian and took him for twice-weekly play therapy-based psychotherapy sessions for a period of five years. This intensive psychotherapy was later augmented with monthly follow-up sessions.

When Brian was around 4 years old, he enjoyed going to a special McDonald's restaurant where he liked the slides in the backyard, and he regularly insisted on staying there for long periods of time. On one occasion, Brian's father noticed that Brian was talking to himself and playing as if he was with someone else even though he was alone. Many months later, Brian was able to disclose that he had been spending the time with his deceased mother. He reported that she was talking to him and hugging him. At that time, Brian believed that his hallucinated mother was real and this was the only place where she could come to him from the sky because of the McDonald's slides. The memory of being hugged and of playing with his mother was Brian's secret and telling the secret to trusted adults made him happy.

When Brian was 9, he and his father moved to a different city, and he had three uneventful years, in spite of some symptoms of anxiety and inattention. However, when Brian was 12 years old, he again became depressed and his father made arrangements for the psychotherapy to resume.

Very young children, like Brian, can become severely depressed after the death of their mother. The severity of Brian's depression could be considered a case of major depressive disorder that might possibly have included psychotic features. But when Brian was playing with his mother and hearing her voice at McDonald's, he was not experiencing a psychotic episode. In accordance with his developing this adaptive coping mechanism for his devastating loss and in conjunction with the psychotherapy, Brian had improved. However, the signs of major depression reoccurred following puberty in Brian, which is common with very early onset, severe mood disorders. In early adolescence, it would be expected that Brian's depressive symptoms would have different cognitive and psychic manifestations than during his early childhood. Like many severely depressed children, Brian unfortunately hadn't responded to antidepressants. In such cases, intensive psychotherapy and mobilizing the family's resources and support remains the main treatment approach.

Brian's history illustrates the complexity of major depression and its relationship to trauma-induced attachment problems and neurobiological dysregulation in some cases (Fischoff, Whitten, and Pettit, 1971). His emotional needs required a flexible treatment approach that included the possibility of very long-term psychotherapy.

Bipolar Disorder with Psychotic Features

Bipolar disorder refers to episodes of depression interwoven with periods of mania or hypomania, with a course of illness that is chronic and that represents a marked change from the individual's habitual moods and functioning. Specific criteria for bipolar I disorder, which is associated with mania, and bipolar II disorder, which is associated with hypomania, are described in great detail in the recently published DSM 5. Many adolescents and adults who suffer from bipolar illness only demonstrate signs of psychosis during episodes of mania (Kennedy, Everitt, Boydell, van Os, Jones, and Murray, 2005). Psychotic symptoms with bipolar disorder occur with greater frequency in childhood and adolescence than at any other period in life. Additionally, psychotic depression in adolescence may represent a precursor of a future course of bipolar disorder (Carlson, 2013). Young children with bipolar illness and psychotic features usually have both visual and auditory hallucinations. Adolescents with bipolar disorder and psychosis often have more auditory hallucinations and delusions than children do. Delusions associated with bipolar disorder at times lack the bizarre, primary process–like content that is more typical of other psychotic disorders. In young children, mood-related hallucinations are often transient and can be difficult to distinguish from the child's make-believe stories and fantasy play. A full medical work-up is essential in order to rule out any medical causes of the severe mood disturbance. Contemporary practice guidelines recommend a thorough medical evaluation in the case of any first episode of psychosis. Furthermore, mania-related psychotic symptoms in young children always need to be carefully evaluated in the context of the child's other symptoms, life circumstances, and the possibility of exposure to traumatic events.

With increasing age, the prevalence rates of bipolar illness increase from childhood through adolescence. In a large study on the course and outcome of bipolar youth, known as the COBY Study, the authors reported a 34.5% prevalence rate of bipolar I disorder (Axelson, Birmaher, Strober, Gill, Valeri, Chiapetta, Ryan, Leonard, Hunt, Iyengar, Bridge, and Keller, 2006), but the prevalence rates of pediatric bipolar illness continue to be highly controversial. The incidence of preschool-onset bipolar disorder is very uncertain, although treatment protocols have been established based on pertinent research (Pavuluri, Henry, Carbray, Sampson, Naylor, and Janicak, 2006). A large percentage of adults with mania have paranoid delusions, but only 8.2% of children and adolescents with mania exhibit symptoms of paranoia (Tillman, Geller, Klages, Corrigan, Bohlofner, and Zimerman, 2008). Adolescents with bipolar disorder have a variable course, although many continue to show some signs of impaired functioning whether or not they meet the full diagnostic criteria for the disorder. The severity of many cases of bipolar disorder in adolescents and its association with psychotic symptoms reinforces the need for early identification and intervention (McGlashan, Walsh, and Woods, 2010).

Bipolar Disorder and Comorbidity

The wide range of comorbid disorders that frequently occur with bipolar disorder further complicates the task of differential diagnosis (Axelson, Birmaher, Strober, Gill, Valeri, Chiapetta, Ryan, Leonard, Hunt, Iyengar, Bridge, and Keller, 2006). Numerous studies indicate that pediatric bipolar disorder frequently co-occurs with ADHD, anxiety disorders, and other disorders (Duffy, 2012). Excessive emotional reactivity is common to oppositional defiant disorder, ADHD, and bipolar disorder in children and adolescents, and the co-occurrence of anxiety disorders and bipolar illness in adolescence is often associated with more severe symptomatic patterns. Substance abuse and alcohol abuse disorders are also highly correlated with worse symptom severity and a greater chronicity of mood episodes in adolescents and adults with bipolar disorder. In an effort to acknowledge the increasing suggestions of underlying genetic ties between bipolar disorder and schizophrenia, the DSM 5 has reorganized current thinking about the position of bipolar illness in the spectrum of psychiatric disorders.

In DSM 5, bipolar disorder and related disorders have been separated from the chapter on depressive disorders and placed between this chapter and the chapter on schizophrenia spectrum and other psychotic disorders. This significant change has been made in recognition of the concept of bipolar disorder as a bridge between schizophrenia and depressive disorders, and an increasing awareness of the commonality between schizophrenia and bipolar illness in terms of symptomatology, family history, and genetics. In the traditional understanding of manic-depressive illness, bipolar I disorder with its emphasis on distinct manic episodes can be considered to be rare in children. Children with unstable mood, irritability, and explosive aggressive episodes, characterized by poor frustration tolerance, have typically been diagnosed as having bipolar disorder, not otherwise specified (NOS). In a recent unpublished study conducted at an intermediary care children's psychiatric hospital, 87% of the children who were admitted in a six-month period had diagnoses of NOS, mainly bipolar disorder, NOS. This trend most likely reflects the convenience of conceptualizing mood lability and extreme volatility as overarching broad categories that incorporate the clinical presentations of children with multiple complex comorbidities that include symptoms of ADHD, oppositional defiant disorder, chronic posttraumatic stress disorder, attachment difficulties, and beginning symptoms of personality disorders. These chronically disturbed, severely emotionally dysregulated child and adolescent inpatients present difficult challenges for diagnosis and treatment. Like many children and youth with bipolar disorder and major depressive disorder, these patients frequently have a number of comorbid psychiatric disorders and require sustained, multimodal treatment.

In a far reaching delineation of the varieties of bipolar disorder in children and adolescents, Leibenluft (2011) and Leibenluft, Charney, Twobin, Bhangoo, and Pine (2003) proposed four categories of pediatric bipolar illness that include a broad phenotype, two intermediary phenotypes, and a narrow phenotype that may be more compatible with the new diagnosis of disruptive mood dysregulation disorder. In her examination of the nature of severe mood dysregulation and the delineation of the diagnostic boundaries of bipolar disorder, Leibenluft (2011) questioned whether extreme non-episodic irritability genuinely reflects an accurate diagnosis of mania. The longitudinal data she reported from clinical and community samples indicated that the non-episodic irritability was associated with an elevated risk of anxiety and unipolar depressive disorders but not bipolar disorder in adulthood. She concluded that frequent severe symptoms of irritability in and of themselves do not constitute either mania or hypomania, unless the manifestations of irritability are accompanied by the DSM-IV criteria B symptoms of mania. In addition to the difficulty of reliably diagnosing bipolar disorder in children and adolescents, clinicians who treat extremely dysregulated children and adolescents with psychotic features over long periods of time may see shifting clinical presentations due to the latent presence of other psychotic disorders (Birmaher, Axelson, Strober, Gill, Valeri, Chiappetta, Ryan, Leonard, Hunt, Iyengar, and Keller, 2006).

Case Example 3

At the age of 3, Arthur was diagnosed with developmental delays and pervasive developmental disorder, but he exhibited the extreme irritability and the aggression that has been associated with pediatric bipolar disorder. Out of desperation, his mother had taken him to a hospital for evaluation. According to his mother, Arthur was very hyperactive, seemed to be driven by a motor, did not rest for a single minute, and had trouble sleeping for more than three hours a night. He also appeared to be unable to pay attention to cartoons, as he had in the past. When Arthur was evaluated, he was unable to speak in words; he did not show interest in any toys for longer than a few seconds, and his interest in others seemed to be superficial, with minimal eye contact. Arthur touched and tried to destroy nearly everything in the examining room. His mother clarified that Arthur was able to say a few random words and that he mainly communicated by grabbing things and showing aggression toward people and objects.

Arthur's mother reported that she had symptoms of untreated depression and that the child's father had been suffering from severe posttraumatic stress disorder. After admission to a pediatric inpatient unit and the establishment of a diagnosis of bipolar disorder, Arthur was treated with the mood stabilizer Depakote. As a result of the medication, he became much calmer, much less aggressive, and his development resumed in many ways as he became more interactive, talkative, and related. His family became much better able to relate to him and to teach him colors, numbers, and letters. Over the next several years, he succeeded in prekindergarten and kindergarten without any significant untoward events.

Arthur's mother stopped giving him the Depakote because he appeared "normal," except that he remained frightened of the dark, had difficulty with separation, and was enuretic. When Arthur was 8 years old, his mother brought him back to the emergency room because he was exhibiting bizarre behavior and paranoid thoughts. After finishing the second grade, he had stopped going to school because of paranoid thoughts about his teacher and anxieties about a group of children whom his mother thought might have been bullying him. Arthur reported what amounted to a fear of being persecuted and annihilated if he went to school. If his mother even mentioned school, he would have a panic attack and describe the presence of hidden traps, cameras, and other devices at his school which he believed the students and teachers had placed there in order to spy on him and to torture him.

Arthur's mother also reported that Arthur had increased in talking to himself and to imaginary friends when he was alone in his room and that he seemed to have created his own complete imaginary world. Retrospectively, we can understand his mental state at that time as indicative of an initial psychotic break. He was given complete medical and neurological evaluations in order to rule out any physical disorders that might have contributed to his deterioration. Arthur continued to show increasingly bizarre behavior, together with the disorganized thinking that is characteristic of some adolescents and many adults with schizophrenia. He developed clear paranoid delusions, experiences of depersonalization, looseness of associations, and auditory hallucinations, with several voices speaking to him and giving him commands. Arthur showed a clinical improvement when he was treated with Risperidone, which was tapered up to 5 mg per day, and he was able to resume living with his family and functioning in the community, but there were residual symptoms of psychosis that continued.

Even though Arthur was first evaluated and treated when he was 3 years old, it was unclear when his psychotic symptoms had first emerged. When he was 8, it originally seemed that his poor reality testing might have been a reflection of features of pervasive developmental delays, an over-reliance on fantasy, and the possible expression of bipolar disorder. Similar children may initially be diagnosed with ADHD, speech and language delays, pervasive developmental delays, and mood disorder symptoms that resemble bipolar illness.

When Arthur began adolescence, it became irrefutably clear that he had been suffering from schizophrenia in addition to comorbid mood symptoms and developmental delays, and he was helped significantly by Clozapine. His pronounced, severe hallucinations and delusions occurred outside of mood episodes, even though first-rank Schneiderian symptoms can sometimes be present in the course of bipolar illness.

Conclusion

Both major depressive disorder and bipolar disorder frequently involve psychotic features in children and adolescents. Effective treatment plans need to deploy nuanced interventions that include psychotherapy and medication algorithms that are based on continuing research. From different conceptual vantage points, cognitive therapies and psychodynamic psychotherapy for mood disorders have similar overall goals in that they seek to restore children and adolescents' compromised functioning and to reduce their emotional suffering. Psychotherapeutic techniques depend on the child's age and maturation, and the severity and chronicity of the mood disorder. The role of family work with depressed and bipolar youth has long been recognized as crucial, since parents and family members are allies in the treatment process and they strongly influence treatment compliance. Some studies of the efficacy of cognitive behavior therapy with depressed adolescents suggest that its impact is greatest with youth who are mildly or moderately depressed (Harrington, Whitaker, Shoebridge, and Campbell, 1998). In the large, federally supported treatment study of depressed adolescents known as the TADS study, about 40% of the adolescent patients improved with cognitive behavior therapy, 60% responded favorably to antidepressant medication, and over 70% improved with combined cognitive behavior therapy and medication. The limited literature on psychotherapy with children and adolescents with bipolar disorder is gradually indicating that dialectical behavior therapy and interpersonal and social rhythm therapy might be promising modalities (Hlastala, Kotler, McClellan, and McCauley, 2010).

Children vary considerably in their responsiveness to psychotherapy for severe mood disorders, just as they do in their reactions to antidepressant, mood stabilizer, and antipsychotic medication. The findings of Geller, Zimmerman, Williams, Bolhofner, and Craney, (2001); Colletti, Leigh, Gallelli, and Kafantaris, (2005); Carlson (2013); Findling, Kafantaris, Pavuluri, McNamara, Frazier, Sikich, Kowatch, Rowles, Clemons, and Taylor-Zapata (2013); and other recent investigators of mood disorders all support treatment with medication that goes beyond short-term interventions aimed at stabilization. The complexity and chronicity of mood disorders symptoms in many youth require coordinated, multimodal treatment that will maximize the likelihood of achieving substantial therapeutic gains. Appropriate treatment for mood disorders and psychosis relies on comprehensive, textured strategies that take the full measure of the child's psychopathology, resources, and developmental needs.

References

American Psychiatric Association, (2013). *Diagnostic and statistical manual of mental disorders* (5th edition). Washington, DC: Author.

Angold, A., Costello, E. J., & Erkanli, A. (1999). Comorbidity. *Journal of Child Psychology, Psychiatry & Allied Disciplines,* 40, 57–87.

Axelson, D., Birmaher, B., Strober, M., Gill, M.K., Valeri, S., Chiapetta, M.S., Ryan, N., Leonard, H., Hunt, J., Iyengar, S., Bridge, J., & Keller, M., (2006). Phenomenology of children and adolescents with bipolar spectrum disorders. *Archives of General Psychiatry,* 63(10), 1113–1148.

Birmaher, B., Arbelaez, C., & Brent, D. (2002). Course and outcome of child and adolescent major depressive disorder. *Child and Adolescent Psychiatric Clinics of North America,* 11(3), 619–639.

Birmaher, B., Axelson, D., Strober, M., Gill, M.K., Valeri, S., Chiappetta, L., Ryan, N., Leonard, H., Hunt, J., Iyengar, S., & Keller, M. (2006). Clinical course of children and adolescents with bipolar spectrum disorders. *Archives of General Psychiatry,* 63(2), 175–183.

Bowlby, J. (2010). *Separation: Anxiety and anger, attachment and loss: Volume 2.* New York, NY: Random House.

Burgin, D., & Meng, H. (2004). *Childhood and adolescent psychosis.* Basel, Switzerland: Karger.

Caldieraro, M. A, Baeza, F.L.C., Pinheiro, D.O., Ribeiro, M. R., Parker, G., & Fleck, M.P. (2013). Prevalence of psychotic symptoms in those with melancholic and nonmelancholic depression. *Journal of Nervous and Mental Diseases,* 201(10), 855–859.

Campbell, R. (1989). *Psychiatric dictionary.* London, UK: Oxford University.

Carlson, G. A. (2013). Affective disorders and psychosis in youth. *Child and Adolescent Psychiatric Clinics of North America,* 22, 569–580;

Cole, D.A., Nolen-Hoeksema, S., Girgus, J., & Paul, G. (2006). Stress exposure and stress generation in child and adolescent depression: A latent trait-state-error approach to longitudinal analyses. *Journal of Abnormal Psychology,* 115, 40–51.

Colletti, D. J., Leigh, E., Gallelli, K. A., & Kafantaris, V. (2005). Patterns of adherence to treatment in adolescents with Bipolar Disorder. *Journal of Child and Adolescent Psychopharmacology,* 15(6), 913–917.

Costello, E. J., Erkanli, A., & Angold, A. (2006). Is there an epidemic of child or adolescent depression? *Journal of Child Psychology and Psychiatry,* 47, 1263–1271.

Duffy, A. (2010). The natural history of bipolar disorder: What we have learned from longitudinal high risk research. *Canadian Journal of Psychiatry,* 55, 477–485.

Duffy, A. (2012). The nature of the association between childhood ADHD and the development of bipolar disorder: A review of prospective high risk studies. *American Journal of Psychiatry,* 169, 1247–1255.

DelBello, M. P, Carlson, G. A., Tohen, M., Bromet, E. J., Schwiers, M., & Strakowski, S. M. (2003). Rates and predictors of developing a manic or hypomanic episode 1 to 2 years following a first hospitalization for major depression with psychotic features. *Journal of Child and Adolescent Psychopharmacology,* 13(2):173–185.

Findling R. L., Gracious, B. L., McNamara N.K., Youngstrom, E.A., Demeter, C.A., Branicky, L.A., & Calabrese, J.R. (2008). Rapid, continuous cycling and psychiatric co-morbidity in pediatric bipolar I disorder. *Bipolar Disorders,* 3, 202–210.

Findling, R. L., Kafantaris, V., Pavuluri, M., McNamara, N.K., Frazier, J. A., Sikich, L., Kowatch, R., Rowles, B. M., Clemons, T. E., & Taylor-Zapata, P. (2013). Post-acute effective treatment in bipolar I disorder. *Journal of Child and Adolescent Psychopharmacology,* 23(2), 80–90.

Fischoff, J., Whitten, C.F., & Pettit, M.G. (1971) A psychiatric study of mothers of infants with growth failure secondary to maternal deprivation. *Journal of Pediatrics,* 79(2), 209–215.

Geller, B., Zimmerman, B., Williams, M., Bolhofner, K., & Craney, J. L. (2001). Bipolar disorder at prospective follow-up of adults who had prepubertal major depressive disorder. *American Journal of Psychiatry,* 158, 135–137.

Harrington, R., Whitaker, J., Shoebridge, P., & Campbell, F. (1998). Systematic review of efficacy of cognitive behavior therapy in adolescent depressive disorder. *British Journal of Psychiatry,* 3(16), 1559–1563.

Hlastala, S. A., Kotler, J. S., McClellan, J. M., & McCauley, E. A. (2010). Interpersonal and rhythm therapy for adolescents with bipolar disorder: Treatment development and results from an open trial. *Depression and Anxiety,* 27, 457–461.

Kennedy, N., Everitt, B., Boydell, J., van Os, J., Jones, P. B., & Murray, R. M. (2005). Incidence and distribution of first-episode mania by age: Results from a 35-year study. *Psychological Medicine,* 35, 855–863.

Leibenluft, E. (2011). Severe mood dysregulation, irritability and the diagnostic boundaries of Bipolar Disorder in youths. *American Journal of Orthopsychiatry,* 168, 129–142.

Leibenluft, E., Charney, D. S., Twobin, K. E., Bhangoo, R. K., & Pine, D. S. (2003). Defining clinical phenotypes of juvenile mania. *American Journal of Psychiatry,* 160, 430–437.

McGlashan, T., Walsh, B., & Woods, S. (2010). *The psychosis-risk syndrome.* London, UK: Oxford University Press.

Newman, C. F., & Beck, A. T. (1990). Cognitive therapy of affective disorders. In: B. B. Wolman & G. Stricker (Eds.), *Depressive disorders: Facts, theories, and methods* (pp. 343–365). New York, NY: Wiley.

Pavuluri, M. N., Henry, D. B., Carbray, J. A., Sampson, G. A., Naylor, M. W., & Janicak, P. G. (2006). A one year open-label trial of risperidone augmentation in lithium nonresponder youth with pre-school onset bipolar disorder. *Journal of Child and Adolescent Psychopharmacology,* 16(3), 336–350.

Pavuluri, M. N., Herbener, E. S., & Sweeney, J. A. (2004). Psychotic symptoms in pediatric bipolar disorder. *Journal of Affective Disorders,* 80, 19–28.

Seligman, M. (1975). *Helplessness: On depression, development, and death.* New York, NY: Henry Holt.

Spitz, R. A. (1965). *The first year of life.* New York, NY: International Universities Press.

Strober, M., & Carlson, G. A. (1982). Bipolar illness in adolescents with major depression: clinical, genetic and psychopharmacologic predictors in a three to four year prospective follow up investigation. *Archives of General Psychiatry,* 39 (5), 549–55.

Tillman, R., Geller, B., Klages, T., Corrigan, M., Bolhofner, K., & Zimerman, B. (2008). Psychotic phenomena in 257 young children and adolescents with bipolar I disorder: Delusions and hallucinations (benign and pathological). *Bipolar Disorders,* 10(1), 45–55.

6

CHILDHOOD TRAUMA AND PSYCHOSIS

Endra K. Henry

The association between the experience of childhood trauma and the range of phenomena we refer to as psychosis remains one of the most fascinating and multifaceted relationships in psychology's memoirs.

That as many as 74% of 12- to 17-year-old youth in a nationally representative survey reported exposure to a traumatic event, including sexual assault, physical assault, and domestic and community violence (Kilpatrick and Saunders, 1999), is a compelling reason to pay close attention to the impact of child victimization and childhood trauma. Another is that we gain valuable knowledge about trauma exposure, traumatic stress, and resilience, facilitating development of more comprehensive and effective prevention and intervention strategies in the war against childhood mental illness, with consequent moderation of the long-term health and social consequences of traumatic exposure.

Some estimates suggest that about one-third of the general population may be affected by adverse childhood experiences, including sexual, physical, and emotional abuse, neglect, and bullying (Varese et al., 2012). Studies suggest that adults who experienced trauma in childhood may have higher rates of criminality (Sarchiapone, Carli, Cuomo, Marchetti, and Roy, 2009), lower educational levels (Scher, Forde, McQuaid, and Stein, 2004), and lower general health and well-being. In addition to negative social outcomes, adverse childhood experiences or traumatic exposure in childhood have also been linked to a greater risk of psychiatric disorder (Kessler et al., 2010; Green et al., 2010; Kessler, Davis, and Kendler, 1997), including psychosis (Morgan and Fisher, 2007). Although the mechanisms by which adverse events in childhood lead to psychotic symptoms remain a source of controversy among psychiatrists, psychologists, and other mental health professionals, there is little debate that childhood traumatic experiences have an impact on mental health.

Posttraumatic Psychosis

Many years ago, I treated a very traumatically exposed adolescent with a long-standing history of mood and psychotic symptoms, including psychomotor agitation, delusions, and command hallucinations. He'd already had seven acute psychiatric hospitalizations under his belt when, at age 15, he was admitted to a state psychiatric facility. He'd also been arrested twice and had been effectively renounced by both parents, who had lost patience with his "antics" and who were, by all accounts, unambiguously emotionally unavailable even before the onset of the antics. He responded favorably, although not fully, to medications intended to moderate his mood and psychotic symptoms, but his complex presentation suggested that there was more to address. What had led this youngster to "see dead people" at age 5, to try to set himself on fire at age 13, and to "see evil shadows" and "hear chatter everywhere" by age 15? How had the boundaries between internal and external become so blurred? What had undermined his reality testing?

Some weeks into his treatment, the young man informed me that he saw his father "almost kill" his mother when he was 4, that he was mainly "ignored" by his parents growing up, and that he was sexually molested by his older brothers between the ages of 5 and 12. With this new information, the recalcitrant psychotic symptoms seemed to make more sense. On further exploration, it became clear that the paranoid delusions and the extraordinary visual, auditory, and tactile hallucinations with which he presented on admission postdated traumatic exposures, which had given rise to what was in this new context understood to be the posttraumatic sequelae of dissociative flashback episodes, recurrent distressing images and a restricted range of affect. This young man had been exposed to multiple traumas, beginning in toddlerhood, and had over time developed some unmistakably psychotic symptoms.

At around the same time, a 16-year-old female with a long history of psychotic symptoms, including disorganized, non-goal-driven behavior and paranoid/disordered thinking, was admitted to the same state psychiatric facility. She, too, had had multiple acute hospitalizations secondary to symptoms of psychosis that seemed resistant to medication management and supportive therapy alone. Her first psychiatric hospitalization followed an attempt to jump out of a second-floor window. On admission, she noted that her mother had made too much of the act because, after all, she would have just "flutter[ed] down to the ground, like a leaf," landing safely. Her psychotic thinking, also illustrated by her assertions that she could "read [people's] minds" and "see their dimensions," postdated an experience of sexual molestation at age 11. This disruptive experience early in development had undoubtedly impinged on this adolescent's functioning.

Another 15-year-old youngster offered on admission to another psychiatric facility that he had "special Kung Fu powers" and could transmit information to other people "just by thinking." He also reported that he could "time travel" and cure diseases. He was routinely anxious and perpetually exhausted secondary to hypervigilance of external stimuli, including dust particles, which he, with great effort, tried to dodge, lest they come into contact with his skin and reduce him to ashes. This young man had been a "straight A" student who was regarded with favor by peers and adults alike owing to his friendly demeanor and his respectful posture. By all accounts, he was "a normal adolescent" with no psychiatric history . . . until his mother died in the 9/11/2001 attacks on the World Trade Center. Around the second anniversary of the attacks, his father became aware of heightened anxiety and a general deterioration of functioning, as indicated, for example, by devolving social connections and an obvious decline in self-care and personal hygiene. This young man had also begun to accuse his father, to whom he'd until that time been very close, of being "an imposter" who'd been sent by the government to steal his disease-modifying agents. By the time he was admitted, he had a two-year period of school refusal. The development of psychotic symptoms in this case, too, postdated traumatic exposure, and symptoms abated incompletely with antipsychotic medication. In this case, as in the others, there was more to tackle than "pure" psychotic symptomatology, so that a treatment plan for this youngster consisting only in medication and supportive therapy, and that overlooked the trauma of losing his mother through an act of terrorism, would have proven woefully ineffective.

The Relationship between Childhood Trauma and Psychosis: Causal, Contributory, Comorbid, or Coincidental?

A number of studies have long established a link between traumatic abuse and the development of depression, anxiety, substance abuse, borderline personality disorder, posttraumatic stress disorder, and suicidal behavior (Widom, 1999; Spataro, Mullen, Burgess, Wells, and Moss, 2004; Widom, DuMont, and Czaja, 2007; Widom, White, Czaja, and Marmorstein, 2007; Johnson, Cohen, Brown, Smailes, and Bernstein, 1999; Cutajar, Mullen, Ogloff, Thomas, Wells, and Spataro, 2010a; Cutajar et al., 2010). Some studies have even established a link between specific forms of abuse and particular disorders (Morgan and Fisher, 2007). Childhood sexual abuse, for example, has been linked to depression (Bifulco, Brown, and Adler, 1991) and borderline personality disorder (Paris, 1994) in adulthood. The link between childhood traumatic abuse and the development of psychotic experience has been less well studied, although the last decade has certainly seen greater awareness of the impact of adverse childhood events, including physical and sexual abuse, on children's difficulty with organization, affect regulation, and reality testing. In the last decade, we have also seen burgeoning interest in understanding the mechanisms by which adverse life events lead to psychotic symptoms. Research groups and networks (e.g., the Trauma-Psychosis Research Network of Northern Ireland) have even been established to study the nature of the association (causal vs. contributory, comorbid, or coincidental) between psychological trauma and the onset and perpetuation of psychosis.

Contributory

In the beginning, researchers set out to merely establish an association, rather than cause, effect, and directionality, between childhood trauma and psychosis. The association between these constructs has now been replicated many times. Indeed, a number of sound studies have identified child maltreatment, peer victimization (e.g., bullying), and experiences of parental loss and separation as risk factors for psychosis and schizophrenia. In a systematic quantitative synthesis of 41 studies examining the association between childhood trauma (defined as sexual abuse, physical abuse, emotional/psychological abuse, neglect, parental death, and bullying) and psychosis (psychotic disorder, schizophrenia, and schizoaffective disorder), Varese et al. (2012) reviewed 18 case-control (n = 2,048 psychotic patients and 1,856 non-psychiatric controls), 10 prospective and quasi-prospective (n = 41,803), and 8 population-based cross-sectional (n = 35,546) studies published in English, Dutch, French, German, Italian, Portuguese, and Spanish. The authors found statistically significant associations between childhood adversity and psychosis across all three research designs. That is, trauma was significantly associated with an increased risk for psychosis in case-control studies comparing the prevalence of adverse events between psychotic patients and controls, in case-control studies comparing the prevalence of psychotic symptoms between traumatically exposed and non-exposed subjects, in prospective and quasi-prospective studies, and in population-based cross-sectional studies. Children who had experienced any type of trauma before age 16 were about three times more likely than controls to develop schizophrenia in later life. Varese et al. (2012) also found a relationship between the level of trauma and the likelihood of psychosis in adulthood—specifically, children who were *severely* traumatized were at a greater risk, in some cases up to 50 times increased risk, than those who experienced less severe trauma. Of note is that the studies included in Varese et al.'s meta-analysis controlled for demographic and clinical confounds, including comorbid psychopathology. Taken as a whole, the findings suggest that childhood adversity is strongly associated with increased risk for psychosis and illustrate the influence of environmental triggers of psychotic disorders. Until recently, research has focused on *biology's* influence (neurological and genetic factors) on conditions like schizophrenia, but the Varese et al. (2012) study presents convincing evidence that these conditions cannot be fully understood without also taking into consideration patients' life experiences.

Other research involving the study of traumatic and psychotic experiences has likewise substantiated the association between childhood trauma and psychosis. In a recent case-control study investigating whether child sexual abuse is a risk factor for later psychotic disorders, Cutajar et al. (2010b) compared a cohort of

2,759 individuals who were sexually abused before age 16, with a community-based control group matched on sex and age groupings. The researchers found that rates of psychotic and schizophrenic illnesses were significantly higher among child sexual abuse subjects compared with controls. Strikingly, children raped in early adolescence by more than one perpetrator were found to have a risk of developing psychotic syndromes 15 times greater than the general population. In a prospective investigation of whether people from the general population who report childhood abuse are more likely to develop psychotic symptoms, Janssen et al. (2004) reported that trauma in early childhood was associated with an increased risk of psychotic symptoms. Spauwen, Krabbendam, Lieb, Wittchen, and van Os (2006), in their longitudinal study of a population sample of 2,524 adolescents and young adults between the ages of 14 and 24 who provided self-reports on psychological trauma and psychosis proneness, also found that self-reported trauma was associated prospectively with onset of psychotic symptoms. In a study assessing the risk of developing psychotic symptoms associated with maltreatment, bullying, and accidents in a nationally representative U.K. cohort of young twins, Arseneault et al. (2011) found that children who experienced maltreatment by an adult or bullying by peers were more likely to report psychotic symptoms at age 12 than were children who did not experience such traumatic events. The risk associated with childhood trauma remained significant after controlling for gender, socioeconomic deprivation, and IQ; for early symptoms of internalizing and externalizing problems; and for genetic liability to developing psychosis. Shevlin, Dorahy, and Adamson (2007) and Shevlin, Houston, Dorahy, and Adamson (2008), in their review of data from the National Comorbidity Survey and the British Psychiatric Morbidity Survey, found that interpersonal trauma (e.g., childhood physical abuse, molestation) predicted psychosis and that experiencing a number of types of early trauma significantly increased the possibility of later psychosis.

Other studies, including Bendall, Jackson, Hulbert, and McGorry's (2008) systematic critical review of 46 studies on childhood trauma and psychotic disorders; Kelleher et al.'s (2008) population based study of early traumatic events in adolescents and their parents; Schreier et al.'s (2009) prospective study of peer victimization in childhood; and De Loore et al.'s (2007) study investigating the longitudinal effects of negative life experiences on the risk for subclinical psychotic symptoms in an adolescent general community sample, all bear out an association between childhood trauma and psychotic symptoms or experiences.

Comorbid

Some studies investigating the link between childhood traumatic abuse and psychotic disorders suggest that psychotic disorders may be secondary to comorbid affective, substance use, personality, or posttraumatic stress disorders, all of which have been linked to early trauma and all of which are common in people with psychotic disorders. Indeed, psychiatric comorbidities, or co-occurring psychiatric disorders, are prevalent among patients with schizophrenia, and some research suggests that rather than trauma predicting psychotic experiences over time, the two in fact co-occur, or happen simultaneously. Some studies suggest that patients with schizophrenia may be at increased risk for exposure to trauma because of environmental influences, comorbid substance use, or "illness-related features" (Buckley, Miller, Lehrer, and Castle, 2009). Famularo, Kinscherff, and Fenton (1992), in their study comparing the diagnoses of 96 children (61 maltreated, 35 controls) between the ages of 5 and 10 years old, found that compared to controls, children who had suffered maltreatment had higher prevalence rates of hyperactive-impulsive behaviors, attention deficits, and posttraumatic stress disorder diagnoses. The authors also found that maltreated children presented with a significant incidence of psychotic symptomatology, in addition to personality and adjustment disorders. De Bellis et al. (2001), in their investigation of psychiatric comorbidity in caregivers and children involved in maltreatment, found that families involved in maltreatment, found significant histories of co-occurring psychiatric diagnoses in families involved in mistreatment. In this study, a majority of maltreated children and adolescents reported experience of mood disorders, suicidal ideation and attempts, disruptive disorders, and anxiety disorders, including posttraumatic stress disorder. Seventy-two percent of maltreated children had co-occurring emotional and behavioral regulation disorders. These studies provide evidence of psychiatric comorbidity vis-à-vis psychotic, affective, personality, and anxiety disorders, all of which have been linked to early trauma.

Coincidental

The profusion of sound case-control, prospective, and population-based studies that have established a connection between childhood trauma and psychotic experiences, and the large sample sizes in many of these studies (large sample sizes help to reduce the chance of a coincidence), are incongruous with the notion that traumatic exposure and psychotic symptoms simply occur at the same time and have no direct relationship to each other. That is, the evidence contradicts the idea that the "relationship" between these constructs is coincidental.

In the Direction of Causal

Although the studies described up to now support an association between child sexual abuse and psychotic disorders, they do not purport evidence of cause, effect, and directionality, or assume that experience of abuse produces psychosis. And as Cutejar et al. (2010) caution, theorizing of a causal relationship is premature until a clear statistical relationship is established.

In an article summarizing the research literature documenting the high prevalence of psychological trauma, including childhood sexual and physical abuse, among people diagnosed psychotic in general and schizophrenic in particular, Read and Ross (2003) note that a review of the literature indicates that the relationship between childhood trauma and psychotic symptomatology later in life may in some cases be a causal one. Bebbington et al. (2011), examining data from a large representative general population sample, concluded similarly that childhood sexual abuse is strongly associated with psychosis and the link may be causal. Morrison, Frame, and Larkin (2003), in an article examining relationships between trauma and psychosis, found evidence both in support of psychosis as a causal factor for posttraumatic stress disorder and of trauma as a causal factor for psychosis. The authors also propose that psychosis and posttraumatic stress disorder could have common links and be part of a spectrum of trauma reactions.

Causal

Although case study reports and decades of personal observation and other anecdotal evidence have established that exposure to adverse childhood events is an important determinant of psychotic disorders, the first systematic scientific evaluation showing cause, effect, and directionality vis-à-vis childhood trauma and psychosis was only very recently published—in July 2013 (Kelleher et al., 2013).

Causal relationships are distinguished by a number of characteristics, including evidence of association, strength of association, and a dose-response effect. The strength of an association is a "probabilistic indicator of causality" (Lanes, 1988). Although it is possible for a strong association to be non-causal and a weak association causal, the stronger the association, the more likely it is that the relation of "variable A" to "variable B" is causal. Moreover, if changes in one variable (in this discussion, trauma exposure) result in changes in the second variable (in this discussion, psychotic experience), a dose–response relationship is presumed, and causality may be inferred, on condition that extraneous or confounding variables are controlled.

The Kelleher et al. study set out to determine whether childhood trauma predicts incident psychotic experiences and whether cessation of trauma predicts cessation of psychotic experiences. It also sought to determine the direction of the relationship between childhood trauma and psychotic experiences. The authors determined that exposure to childhood trauma was strongly predictive of the onset of psychotic symptoms. They reported a dose-response relationship between severity of bullying and risk for psychotic experiences, such that more severe bullying was associated with higher risk of developing psychotic symptoms. The study also found that discontinuance of traumatic experiences led to a reduced incidence of psychotic experiences, such that individuals whose exposure to trauma was discontinued in the course of the study had a significantly lower occurrence of psychotic experiences than for those for whom traumatic experiences were continued (Kelleher et al., 2013). The study, having provided evidence of a strong association between childhood trauma and incident psychotic experiences; of a dose-response effect in which cessation of traumatic experiences led to a reduced incidence of psychotic experiences; and having controlled for confounding variables, provides persuasive evidence that childhood trauma may indeed be a cause of psychotic experiences.

Clinical and Theoretical Implications

Exposure to trauma and other stressful life events does not, of course, inevitably lead to psychosis: Although some traumatized children go on to develop psychosis or other mental illness, many grow up to be psychologically healthy. And although research has now shown "cause, effect, and directionality" with regard to childhood trauma and psychosis, the full story has yet to be understood.

Indications are that type of trauma (i.e., chronic/repeated [e.g., neglect/maltreatment, sexual abuse, domestic violence], circumscribed [e.g., serious accident, sexual assault/rape], loss/separation [e.g., traumatic bereavement, displacement]); genetic liability; developmental stage and age of exposure; diversity of exposure (poly-victimization vs. individual victimization); and severity and duration of exposure, all influence how children experience and react to trauma (Morgan and Fisher, 2007; Finkelhor, Ormrod, and Turner, 2007). Although many studies (e.g., Bentall, Wickham, Shevlin, and Varese, 2012) have sought to clarify the relationships between, for example, type of trauma and reaction to exposure; between developmental stage and age of exposure and reaction to exposure; and between severity and duration of exposure and reaction to exposure, the results reported persuade further study.

As a review of the literature has illustrated, the association between childhood trauma and psychosis has been replicated many times. Studies suggesting the likelihood of or substantiating a causal relationship between childhood trauma and psychotic symptoms are significantly less numerous. But establishing that adverse childhood experiences are risk factors for psychosis has important clinical implications regardless of questions of causality.

The Multimodal Treatment Approach

Once it became clear that the paranoid delusions, the hallucinations of "dead people," "shadows," and "chatter," and the attempts to set himself ablaze were associated with his history of traumatic exposure, we better understood the presentation and treatment goals of that 15-year-old youngster who had been sexually molested by his older brothers. His disturbed behavior, understood in context of his traumatic exposure, demanded a multi-systemic approach that had the capacity to address a broad range of problems and contributory determinants. A measure of Trauma-Focused Cognitive Behavioral Therapy (TF-CBT), with its incorporation of elements of cognitive behavioral, attachment, humanistic, empowerment, and family therapy models (Child Sexual Abuse Task Force and Research & Practice Core, National Child Traumatic Stress Network, 2004), seemed both useful and essential. This components-based psychosocial treatment is recognized as being one of the most effective interventions for children with psychological symptoms related to trauma exposures. It improves mood, increases interpersonal trust and social competence, and decreases anxiety, disruptive behaviors, and trauma-related shame (Child Sexual Abuse Task Force and Research & Practice Core, National Child Traumatic Stress Network, 2004).

Favorably, this youngster was receptive to the provision of psychoeducation about the impact of trauma and common childhood reactions to trauma; to learning and practicing relaxation and stress management, affective expression and modulation, and cognitive coping and processing skills; to developing a trauma narrative and an in-vivo desensitization plan to resolve avoidant behaviors; and to learning problem-solving and social skills to help reduce the risk of re-victimization. He was also receptive, in due course, to sharing his trauma narrative with his mother.

A unique component of TF-CBT, the goals of the trauma narrative are to "un-pair" fearful associations between innocuous stimuli (e.g., the dark) and danger; to identify and correct unhelpful and inaccurate thoughts related to the trauma (e.g., "It was my fault because I didn't tell them to stop"); and to share information with the involved parent or caregiver about the child's experience, with the aim of enhancing parent–child communication.

In the course of his trauma-focused cognitive behavioral therapy, my very traumatically exposed 15-year-old patient, after becoming skilled in the use of relaxation and cognitive coping skills, developed a thorough trauma narrative, in which he described his personal traumatic experiences of sexual abuse and emotional neglect. He reported on completion of the narrative that the experience of "finally" giving voice to and sharing his traumatic experiences was "freeing." Indeed, evidence suggests that remembering and processing trauma is crucial to resolving its impact (Child Sexual Abuse Task Force and Research & Practice Core, National Child Traumatic Stress Network, 2004). As treatment progressed, the patient reported significantly fewer re-experiencing, avoidance, and increased-arousal symptoms. His paranoid delusions were less readily elicited and his experiences of visual, auditory, and tactile hallucinations became less frequent and less intense. As well, he related to his mother with less difficulty, thanks in some measure to our own therapeutic alliance, which was the foundation for his improved relationship with his mother, and, of course, for the successful outcome of our trauma work.

With his posttraumatic symptoms appreciably moderated on completion of a measure of TF-CBT, we moved on to the next modality in our integrated model of treatment, in which cognitive behavioral therapy and psychodynamic psychotherapy each played a crucial role at different points in the course of treatment. In this stage of the treatment, our goal was to improve capacity for self-examination, self-observation, and insight. Admittedly, there was some resistance early on, born perhaps of a fear of being "too aware" of his inner experience, or perhaps because all patients resist therapeutic process. As well, there were repeated crisis situations (e.g., the hospitalization of his grandmother secondary to deteriorating physical health) that prolonged the course of treatment. But as it had been in our trauma-focused work, our therapeutic relationship was valuable in facilitating a working through of the resistance, and a coping with of the surfacing crisis situations, as we engaged in this measure of psychodynamic psychotherapy. In due course, the patient demonstrated a considerably improved ability to identify, explore, and cope with his feelings, including his fear of not being able to establish and maintain healthy romantic relationships in the future. He also demonstrated an improved ability to recognize the connection between his current attitudes and functioning and his past experiences, and was in time able to understand (and move beyond) his negative relationship patterns.

The combination of the short-term treatment approach of TF-CBT to address this youngster's difficulties related to his traumatic life experiences; our subsequent engagement in a psychodynamic psychotherapy intended to shore up his reality testing and replace his primitive defense mechanisms with more mature tactics to protect against anxiety; and a medication regimen that targeted his mood and psychotic symptoms, restored once-blurred boundaries between internal and external and led to sustained psychosocial improvements.

Not unlike the case described above, what was mutative in treatment for the 16-year-old youngster who had imagined that she would "flutter down to the ground, like a leaf" and land safely after jumping out of a second-floor window; and for the 15-year-old youngster who had lost his mother in the 9/11/2001 attacks on the World Trade Center, was an integrated, multimodal approach that straightforwardly addressed their trauma exposure, posttraumatic symptoms, and associated mood and psychotic symptoms, and that also sought to develop their capacity for self-examination, self-observation, and insight.

The latter youngster, who was also actively abusing marijuana, completed a substance abuse treatment program before starting TF-CBT, since this psychosocial treatment is not the first-line treatment of choice for patients with active substance abuse (Child Sexual Abuse Task Force and Research & Practice Core, National Child Traumatic Stress Network, 2004). With his substance abuse treated, and with the benefit of a solid therapeutic alliance, we undertook a measure of TF-CBT, including developing a trauma narrative, in which the patient described his personal traumatic experience of parental loss. In view of the fact that the family, en bloc, was deeply affected by this trauma, and recognizing the critical role of the family system in this patient's world, it was important to actively engage the family in decision-making about how, within the guidelines of the model, the therapy should proceed. Owing largely to this emphasis on empowerment, family, and a collaborative approach, the family was in every respect committed to the treatment. As "phase one" (trauma-focused cognitive behavioral therapy in combination with an optimized medication regimen) of the treatment progressed, the patient reported increasingly fewer re-experiencing, avoidance, and arousal symptoms, and exhibited improved social behavior. As "phase two" (psychodynamic psychotherapy in combination with an optimized medication regimen) of the treatment progressed, his delusions and paranoia subsided and he demonstrated significantly improved insight and executive functioning.

The 16-year-old whose reality testing had been undermined after being sexually molested at age 11 likewise benefited from an integrated, two-phase model of treatment, comprised, again, of a measure of trauma-focused cognitive behavioral therapy in combination with an optimized medication regimen, followed by a measure of psychodynamic psychotherapy in conjunction with an optimized medication regimen. She reported significantly fewer intrusive, avoidance, and arousal symptoms, engaged in fewer disruptive and sexualized behaviors and reported improved social competence and decreased trauma-related shame by the end of "phase one." By the end of "phase two," her behavior was organized and appropriately goal-driven; her thought processes were coherent, articulate, and logical; and her insight and judgment were markedly improved. As well, she demonstrated improved abilities to plan and self-monitor.

In the three cases described, the patients' psychotic symptoms postdated experiences of traumatic exposure. Appropriately, in *none* of the cases was the sole focus of treatment their psychotic symptomatology. To be sure, resolving the impact of their traumas was essential to treating the psychotic and affective symptoms with which these patients presented.

Although the debate over the nature of the relationship (causal vs. contributory, comorbid, or coincidental) between childhood trauma and psychosis has not been settled absolutely, we do know, beyond a reasonable doubt, that these phenomena are associated. We also know, at least anecdotally, that the combination of the short-term treatment approach of TF-CBT, psychodynamic psychotherapy, and psychopharmacology comprises a comprehensive treatment that restores blurred boundaries between internal and external and that effects improvements in depression, anxiety, disruptive behaviors, and social competence.

Taking Social Context into Account

In consideration of the established association between childhood trauma and psychotic experiences, and of the evidence that conditions like schizophrenia cannot be fully understood without taking into consideration patients' life experiences, in addition to neurological factors and genetic liability, our approach to treating psychotic disorders should be rooted in an integrated model that takes patients' socio-environmental experiences into account (Read, van Os, Morrison, and Ross, 2005). Fundamentally, this means that clinicians should be engaging, as a matter of course, in thorough history taking (i.e., asking about abuse histories and adverse events in childhood) and going beyond the usual reductionistic focus on biological phenomena. After all, understanding *why* someone has developed psychosis is a fundamental part of his adjustment to a first episode (Bendall et al., 2008). In addition to being more conceptually useful, an integrated model of mental illness allows for more optimism about the potential for recovery versus a strictly medical model, which is associated with harmful pessimism apropos of recovery potential (Read, Bentall, and Fosse, 2009).

If exploration of the presence of early adverse life events in patients diagnosed psychotic reveals a history of traumatic exposure in childhood, a comprehensive treatment plan, including pharmacotherapy, psychodynamic psychotherapy, and a psychosocial intervention like TF-CBT, should be recommended. Indeed, a range of psychosocial treatment approaches to psychosis that address the sequelae of adverse childhood events have been found to be effective for many patients (Read and Dillon, 2013). Further, recognizing the possibility that traumatic childhood experiences may have contributed to psychotic symptoms primes us to attend to these issues in psychotherapeutic management. Psychotherapeutic treatment of patients who report traumatic life events in the context of psychotic experiences should focus on teaching adaptive coping strategies; on processing the trauma in view of evidence that remembering and talking about trauma in a way that creates meaning and that decreases the intensity of the emotional charge is central to resolving its impact; and on increasing self-observation, insight, and executive functioning, with the essential aim of improving the patient's ability to cope effectively with the demands of adulthood.

Implications for Primary Prevention

The reality that child maltreatment, including sexual abuse, physical abuse, emotional/psychological abuse, neglect, and peer victimization, is a risk factor for psychosis prescribes that children who come to the attention of mental health professionals following maltreatment should receive ongoing and comprehensive clinical and social support, with focus on facilitating trauma processing and improving coping ability and insight, and with the aim of reducing the risk of developing a post-trauma anxiety disorder or a psychotic illness. In fact, ongoing clinical and social support is likely to benefit all victims of child maltreatment, irrespective of their risk of developing a psychotic illness.

Conclusion

Treating schizophrenia and other psychotic disorders effectively requires routine taking of trauma histories, a conceptualization that includes the influence of life experiences and that goes beyond the narrow focus on genes and brain functions; a comprehensive treatment plan; and continued study of the long-term effects of traumatic exposure. As Read and Ross (2003) note, addressing the high rates of trauma in people diagnosed with schizophrenia requires a broader, not a more restrictive, approach to treatment. Only by adopting an integrated approach that takes patients' socio-environmental experiences, as well as biological and psychological factors, into account can we understand mental health and illness in their fullest contexts, and only when we understand mental health and illness in their fullest contexts can we provide the comprehensive care that will allow the remission of symptomatology, functional recovery, and improved quality of life we strive to provide for all of our patients.

References

Arseneault, L., Cannon, M., Fisher, H. L., Polanczyk, G., Moffitt, T. E., & Caspi, A. (2011). Childhood trauma and children's emerging psychotic symptoms: a genetically sensitive longitudinal cohort study. *American Journal of Psychiatry,* 168, 65–72.

Bebbington, P., Jonas, S., Kuipers, E., King, M., Brugha, T., McManus, S., & Jenkins, R. (2011). Childhood sexual abuse and psychosis: data from a cross-sectional national psychiatric survey in England. *British Journal of Psychiatry*, 199, 29–37.

Bendall, S., Jackson, H. J., Hulbert, C. A., & McGorry, P. D. (2008). Childhood trauma and psychotic disorders: A systematic, critical review of the evidence. *Schizophrenia Bulletin,* 34, 568–579.

Bentall, R. P., Wickham, S., Shevlin, M., & Varese, F. (2012) Do specific early-life adversities lead to specific symptoms of psychosis? A study from the 2007 The Adult Psychiatric Morbidity Survey. *Schizophrenia Bulletin,* 38(4), 661–671.

Bifulco, A., Brown, G. W., & Adler, Z. (1991). Early sexual abuse and clinical depression in adult life. *British Journal of Psychiatry,* 159, 115–122.

Buckley, P. F., Miller, B. J., Lehrer, D. S., & Castle, D. J. (2009). Psychiatric comorbidities and schizophrenia. *Schizophrenia Bulletin,* 35(2), 383–402.

Child Sexual Abuse Task Force and Research & Practice Core, National Child Traumatic Stress Network. (2004). *How to Implement Trauma-Focused Cognitive Behavioral Therapy.* Durham, NC, and Los Angeles, CA: National Center for Child Traumatic Stress.

Cutajar, M. C., Mullen, P. E., Ogloff, J. R., Thomas, S. D., Wells, D. L., & Spataro, J. (2010a). Psychopathology in a large cohort of sexually abused children followed up to 43-years. *Child Abuse and Neglect: The International Journal*, 34(11), 813–822.

Cutajar, M. C., Mullen, P. E., Ogloff, J. R., Thomas, S. D., Wells, D. L., & Spataro, J. (2010b). Schizophrenia and other psychotic disorders in a cohort of sexually abused children. *Archives of General Psychiatry,* 67(11), 1114–1119.

Cutajar, M. C., Mullen, P. E., Ogloff, J. R., Thomas, S. D., Wells, D. L., & Spataro, J. (2010c). Suicide and fatal drug overdose in child sexual abuse victims: a historical cohort study. *Medical Journal of Australia,* 192(4), 184–187.

De Bellis, M. D., Broussard, E. R., Herring, D. J., Wexler, S., Moritz, G., & Benitez, J. G. (2001). Psychiatric comorbidity in caregivers and children involved in maltreatment: a pilot research study with policy implications. *Child Abuse & Neglect,* 25(7), 923–944.

De Loore, E., Drukker, M., Gunther, N., Feron, F., Deboutte, D., Sabbe, B., Mengelers, R., van Os, J., & Myin-Germeys, I. (2007). Childhood negative experiences and subclinical psychosis in adolescence: a longitudinal general population study. *Early Intervention in Psychiatry,* 1, 201–207.

Famularo, R., Kinscherff, R., & Fenton, T. (1992). Psychiatric diagnoses of maltreated children: preliminary findings. *Journal of the American Academy of Child and Adolescent Psychiatry,* 31(5), 863–867.

Finkelhor, D., Ormrod, R.K., & Turner, H.A. (2007). Poly-victimization: A neglected component in child victimization. *Child Abuse & Neglect,* 31, 7–26.

Green, J.G., McLaughlin, K.A., Berglund, P.A., Gruber, M. J., Sampson, N.A., Zaslavsky, A.M., & Kessler, R.C. (2010). Childhood adversities and adult psychiatric disorders in the national comorbidity survey replication I: Associations with first onset of DSM-IV disorders. *Archives of General Psychiatry,* 67, 113–123.

Janssen, I., Krabbendam L., Bak, M., Hanssen, W., Volleberg, W., de Graaf, R., & van Os, J. (2004). Childhood abuse as a risk factor for psychotic experiences. *Acta Psychiatrica Scandinavica,* 109(1), 38–45.

Johnson, J.G., Cohen, P., Brown, J., Smailes, E.M., & Bernstein, D.P. (1999). Childhood maltreatment increases risk for personality disorders during early adulthood. *Archives of General Psychiatry,* 56(7), 600–606.

Kelleher, I., Harley, M., Lynch, F., Arseneault, L., Fitzpatrick, C., & Cannon, M. (2008). Associations between childhood trauma, bullying and psychotic symptoms among a school-based adolescent sample. *British Journal of Psychiatry,* 193, 378–382.

Kelleher, I., Keeley, H., Corcoran, P., Ramsay, H., Wasserman, C., Carli, V., Sarchiapone, M., Hoven, C., Wasserman, D., & Cannon, M. (2013). Childhood trauma and psychosis in a prospective cohort study: Cause, effect and directionality. *American Journal of Psychiatry,* 170(7), 734–741.

Kessler, R.C., Davis, C.G., & Kendler, K.S. (1997). Childhood adversity and adult psychiatric disorder in the U.S. National Comorbidity Survey. *Psychological Medicine,* 27, 1101–1119.

Kessler, R.C., McLaughlin, K.A., Green, J.G., Gruber, M. J., Sampson, N.A., Zaslavsky, A.M., Aguilar-Gaxiola, S., Alhamzawi, A.O., Alonso, J., Angermeyer, M., Benjet, C., Bromet, E., Chatterji, S., de Girolamo, G., Demyttenaere, K., Fayyad, J., Florescu, S., Gal, G., Gureje, O., Haro, J.M., Hu, C.Y., Karam, E.G., Kawakami, N., Lee, S., Lepine, J.P., Ormel, J., Posada-Villa, J., Sagar, R., Tsang, A., Ustun, T.B., Vassilev, S., Viana, M.C., & Williams, D.R. (2010). Childhood adversities and adult psychopathology in the WHO World Mental Health Surveys. *British Journal of Psychiatry,* 197, 378–385.

Kilpatrick, D.G., & Saunders, B.E. (1999). *Prevalence and consequences of child victimization: Results from the National Survey of Adolescents.* U.S. Department of Justice, Office of Justice Programs, National Institute of Justice, Grant No. 93-IJ-CX-0023.

Lanes, S.F. (1998). Error and uncertainty in causal inference. In K. J. Rothman (Ed.), *Causal inference* (pp. 173–188). Chestnut Hill, MA: Epidemiology Resources Inc.

Morgan, C., & Fisher, H. (2007). Environment and schizophrenia: environmental factors in schizophrenia: childhood trauma—a critical review. *Schizophrenia Bulletin,* 33, 3–10.

Morrison, A.P., Frame, L., & Larkin, W. (2003). Relationships between trauma and psychosis: A review and integration. *British Journal of Clinical Psychology,* 42(4), 331–353.

Paris, J. (1994). *Borderline personality disorders: A multidimensional approach.* Washington, DC: American Psychiatric Press.

Read, J., Bentall, R.P., & Fosse, R. (2009). Time to abandon the bio-bio-bio model of psychosis: Exploring the epigenetic and psychological mechanisms by which adverse life events lead to psychotic symptoms. *Epidemiologia e Psichiatria Sociale,* 18(4), 299–310.

Read, J., & Dillon, J. (Eds.). (2013). *Models of madness: Psychological, social and biological approaches to psychosis, 2nd edition.* New York, NY: Routledge.

Read, J., & Ross, C. A. (2003). Psychological trauma and psychosis: another reason why people diagnosed schizophrenic must be offered psychological therapies. *Journal of the American Academy of Psychoanalysis and Dynamic Psychiatry,* 31(1), 247–68.

Read, J., van Os, J., Morrison, A. P., & Ross, C. A. (2005). Childhood trauma, psychosis and schizophrenia: a literature review with theoretical and clinical implications. *Acta Psychiatrica Scandinavica,* 112(5), 330–50.

Sarchiapone, M., Carli, V., Cuomo, C., Marchetti, M., & Roy, A. (2009). Association between childhood trauma and aggression in male prisoners. *Journal of Psychiatric Research,* 165, 187–192.

Scher, C. D., Forde, D. R., McQuaid, J. R., & Stein, M. B. (2004). Prevalence and demographic correlates of childhood maltreatment in an adult community sample. *Child Abuse & Neglect: The International Journal,* 2004(28), 167–180.

Schreier, A., Wolke, D., Thomas, K., Horwood, J., Hollis, C., Gunnell, D., Lewis, G., Thompson, A., Duffy, L., Salvi, G., & Harrison, G. (2009). Prospective study of peer victimization in childhood and psychotic symptoms in a nonclinical population at age 12 years. *Archives of General Psychiatry,* 66, 527–536.

Shevlin, M., Dorahy, M. J., & Adamson, G. (2007). Trauma and psychosis: an analysis of the National Comorbidity Survey. *American Journal of Psychiatry,* 164, 166–169.

Shevlin, M., Houston, J. E., Dorahy, M. J., & Adamson, G. (2008). Cumulative traumas and psychosis: an analysis of the National Comorbidity Survey and the British Psychiatric Morbidity Survey. *Schizophrenia Bulletin,* 34, 193–199.

Spataro, J., Mullen, P. E., Burgess, P. M., Wells, D. L., & Moss, S. A. (2004). Impact of child sexual abuse on mental health: prospective study in males and females. *British Journal of Psychiatry,* 184, 416–421.

Spauwen, J., Krabbendam, L., Lieb, R., Wittchen, H. U., & van Os, J. (2006). Impact of psychological trauma on the development of psychotic symptoms: relationship with psychosis proneness. *British Journal of Psychiatry,* 188, 527–533.

Varese, F., Smeets, F., Drukker, M., Lieverse, R., Lataster, T., Viechtbauer, W., Read, J., van Os, J., & Bentall, R. O. (2012). Childhood adversities increase the risk of psychosis: A meta-analysis of patient-control, prospective- and cross-sectional cohort studies. *Schizophrenia Bulletin,* 38(4), 661–671.

Widom, C. S. (1999). Posttraumatic stress disorder in abused and neglected children grown up. *American Journal of Psychiatry*, 156, 1223–1229.

Widom, C. S., DuMont, K., & Czaja, S. J. (2007). A prospective investigation of major depressive disorder and comorbidity in abused and neglected children grown up. *Archives of General Psychiatry,* 64(1), 49–56

Widom C. S., White, H. R., Czaja, S. J., & Marmorstein, N. R. (2007). Long-term effects of child abuse and neglect on alcohol use and excessive drinking in middle adulthood. *Journal of Studies on Alcohol and Drugs,* 683(3), 317–326.

PART III

Treatment and Future Directions

7

PLAY THERAPY WITH PSYCHOTIC AND BORDERLINE CHILDREN

James B. McCarthy and Gladys Branly Guarton

> *Analysts have always been proud of the distinction that theirs is a causal therapy, aiming at the conflicts and stresses which are hidden in the patient's personality and underlie their psychopathology.*
>
> —Anna Freud, 1970, p. 19

This chapter's primary goal is to depict the transformative value of psychodynamic play therapy as a medium for redressing pathological variations in psychological development and promoting psychotic and borderline children's resilience. Interwoven with concepts from Freudian theory, ego psychology, object relations theories, interpersonal and relational psychoanalysis, and self-psychology, psychoanalytic models of play therapy explicate the mutual interaction of developmental delays and unresolved psychological conflicts with family and social influences on the formation of children's emotional problems. Based on an integration of Anna Freud's (1946) revolutionary ideas about development, Winnicott's (1953) formulation of transitional objects, and the contributions of other theorists, the psychoanalyst's therapeutic objective is to encourage the disturbed child's growth by embellishing the play in ego-enhancing ways and capitalizing on its transitional elements. Engagement with seriously disturbed children in play frees their innate capacities for resilience.

The Functions of Play

Play has a universal, critical significance in the mental life of children. It generally entails unhurried, non-goal-directed activity, which is consistently fueled by the child's fantasy life. The ability to play presents children with an endless source of pleasure and opportunities for ultimately attempting conflict resolution through action and fantasy. Play invokes crucial functions in children's cognitive, emotional, and social development (Greenspan and Lourie, 1981). From infancy, play with the body, playful interactions with adults, and negotiating with toys all facilitate tension regulation and the expression of complex emotional states. Play with important adults enhances speech and language development along with a gradually intensifying awareness of the modes of emotional and social communication. Through play, especially fantasy play, the 1- to 2-year-old establishes self-differentiation and animates capacities for self-regulation. For toddlers, the organization of sequences and thematic development in play may be related to their degree of success with separation-individuation (Slade, 1986, 1987). Once pretend play flourishes and includes descriptions of interactions with others by around age 2, fantasy play becomes more interactive. For the 2- to 3-year-old, play fantasies inevitably evolve into imaginative games. The representation of attachment relationships through the use of symbols further coincides with imaginative play as children deepen identifications with others and develop greater empathy through a burgeoning awareness of others' inner experience. In a synthesis of the literature, Schaefer (1999) enumerated 25 therapeutic functions of play that include the inspiration of creativity, desensitization to negative affect, and improvements in children's self-esteem. Children's reliance on play in order to become more communicative remains another paramount aim.

Play activities trigger neuronal activity in the developing brain. They foster cognitive abilities by stimulating more advanced planning and problem-solving ability as well as social skills, as play with peers progresses along with the popularity of rule-based games (Fisher, 1992). When the 3- to 5-year-old child becomes capable of a richer fantasy life as part of the increasing use of symbols, play enhances social competence and the capacity to sustain dysphoric feelings without prolonged regressions in functioning (Bretherton, 1984; Connolly and Doyle, 1984). As action is steadily transmuted into the capacity to use metaphors in play, affect-regulation progresses in concert with cognitive development (Fonagy, Gergely, Jurist, and Target, 2004). In the course of maturation, fantasy play at increasingly sophisticated levels enriches the growing, school-aged child's concentration and sequential thinking ability. In accordance with children's more mature cognitive and emotional functioning, greater sensitivity to oneself and others, and resourcefulness in tolerating ambivalence and ambiguity can be observed in their play themes. Opportunities for making multiple identifications and improving empathy by elaborating emotional themes in imaginative play further augment latency-aged children's relatedness and social competence. Piaget (1965) first maintained that play also serves as an essential arena for the older child and young adolescent's expanding ability to alternate between making use of concrete operations and abstract thinking. By itself, play thus fulfills multiple therapeutic purposes for children as a readily available framework for lowering anxiety, eliciting fantasies and wish fulfillment, integrating potentially overwhelming life experience, achieving a sense of mastery in developmental tasks, offering a respite from superego demands, and stimulating healthy ego functioning (Waelder, 1932.) In addition, as a medium of exchange in psychotherapy, play offers disturbed children suitable circumstances for representing themselves symbolically through narratives (Slade, 1986, 1987) and feeling valued and understood without being judged (Sperling, 1997).

Play in Psychoanalytic Theory

Play therapy holds a great conceptual importance in the history of psychoanalytic theory. Beginning with his discussion of the case of phobic Little Hans, the first attempted analysis of a child, Freud (1909) stated his original position that play performs the function of allowing children to discharge libidinal energy and achieve a forceful mastery of the drives. In his subsequent writing, Freud (1911, 1915, 1920) enlarged this view by explaining that children compulsively re-enact emotionally traumatic events in play, creating opportunities to reduce anxiety and unconsciously find resolutions. In early accounts of child psychoanalytic psychotherapy, Anna Freud (1965) characterized play as the precursor of work for children and the most natural outlet for their expression of inner experience, which can't be fully articulated and communicated. Although Hug-Hellmuth (1921) probably conducted the first complete psychotherapeutic treatment of a child, Anna Freud's (1936, 1946) nuanced delineation of the stages of ego development provided the most influential depiction of play as the avenue for the unfolding of children's unconscious anxieties and their gradual resolution through repetition and compromise formations. Since the early 1920s and 1930s when Anna Freud (1928) and Melanie Klein (1932) began to rely on play techniques as fitting alternatives to verbalization and free association in clinical work with children, play therapy approaches have been broadly applied to help children concretely convey and symbolically express their emotional suffering and developmental conflicts.

In some of her preliminary papers, Klein (1955) indicated the need for ongoing interpretation of the unconscious meaning of children's fantasies in play, since it substituted for free association, while Anna Freud (1965) endorsed a more balanced, comprehensive psychoanalytic perspective with children. For Klein, rather than being inherently therapeutic, play's value was as the best vehicle for providing unencumbered access to the child's unconscious. For Anna Freud, engaging children with toys and play material was inextricably tied to the therapist's significance as a powerful figure in their emotional life. Far from rejecting the primacy of interpretation as essential to psychotherapy, Anna Freud observed that the child therapist remains not only a transference figure, but also a very real object who functions as an *auxiliary ego* during the treatment. She recommended first strengthening the positive alliance with the child and family and examining the play activities in relationship to the child's ego immaturities and developmental profile before the interpretation of defenses (Anna Freud, 1946).

Winnicott (1953) argued persuasively that the baby's survival and healthy individuation rest on the foundation of combined me and not-me experience that originally arises as a result of shared oneness with the mother. This simultaneous sense of both oneness and separateness that Winnicott (1968) labeled *transitional experience* is exercised during play and can later be recreated and strengthened in the therapeutic relationship in psychoanalytic psychotherapy. Consistent with Winnicott's (1971, 1975) principle that play represents transitional phenomena, Winnicott concluded that psychotherapy is equivalent to play. His development of the Squiggle Game illustrated his exposition of the therapist's need to engage the child in play, thereby participating in the child's transitional experience between self and not-self as a temporary blurring of the distinction between internal and external reality. The Squiggle Game has been routinely employed as a projective-like technique that can assist children with communicating and understanding their conflictual feelings through the use of drawings in play. Like other forms of interactive therapeutic play, such games perpetuate the child's ability to prosper from inhabiting the internal world and the external world at the same time as a pathway to self-differentiation, a capacity that can be heightened by internalizing transitional play with the therapist. As a result of Mahler's (1967) infant–mother observation studies, she was able to record the sequence of the stages of separation–individuation as reflected in infants and toddlers' emotional communication during solitary and interactive play. In a compelling extension of Mahler's work, Kaplan (1978) portrayed struggles with the simultaneous fear of oneness and separateness as central to the developmental origin of severe psychopathology in children.

In psychoanalytic psychotherapy, children's play can have enormous curative value, even if its latent psychodynamic meaning isn't interpreted. Within an interpersonal–relational psychoanalytic framework first advocated by Sullivan (1956) and highlighted by his thesis that participant-observation and detailed inquiry are crucial for meaningful psychotherapy, the investigation of the patient's and the therapist's mutual influence constitutes a vital therapeutic task with children, as it does with adult patients (Spiegel, 1989; Altman, Briggs, Frankel, Gensler, and Pantone, 2000). Interpretation inevitably amounts to only one possible form of participation with the patient, since the child and adolescent psychotherapist also observes and tries to understand and expand on the emotional communication. These goals are accomplished by examining transference–countertransference configurations and considering the child's experience of the therapist while making an effort to identify intrapsychic and environmental obstacles to the child's maturation. Along with scrutinizing the transactional aspects of the process, the psychoanalyst explores the child's symptoms and behavior along multidimensional axes that locate the unconscious conflicts in their relevant developmental, neurocognitive, family, and social contexts. In keeping with contemporary relational psychoanalytic models and Anna Freud's (1965) and Winnicott's (1971) beliefs that children blend their participation in the internal world and the external world through play, coping strategies are frequently taught by means of metaphors and comments that are made about the child's drawings and play themes. More direct observations about the child's feelings that circumvent the use of metaphors might be ameliorative with some children but can be destructive with others when the links between the child's feelings, unconscious psychodynamics, and behavior aren't offered sensitively at appropriate times (Bornstein, 1945). The therapist needs to attentively monitor the impact of the interventions on the child's feelings, on the therapeutic relationship with its transference elements, and on the family relationships. The patient–therapist interactions with children mirror parent–child interactions, which build psychological structure in the child and support nascent developmental processes. From the perspective of each of the psychoanalytic orientations, the therapeutic relationship therefore has a number of reparative dimensions beyond the enactment of the emotional conflicts and the repetition of dynamic family transactions with the therapist.

For heuristic purposes, we contrast psychoanalytic play therapy with cognitive-behavioral play approaches, as a more structured psychotherapy in which prescriptive interventions outweigh listening for unconscious communication. However, this distinction represents a partially false dichotomy, since psychoanalytic play therapy always involves the child learning and practicing new psychological skills, and effective cognitive behavior therapy must be based on the presence of a positive therapeutic relationship. Even though our commentary is about individual psychotherapy with the child, play therapy always has to be integrated with clinical work with the family. From a psychoanalytic vantage point, play therapy can uncover the continuum of the child's feelings and anxieties, along with their role in defensive breakdowns and their impact on the emergence of symptoms in the child's life and in relation to the psychotherapist. For the seriously disturbed child with borderline personality disorder traits or psychotic features who is often not particularly psychologically minded, psychoanalytic play therapy sessions especially offer clinicians continuous opportunities for assessment and an appreciation of the child's psychopathology and developmental needs. Even though psychotherapists dictate the setting and the limits of the therapy, as long as the play in sessions continues to be largely the child's creation, the therapist can remain open to finding interpretative interventions that will support the child's transitional experience and the promotion of psychological structure.

Empirical Support for Play Therapy

Although psychoanalytic play therapy techniques have been used in the treatment of emotionally disturbed children and adolescents for over 100 years, with few exceptions the relative absence of play therapy as a general topic in the scientific literature reflects the difficulty of applying scientific methodology to an often unstructured activity with the potential for infinite variations. There has been a longstanding consensus among child clinicians that play techniques frequently offer therapeutic possibilities, but scientific methodology has been used to assess play therapy principally only in the last 25 years. Nevertheless, unpressured play therapy techniques offer the advantage of appealing to the child as a whole person with full cognizance of the child's age-appropriate interests and preference for freedom with games and imaginative play (Guerney, 2001; Kaduson and Schaefer, 2006). Play therapy approaches have been successfully tried in a multitude of outpatient, inpatient, school, and agency treatment endeavors with highly traumatized children as well as those with a variety of other emotional and behavioral problems (VanFleet, Lilly, and Kaduson, 1999; Schaefer, 1993, 2011).

In spite of the developmentally sensitive reliance on the use of age-appropriate materials with children and young adolescents, play therapy has been regularly criticized for lacking an empirical basis, since it can be difficult to measure and there is only limited research supporting its overall effectiveness. Few carefully designed, well-controlled studies of play therapy and its efficacy have been carried out, although there has been an abundance of theoretical models of play therapy strategies. These models range from relatively unstructured approaches, such as psychoanalytic play therapy, nondirective therapeutic play (Axline, 1947), and child-centered play therapy (Moustakas, 1953; Landreth, 1991), to more structured interventions, such as improving parenting techniques by coaching parents' play with children (VanFleet, 1994) and including their participation in the play (Gurney, 2000). Prescriptive play therapy interventions and cognitive-behavioral play therapy represent the most highly structured play therapy approaches. In cognitive-behavioral play therapy with children, the interventions are generally more standardized and can be more readily translated into measurable outcomes. Modeling is frequently used and adaptive cognitive skills are taught, at times indirectly with the goal of generalization and eventual response prevention of maladaptive behavior (Knell, 1998). Drewes (2006, 2009) recently explored a variety of children's disorders and emotional problems that have been successfully treated by combining play therapy techniques with cognitive behavior therapy, resulting in a steadily developing body of empirical support for the therapeutic uses of play techniques. Aside from the use of cognitive behavioral techniques with symptom inventories completed prior to and after treatment interventions, there has been little agreement about what constitutes acceptable outcome measures for play therapy's effectiveness given the expansive scope of its applications.

Concern about the variety of therapeutic techniques employed with children and how to quantify and objectively assess them was voiced as long ago as the 1930s (Solomon, 1938). Perry and Landreth (1991) developed the Play Therapy Observation Instrument (PTOI) as one initial effort to create a standardized treatment outcome measure. In another attempt to quantify play therapy and establish a standardized scale for measuring its impact, Kaduson, Cangelosi, and Schaefer (1997) examined the efficacy of play therapy and endorsed its value with a variety of emotional and behavioral problems in children. Kernberg, Chazan, and Normandin (1998) developed and conducted reliability studies with the Children's Play Therapy Instrument (CPTI), which has had considerable promise as a measure of play activity during individual therapy sessions. However, it has apparently not yet been widely used to differentiate an array of diagnostic groups or to broadly assess the efficacy of related treatment outcomes. In several of the most thorough meta-analytic studies of play therapy's effectiveness, LeBlanc and Ritchie (1999, 2001) investigated 42 controlled studies conducted between 1950 and 1996, with an emphasis on which characteristics predicted the most positive therapeutic outcomes. Based on their assessment of the studies that successfully met the criteria of having had experimental designs, they found that play therapy has a moderately positive effect with children (an average effect size of 0.66 standard deviations). They also reported strong relationships between the overall effectiveness of play therapy, including parents in the child's play therapy, and the duration of the treatment with therapy that involved 30 to 35 sessions having the most beneficial outcome.

In the first of a series of meta-analytic investigations of the play therapy literature, Bratton, Ray, Rhine, and Jones (2005) summarized studies of its effectiveness with specific presenting problems and noted generally positive outcomes with behavioral problems, self-concept, emotional adjustment, proneness to anxiety, and social skills weaknesses. Rennie and Landreth (2000) reported the demonstrable effects of filial play therapy approaches on children's behavior and parental attitudes. Ray, Bratton, Rhine, and Jones (2001) reviewed 94 research studies about play therapy and found positive effects across gender, age, population characteristics, and theoretical models of play therapy. The outcome effects of play therapy were found to be even more significant when there was parental involvement. In a more recent meta-analysis of 93 outcome studies of play therapy's effectiveness with over 3,200 girls and boys who did not have cognitive delays, Bratton, Ray, Rhine, and Jones (2005) found an overall treatment effect of 0.80 standard deviations for play therapy, with even more positive effects when parents were included in the therapy. Humanistic play therapy interventions demonstrated the largest effect size, whereas non-humanistic treatment approaches had a moderate effect size. The mean age of the children in the studies they reviewed was 7, and most were completed with children under age 10, even though play therapy's effectiveness remained true across age groups and genders, regardless of whether the children were in treatment for internalizing or externalizing disorders and other presenting problems. Since this meta-analytic review of play therapy included children in residential settings, the data revealed that when play therapy was done in residential settings it had significantly larger treatment effects than when it was conducted in outpatient clinics or school settings. The children who were seen in residential programs received the largest number of play therapy sessions and derived the greatest benefit from treatment. Even though emotional and behavioral disturbances were included among the patient characteristics in the studies and six of them were done in residential programs, no controlled studies were identified that involved children with severe psychiatric disorders, such as borderline personality features or psychotic disorders.

Russ (2004) has made considerable effort to emphasize an empirical foundation for play therapy by synthesizing and integrating developmental research on the functions of play with clinical research studies and by underscoring the need for careful assessments prior to and subsequent to play therapy interventions. More recently, play therapy has accumulated steadily developing research support for its effectiveness although the challenge of constructing methodologically sound studies for unstructured play activities continues (Baggerly and Bratton, 2010; Schaefer, 2011). Nevertheless, as far as we know, no controlled studies have been done to assess the outcome effectiveness of play therapy with psychotic children and those with borderline personality disorder features, and none have thoroughly compared psychodynamic and psychoanalytic interventions with cognitive behavioral strategies for severely disturbed children and adolescents.

Play Therapy Techniques

Based on the bedrock of its flexibility, the use of play can be thoughtfully employed in therapy to discern the sources of anxiety in most children and young adolescents who aren't comfortable speaking with adults. Play therapy techniques that allow for the possibility of symbolic interventions at appropriate moments constitute an ideal modality for helping children learn about their problematic thoughts and emotional reactions. In accordance with their cognitive development, preschool children vary in when they begin to express symbolic thinking and thematic content in play. Young children's egocentricity and concrete thinking typically lead them to attribute their own feelings to their parents and to likewise automatically feel that they are the direct cause of their parents' distress. Even latency-aged or adolescent children's concreteness might contribute to their having a limited ability to understand sequential feelings and to grasp the nature of contradictory, ambivalent feelings. Hence, the psychotherapist frequently creates concrete metaphors in order to identify and reflect children's thoughts and feelings in play therapy sessions. Either using metaphors that children have created themselves or constructing new ones can help expand the child's use of symbolism in play to convey inner experience. For example, a therapist might draw a picture of children playing a tug of war game in order to begin to explain the concept of an internal conflict. A picture of a layer cake might help children grasp the possibility of experiencing more than one feeling at a time, and a picture of a seesaw in a park could be used to illustrate someone having up and down, ambivalent feelings about the same person. With latency-aged children and young adolescents, drawing a picture of a stop sign with the child might be a way to convey the use of external cues to guide behavior and their internalization in the development of self-regulatory capacities. The psychotherapist's reflective statements about the play themes and associated interpretative comments can link the patient's thoughts, feelings, and actions in many ways that support psychological development. For example, with a highly aggressive 8-year-old boy who has been traumatized by witnessing his father physically assault his mother and who is unconsciously threatened by his own aggressive behavior, the therapist might eventually respond to a play theme involving a violent fight between toy bank robbers at an appropriate time by asking: Has anyone thought of calling the police? This kind of interpretative question, conveyed metaphorically, might gradually help the child feel in greater control by becoming more aware of ego-enhancing internal dialogue and by generating healthier representational models of identification.

In contrast to the twofold psychoanalytic emphasis on discerning unconscious symbolization and developmental weaknesses in children's play and analyzing how interventions impact the therapeutic process, Gardner (1971) proposed relying on structured game playing techniques, such as the Talking, Feeling, Doing Game, as therapeutic strategies for inducing positive emotional changes. These techniques were designed to circumvent latency-aged children's natural reluctance to be introspective and psychologically minded due to their limited frustration tolerance and action orientation (Gardner, 1975). As strategic interventions, they reflect the misleading assumption that the development of insight is the *sine qua non* of psychoanalytic psychotherapy, rather than the use of the process with the therapist as a means of facilitating more adaptive ego functioning through the play. For example, although the use of board games with children can have a very significant therapeutic value, Gardner advised playing checkers with children indefinitely as a way of potentially avoiding resistances in therapy. However, children may at times use board games as a distancing mechanism and a way of avoiding any anxiety about experiencing emotional contact with the therapist; resistance is as much a central part of the therapeutic process with children as it is with adults. Based on Gardner's work, Kritzberg (1975) formulated more flexible, structured therapeutic games for use with children that allowed for crafting metaphors and for the therapist to be guided by the content of the child's games and stories.

Harter's (1977) elucidation of the use of drawings in play therapy and the benefit of initially making interpretations about play themes that are closely tied to children's emerging cognitive capacities is very similar to the play therapy approach we are describing as one that is completely compatible with psychoanalytic developmental theory. Based on a Piagetian model of cognitive development, children can gradually be helped to understand some of the motivation underlying their behavior. In light of Piaget's (1962, 1965) descriptions of preoperational and concrete-operational thinking, play therapy techniques need to be aligned with the child's fluctuating levels of concrete and more abstract thinking. Also consistent with a developmental framework that takes cognition into account, Scarlett (1994) added that children try to regulate optimal levels of anxiety through play, whether the spontaneous productions involve imaginative fantasy creations or toys and action sequences. Assiduous discussions of the interconnections between symbolization, the use of metaphor, and pretend play in psychotherapy have been elaborated by Schaefer, Gitlin, and Sandgrund (1991); Drucker (1994); First (1994); Slade (1994), Landreth (2002); Kaduson and Schaefer (2006); and Schaefer (2011).

Psychoanalytic Views of Play Therapy

Even though psychoanalytic play therapy approaches have not been rigorously tested empirically, there is a substantial history of their successful use with developmentally delayed, borderline, and psychotic children. Play therapy is congruent with each of the psychoanalytic orientations through its emphasis on using the therapeutic relationship to facilitate the child's innate developmental capacities and listening for unconscious communication that clarifies the impediments to the child or adolescent's psychological maturation. Slade (1994) hypothesized that as a result of play, the disturbed child can rely on the safety and security of being recognized by the therapist in order to integrate self-experience. For Frankel (1998), emotionally troubled children derive considerable benefit from play therapy simply by recognizing and accepting their experience of themselves. Moran (1987), Cohen and Solnit (1993), and Rosegrant (2001) worked out in detail how a psychoanalytic approach adds optimal tension and motivation for participating in the therapeutic interaction among children who have difficulty creating transitional phenomena in play. The tremendous clinical value that children with marked ego deficits can derive from psychoanalytic play therapy has also been discussed by Erikson (1950); Anna Freud (1965); Steingart (1983); Spiegel (1989); Cohen, Solnit, and Neubauer (1993); Neubauer (1993); Slade and Palmer Wolf (1994); Altman, Briggs, Frankel, Gensler, and Pantone (2000); Gaines (2003); and Levy (2008).

Psychoanalytic concepts of psychotic and borderline psychopathology in children and adolescents have similarly stressed the significance of underlying developmental delays and ego impairments that influence the child or adolescent's emotional lability and marked variability in thinking and reality testing. Delays and weaknesses in self- and object-constancy and anxiety about self-preservation are frequently apparent in the seriously disturbed child's disorganized play and anxiety-laden play themes. The severely disturbed child or adolescent's anxieties and overwhelming experiences of panic often occur simultaneously with temporary decompensations that are characterized by intrusions of primary process material (Chetick and Fast, 1970); a tenuous ego organization that is the basis for fluctuations between neurotic and psychotic experience (Ekstein and Wallerstein, 1954); shifting levels of functioning and a poor identity sense (Kernberg, 1980); impairments in object relations and separation-individuation (Mahler, 1967; Mahler, Pine, and Bergman, 1975); withdrawal from autonomous functioning in favor of regressed behavior (Masterson, 1978; Rinsley, 1980); developmental delays that intensify difficulties with affect regulation (Towbin, Dykens, Pearson, and Cohen, 1993); states of psychic fusion in symbiotic transference reactions (McCarthy, 1996); annihilation anxiety (Hurvich, 2000, 2002, 2003); disorganizing rage, the splitting of self and object representations; and feelings of helplessness brought about by a combination of a genetic predisposition, trauma, and broad-based developmental problems (Bleiberg, 1994, 2001).

With borderline and psychotic children and adolescents, their tenuous distinctions between internal and external reality reflect more primitive anxiety and more severe internalizing and externalizing symptoms that may be associated with considerable impairment in functioning (McCarthy, 1997). The psychoanalyst's empathic involvement with these children's most disorganizing anxieties recreates the internalized dangers in the midst of a supportive relationship that encourages transitional play. The therapeutic interventions are less focused on uncovering unconscious derivatives in the play and more focused on providing a greater organizing function. Through the engagement with the therapist and the continuity of the sessions, children and adolescents become better able to create meaning despite their disruptive anxieties and changing levels of psychic functioning. Significant attention is paid to these shifts and to the intrapsychic and interpersonal stimuli for the child's regressions, which are frequently recreated in the therapeutic relationship. As we will attempt to demonstrate through a case presentation, the interpretative interventions are designed to facilitate the play as a curative process. The immediacy of the therapeutic engagement renews the child and family's inherent potential for maturation and emotional growth. As Winnicott (1971) noted, the transitional nature of the engagement allows the child to merge with, make use of, and then separate from the analyst. This kind of therapeutic involvement with the borderline or psychotic child's inner world of annihilation anxiety shapes mutative opportunities for counteracting regressions through the gradual emergence of healthier defenses and more mature object relationships that bring about better functioning.

In order to illustrate the curative possibilities offered by psychoanalytically informed play therapy with children who have psychotic features and precursors of borderline personality disorder symptoms, in this chapter we present material from the play-based treatment of a 7-year-old girl who was seen in twice-weekly therapy sessions during the time she was enrolled in a special school for children with severe behavioral and emotional problems. By presenting actual clinical material and the thoughts it immediately generated, our goal is to focus a narrative lens on invoking resiliency. The reflective reactions to the disorganizing anxieties that occurred in the treatment sessions helped to free this child's inborn capacities for resilience. Bertha was a highly withdrawn, sporadically aggressive child of at least average intelligence who had intermittently bizarre behavior that on the surface appeared to be autistic or psychotic. She struggled with developmental delays in expressive language, attention, and impulse control and she demonstrated curtailed anxiety tolerance and frequent stereotypical behavior such as hand flapping. Bertha was seen in play therapy for a year and a half beginning in the late 1970s by Dr. Guarton, in consultation with Dr. McCarthy. Her behavior and her play themes during the sessions suggested her great difficulty preserving and integrating self and object representations, which is typical of disturbed children whose anxiety about self-preservation can become overwhelming even with the physical presence of the parent. Our report of the treatment begins with a description of Bertha's overall adjustment difficulties, followed by a summary of process notes and reactions to several of her sessions. We also include a brief discussion of her borderline and psychotic features and her developmental delays as they would be understood at present, in contrast to the dynamic formulations and the diagnostic considerations of 35 years ago.

Case Example

Bertha was an only child who lived with her parents, both immigrants from Argentina. She was an isolated, self-abusive girl with incapacitating anxiety symptoms who was originally described as being psychotic. She suffered from phobias about animals and had violent outbursts with her mother that had resulted in a brief psychiatric hospitalization when she was diagnosed with childhood schizophrenia and autistic features. Bertha's bizarre, illogical statements detracted from her limited ability to engage other children in spite of her warmth, and her stereotypical movements frightened them. Bertha was intensely afraid of dogs and garbage trucks, and would run away from her parents if she saw a dog in the street. She was highly oppositional, refusing even simple requests to change her clothes or to follow any routine at home. Bertha frequently had temper tantrums at home, in which she hit her mother or herself, pulled her own hair, or banged her head into the wall when she was asked to do something. At the time of Bertha's admission to a psychiatric hospital, she was found to be in a psychotic withdrawal, highly anxious, probably hallucinating, and incoherent in her communications. Bertha's description of her body at the beginning of therapy conveyed her disturbed body image: "*In my head I have water, animals, and things that kill. In my chest there are flowers.*" She was referred for outpatient therapy with little improvement after her hospital stay.

Developmental History

Bertha's early history was characterized by a prolonged separation from her parents who visited her periodically. At the age of 18 months, she was taken by her parents to live with her maternal grandmother in Argentina because of their financial difficulties trying to balance employment and childcare as recent immigrants. Bertha returned to live with her parents when she was 4 years old. Her early developmental history was reported as uneventful, except for delays in toilet training, and there was no reported history of mental illness in either of her parents' families. There were no early signs of deficits in her receptive or expressive language, her ability to form attachments to her parents and her grandmother, her social interactions with playmates, or any disturbances in reality testing. However, her oppositional behavior and temper tantrums and her regression became apparent at the time she returned home to her parents. At that time, Bertha began to limit much of her conversation to two- or three-word utterances, and to become increasingly moody and withdrawn. When she started psychotherapy at age 7, her aggressive outbursts occurred daily, mostly at home, and she was making minimal academic or social progress in school. In addition to Bertha's individual analytic sessions, her mother was seen in collateral sessions for supportive guidance concerning her daughter's behavior. Efforts to engage the parents in family sessions were unsuccessful, even though Bertha's mother eventually formed a very positive alliance with her therapist. The following session notes were written by Dr. Guarton shortly after the therapy sessions.

Attempt at a First Session

Bertha had been in the school for four days when I came to her classroom to meet her and to take her for play therapy. After her teacher introduced us, I sat by her on one of the chairs and explained that I worked with the children and that I had a room with toys that she might want to see. Bertha smiled in a friendly way and seemed eager to show me what she was working on in class until I mentioned the playroom, and she made it clear with gestures that she wouldn't leave the classroom. She remarked, "Not going to the hospital" several times, and I replied that I wasn't taking her to the hospital. I thought that she was probably reliving her experience of being left at the hospital without fully understanding that she was going to stay there. Although I could have reassured Bertha more, I felt that it was more important to help her to feel comfortable and to gradually develop her sense of trust. Bertha then walked around me singing a tune and repeating the phrases, "I am going home," "A dog bit me" (showing me a pimple on her arm), and "I like your dress." I answered with short phrases. "Yes, after school you are going home," "Oh, I see, how did it happen?" to which she replied: "In the street." I told her that I would come to see her another day when, if she wanted, she could accompany me to see the toys. She smiled, and I felt that we had made some emotional contact. The therapy had begun.

The First Session

Bertha readily took my hand and came to the playroom after I assured her that she could play with the toys and that I would stay with her for an hour before I would bring her back to the classroom. She looked at me intently, picked up a checkerboard, removed the checkers, and replaced them. Bertha then took a crayon and drew a person with a complete face, a torso, a rudimentary skirt, and much hair on the head but no arms and legs, and she noted, "It's a mommy." Since the figure seemed to be smiling, I commented, "She is smiling." Bertha answered, "She is happy now." At that point, Bertha went to the toy box and took out a baby doll as she started to hum a rhythm. She began playing with the doll, holding her close to her body and then moving her away. She laid down on the floor and gently placed the doll beside her as she continued to move it back and forth. The doll was never further away than an arm's length. When Bertha started to put the doll back in the toy box she noticed a brown spot on its thigh and said, "She has poop." I responded, "Yes, I see. She wants to make poop?" and she nodded, "Yes." I then pointed to a chair as I prompted her, "Let's use this as a toilet." She sat the doll on the chair, took her off, and complained, "This is not a toilet." I asked, "Do you want to take her to a real toilet?" When she said "Yes," I took Bertha and the doll to a ladies' room that could be locked from the inside.

Bertha looked at the toilet in a frightened way and tried to sit the doll on the toilet seat, but she was hesitant and unable to do so. I helped her hold the doll on the toilet seat. Bertha looked surprised and smiled as she said, "She is not afraid. No, she is not afraid." I answered, "She made poop. Does she want me to flush?" When I flushed the toilet as we both held the doll, Bertha's whole body trembled and she stated, "She is angry. She was beaten." She then stroked the seat of the toilet, while carefully looking inside. I asked if she was still angry, and she said, "No." She looked at the baby doll, which she was now holding, and I asked, "How does the doll feel?" She answered, "Well." By then, Bertha was standing close to me. She looked at my face and slowly moved her face closer to mine until her lips were touching my face, but she did not kiss me. I stayed there contentedly as Bertha had the doll kiss my face, and I returned the kiss. After Bertha washed her hands, she calmly returned to the playroom and went back to her classroom without saying anything.

Reflections on the First Session

Although I expected that Bertha would come to the session, I was relieved that she did. Leaving the classroom with a stranger had frightened her. I remembered other young children and their reactions to unfamiliar people and surroundings. I was convinced that I had to allow Bertha to trust and to mistrust me in order to struggle with her fears of separateness and growth. In the session, she had initially approached safe, familiar play material. When she completed a picture of a mother and described her as being "well," she was communicating something positive about herself and probably also something that was comforting about my presence. She could have been expressing a desire for a deeper, more stable, predictable relationship with her mother. Developmentally, her drawing corresponded to that of a 4- or 5-year-old child, and her expressive language was at the level of a 3-year-old child.

When Bertha played with the baby doll, she seemed to be enacting ambivalent early attachment experiences. She had been separated from her parents when she was 18 months old. During her play fantasy in the bathroom, I had hoped that her fear and excitement would not become too over stimulating. Much had been accomplished as she held the doll and later approached and avoided the toilet. Bertha's holding of the doll, her symbolic letting go of the feces with a fear of disappearing and of being dissolved, and her fear of her own aggression and later retaliation, all pointed to developmental issues of object constancy and toddlerhood. I shared the changing emotions that Bertha experienced as we recreated critical moments. Since I experienced the cascading shifts in Bertha's feelings, I was struck by my limited understanding of what had taken place even though I sensed that Bertha might be starting to feel more secure. The immediacy of her dramatization of her conflicts suggested their disorganizing quality and the vulnerability of her ego functions.

The Fifth Session

After Bertha showed me a picture of fruit she had colored, she picked up a stuffed toy shark and said, "Shark, monster, it's going to eat me. It's going to eat me." She cuddled the "baby" shark, opening and closing its mouth, and added, "It's a baby shark. He is going to eat you. He is angry, was bad to his mother. His mother scolded him. Tell him to 'shut up'. Tell him to 'shut up'." At that point, I hesitated because I did not know whether to consider the shark as a "bad" part of Bertha that wanted to be controlled, or as a representation of another aspect of Bertha that was being shut up by her mother. Finally, I instructed her that "I might tell him to 'shut up,' but first I would like to hear what he has to say." Bertha continued: "Now, he didn't put his pants on, didn't put his pants on because he was angry. His mother scolded him because he didn't wear his pants." I agreed that, "He was angry at his mother and that's why he didn't wear his pants." She then opened the shark's mouth wide and put her head inside, asking, "Can you lie down, sir? Lie down," and she placed the shark carefully on the toy shelf. Although I sensed that I was missing some important material during this sequence, I was very impressed by Bertha's affectionate cuddling of the angry shark, and I wondered how much of her anger expressed dissociated grief.

Bertha next picked up a baby doll from a crib, saying, "That's my doll. She put a dress on, see. She is not naked." I confirmed, "She likes to get dressed." "Yes," she replied, "but he (the shark) doesn't wear pants. The mommy dressed her, but the shark doesn't let her dress him. He is angry. See how pretty she looks, but he doesn't let her put his pants on. He is naked. She doesn't have shoes, didn't put any shoes on. Let's find shoes, okay?" "What kind of shoes should we look for?" I asked. "Pretty shoes," she replied. "Poor baby, she has no shoes, okay?" Since I sensed that she wanted me to provide for her while testing my availability I created a pair of shoes out of tissue paper and taped them to the doll's feet. Bertha smiled in response, hugged the doll, put her in a crib, and rocked her.

Bertha then shifted with no apparent transition and looked at the male doll. "The mommy is beating him and he is crying, because he doesn't listen." Next, she picked up a Barbie doll, "This is his mommy. He took her blouse and he pulled her hair. The poor mommy. He pulls because the mommy beat him." Next, Bertha turned to me and asked, "Is your name Grandmother?" I was surprised and touched. I answered, "My name can be Grandmother if you want it to be." Bertha approached the male doll and observed, "Yes, he put the pants on. He didn't get angry at the pants. No. Please don't get angry at the pants. He put them on. He is not angry at them."

Reflections on the Fifth Session

Bertha and I had met for only five sessions, and although the gains she made were by no means stable, she seemed to be deeply involved in an effort to enact her conflicts. She had demonstrated trust openly by asking me whether my name was "Grandmother" as a wish that she could endow me with greater strength and more nurturing attributes. However, I believed that I did not exist for Bertha outside of the playroom. Her difficulty retaining an internal image of me stemmed from her regressed psychic development in addition to her cognitive difficulties in sustaining thoughts and sequential thinking. There had also been some irregularity in the schedule of sessions because of holidays and vacations.

I was fascinated by Bertha's eagerness to recreate her conflicts in the sessions in spite of her anxieties, and I was pleased that her grimacing and her biting herself had significantly decreased. Not only was Bertha becoming more focused and more engaged during the play, but her speech was also gradually improving with fewer reported periods of muteness in school. In the previous sessions, she hadn't been able to state that a doll was angry without immediately denying it or projecting the anger, and then becoming frightened and confused about what was real. As I gained greater trust in my own reactions to Bertha, my feelings changed from awe, curiosity, and protectiveness, to awareness of the need for Bertha to experience her hateful feelings and to test my hope that the treatment would reinforce her resilience in the face of her developmental delays and ego impairments. In the session, Bertha had expressed her fear of her own anger, attributed to the shark, and her disavowed perception of herself as "bad" because of her defiance and her anger with her mother. She had urged me to tell the shark to "shut up," but I had initially declined out of concern that I would reify her designation of the doll as socialized and "good," and add to her uncertainty about whether I was afraid of her anger. Bertha's affection with the shark as a self-representation seemed promising. Her pulling of the mother doll's hair was done carefully with some restraint, perhaps as an expression of appreciation that there was now a grandmother participating in her life and in her internal representational world.

The Sixth Session

Bertha began the session by silently taking the baby doll and sitting her on a training toilet that I had put in the playroom. "She made pee," she said. Bertha then played with toy cars and trucks until she laid down on the floor and admitted, "The bathroom scares me. I am going to make poop and pee here. The other one scares me." She then sat on the potty and said, "I need paper." After I gave her some tissue paper, she pretended to defecate and to wipe herself. She added, "The doggie is going to make poop," as she sat the toy dog on the toilet. "He made it now, and the shark is going to make poop. They are happy." I asked if they were happy before, and she replied, "No, they were scared that the toilet was angry." She continued, "The doggie washes her hands, takes a bath . . . The mommy doesn't take a bath." I asked, "How come the mommy doesn't take a bath?" She answered, "The mommy likes to be dirty. She beat me on the head." Bertha then tried to put the potty inside the dollhouse even though it was obviously too big, and she explained, "This is the toilet. The mommy makes poop here. Bertha also makes poop here, and she is not scared anymore."

Bertha then switched affective themes. She began to appear agitated as she started singing and smiling. She suddenly yelled, talking to the air, "Go to hell." I asked, "Was someone bothering you?" She did not answer, but smiled, approaching the toilet, and softened: "I am going to make poop for real. Now throw it out. You throw it out?" At that point, she grimaced, engaged in some hand flapping, and stated, "You throw the toilet out. Look, this is named toilet. No, it's a girl toilet. The girl toilet is angry." "The girl toilet is angry?" I asked, and she replied, "Yes," before remaining silent for a prolonged period. Bertha then began to open and close some toy purses. "Kim hit me yesterday." I asked, "How did you feel then?" and she said, "Angry." She next took a girl doll, pulled its pants down and then pulled them up. Bertha noted, "She gets dressed . . . she gets dressed. He doesn't," (pointing to the shark). Prior to the end of the session, Bertha approached the potty again and asked me to clean it. As I did, she watched intently and promised: "Next time I will go to the bathroom by myself. I am not scared."

Reflections on the Sixth Session

Bertha's parents had reacted to her violent outbursts by feeling overwhelmed and hopeless, but there had been no indications of any physical punishment or abuse. I wondered whether Bertha's rage and anxiety about toilet training had fused her anxiety about annihilation with her confusion and despair about the separations from her mother and her grandmother. As these anxieties had intensified in the session, Bertha had regressed in reality testing and revealed momentary thought disorder. Her exclamations, "Go to hell . . . is here. Go to hell," seemed designed to try to overcome persecutory anxiety. For the first time, Bertha had spoken to someone or something that was not identifiably present. Although I wondered if she had been hallucinating, I imagined that she might also have been courageously challenging her fears. Her statement, "The girl toilet is angry," had suggested multiple explanations. Was Bertha at last feeling safe enough to risk feeling anger and rage with me? Was the toilet angry at Bertha and at me? Her remarks about the female doll getting dressed, even though the male shark didn't, also offered many possible meanings that I had decided not to interpret for the present. The happy ending to the session seemed to reflect Bertha's need for continued attachment in the face of her destabilizing anxieties. Her promise to go to the bathroom by herself reinforced my hope that true internalization might be possible on the way to her development of more whole object-relationships.

Summary

At first, Bertha's play in the sessions suggested that her anxieties about aggression and survival had disrupted her development of stable object relations and rational thought. For the first few months, Bertha's behavior in the sessions often resembled that of a one-and-a-half- to 2-year-old child, who had not yet achieved psychic integration or age-appropriate abilities to localize aggression and to process reality-based language. Her bizarre body image and her self-abuse indicated that she had not learned to distinguish between the internal and the external, or fantasy and reality, distinctions that should be well established by latency. When Bertha designated the "girl toilet" as an important element in her play, she signaled that she could not fully differentiate either herself or her internal objects from inanimate objects in her environment. Her capacity for reality testing became temporarily impaired in the face of annihilation anxiety, and her play generally lacked Oedipal material and symbolic themes that would be expected of a latency-aged child.

Even though the drawings that Bertha completed in the sessions resembled those of a 4- or 5-year-old child, she made excellent use of drawing to convey her shifting internal preoccupations, such as with the dangerous doll/mommy who could be brought close for unconscious merger or moved away for greater separateness with accompanying fears of retaliation. Although there was little content interpretation during the sessions, the play itself was crucial for Bertha's mastery of her fears of annihilation, of being eaten and swallowed by the hungry shark or by the aggressive, devouring toilet. Bertha's willingness to be soothed by having her doll held over the toilet proved to be a turning point, which ensured that neither she nor her analyst would be destroyed by their intimate connection or by her own feces. This bad, "angry" doll who had been "beaten" sought the unconditional mirroring and loving protection of a "grandmother" who provided her with ego and body definition without interpreting her disturbing conflicts. Bertha's willingness to straighten up and clean the playroom suggested that she sought containment while she initiated a more adaptive use of her compulsive doing and undoing. Her fears of abandonment and identity loss as a result of her rageful impulses and her anger at separation became less destabilizing as she symbolically differentiated her own feelings from those of her analyst/mother.

By the time of the termination of the treatment, which occurred when the family returned to Argentina, Bertha's overall functioning showed a remarkable improvement. Her phobias, as well as her aggressive and self-abusive behavior, had been eliminated. Speech and language services had not been available for Bertha and she continued to lag behind other children her age in grasping some nuances of social interactions, but she acquired several friends. She began participating in a relatively active social life and communicating with both adults and peers with less anxiety and hesitation. Bertha's concentration and her learning blossomed. Her relationship with her mother became closer, with greater spontaneity and playfulness in their interactions. Bertha's mother reported that the discussions about her lengthy separation from her daughter had empowered her to take a more active role as a mother. She had begun to view Bertha and relate to her as a child who needed her and whom she could help, instead of seeing her as someone whose defiant, strange behaviors were a shameful reflection of her incompetence.

Discussion

During Bertha's early period of hospitalization, her emotional and behavioral problems had been diagnosed as an expression of a subtype of childhood schizophrenia in which infantile autism was accompanied by widespread, nonspecific neurodevelopmental delays that might have been exacerbated by pervasive anxieties and neonatal sequelae (Bender, 1969), and she was treated with antipsychotic medication and speech therapy. Mahler (1972), and Mahler, Pine, and Bergman's (1975) concept of an impaired infantile symbiosis was gaining increasing dominance at that time as possible psychodynamic factors in childhood psychosis and developmental delays that stemmed from early disturbances in the separation-individuation phase of psychological development. The concept of impaired symbiotic relatedness shares common conceptual ground with Winnicott's (1971) portraits of disturbed transitional experience in children with severe ego impairments. Bertha either had not experienced or had not retained internalizations of transitional phenomena and play, and had been left without stable me/not-me experience that could sustain self-differentiation. Although there had been no evidence of any physical or sexual abuse during Bertha's stay in Argentina, we were mindful of the possibility of its occurrence. Despite Bertha's exhibiting sporadic psychotic signs of unrelatedness and marked thought disorder during the course of her psychoanalytic treatment, her adjustment difficulties were viewed in the sessions as manifestations of emergent borderline personality features in a traumatized child whose ego organization had been crippled by destabilizing anxieties about permanence and survival (Ekstein and Wallerstein, 1956). In addition, her impairments also fit with the possibility that, far from constituting a psychotic disorder, her hallucinations and thought disorder could be accounted for, in part, as a reflection of receptive and expressive language delays, which had contributed to her bizarre communication and adversely affected many aspects of her ego development (Dossetor, 2007). Research has demonstrated that children with autistic-like features often have marked weaknesses in social cognition and the theory of mind associated with their pragmatic language impairments (Cicchetti, Beeghly, Carlson, and Toth, 1990). Our retrospective review of the treatment more the 35 years later endorsed the relevance of both of these hypotheses.

Bertha used the transference relationship in order to sustain a maturational process of play and to strengthen her ego functions, especially her relatedness and reality testing. Her treatment provided an opportunity for speculating about the spectrum of psychoanalytic developmental theories of borderline psychopathology. At the time of Bertha's analytic treatment, the role of her transference attachment in her achieving psychic stability and overcoming her vacillation between fluctuating psychotic and neurotic experience could have been conceptualized as improved mastery of the drives (Freud); enhanced ego autonomy and the resolution of drive fixations (Anna Freud); the establishment of the depressive position (Klein); the fortunate attainment of a compensatory holding environment (Winnicott) through play; the consolidation of a more stable, nurturing self object through the development of a mirror transference (Kohut); and a more secure re-experiencing of the rapprochement phase of separation-individuation with the analyst (Mahler). If it was reported accurately, Bertha's marked deterioration from "normal" functioning in speech and relatedness during her first year and a half to her anxiety-filled withdrawal at age 4 fit clearly with Mahler's conception of regression in a symbiotic psychosis of infancy. Bertha's consistent reliance on emphatic interpretative clarifications of her moods and feelings throughout the treatment seemed to indicate the presence of a closely attuned mirror transference, which helped to stabilize her experience of self in spite of her psychotic level of anxiety about oral aggression and identity loss. The recreation in the therapeutic relationship of the dissociated obstacles to Bertha's maturation was consistent with how the treatment might be understood from a current interpersonal, relational perspective (Altman, Briggs, Frankel, Gensler, and Patone, 2000). Her use of the identification of her anxieties as the groundwork for the elaboration of psychological tructure resonated with Kohut's concept of transmuting internalizations of maternal functions. It also illustrated Anna Freud's emphasis on the essential nature of positive transference for the successful treatment of children, as well as Winnicott's underscoring of transitional experience in play as involving the child's use of both internal and external reality in order to become integrated.

Conclusions

Bertha had been able to say very little about her feelings and her prolonged separation from her mother, but aspects of their relationship seemed to be present in the partly nonverbal interactions in the therapy. The interactions were curative by providing an atmosphere for Bertha to play and to rely on the therapeutic relationship to develop better reality testing and self-regulatory capacities. The sessions with Bertha emphasized the psychoanalytically informed play itself as the therapy, rather than unearthing and interpreting unconscious psychodynamic meaning. Bleiberg (1994, 2001) emphasized the role of trauma in personality disorder symptoms in children, particularly borderline personality disorders, which entail a kind of reversal of traumatic helplessness that has permeated the child's maladaptive defenses and relationships. Towbin, Dykins, Pearson, and Cohen (1993) used standardized measures to validate criteria for an early onset, multiple complex development disorder, defined by disturbances in thinking, affect regulation, and social relatedness that are present in children with schizophrenia, borderline syndrome of childhood, and pervasive developmental disorder. Today, Bertha's clinical features would no longer be conceptualized as indicative of childhood schizophrenia. Her severe symptoms and developmental anomalies would be congruent with both Bleiberg's (2001) and Towbin, Dykens, Pearson, and Cohen's (1993) views about the etiology and the persistence of borderline phenomena in childhood. They would likewise be consistent with research findings about comorbidity and the confluence of developmental disorder deficits and psychotic symptoms in atypical early development. Signs of psychosis, such as hallucinatory experience, in a child with marked developmental disabilities can easily be misinterpreted as being diagnostic of a true psychotic disorder.

Rather than attempting to reconstruct a comprehensive case presentation or a complete summary of the relevant scientific literature, we have placed the powerful connection with this extraordinary child at the center of the interpretative inquiry. We have limited our review by offering a glimpse of the fiercely emotional atmosphere that evolved in the psychoanalytic relationship with a child who demonstrated remarkable recuperative powers. Advances in knowledge about developmental disabilities, early psychopathology, attachment theory research, and voluminous studies about brain structure and functioning have all added substantially to the understanding of the diverse interacting developmental trajectories that give rise to early signs of disturbance. Bertha's ability to accept her own fears and destructive wishes without being condemned by an admired other and substitute parent figure facilitated her efforts to play and to delineate an integrated sense of self. Her success in tolerating an emotionally intense therapeutic alliance reflected considerable resilience. The terror and the tender longings that she revealed in her sessions epitomized the conflicts about relatedness and the emotional dilemmas of borderline and psychotic children.

References

Altman, N., Briggs, R., Frankel, J., Gensler, D., & Pantone, P. (2000) *Relational Child Therapy.* New York, NY: Other Press.

Axline, V. (1947). *Play Therapy: The Inner Dynamics of Childhood.* Boston, MA: Houghton Mifflin.

Baggerly, J., & Bratton, S. (2010). Building a firm foundation in play therapy research: Responses to Phillips. *International Journal of Play Therapy,* 19, 26–38.

Bender, L. (1969). A longitudinal study of schizophrenic children with autism. *Hospital and Community Psychiatry,* 20, 28–35.

Bleiberg, E. (1994). Borderline disorders in children and adolescents: The concept, the diagnosis and the controversies. *Bulletin of the Menninger Clinic,* 58, 169–196.

Bleiberg, E. (2001). *Treating Personality Disorders in Children and Adolescents: A Relational Approach.* New York, NY: Guilford Press.

Bornstein, B. (1945). Clinical notes on child analysis. *Psychoanalytic Study of the Child,* 1, 151–166.

Bratton, S. C., Ray, D., Rhine, T., & Jones, L. (2005). The efficacy of play therapy with children: A meta-analytic review of treatment outcomes. *Professional Psychology: Research and Practice,* 36, 376–390.

Bretherton, I. (1984). *Symbolic Play: The Development of Social Understanding.* Orlando, FL: Academic Press.

Chetik, M., & Fast, I. (1970). A function of fantasy in the borderline child. *American Journal of Orthopsychiatry,* 49, 756–765.

Cicchetti, D., Beeghly, M., Carlson, V., & Toth, S. (1990).The emergence of the self in atypical populations. In D. Cicchetti & M. Beeghly (Eds.), *The Self in Transition: Infancy to Childhood* (pp. 309–344). Chicago, IL: University of Chicago Press.

Cohen, D., & Solnit, A. (1993). Play and therapeutic interaction. *Psychoanalytic Study of the Child,* 48, 49–63.

Cohen, D. J., Solnit, A.P., & Neubauer, P. (1993). *The Many Meanings of Play.* New Haven, CT: Yale University Press.

Connolly, J.A., & Doyle, A. (1984). Relation of social fantasy play to social competence in preschoolers. *Developmental Psychology,* 20, 797–806.

Dossetor, D.R. (2007). 'All that glitters is not gold': Misdiagnosis of psychosis in pervasive developmental disorder: A case series. *Clinical Child Psychology and Psychiatry,* 12, 537–548.

Drewes, A.A., (2006). Play-based interventions. *Journal of Early Childhood and Infant Psychology,* 2, 139–156.

Drewes, A.A. (2009). *Blending Play Therapy with Cognitive Behavior Therapy: Evidence–Based and Other Effective Treatments and Techniques.* Hoboken, NJ: John Wiley.

Drucker, J. (1994). Constructing metaphors: The role of symbolization in the treatment of children. In A. Slade & D. Palmer Wolf (Eds.), *Children at Play: Clinical and*

Developmental Approaches to Meaning and Representation (pp. 62–80). Oxford, UK: Oxford University Press.

Ekstein, R., & Wallerstein, J. (1954). Observations on the psychology of borderline and psychotic children. *Psychoanalytic Study of the Child,* 9, 344–369.

Ekstein, R., & Wallerstein, J. (1956). Observations on the psychotherapy of borderline and psychotic children. *Psychoanalytic Study of the Child*, 11, 303–311.

Erikson, E. (1950). *Childhood and Society.* New York, NY: Norton.

First, E. (1994). The leaving game, or I'll play you and you play me: The emergence of dramatic role play in 2 year olds. In A. Slade & D. Palmer Wolf (Eds.), *Children at Play: Clinical and Developmental Approaches to Meaning and Representation* (pp. 111–132). Oxford, UK: Oxford University Press.

Fisher, E. (1992). The impact of play on development: A meta-analysis. *Play and Culture,* 5, 159–181.

Fonagy, P., Gergely, G., Jurist, P., & Target, M. (2004). *Affect Regulation, Mentalization, and the Development of the Self.* New York, NY: Free Press.

Frankel, J. (1998). The play's the thing: How the essential processes of therapy are seen more clearly in child therapy. *Psychoanalytic Dialogues,* 8, 149–182.

Freud, A. (1928). *Introduction to the Technique of Child Analysis.* New York, NY: Nervous and Mental Disease Publishing.

Freud, A. (1936). *The Ego and the Mechanisms of Defense,* New York, NY: International Universities Press.

Freud, A. (1946). *The Psychoanalytic Treatment of Children.* London, UK: Imago.

Freud, A. (1965). *Normality and Pathology in Childhood.* New York, NY: International Universities Press.

Freud, A. (1970). Child analysis as a subspecialty of psychoanalysis. *The Writings of Anna Freud,* 7, New York, NY: International Universities Press.

Freud, S. (1909). The analysis of a phobia in a five year old boy. In J. Strachey (Ed.), *The Standard Edition of the Complete Psychological Works of Sigmund Freud* (Vol. 10, pp. 5–147). London, UK: Hogarth Press.

Freud, S. (1911). Formulations regarding two principles in mental functioning. *Collected Papers,* 4, 13–21, London, UK: Hogarth Press, 1948.

Freud, S. (1915). Repression. In J. Strachey (Ed.), *The Standard Edition of the Complete Psychological Works of Sigmund Freud* (Vol. 14, pp. 141–158). London, UK: Hogarth Press.

Freud, S. (1920). Beyond the pleasure principle. In J. Strachey (Ed.), *The Standard Edition of The Complete Psychological Works of Sigmund Freud* (Vol. 18, pp. 7–67). London, UK: Hogarth Press.

Gaines, R. (2003). Therapist self-disclosure with children, adolescents, and their parents. *Journal of Clinical Psychology,* 59, 569–580.

Gardner, R. A. (1971). *Therapeutic Communication with Children: The Mutual Story Telling Technique.* New York, NY: Aronson.

Gardner, R. A. (1975). *Psychotherapeutic Approaches to the Resistant Child.* New York, NY: Aronson.

Greenspan, S. I., & Lourie, R. S. (1981). Developmental structuralist approach to the classification of adaptive and pathologic personality organizations: Infancy and early childhood. *American Journal of Psychiatry,* 138, 725–735.

Guerney, L. (2001). Child-centered play therapy. *International Journal of Play Therapy,* 10(2), 13–31.

Harter, S. (1977). A cognitive-developmental approach to children's expression of conflict feelings and a technique to facilitate such expressions in play therapy. *Journal of Consulting and Clinical Psychology,* 45, 417–432.

Hug-Hellmuth, H. (1921). On the technique of child analysis. *International Journal of Psycho-Analysis,* 2, 287.

Hurvich, M. (2000). Fears of being overwhelmed and psychoanalytic theories of anxiety. *Psychoanalytic Review,* 87, 615–649.

Hurvich, M. (2002). Symbolization, desymbolization, and annihilation anxieties. In R. Lasky (Ed.), *Symbolization and Desymbolization: Essays in Honor of Norbert Freedman* (pp. 347–365). New York, NY: Karnac Books.

Hurvich, M. (2003). The place of annihilation anxieties in psychoanalytic theory. *Journal of the American Psychoanalytic Association,* 51, 59–66.

Kaduson, H. G., Cangelosi, D, & Schaefer, C. E., (1997). *The Playing Cure: Individual Play Therapy for Specific Childhood Problems.* Northvale, NJ: Aronson.

Kaduson, H. G., & Schaefer, C. E. (2006). *101 Favorite Play Therapy Techniques.* Lanham, MD: Rowan & Littlefield.

Kaplan, L. (1978). *Oneness and Separateness: From Infant to Individual.* New York, NY: Simon & Schuster.

Kernberg, P. F. (1980). Issues in the psychotherapy of borderline conditions in childhood. In K. Robson (Ed.), *The Borderline Child.* New York, NY: McGraw Hill.

Kernberg, P. F., Chazan, S. E., & Normandin, L. (1998). The Children's Play Therapy Instrument (CPTI): Description, development, and reliability studies. *Journal of Psychotherapy Practice and Research,* 7, 196–207.

Klein, M. (1932). *The Psycho-Analysis of Children.* London, UK: Hogarth Press.

Klein, M. (1955). The psychoanalytic play technique. *American Journal of Orthopsychiatry,* 25, 223–237.

Knell, S. M. (1998). Cognitive-behavioral play therapy. *Journal of Clinical Child Psychology,* 27(1), 28–33.

Kritzberg, N. I. (1975). *The Structured Therapeutic Game Method of Psychoanalytic Psychotherapy.* Hicksville, NY: Exposition.

Landreth, G. (1991). *Play Therapy: The Art of the Relationship.* Bristol, PA: Accelerated Development.

Landreth, G. (2002). *Play Therapy: The Art of the Relationship.* New York: NY: Brunner-Mazel.

LeBlanc, M., & Ritchie, M. (1999). Predictors of play therapy outcome. *International Journal of Play Therapy,* 8(2), 19–34.

LeBlanc, M., & Ritchie, M. (2001). A meta-analysis of play therapy outcomes. *Counseling Psychology Quarterly,* 14, 149–163.

Levy, A. (2008). The therapeutic action of play therapy in the psychodynamic treatment of children: A critical analysis. *Clinical Social Work Journal,* 36, 281–291.

Mahler, M. (1967). On human symbiosis and the vicissitudes of individuation. *Journal of the American Psychoanalytic Association,* 15, 740–763.

Mahler, M. (1972). A study of the separation-individuation process and its possible application to borderline phenomena in the psychoanalytic situation. *Psychoanalytic Study of the Child,* 26, 403–426.

Mahler, M., Pine. F., & Bergman, A. (1975). *The Psychological Birth of the Human Infant.* New York, NY: Basic Books.

Masterson, J. (1978). The borderline adolescent: An object relations view. *Adolescent Psychiatry,* 6, 344–359.
McCarthy, J. (1996). Paranoia and omnipotent symbiosis in borderline adolescents. *Journal of the American Academy of Psychoanalysis,* 24, 45–59.
McCarthy, J. (1997) Narcissistic adolescents' object relations. *Psychoanalytic Psychology,* 14, 95–112.
Moran, G. (1987). Some functions of play and playfulness. A developmental perspective. *Psychoanalytic Study of the Child,* 42, 11–29.
Moustakas, C. (1953). *Children in Play Therapy.* New York, NY: McGraw Hill.
Neubauer, P. (1993). Playing: Technical implications. In A. Solnit, D. Cohen, & P. Nuebauer (Eds.), *The Many Meanings of Play.* New Haven, CT: Yale University Press.
Piaget, J. (1962). *Play, Dreams and Imitation in Childhood.* New York, NY: Norton.
Piaget, J. (1965). *The Moral Judgment of the Child.* New York, NY: Free Press.
Perry, L., & Landreth, C. (1991). Diagnostic assessment of children's play therapy behavior. In C. Schaefer, K. Gitlin, & S. Sandgrund (Eds.), *Play Therapy: Diagnosis and Assessment.* (pp. 643–660). New York, NY: John Wiley.
Ray, D., Bratton, S., Rhine, T., & Jones, L. (2001). The effectiveness of play therapy: Responding to crisis. *International Journal of Play Therapy,* 10(1), 85–108.
Rennie, R., & Landreth, G. (2000). Effects of filial therapy on parent and child behaviors. *International Journal of Child Therapy,* 9, 19–37.
Rinsley, D. (1980). Diagnosis and treatment of borderline and narcissistic children and adolescents. *Bulletin of the Menninger Clinic,* 44, 147–170.
Rosegrant, J. (2001). The psychoanalytic play state. *Journal of Clinical Psychoanalysis,* 10, 323–343.
Russ, S. (2004). *Play in Child Development and Psychotherapy: Towards Empirically Supported Practice.* Mahwah, NJ: Lawrence Erlbaum Associates.
Scarlett, M. W., (1994). The relation between anxiety and pretend play. In A. Slade & D. Palmer Wolf (Eds.), *Children at Play: Clinical and Developmental Approaches to Meaning and Representation* (pp. 48–61). Oxford, UK: Oxford University Press.
Schaefer, C. E. (1993). *The Therapeutic Power of Play.* Northvale, NJ: Aronson.
Schaefer, C. E. (1999). Curative factors in play therapy. *Journal for the Professional Counselor,* 14, 7–16.
Schaefer, C. E. (2011). *Foundations of Play Therapy.* Hoboken, NJ: John Wiley.
Schaefer, C. E., Gitlin, K., & Sandgrund, S. (1991). *Play Therapy: Diagnosis and Assessment.* New York, NY: John Wiley.
Slade, A. (1986). Symbolic play and separation-individuation: A naturalistic study. *Bulletin of the Menninger Clinic,* 50, 78–85.
Slade, A. (1987). The quality of attachment and early symbolic play. *Developmental Psychology,* 23, 78–85.
Slade, A. (1994). Making meaning and making believe: Their role in the clinical process. In A. Slade & D. Palmer Wolf (Eds.), *Children at Play: Clinical and Developmental Approaches to Meaning and Representation* (pp. 81–110). Oxford, UK: Oxford University Press.
Slade, A., & Palmer Wolf, D. (1994). *Children at Play: Clinical and Developmental Approaches to Meaning and Representation.* Oxford, UK: Oxford University Press.
Solomon, J. C. (1938). Active play therapy. *American Journal of Orthopsychiatry,* 8(3), 479–498.

Sperling, E. (1997). The role of play in child psychotherapy. *Child and Adolescent Psychiatric Clinics of North America*, 6(1), 69–79.
Spiegel, S. (1989). *An Interpersonal Approach to Child Therapy.* New York, NY: Columbia University Press.
Steingart, I. (1983). *Pathological play in Borderline and Narcissistic Personalities.* New York, NY: S. P. Scientific Books.
Sullivan, H. S. (1956). *The Interpersonal Theory of Psychiatry.* New York, NY: Norton.
Towbin, K., Dykens, E., Pearson, G., and Cohen, D. (1993). Conceptualizing a borderline syndrome of childhood and a childhood schizophrenia as a developmental disorder. *Journal of the American Academy of Child and Adolescent Psychiatry,* 32, 775–782.
VanFleet, R. (1994). *Filial Therapy: Strengthening Parent–Child Relationships through Play.* Sarsota, FL: Professional Resources Press.
VanFleet, R., Lilly, J., & Kaduson, H. (1999). Play therapy for children exposed to violence: Individual, family, and community interventions. *International Journal of Play Therapy,* 8(1), 27–42.
Waelder, R. (1932). The psychoanalytic theory of play. *Psychoanalytic Quarterly,* 2, 208–224.
Winnicott, D. W. (1953). Transitional objects and transitional phenomena; a study of the first not-me possession. *International Journal of Psycho-Analysis,* 34, 89–97.
Winnicott, D. W. (1968). Playing: Its theoretical status in the clinical situation. *International Journal of Psycho-Analysis,* 49, 591–599.
Winnicott, D. W. (1971). *Playing and Reality.* New York, NY: Basic Books.
Winnicott, D. W. (1975). *Through Pediatrics to Psychoanalysis.* London, UK: Hogarth Press.

8

CORE ELEMENTS OF PSYCHODYNAMIC TECHNIQUE

Allan M. Eisenberg

The following chapter represents an effort to extract some essential principles of technique from more than twenty-five years of psychotherapeutic practice with deeply troubled children, as well as with many adults whose lives display the aftereffects of difficult childhoods. It also reflects a distillation of my work as a clinical supervisor—what it is I have sought to convey to supervisees, and what they report to have found most useful clinically. While there is currently an array of supposedly new, more efficient approaches to psychotherapy in the mental health marketplace, I believe, with Shedler (2010), that the psychoanalytic tradition and some of its core concepts underlie many of these approaches. In fact, psychoanalytic ideas have so permeated our culture that it would be difficult to undertake almost any form of psychotherapy without revealing their pervasive influence. Contemporary views of human functioning almost invariably make use of such phenomena as unconscious motivation, projection, denial, regression, identification, fixation, the recurring effects of childhood conflicts, the connection between anxiety and defense, and other ideas of psychological functioning too numerous to mention, but whose origins lie within the psychoanalytic tradition. My own work has been firmly rooted in the psychoanalytic or psychodynamic (I use these terms interchangeably) tradition, which for me remains the most comprehensive and effective approach for exploring and ameliorating psychological distress at all levels.

In referring to the "psychoanalytic" or "psychodynamic" tradition I am including a very broad array of thinkers, starting with Freud, but including the contributions of ego psychology, object relations theory, attachment theory, self-psychology, relational psychoanalysis, and other currents within this well-known tradition, especially psychoanalytic developmental theory. In spite of their enormous therapeutic value with children, adolescents, and adults, the approaches that reflect this tradition are currently out of favor in most institutional settings, discouraged in private practice, and are at risk of falling out of the curricula of many university graduate departments. Notwithstanding the short-sightedness of the current climate in its enthusiasm for time-limited treatments which are not always matched with patients' needs, psychodynamic thinking continues to permeate the atmosphere of psychotherapy and continues to provide therapists and patients alike with opportunities to think in depth about their lives, their relationships, their origins and their possibilities, and to help them to chart pathways toward meaningful change.

There has been significant change over the last thirty to forty years both in approaches to mental health treatment in general and within the psychodynamic tradition in particular. No working clinician can fail to have registered or in some fashion been affected by these changes. And yet, for those of us in the psychodynamic tradition who have practiced over many years, what is perhaps more striking than change is a remarkable theme of consistency in the clinical encounter with patients—a consistency across differing theoretical orientations within psychoanalysis and a consistency from early practice to contemporary practice. This consistency of clinical approach within the psychoanalytic tradition also runs across diagnostic categories and clinical settings. In this chapter, I will attempt to identify some of the abiding characteristics of clinical technique that characterize all of the psychodynamic approaches to treatment. By looking closely at what dynamically oriented therapists actually do in their up-close interactions with patients, I hope to extract the implicit guidelines that inform and regulate the clinical encounter. The microscopic attunement that characterizes this kind of clinical engagement is at the heart of psychodynamic approaches to therapy, promoting emotional growth as well as behavioral and symptomatic improvement.

Clinical Exchanges and Core Elements of Technique

Clinical discussions and consultations with colleagues and supervisees have helped to cement my conviction that there are core aspects of clinical technique that reflect an amalgam of theory, values, and cultural norms that guide the practice of dynamically oriented clinicians. While we may wish that theory could guide practice in a reliable and predictable way, it is ill suited to such a task. Theory may provide us with concepts of mental functioning, such as unconscious motivation, super-ego anxiety, defensive splitting, and even concepts related to clinical phenomena—such as resistance, enactment, and counter-transference—but it lacks the specificity to guide the clinician in the moment. The clinician may utilize theory to conceptualize an exchange as indicating "transference," but he must draw upon many other resources, including his own life experiences, temperament, general knowledge of prevailing culture, expressive capacities, and sense of the patient at that moment in order to marshal an appropriate response.

Theoretical ideas are clearly in the background mix, but the exigencies and uniqueness of each clinical exchange requires of the clinician an experiential attunement that guides her in the moment-to-moment management of the clinical encounter. Clinical moments, in other words, are fraught with a multitude of exigencies unique to that clinical moment, guided in the background by theory, but governed in the moment by more experiential factors. It has often been noted, in fact, that clinicians from different schools within the analytic tradition may show striking similarities in their actions as practitioners, while those who share a common theoretical perspective may diverge widely in how they handle the clinical moment.

In a similar vein, we can get only limited guidance in the clinical moment from the diagnostic category into which a patient may fall. To know that a child or adult suffers from psychotic depression, borderline personality disorder, or bipolar disorder provides only the most general parameters of what we might expect to encounter in sessions. Since, beyond the most general symptomatic features, each depressed person is depressed in their own way, within the confines of their own personality and history, one must meet them, speak with them, and be with them to know how one might respond to their depression. At that point, one is responding to the *person* in their unique developmental context, guided by the possibilities of that clinical moment, rather than by some generalized set of techniques for how one responds to people who suffer from "depressive disorders."

Within the broad tradition of psychodynamic therapy, there are shared informing guidelines that underlie clinical technique, and these guidelines cut across differences among the various schools within that tradition. What I consider to be the core elements of technique in psychodynamic psychotherapy do not change automatically with level or type of disturbance. That is, they underlie our work with those seen as psychotic as well as those who are judged more psychologically intact. Some elements of what I have to say on this subject have been said by others in different ways, and here I have in mind the work of Anna Freud (1946), Escalona (1948), Ekstein and Wallerstein (1956), Winnicott (1960), Kernberg (1983), Pine (1985), Stern (1985), Settlage (1989), Donnellan (1989), Slade (1994), Jones (2002), and others. It is my expectation that these observations will have a familiar ring to those whose lives are taken up with the practice of psychotherapy. What I hope may be of value is the attempt to make explicit some ideas and beliefs that are implicit in much of our work, and to link certain ideas together in ways that may prove useful to practitioners, especially those who work with borderline, psychotic, and other severely disturbed children and adolescents.

I would like to make manifest, then, some of the principles that may lie hidden beneath much of our dynamically informed clinical work in the up-close moments with patients. Theoretical commitments are always somewhere in the background mix—ego psychologists take special note of defenses and adaptations;

object-relations theorists are sensitive to patterns of internalizations, and so on. But, *in the moment,* what guides the clinician are phenomena that are more diffuse, more implicit, more spontaneous, and experientially driven—and yet rooted in the broad psychoanalytic tradition. These guiding principles of therapeutic work cluster in three general areas that are present in, valued by, and supported by therapists in all variants of the analytic tradition. It will come as no surprise to psychodynamic clinicians to register the fact that we are guided by processes that promote in the patient:

1. a sense of psychological safety, security, and trust in the presence of the therapist;
2. a sense of engagement, commitment, and relatedness with the therapist; and
3. an expanding capacity for curiosity, interest, and reflection upon themselves.

Although these processes may not always be easily differentiated from each other, and further, many clinical exchanges will embody more than one, they nevertheless capture different aspects of what dynamically oriented therapists seek to promote.

The analytic tradition, broadly speaking, teaches us to attend to the subtle manifestations of internal experience and conflict, taking note of feelings of shame, patterns of attachment, disavowed affect, types of adaptation to developmental challenges, repetitive habits of behavior, the importance of self-feelings and self-identity, the symbolic meanings of behavior, feelings of isolation and experiences of abandonment, the internalized effects of seduction and of trauma, and most of all, the recurrent threat of anxiety to the equilibrium of the organism. Analysts also take note of feelings of wholeness and well-being, as well as experiences of excitement and exhilaration, love and tenderness, calmness and serenity. The subtle and rapidly changing play of emotional states across the landscape of behavior are the focal points of analytic attention—they are noticed, evaluated, and selectively responded to by the analyst. Increasingly in the modern era, analysts have become more cognizant of the wide range of expressive tools at their disposal and more comfortable with utilizing them: an expression of surprise or concern, a question, a smile, a lingering look, a sigh, a chuckle, a gesture with hand or head, a tonal shift, or, often enough, an attentive silence.

When we speak of the three core elements of technique in the clinical setting, we are referring to the quality of experience that is engendered in the patient through these minute and subtly changing interactions. The therapist's words, but more powerfully his tone, facial expression, gestures, pacing, and overall demeanor, seek to convey an atmosphere of safety to the patient and to tender an invitation to engage and to reflect on themselves and their lives in this most private of settings. This is not to say that nothing threatening or unwelcome should ever happen in the therapeutic hour, but rather that when they happen, the atmosphere created by these three underlying principles of analytic technique will enable those feelings to be endured by the patient and utilized in the service of growth and healing.

Because of their focus on the dynamics of intrapsychic and interpersonal phenomena, then, analysts engage in a constantly shifting and microscopically adjusting series of stratagems, often unnoticed even to themselves, designed to facilitate a sense of safety, engagement, and reflectivity in the patient. Without this flowing undercurrent of adaptation on the part of the analyst, little effective therapy can take place. With it, therapeutic change often occurs, even when little else is done in the sessions. Theorists have variously referred to this aspect of therapy as a "corrective emotional experience" (Alexander, 1956), as providing a "holding environment" (Winnicott, 1960), as offering a "secure attachment" opportunity (Ainsworth and Bowlby, 1991), or a "new object experience" (Fairbairn, 1952, Wallin, 2007). Without taking issue with any of these and other theoretical formulations, my preference is to offer a rendering of what analysts actually do in those up-close moments with patients that contribute to the experience of safety, engagement, and reflectivity.

I am not suggesting that analysts do or should refrain from introducing material into sessions that causes disturbance in the patient, creates discomfort, or raises anxiety, or that therapists should only provide a feather-like surrounding of warmth and comfort. It is the context or background against which this is done that is critical. Just as the good-enough mother may sharply rebuke, chastise, and raise anxiety or even fear in a child at certain moments without fear of rupturing the relationship or inflicting lasting damage, so too the therapist may engender moments of anxiety in a patient—sometimes inadvertently but often enough purposefully, without fear of damage. This is because, as with mothers, there are an infinite number of subtle, sometimes transient and sometimes sustained moments between the two that compellingly convey an atmosphere of sustained relatedness and security.

Promoting a Sense of Safety, Security, and Trust

Contemporary analysts working with adults have gradually come to appreciate what child analysts have implicitly known for decades—that the quality of the felt relationship with the therapist is crucial for patients in generating changes in their feelings, outlook, and behavior. A sense of security and vital engagement with the therapist is both the setting in which new growth can occur, and often the instrument though which change and growth are brought about.

Psychotherapy with adults relies primarily on the medium of words. The situation with children and adolescents is different. Here, many forms of interaction are mobilized in the service of therapy, such as games and activities, role-playing, storytelling, joint projects, and often exaggerated and dramatized forms of speech. Since children rarely refer themselves to therapy with the intention of discussing problem areas they have encountered but more typically find themselves thrust into therapy without any clear idea of what it is about, it becomes the task of the therapist to both help the child to feel comfortable and to guide them in the use of the therapeutic experience. While some children come reluctantly or resentfully, others are so burdened by their own suffering or confusion that they are willing to come to the therapist even when they don't know what to do when they get there.

Facilitating a sense of safety and trust is therefore both an initial and an ongoing task for the therapist working with young children as well as with adolescents. While it is true that some very young children may enter guilelessly into comfortable relationships with any warm and engaging adult, most older children are cautious, guarded, or openly suspicious. They have no template for this encounter with an adult who is neither teacher, parent, sibling, babysitter, aunt or uncle, policeman, warden, or foster parent. An initial period, which may extend for weeks or months, must therefore be devoted to creating a sense of comfort and to helping the child come to the realization that this relationship with the therapist is not exactly like any of the other relationships they may have experienced. It is not totally unrelated, and at moments may remind the child of other relationships, but it is different. If things go well, the youngster will gradually realize that much more is *allowed* here both in behavior (you can make a mess!), in expression (you can show ragefulness, even curse!), and you can think and maybe tell thoughts that you know you are not supposed to have—thoughts and feelings that may be confusing, shameful, and even frightening.

Providing for the sense of security, safety, and trust is an enterprise so microscopically attuned and exquisitely nuanced that it is difficult to capture or describe on the printed page. It is also so embedded in the routine exchanges between therapist and patient that most therapists most of the time are unaware of how they facilitate it. A fine illustration of the processes I am alluding to is offered by Dan Stern in his description of mother–infant interaction through which the mother naturally and spontaneously promotes in her infant the sense of an intersubjective world and helps to generate the awareness in the child that his inner states can be shared with others, understood, and appreciated:

> The sharing of affective states is the most pervasive and clinically germane feature of intersubjective relatedness. . . . What are the acts and processes that let other people know that you are feeling something very like what they are feeling? How can you get "inside of" other people's subjective experience and then let them know that you have arrived there . . .?
>
> When the infant is around nine months old . . . one begins to see the mother add a new dimension to her imitation-like behavior, a dimension that appears to be geared to the infant's new status as a potentially intersubjective partner. . . . a new category of behavior we will call *affect attunement*. . . . Affect attunement is often so embedded in other actions and purposes that it is partially masked. . . .

> A ten-month old girl finally gets a piece in a jig saw puzzle. She looks toward her mother, throws her head up in the air, and with a forceful arm flap raises herself partly off the ground in a flurry of exuberance. The mother says 'YES, thatta girl.' The "YES' is intoned with much stress. It has an explosive rise that echoes the girl's fling of gesture and posture. Affect attunement, then, is the performance of behaviors that express the quality of feeling of a shared affect state. . . . The evidence indicates that attunements occur largely out of awareness and almost automatically.
>
> (Stern, 1985, pp. 138–145)

A 9-year-old boy, seen in a hospital clinic, was referred by his teacher with some sense of alarm at his increasingly remote, non-responsive, and at times angrily eruptive behavior in class. He had become increasingly pre-occupied with incomprehensible fiddling at his desk—doodling or repetitively playing with a pen or some other small item, clicking it or snapping it, or seemed randomly focused on private activities and oblivious to or at best slow to respond to the teacher's communications. He could also become rageful if intruded upon too assertively by the teacher or other students. At home, his mother reported that he often ignored her or pretended not to hear, that he spoke little and often only to demand what he wanted, and seemed to live in his own world. He rarely smiled, rarely initiated contact or communication, and his most frequently noted emotional communication was a look of impatience or irritation when intruded upon or when some undertaking with a small object did not go his way.

Sandor walked compliantly but silently to his female therapist's office for his first session, after she had come to cheerily greet him in the lobby where he waited with his mother. The therapist immediately noted his lack of greeting or eye contact and his neutral facial expression. The therapist's upbeat and cheery tone became a bit quieter as they walked toward her office and she told him he could call her "Laura" and asked what name he usually went by. "Sandor," he said softly, looking down. "And here's my office," Laura said with a smile as she opened the door to reveal two play tables and shelves containing a wide variety of games and toys. As Laura preceded Sandor into the room, he hesitated for a moment in the doorway, his eyes rapidly scanning the room, seemingly taking note of everything that was there. At once, he proceeded rapidly and silently into the room, going to the farthest shelf of toys, reaching out with his hands to touch, pick up, nudge, turn around, replace, and move on until he had seemingly catalogued everything that was there. Aside from his name, he had yet to say a word.

Laura, noting the intensity and urgency of his exploration and his silence, stood quietly by and observed. Sandor picked up a bunch of half-constructed Lego clusters, brought them to a table, and began taking them apart. As he stood at a table working at the Legos, Laura stepped toward the table and quietly observed, "You seem to be good with Legos." Sandor turned slightly to the side so that his back was to her, clearly shielding his activities from her and, in effect, closing the door in her face. Only 15 minutes had passed since they had first met, and barely a word exchanged, but Laura was rapidly adjusting and adapting herself to ensure that Sandor could proceed in her presence without impingement. She did want, however, to register her presence even if only to convey that he need fear no intrusion. "Okay," she said softly, "I'll be working with some Play-Doh here at this other table" and she sat down and proceeded to busily engage herself in making pizza and cupcakes with the Play-Doh.

Sandor worked for another 10 or 15 minutes at his Legos, but Laura noted that he gradually shifted his position so that his back was no longer to her and he had turned sideways to her at his table, a few steps from hers. He also at one point glanced quickly, almost furtively, at what she was doing before returning intently to his project. At another point, he muttered something under his breath, slapped his construction on the table, and walked rapidly past Laura to the shelf from which he had taken the Legos. He rummaged around and a grunt of satisfaction signaled that he had found what he wanted. Laura noted that these mutterings from Sandor might be his way of letting her know that he was present too, in his fashion. Laura became aware that the end of the session was rapidly approaching and was unsure what to do. She decided to alert Sandor to this fact by saying softly, "We will have to stop our work here in about five minutes." She had decided to use the term "work" to convey that she took their time together seriously, that it wasn't just "play," and to slightly prick his interest by saying something a bit unexpected but which required no response from him. A few moments later, Laura told Sandor that their time together was up and it was time to go. He quickly put down his Legos, stepped over to her table, pointed to her Play-Doh constructions, and said peremptorily, "What's that?" Laura laughed and said, "Hmmm, I thought it would be obvious—it's a slice of pizza and a vanilla cupcake." Sandor gave a single firm nod of acknowledgement, turned, and walked to the door. The session was over.

Moments such as this are commonplace in clinical practice, much like the routine exchanges that occur dozens of times a day between mother and child. Despite the fact that such interchanges are common and typically unremarked upon, they display enormous complexity and subtlety in the refined attunement of each party to the other. In our case, Laura's voice tone, verbal expression, physical movements, facial expression, physical location, and other forms of response too microscopic to render, all display a finely tuned adaptation to her patient's needs and capacities as they evolve from moment to moment. Laura's sensitivity to Sandor's need for control, for distance, for freedom from impingement, for exercising his own initiative and yet for some form of experience of presence, enabled her to steadily adjust, adapt, engage, and modulate her responses so that Sandor could have an experience of himself in the presence of another that did not feel disturbing. And all in the service of engendering a sense of safety, security, and trust in the patient. It was a good first session.

This pattern would repeat itself in one form or another for many weeks. Sandor would enter the playroom silently, rapidly select the toys he wanted to use, and busy himself at one of the play tables. Laura would make one or two simple observations and then proceed to sit at her table and engage in some related activity. After many weeks, Sandor asked her to bring him an object from the shelf. Gradually he would tolerate her standing or sitting next to him. Later he would direct her to take up an object in relation to the one he was playing with. Even later, he would direct her in what to do or say with the object. As he gradually included her more in his play, Laura was able to comment, make observations, or ask questions to which he became increasingly responsive.

By then end of a year's work, Sandor entered therapy with a smile on face and usually with a plan of what they were going to do that day. The play was mutual, enlivened by his steady commentary, and more physically animated. The rigidity of the early weeks had faded, the mask-like facial expression had dropped away, and there were occasional sessions in which he would enter and say. "What should we do today?" The achievement of mutuality, reciprocity, and expressiveness in the sessions was facilitated by Laura's willingness to map herself along the paths that Sandor would lay out, adapting herself spontaneously to the moment-to-moment signals from Sandor. By the end of eight months, their exchanges included lively laughter, mutual teasing, and even friendly competition.

Symptomatic improvement both at home and at school was evident by the fifth month of treatment. Interestingly—and this is common in child treatment—improvement occurred despite the fact that Laura and Sandor had virtually no exchanges regarding the difficulties in his life that had prompted treatment in the first place. At most, there were some brief references by Sandor to things that bothered him: "I hate the kid that sits next to me at school." "My sister is a spoiled brat." Laura invariably responded with quiet interest, but Sandor never elaborated and seemed content to simply report these phenomena. And Laura, while expressing interest and curiosity, never pushed for more. The therapy hours consisted in a wide range of play—Legos, clay, drawing, constructions, competitive games, and all manner of made-up activities. At times, symbolic aspects of the play seemed to fleetingly allude to personal issues, but more often, the active process of play and Laura's happy engagement with it seemed to be the overriding issue.

One could discern in the play many aspects of Sandor's modes of functioning—his approach to problem solving, his creativity, his ambivalence regarding competition, his relatively greater comfort with fine rather than gross motor activities, etc. Emotional issues were also at times evident—the gleeful excitement with victory, a capacity to get carried away when aggression was tapped, an avoidant attitude regarding emotional needs, a tendency to get despondent in defeat, but also a resilience that supported renewed effort. It cannot be reliably said that these issues were "worked on" in therapy. It would be more accurate to say that they were manifested in therapy, revealed, allowed to be seen, or just lived out. But they were lived out with Laura, who might notice and convey interest but made very little effort to influence or change these manifestations. It seems reasonable to suppose, therefore, that for Sandor, there was something intrinsic to the experience of being with Laura, of being who he was *with* Laura, that facilitated his change both within and outside of therapy.

The relationship elements that I have been addressing in the discussion of Sandor and Laura have to do with the facilitation of safety, security, and trust. These aspects of the relationship are essential for therapy to proceed and need to be consistently attended to in an ongoing way throughout therapy. For many patients, a relationship marked by these features—that is, just *having* a relationship in which one can experience these phenomena, is itself the most potent and change-inducing element in therapy.

Promoting a Sense of Engagement, Commitment, and Relatedness

Engagement in the therapeutic encounter is the second of the clinical dispositions that are embodied in contemporary psychodynamic practice. It refers both to an attitude on the part of the therapist and a clinical goal with regard to the patient. This element in current practice follows many decades of extreme cautiousness on the part of analysts, during which anonymity and abstinence were taken to be the defining postures of the analyst toward the patient. While quiet, attentive listening was often held up as the ideal of practice, providing the "blank screen" for transference projections, and with only intermittent and judiciously selected comments from the therapist, this portrait and recommendation was finally seen as unrealistic, and even, at times, dysfunctional. Many contemporary analysts have gradually moved away from this approach to treatment, and anecdotal evidence suggests it may always have been honored more in the breach than in the observance. In any case, what I mean by "engagement," and its rationale, is not dependent on any particular theoretical orientation within psychoanalysis, but flows from shared sensitivities with regard to human dynamics.

A series of exchanges from a recent supervision group may serve to illustrate this point. A trainee presented a case involving Daryl, a reticent and guarded 14-year-old boy being seen in a hospital clinic subsequent to being hospitalized for rage episodes, inappropriate sexual behavior, and an episode of fire setting. He had never known his father and lived with his mother and older sister. He was often sullen and inarticulate and clearly resented having to come to therapy. The young male trainee who was working with him was patient and empathic, but often found himself at a loss about what to say or what to do to facilitate a more open communication process between them.

In the session reported, Daryl described, in his typically sparse, flat, and slightly bitter tone, a confrontation the night before between him, his mother, and

16-year-old sister ("the angel" in the family, in his words). His sister's cell phone was missing and she immediately assumed he had taken it and began yelling at him and cursing him out. His mother (as usual, he claimed), joined the sister and they both proceeded to yell and curse at him, calling him "useless," "fucked up," "a loser." Daryl did not say anything and walked out of the house and sat on a park bench across the street. (He had not taken the phone and it was, in fact, found by the sister later that evening under the covers of her bed.)

Given Daryl's history with dangerously explosive behavior and some aspects of how he told the story, the therapist was particularly interested in what Daryl was experiencing while sitting on the park bench across from his house. The therapist felt, appropriately, that the psychological isolation in which Daryl normally lived was both painful to him and potentially dangerous for him and others. But the therapist found himself at a loss for words and waited in concerned silence before finally asking quietly, "So what did you do then?" Daryl shrugged in silence. The therapist asked some further questions, such as how long he had stayed out, when did he finally go back in, etc., but Daryl was finished and said, "It's alright, man. It's over. That's just the way it is."

But the therapist felt that he had missed an opportunity to engage the patient and wished that he had found a way to reach out and to connect. He sensed that the very fact that the normally reticent Daryl took the trouble to tell the story in the first place was itself meaningful, a gesture of communication that called for a response, and that his response was not what was called for or needed.

The other trainees listened carefully to the discussion, easily identifying with the therapist's quandary. Many suggestions were proposed about what the therapist could have said or done about the park bench moment and in the end they seemed to come down to one of two types of responses from the therapist. One was a question—some version of, "What were you feeling as you were sitting there alone on the park bench?" A question, it was suggested, that could have been asked with gentleness and quiet concern. The other was a statement, hopefully of understanding or validation, "You must have been so angry sitting there, after what they had said and accused you of." The therapist felt that either one of these would have been better than what he did, but he did not feel either of these comments would have had much impact. Finally, someone said, "You know what? After hearing that story, the only thing I would have liked to say to Daryl is, 'Man, that sucks!' " The group laughed at this obviously heart-felt expression, but after a moment, when the laughter had died down, the therapist said, "You know, I wish I *had* said that. I think he would have responded to that. I think we might have gone on from there." As the group paused to take that in, one member said, "Are we allowed to say that?"

"Are we allowed to say that?" The very question itself testifies to the long-standing inhibition placed on analytic therapists with regard to revelatory comments about their own feelings or personal reactions to a patient's comments. And yet, as Daryl's therapist clearly sensed, this would have been the most effective comment, the most "related" and the most engaged. The engagement we are discussing has many forms, of which this last comment to Daryl is only one type. Consider an episode from much earlier in life that seems to convey the same message:

> The mother of a 10-month-old child watches him crawl across the room, pull himself up to stand at a coffee table, and then reach across it to grab a toy just beyond his reach. As he leans in and stretches, pressing his belly against the table, wiggling his fingers towards the desired object just beyond his reach, the mother matches his muscular effort with an echoing vocal effort of her own, "Aah, aaahhh, Ahhhh, AAAHHH . . . !" until he finally grasps it and she says with excitement, "YOU GOT IT!" At that moment the child turns to her with a big smile which she returns with an expansive smile of her own and a clap of her hands. The child then turns to crawl rapidly away, clutching the precious toy in his hand as he crawls.

It is not hard to suppose that in exchanges like this, and dozens more of its kind repeated throughout the day, the mother slowly builds up the expectation in her child that his private effort and triumph is seen, felt, known, and shared by another, that he lives in a world where private states can be grasped by others, and that this intersubjectivity can be a source of joy, comfort, and solace. Interwoven and developing along with this is the child's growing capacity to use language to intentionally communicate his inner states, and to thereby engage in complex interpersonal exchanges about inner experiences—thoughts, feelings, wishes, and so on. For patients who have lacked adequate opportunity for intersubjective experiences, or for whom it is poorly developed, or has been lost, or has proved more painful than joyful and is therefore avoided or defended against, the therapist's willingness to engage affectively ("Man, that sucks!") may be just what the doctor ordered.

As with the processes that support safety, security, and trust, moments reflecting clinical engagement are often subtle, fleeting, rapidly shifting and not consciously registered by the therapist. As with the previously discussed phenomena, manifestations of engagement inevitably reflect the personality and personal style of the therapist along with the particular chemistry or "feel" between patient and therapist at a given moment. That is why it is so difficult to capture in rules, principles, or guidelines to treatment. Despite this difficulty, there appears to me to be a strong common element underlying effective therapists' approach to engaging the patient. What they have in common is the vitality of the therapist's *interest in* and *curiosity about* the patient's experience, and a willingness to *communicate* that interest and curiosity in whatever ways may suit the moment.

And it is most typically through the therapist's willingness to engage that many patients find a way to reciprocate and to become, in turn, engaged with the therapist. For our more disturbed children and adolescents, in whom the very capacity to form relationships—to differentiate self from other, to separate reality from fantasy, to retain the existence of an other in their minds, to manage their own overwhelming emotions in the presence of an other, to experience their own existence with a sense of continuity—to be drawn into an engaged relationship with the therapist is itself a major step toward health.

For the most part, the therapist's efforts at engagement are ultimately directed at helping the patient toward sharing increasing elements of conflicted, disavowed, or previously unformulated affect. Often enough, the therapist's willingness to be vitally engaged with the patient in one dimension opens up the possibility of engagement in a more sensitive area or one not readily accessed or shared by the patient. If the therapist allows himself to participate with gusto in a board game, to get caught up with the patient in a construction project, or to follow with patience and curiosity the child's effort to explain the latest computer game, the soil becomes fertile for the growth of more personal forms of engagement. Sometimes the therapist's willingness to engage intellectually with a patient becomes the pathway for a more emotionally revealing encounter.

Sara was an 11-year-old whose school attendance had been intermittent until she had finally stopped attending two months prior to the start of therapy. She had become increasingly socially withdrawn, spoke very little even at home, was losing weight, and spent most of her time in her room. She expressed multiple fears—of the dark, of sounds in the house, of birds, of teachers, of people on the street, etc. She had periodic hallucinatory experiences and episodes of depersonalization and she presented as anxious, hyper-alert, and overwhelmingly sad. She spoke haltingly, barely above a whisper, usually in response to questions or observations of the therapist. She wore baggy clothes over her slender frame and often her hood or her hair would partially conceal her face.

Over a period of months, Sara was gradually able to make periodic eye contact with her male therapist, to smile briefly in response to his gentle teasing, and to share such thoughts as "the kids at school are phony," her mother was "annoying and like a child sometimes," and that she "hated" her father because he was "mean and loud." (Her parents were in the midst of a contentious divorce.) She found it difficult, however, to elaborate on these blunt statements and quickly seemed embarrassed or confused if the therapist showed interest or curiosity.

Sara would typically enter the office with eyes cast down and sit silently on the edge of the couch with her hands tensely gripping each other in her lap. Often she appeared pale, bleak, and helpless, unable to say what she was thinking or feeling. An agony of self-consciousness seemed to consume her, and she was invariably relieved when the therapist began speaking on some topic that didn't focus directly on her. On rare occasions, she managed a brief conversational exchange, displaying flickers of a sharp, whimsical intelligence in the form of clipped observations of others. When invited to talk about personal matters such as what bothered her about school, why she refused to talk with former friends, how the divorce was affecting her, what her feelings or inner experience was like, Sara would freeze, look forlorn, and silently shake her head. Withdrawal and panic were always, the therapist sensed, just around the corner.

On one occasion, close to a year into treatment, Sara entered the office silently, eyes averted, with a barely whispered "Hi" and sat on the edge of the couch, as usual. After she had been sitting silently for a few minutes, staring at her hands in her lap, she asked softly, "Is it possible that everything is just a dream?" Struck by her asking a question of him for the first time, and by the question itself, the therapist said it was an intriguing question and asked if she could explain more what she meant. Sara responded haltingly,

> Sometimes I just wonder . . . if, well, if anything is really real. I . . . mean, maybe it's all a dream . . . like everything . . . I mean . . . like, maybe we just think things are real . . . and . . . maybe they aren't. I . . . don't know. . . . It's nothing really . . . it's just stupid . . . never mind. . . .

Seeing her growing embarrassment and anxiety about having exposed something about herself, the therapist said that he was impressed that this question had occurred to her, that it was an ancient question, that the smartest philosophers had struggled with it for centuries, and that it was part of what was called "epistemology." Sara stared at him.

"You mean you don't think it's weird?"

"Not at all," the therapist replied, and went on to tell her of the famous philosopher Descartes and how he had looked at a ball of wax and asked himself, "How do I know that I am not *dreaming* that there is a ball of wax in my hand?"

"That's it! Right! That's just what *I* am thinking!" Sara said excitedly, her face beaming. The therapist went on a bit about Descartes' puzzlement about how can we know what is real and what is unreal, about pinching oneself to tell if one was dreaming, but then how one could just be dreaming that one was pinching oneself, etc. Sara was nodding and smiling, almost giggling at the infinite regress about dreaming that one was dreaming.

"No, Sara, it's not weird at all to wonder what is real and what is unreal. In fact, it is one of the deepest questions one could ask."

A slight smile flickered across her face, almost of satisfaction. She grew quiet again.

"My mother thinks I'm weird. . . . So do the kids at school." The therapist asked her why the kids thought she was weird.

"Because I'm quiet. . . . I never talk. . . . It's like I'm a shadow along the wall . . . they don't even see me. . . . I'm invisible. . . ."

"Is that, then, when you begin to feel like you're not real?"

"Mm hmm," she nodded.

"Just a shadow, that doesn't even exist?"

"Mm hmm," she nodded, biting her lip and looking down. A bleak look came over her face, and for the first time her eyes began to glisten with tears.

After a moment, the therapist asked quietly, "But would you like it if they saw you, if they talked to you?"

"NO!" She almost shouted, her head snapping up to look at him in panic.

To the therapist's puzzled look, she added, looking down again, "I'd die if they talked to me. . . . I wouldn't know what to say. . . . I'd just be stupid and weird. . . ."

"I see," he said softly. "I think I get it. You really are stuck. You hate being a silent shadow at school. It makes you look weird and makes you feel unreal, like you don't even exist. But the idea of changing it by talking and acting normal scares you because you don't quite know how to do that. So you are really stuck. . . ."

Sara nodded glumly, gave a sigh, and looked at the therapist briefly, as if to say, "So now you know."

For Sara, in that session, it felt safe and reassuring to be engaged around some thoughts and ideas that had been confusing to her. The strictly intellectual, even didactic remarks of her therapist on the epistemological conundrum echoed her own questions, dignified her own thinking processes, and reassured her that she was not "weird." Feeling this sense of mutuality and connectedness in the realm of ideas enabled Sara to venture farther, to share the deeply painful and mortifying experience of feeling like an invisible shadow at school, sliding along the wall—unknown, wishing to be known, terrified of being known. It was safer to stay at home.

Contemporary psychodynamic therapists will not find this clinical vignette particularly surprising or unusual. It is, almost routinely, the thing we do. But the fact that it is so much a part of the fabric of discourse with patients should not mask its significance. The therapist's efforts to engage with Sara are pursued in different ways at different moments. The shifting choices and decisions of the therapist as the session unfolds are guided by his effort to stay attuned to what the moment requires for Sara to be encouraged into a closer, more trusting, more confiding engagement. At one moment a therapist might crack a joke, at another he might murmur something softly empathic, at another roll his eyes, at another say something provocative—all driven by the constantly shifting nature of what he senses the patient needs and what he can do to maintain and deepen their engagement with each other.

For many of our patients, the prospect of genuine engagement with another person is fraught with danger or—even more disheartening—is a completely unknown experience. And for many of our patients suffering from severe disorders, the main function of therapy will be to create, if not sustained engagement, at least increasingly extended moments of it. The overt content of a session may be focused on any manner of subject (a TV show, how bad the cafeteria lunch was), but the therapist is implicitly, and often intuitively, tracking and mapping himself along the patient's path, seeking opportunities for extending, expanding, and deepening the moments of engagement. If we do our jobs well, we may reduce the danger of engagement for many of our most troubled patients, and with time, demonstrate that engaged relationships are not only possible, but also add immeasurably to the vitality of life.

Expanding the Capacity for Curiosity, Interest, and Self-Reflection

At the beginning of this discussion I listed three areas of focus that seem to me to guide the clinical processes that underlie the broad range of psychoanalytic approaches to treatment. It is, of course, not easy to sharply differentiate one area from another. They inevitably blend into each other—a therapeutic gesture that may serve to enhance the sense of trust and security may simultaneously facilitate a moment of engagement. It is more the rule than the exception that therapists' communications—like all communications—have multiple determinants and multiple functions. So it is with the third area that I would like to discuss—processes that facilitate in the patient an expanding capacity for curiosity, interest in, and reflection upon themselves. There is no single type of communication from the therapist that specifically targets this goal, but I would argue that facilitating this capacity in patients is implicit in the entire process of therapy from an analytic perspective and that this is one of its most profound and potent aspirations.

While most therapists—and emphatically those with a psychodynamic orientation—would heartily endorse the idea of "Know Thyself" as an important value and continuing goal in life, therapists themselves are not always aware of how pervasive this guideline is in their work, or, for some of their patients, how revolutionary it is. The effort to promote processes of curiosity, interest, and self-reflection in their patients is so embedded in analysts' clinical stances that they often fail to see the myriad ways in which this endeavor is pursued. Even with our most troubled patients, we promote processes of self-awareness that can serve as a bulwark against their own chaotic, impulse-driven, and seemingly thoughtless behavior. Being able to *think* about oneself, to make sense of one's own behavior, to see patterns and meanings in one's behavior, to discern underlying motivations that are not immediately obvious, to understand that there are reasons for our choices—even the most seemingly irrational or dysfunctional ones, is for many patients a revelatory experience, and often the beginning of hope. And this is the persistent undercurrent of all psychoanalytic work. Such work does not necessarily focus directly on "symptom relief" but rather on engendering a reflective process through which the symptom begins to make sense. That is, the symptom or troubling behavior, upon reflection, comes to be seen as a solution to an often unacknowledged problem, and ultimately to be rejected as a poor solution to the actual problem that gave rise to it. For most children and adolescents, even those with severe afflictions, the realization of a measure of comprehensibility in their behavior and feelings and the dawning awareness that it all makes a certain kind of sense, is the first step toward change.

José was a burly 13-year-old youngster hospitalized for attempting to choke his mother and for a pattern of explosively violent and dangerous behavior over seemingly trivial slights. His single mother was physically handicapped and had difficulty controlling him, whereas his father was reportedly a brutal man who had abandoned the family when José was less than 5 years old. As with many treatment-resistant youngsters, José invariably located all of his troubles outside of himself in the form of mean parents, unfair teachers, nasty kids, insulting shopkeepers, and a generally predatory world against which he had to defend himself. At times of threat, paranoid ideation would consume him and unbridled rage would erupt as he fought for what felt to him to be his very life.

After a period of hospitalization during which he was stabilized on medication, José entered the day treatment program, which consisted of school plus therapeutic activities, including twice-weekly psychotherapy. José was overweight and often unkempt, with a clumsy, waddling swagger in his movements and a tendency to make fun of other kids and to use his large, heavy body to intimidate them. Although not very expressive verbally, he was clearly intelligent, perceptive about others, and, when not guarded or belligerent, capable of both good-natured humor and funny wisecracking.

After sitting down heavily in a chair in the therapist's office, José began his familiar litany of complaints about the teachers and hospital staff who seemed determined to treat him unfairly. Racial, sexual, and ethnic epithets poured from his mouth as he excoriated now this one and now that of the people he had encountered that day. When his eye caught the checkerboard on the table, he interrupted his invectives and said, "Wanna play?"

"Sure," the therapist responded, and they proceeded to set up the board and began to play. After playing for a while, the therapist, perhaps preoccupied with whether to revisit José's earlier remarks, found himself in a winning position. This awareness was borne in on the therapist by José's increasing restlessness and his suggestions that the therapist was cheating. In a sudden explosion and an angry swipe of his arm, José knocked all the pieces to the floor, got up, yelled, "You're a fuckin' cheater!" and stormed out of the office, slamming the door. After alerting staff to José's sudden departure and making sure that he was in good hands, the therapist returned to ponder what had just happened, feeling a bit sheepish about not having been more mindful about how the game was developing and José's likely reaction.

It was not until the next week that the two met again in the therapist's office. Amid the multitude of high-intensity events that typified the days in a day-hospital setting for adolescents, some of which involved José, both had forgotten the checker episode of the week before. As José sat down in his usual seat, the therapist suddenly remembered their previous session and said with exaggerated casualness, "Say, José! Would you care for a game of checkers?" José instantly remembered, looked at the therapist and, chuckling, said, "Sure."

As they proceeded to engage, the therapist was careful this time not to dominate the play. In fact, José was on the verge of winning when the therapist suddenly slapped the board upward with a bang from underneath, sending the pieces flying around the office. José, stunned, jumped back in his seat, eyes wide open, jaw dropped.

"What the fuck! You crazy, man?" They stared at each other for a moment before the therapist said, "Yeah, I guess it takes one to know one. . . ." The two stared at each other for a split second before simultaneously bursting out in laughter. José, shaking his head and laughing, "Man, you some crazy therapist." And then, muttering, laughing, and shaking his head as he stooped to help the therapist pick up the pieces, "Okay, you got me, you got me. . . ."

After they put the checkers away and sat down again, the therapist said, "So seriously, José, why do you think I did that?"

"'Cause you crazy. . . ." he said smiling.

"C'mon . . . seriously . . ."

"You just getting back at me . . . ahh . . . no . . . no . . . you ain't like that . . . ahhh . . . I guess maybe you just tryin' to teach me a lesson. . . ."

"Okay . . . maybe there is something to that. . . . What would the lesson be, though?"

"Mmmm . . . I dunno. . . . Maybe that its crazy to lose your shit over a game of checkers? Man! You had me freaked!" José said, laughing again.

"Well, what do you suppose *I* thought when you did it last week?" the therapist asked.

"Yeah, I got it. 'Another wacko crazy kid.'"

"Losing your shit over a game of checkers. . . ." repeated the therapist, musing and slowly shaking his head. And after a pause, he looked directly at José and added, "It's kind of the story of your life, isn't it?"

After an unusually long, pensive moment, José said soberly, "Yeah. . . . I don't know why I get so mad. . . ."

Therapy begins with curiosity about oneself, but this curiosity is not always there at the beginning. For many of our patients, old and young, the whole therapeutic enterprise is uncomfortable and a bit mystifying. Often it is quickly evident that this 50 minutes or so with the therapist is the longest period of time that the patient ever spends in a one-to-one encounter with another person. Many children have never played alone for any period of time with an adult. Many adolescents have never had an extended conversation with anyone—they have "hung out," played ball, goofed around, watched TV, played video games. Even with parents or teachers, verbal exchanges are often brief, and fraught with the weight of expectations, disappointments, reprimands, or other real-life concerns that are part of that relationship. So, the time with the therapist is often unusual for the patient, particularly because the focus is exclusively on the patient himself. For some, it arrives as a relief, a pleasure, or an opportunity that has been long desired. For others, it is simply awkward, puzzling, and uncomfortable.

But as the relationship proceeds, and the therapist works both consciously and intuitively to establish a sense of trust and security and to enrich the engagement with the patient, it becomes apparent that something else is also going on between them. The therapist exerts a recurring and relentless pressure on the patient to be curious and to wonder. That is, to wonder about themselves—about why they do the things they do and feel the things they feel. To be curious about things in themselves that they have never, or only dimly, thought about before. To reflect on how they came to be the kind of person they are, and on whether they could, or would, or would want to be different. And this process—the cultivation and encouragement of curiosity about oneself—to which the analytically oriented therapist returns again and again, is the most potent of instruments for change.

As with so many aspects of technique common to the psychoanalytic approaches to clinical work, the effort to expand the patient's capacity for curiosity, interest, and reflection upon themselves is so woven into the very fabric of the relationship that it is taken for granted. Clinicians are not always aware themselves of the multiplicity of stratagems they use to move the patient in the direction of self-reflection. They may tease or joke, express puzzlement, challenge and provoke, wonder out loud, invite, entice, play devil's advocate, share a personal story—and sometimes simply ask, "Why do you think you did that?"

And the answer may not be that important. Whether the patient can offer an answer or not, whether the answer is simple, or partial, or vague, or elaborately detailed, or simply "I don't know," is only of provisional interest and will likely change over time. Of greater interest, and likely of greater permanence, is the patient's increasing ability to see the question itself as important. While therapy often generates surprising insights and discoveries that may prompt a patient to re-evaluate aspects of his life and behavior, the more lasting impact of the therapeutic experience lies in its capacity to engender an ongoing inquisitiveness on the patient's part with regard to the meaning of his own patterns of living.

The lack of inquisitiveness about themselves among many of our patients can often be startling, and may stem from a variety of sources. For some, parental inadequacy or pathology may have removed the parent from adequate engagement with the growing child. For others, multiple changes in parenting figures, as in sequential foster care placements, may have deprived the child of a sufficiently invested parent to sustain and nurture a consciousness of self. For others, dynamic factors mitigate against the opening up of self-reflection. Here one often encounters a fierce avoidance, denial, a deliberate concreteness in thinking, a refusal to wonder about themselves for fear that the wondering can only lead to humiliation and shame.

Justin was a tall, stocky 15-year-old boy who had been hospitalized twice during the previous year for suicidal gestures and attempts. The son of two busy professional parents, he had always been a reasonably successful student, participated in sports, and had a group of friends. The parents noted that he had always been a quiet boy, but over the last three years he had become even quieter, less interested in seeing friends, less interested in participating in sports, and gruffer and more remote at home. He was minimally responsive when queried about what was wrong, irritably brushing off inquiries with a surly look and dismissive gesture. It was Justin's younger brother who found him crying on the roof one day and pulled him back from the ledge.

Justin came to therapy without apparent objection, but he was remarkably unable or unwilling to make use of his time there. He was visibly sad and stunningly silent. Over many months of weekly sessions, punctuated by a second hospitalization for suicidal behavior, he communicated primarily with shrugs, nods or shakes of the head, and on occasion a "Yeah" or "Maybe." His despondency was profound, and on some days he would sit with tears rolling down his cheeks and would only respond, "Bad day," to the therapist's varied inquiries.

Justin's parents were understandably frightened and exasperated by his refusal to see old and close friends, to engage in activities he had always enjoyed, to join or interact with the family, or to clarify in any way what was troubling him. School personnel, as well, were alarmed by Justin's withdrawal and isolation and by the "zombie-like" demeanor he displayed at school. There were, to be sure, moments in therapy when brief exchanges would take place and Justin would reveal a sardonic sense of humor. These moments were always at the therapist's initiative, usually on a fairly neutral topic, and would at times evoke a wry smile and ironic remark. In fragmentary exchanges over the course of a year, Justin managed to convey something of his bleak outlook: his "friends" were not really friends but were faking it; people talked about him negatively behind his back; no girl would ever like him because he was too fat; when he was with people he could never think of anything to say and looked stupid; he would always be alone. These observations emerged fitfully, over the course of many months, often toward the end of a session that had been filled with silence, shrugs, and monosyllabic responses. Such observations were offered as simple facts, unhappy ones, but not ones that were open to discussion. Any effort to engage Justin in some reflection on these "facts" was met with a dismissive shrug.

Despite this rather unhappy portrait, over the course of a year and a half of therapy, things began to moderate for Justin. Both his parents and school personnel reported that Justin was observed increasingly laughing and joking around with a group of people, had invited kids over to the house, had accepted invitations to sleep at friends' houses, and had gone to a few basketball games with friends. However, his demeanor when at home, when talking to adults at school, or with his therapist remained unremittingly dark. He insisted that if he appeared to be having a good time it was just because he was pretending. He had decided to fake it because he knew that was what people wanted, but he still thought it would be better to be dead and not be a burden to his family or anyone else.

Toward the end of the school year, in his second year of therapy and during this period of "pretend" improvement, Justin was getting ready to go to the summer camp he had attended for a number of years. He expressed no particular pleasure at this prospect, although reports from the previous summer seemed to indicate that he appeared to enjoy the experience. Taking the opportunity to invite some reflection on his current state of mind, the therapist asked if he felt that this year at school had been any different for him from the previous year when he had experienced two hospitalizations. After watching him shrug and stare at the ground, the therapist pressed him again.

"So? Any difference?"

"Maybe a little . . . I guess . . . maybe . . . it wasn't as bad this year. . . ."

"In what way were you different?"

"Uh . . . tried, I guess . . . uh, tried to be more social. . . ."

Hesitant to press the point, the therapist waited a bit and Justin volunteered,

"I might go to a party this week."

"Who's having the party?"

"Alex."

"Kids from school?"

"Uh huh . . . but I might not go. . . ."

"I see . . . You're not sure. . . ."

"Uh uh . . ."

Then quiet. Justin looked a bit glum, maybe bored, or sleepy. The therapist waited and pondered for a few minutes. Then, abruptly sitting up straighter in his chair, he leaned forward, looked at Justin, and said with a sudden urgency, "Let me ask you a question . . ."

Justin looked at him quickly, suddenly alert. The therapist continued, "Let's entertain a hypothesis together, you know, like in science? Let's entertain the possibility that you go to the party—just for argument's sake, okay?"

"Uh huh . . ."

"So you go to the party, and you have a good time . . . no, a great time. You're really having fun . . . You're dancing, and joking, and talking with people, you know . . . just having fun at a party. . . ."

"Uh huh . . ."

"And let's say we have an appointment the next day, you and me. And you come in and I ask you: 'So how was the party? Did you have a good time?' So here's my question: Would you tell me that you had a good time?"

Shifting his weight on the couch and looking down at the carpet, Justin finally says, "Nope."

After a pause to let this exchange sink in, the therapist says, "And why wouldn't you tell me?"

Justin shrugs and looks away.

"No, really. . . . Why wouldn't you tell me if you had a good time? What's the big deal?"

Shrugging more and looking increasingly uncomfortable, Justin says, "I dunno . . . just wouldn't. . . . "

"I'M YOUR THERAPIST, FOR CHRISSAKE!" says the therapist loudly, in mock anger, beginning to laugh. "Who *would* you tell?"

"No one . . ." says Justin, starting to laugh now himself.

"Can you see how ridiculous that is?"

Justin raises his eyebrows and smiles a bit sheepishly, "I guess so. . . . "

"So you wouldn't want to *admit* that you had a good time. Not to me or anyone else . . . it has to be kept a secret . . . everyone should think you had a bad time, just another miserable time like you always have. . . . "

"I guess," he says, still smiling, but clearly flustered.

"So this is a puzzle to me. . . . And it makes me want to ask another question." The therapist turns more serious now and asks more softly, "Why do you feel it's so important to hide it from everyone if you are feeling good? Why do you want everyone to think you are depressed, even when you are not?"

Justin shrugs again and says, "I dunno. . . . "

It's quiet in the room now. Justin is looking down. After a few moments, there are tears in his eyes, which soon spill over to run down his cheeks.

"What is it?" asks the therapist quietly.

"I guess . . . 'cause . . . there's nothing special about me . . . it's just . . . at least people are worried? . . . I don't know . . . maybe I need the attention. . . . At least . . . if I were okay maybe they wouldn't think to notice. . . ." And then, shaking his head, and holding it, rocking back and forth, crying, "I don't know. . . . I don't know. . . . 'Cause I'm fucked up! . . . I don't know . . . "

A cry of anguish and confusion, to be sure, but at the same time an acknowledgement that something here demands to be understood. The terrible moment of shame that Justin feels as he realizes that the only claim he has on anyone's interest or attention is his misery, that there is nothing else about him that would engage the concern of others, that he cannot risk allowing himself to embrace a moment of pleasure because rejection or abandonment would follow quickly in its wake—is suddenly clear to him and it fills him with shame and self-loathing.

Painful as it is for Justin to look at himself, it is nevertheless a necessary beginning. He cannot continue to live within the world he has constructed for himself, built as it is on denial, isolation, deflection, and acting out. He must learn to question himself, to wonder about himself, and to ask himself why he does and feels the things he does and feels; to learn what it is he struggles against and what it is he wishes for. The processes implicit in analytically oriented therapy are relentless in their pursuit of this goal. These processes may not be overt or direct or present in every exchange, but they are returned to over and over again as the therapist solicits, provokes, cajoles, challenges, teases, dares, and sometimes simply invites the patient's curiosity about his own experience. And it is remarkable how often dysfunctional behavior begins to fade away—not as the result of interpretive understanding or because its underlying hidden meaning or motivation has been fully grasped—but simply because it has been questioned. That is, it has been seen as something that could be, that is worthy of questioning, rather than as something that just is, or as patients often say, "That's just the way I am." Because once patients begin to wonder and to be curious about themselves, to take their behavior and feelings as objects of reflection and interest, they cannot help but wonder, "Does it have to be this way?" And the answer to this question is almost never simply, "Yes."

Conclusion

I have been seeking to identify some underlying clinical guidelines that are held in common by all of the psychoanalytically oriented theories. These concerns with safety and trust, with engagement, with reflectivity and curiosity function as implicit values in clinical practice and extend beyond theoretical differences regarding mental structure, motivational systems, or personality origins. They operate as clinical values that push the therapeutic process powerfully along certain paths. As I have tried to show, this powerful thrust is often accomplished intuitively or unconsciously by therapists. While it is true that therapists trained in the dynamic tradition are taught to be on the alert for their own countertransference reactions to patients, to be mindful of moments of idiosyncratic or personalized responses in the clinical encounter, the phenomena I have been discussing are both less and more significant. Less significant, because they are generally not the product of therapists' conflicts or sensitivities likely to intrude upon or distort what the patient is trying to say. But perhaps more significant because they are so imbedded in the natural-feeling flow of communication with patients that we often don't notice them. And yet it is important that we do notice them precisely because they are the fleeting but powerful exchanges through which therapy takes place. They are, more than anything else, the things we do.

I have also sought to make the point that these analytically derived clinical guidelines are deployed without regard to level of pathology, diagnosis, or age of the patient. They may be pursued in different ways, with different language or behavior on the part of the therapist, varying according to who the patient is and what the relationship with the therapist can sustain at any moment. But safety and trust, engagement, and the push toward reflection are the bedrock of the therapeutic enterprise for any analyst, with any patient. For the paranoid patient, it may be moments of trust that are most valuable. For the withdrawn and depressed patient, it may be the solicitation of and tentative experience of engagement that may have the most powerful effect. For the highly constricted, concrete, or acting-out patient, the dawn of curiosity and self-reflection may be the opening through which change and healing begin to happen. But all three of these interlocking components of the therapeutic enterprise are always percolating beneath the surface of the relationship, woven deep into the fabric of almost every exchange, enacted implicitly and sometimes explicitly by the therapist, as he sustains and encourages the patient toward the possibility of change.

But the process takes time. It should be evident from the clinical examples above that these delicately nuanced exchanges attuned to the rapidly shifting play of affect and defense, of engagement and withdrawal, of fear and hope must be cultivated over time, with enormous care and patience. These are not 12-session treatments, or 16-session or even 30-session treatments. Nor can they be seen as strictly symptom-focused treatments. The symptoms, or presenting problems, are often the least approachable aspects of a patient's functioning and often serve as deflections from what really ails them. Certainly in the case of children and adolescents, the presenting symptoms are more often those aspects of a youngster's behavior that have become troublesome to someone else. If they are ever to become troublesome to the young patient himself, it is only on the basis of a therapeutic relationship that embodies these core ideas of trust, engagement, and the solicitation of reflective curiosity. And again, this takes time.

The current enthusiasm for short-term, symptom-focused mental health treatment—often guided by a step-by-step manual—abbreviates the interpersonal exchange. But the interpersonal exchange, with its cues and miscues, its complex layering of gesture, tone, words, and glances, its boldness and feints, revelations and deceptions, is where most patients experience their lives going sadly awry. And when things go wrong in this domain, when relationships are fractured, hurtful, empty, devoid of meaning, or simply nonexistent, the therapeutic task is to unwind the complex web of developmental experiences and of misguided adaptations in order create the possibility for future growth. Treatment protocols that focus simply on symptom reduction do not address these issues.

The symptom, as Freud taught us, is a compromise formation, the distorted vestige of powerful abiding conflicts and throttled longings—hopes, wishes, and fears that dare not emerge lest we shrivel with shame and self-loathing. If we limit our treatment to symptom reduction, we overlook the complex sediment in which these symptoms grow, and risk that they, or others, will grow again in the same unexamined soil. The therapeutic relationship, as it has come to be understood by those dynamic psychotherapists working within the psychoanalytic tradition, is the setting in which symptoms, and more importantly the reasons for symptoms, are made available for reflection and for change. And that relationship, guided as it is by providing for trust and security, for vital engagement, and for reflective self-awareness holds out the greatest hope for lasting change.

References

Ainsworth, M. D., & Bowlby, J. (1991). An ethological approach to personality development. *American Psychologist,* 46, 333–341.

Alexander, F. (1956). *Psychoanalysis and psychotherapy: Developments in theory, technique and training.* New York, NY: Norton

Donnellan, G. J. (1989). Borderline children and the dilemma of therapeutic efficacy. *Contemporary Psychoanalysis,* 25, 393–411.

Escalona, S. (1948). Some considerations regarding psychotherapy with psychotic children. *Bulletin of the Menninger Clinic,* 12, 126–134.

Ekstein, R., & Wallerstein, J. (1956). Observations on the psychotherapy of borderline and psychotic children. *Psychoanalytic Study of the Child,* 11, 303–311.

Fairbairn, W. R. (1952). *Psychoanalytic studies of the personality.* London: Routledge & Kegan Paul Limited.

Freud, A. (1946). *The Ego and the mechanisms of defense.* New York, NY: International Universities Press.

Jones, J. D. (2002). Plea for a measure of understanding: the importance of intensive psychotherapy in the treatment of children with ADHD. *Psychotherapy: Theory/Research/Practice/Training,* 39, 12–20.

Kernberg, P. (1983).Issues in the treatment of borderline conditions in children. In K. Robson (Ed.), *The borderline child: etiology, diagnosis and treatment* (pp. 224–234). Northvale, NJ: Aronson.

Pine, F. (1985). *Developmental theory and clinical process.* New Haven, CT: Yale University Press.

Settlage, C. F. (1989). The interplay of therapeutic and developmental process in the treatment of children: an application of contemporary object relations theory. *Psychoanalytic Inquiry,* 9, 375–396.

Shedler, J. (2010). The efficacy of psychodynamic psychotherapy. *American Psychologist,* 65, 98–110.

Slade, A. (1994). Making meaning and making believe: their role in the clinical process. In A. Slade and D. Wolf (Eds.), *Children at play* (pp. 81–107). New York, NY: Oxford University Press.

Stern, D. (1985). *The Interpersonal world of the infant.* New York, NY: Basic Books.

Wallin, D. J. (2007). *Attachment in psychotherapy.* New York, NY: Guilford Press.

Winnicott, D. W. (1960). The theory of the parent–infant relationship. *International Journal of Psychoanalysis,* 41, 585–595.

9

EVIDENCE-BASED PRACTICE AND CHILDHOOD PSYCHOSIS

Emily Kline, Jason Schiffman, Jimmy Choi, Christiana Laitner, and Jon Rogove

> *The voices are so frightening and annoying. They tell me to do things I don't want to do, and sometimes I can't stop myself from doing what they say. I hate them. I want them to go away and never come back . . . When I get better I'm going to go to move back home, go to college, and become a social worker.*
>
> —Emma (April 2013)[1]

The quotation printed above reflects an appreciation for the emotional and maladaptive impact a psychotic disorder can have on a child's life. The contributor, Emma, is a 16-year-old inpatient with a penchant for playing basketball and dreams of becoming a psychotherapist, who has, over the past several years, experienced an insidious and debilitating cognitive, emotional, and social devolution. The years between her 13th and 16th birthdays were characterized by increasingly incapacitating negative symptomatology, frequent auditory command hallucinations, persecutory delusions, compromised impulse control, and recurrent episodes of agitation, anxiety, and dysphoria.

Just as debilitating are the secondary social ramifications of her illness. Despite the fact that Emma is usually soft-spoken and reserved, her unpredictable odd behavior and interpersonal deficits are off-putting to her peers, who have begun to actively dislike and victimize her. Fortunately, her family has been exceptionally supportive and understanding, and some of Emma's positive symptoms have responded well to medication treatment. More recently, she has begun to respond favorably to a number of psychosocial and psychoeducational interventions. Although the road to recovery is likely to be long and challenging, Emma, her family, and her treatment team are hopeful that she will continue to improve.

In many ways, Emma's story is typical of early-onset schizophrenia (EOS). Schizophrenia remains one of the top causes of disability in the world (Knapp, Mangalore, & Simon, 2004), and individuals with psychotic disorders (including schizophrenia) are at significant risk for compromised psychosocial functioning, a host of medical and psychosocial sequelae, and impoverished quality of life (QOL). Furthermore, the functional outcomes of early-onset psychosis are typically poorer than those associated with adult-onset psychosis, with earlier onset being associated with worse prognosis (Asarnow, Tompson, & Goldstein, 1994; Deakin & Lennox, 2013; Fleischhaker et al., 2005; I. C. Gillberg, Hellgren, & Gillberg, 1993; Lay, Blanz, Hartmann, & Schmidt, 2000; Maziade et al., 1996; Werry, McClellan, & Chard, 1991).

Despite the very serious developmental and functional ramifications of EOS and other psychotic disorders, the majority of available psychosocial treatments have been validated for use in adults, and the evidence base is surprisingly sparse with regard to psychosocial treatments for children with psychosis. The current chapter was written with two purposes in mind: to (a) summarize the current state of knowledge regarding non-pharmacological interventions for psychotic disorders in children and adolescents, and (b) provide the reader with a concrete framework for the provision of evidence-based treatment.

Recovery-Oriented Treatment for Youth with Psychosis

Within the current nosology, primary psychotic disorders include schizophrenia, schizoaffective disorder (applied for individuals with significantly impairing mood episodes in addition to periods of non-affective psychosis), delusional disorder (for individuals with one or more delusions but not meeting full criteria for a diagnosis of schizophrenia), and "brief psychotic" or schizophreniform disorder (for individuals with recent-onset symptoms or symptoms lasting no longer than one and six months respectively) (American Psychiatric Association, 2013). These disorders, along with schizotypal personality disorder, are sometimes referred to collectively as the "schizophrenia spectrum."[2]

A schizophrenia spectrum or psychotic disorder diagnosis can imply the expectation of a long struggle with a highly stigmatizing condition. Precisely because of this stigma, psychotherapists and other mental health care providers are advised to emphasize *recovery* during every stage of diagnosis and treatment for patients with psychosis. Recovery refers broadly to leading a satisfying and engaged life within consumers' communities of choice, and serves as a guiding principle for evidence-based care (Liberman, 2012). Recovery implies investment in long-term management of symptoms of mental illness; however, within a recovery framework, treatment goals should go beyond "symptom reduction" to encompass meaningful social and occupational contributions (Barber, 2012). For example, rather than focusing narrowly on illness-related aims such as eliminating hallucinations or managing suicidal ideation, a more personal recovery-oriented treatment program might emphasize goals such as living independently, finishing college, obtaining employment within a desired field, or maintaining an active social and romantic life.

Recovery-oriented interventions should promote long-term goal setting and community integration, with an understanding that most adolescents with psychosis will require psychosocial, educational, and/or vocational supports beyond psychiatric medication management or psychotherapy alone (McClellan et al., 2001; Schiffman, Chorpita, Daleiden, Maeda, & Nakamura, 2008; Schiffman & Dixon, 2011). Thus, practice parameters for individuals with psychosis emphasize a multi-dimensional approach to treatment involving complementary services to support recovery from illness (Dixon et al., 2010; McClellan et al., 2001).

A related principle of recovery-oriented treatment reflects respect for patients' and families' autonomy to choose among treatment options. Taking time to understand families' goals and preferences—for example, by carefully helping to explain the potential risks and benefits associated with medications, taking concerns about stigma seriously, and engaging parents and caregivers as allies (rather than obstacles) in treatment—may help to build therapeutic rapport, enhance clients' and families' motivation to adhere to complex treatment plans, and instill a sense of optimism and empowerment regarding mental health treatment. Although family engagement is listed as a highly supported treatment within the schizophrenia Patient Outcomes Research Team recommendations (Dixon et al., 2010), caregivers of psychotic-disordered youth often report considerable barriers with respect to both identifying appropriate services and engaging with care providers (Knock et al., 2011). Thus, family engagement remains an area for particular emphasis within a recovery-oriented treatment framework.

Finally, the recovery movement places importance on clients' abilities to live within "communities of choice," as opposed to long-term residential treatment facilities or other potentially marginalizing spaces reserved for mentally ill residents. This principle echoes the legal mandate embedded within the Individuals with Disabilities Education Act to educate children with mental health and behavioral concerns within the "least restrictive environment." In other words, although inpatient hospitalizations may be necessary to manage acute crises and initiate treatment, long-term care for adolescents with psychosis should generally take place within clients' preferred communities. In fact, most teens with schizophrenia do not require residential treatment or lengthy hospital stays (Dyer, 1998), and maintaining (or establishing) connections to natural support systems is important for both young and older consumers with psychosis. Although safety is an important concern for this vulnerable population, many youth can receive effective treatment in outpatient settings. Comprehensive programs such as Assertive Community Treatment (ACT) and family-oriented "wraparound" services were designed specifically to support individuals with significant need who are at risk for hospitalization.

Adapting the Evidence Base

Unfortunately, the evidence base for psychotherapeutic interventions developed specifically for the treatment of EOS in children and adolescents is slim. Psychotherapists treating adolescents with schizophrenia and other psychotic disorders are encouraged to adapt empirically supported treatments developed for adults with schizophrenia to address younger clients' needs (McClellan et al., 2001). Alternatively, therapists may find that evidence-based practices (EBPs) developed for adult populations are inappropriate for school-age clients; in this case, a second strategy is to adapt empirically supported interventions developed for similar child populations. For example, young clients experiencing anxieties or phobias stemming from delusions and hallucinations may benefit from exposure and desensitization therapy originally developed for anxious children (Nakamura, Schiffman, Lam, Becker, & Chorpita, 2006).

Psychotherapists treating children with psychotic disorders are likely to work alongside psychiatrists, medical specialists, educators, and case managers to provide multiple treatment components that aim to facilitate recovery across settings. The existing evidence supports the use of an array of treatment options, including pharmacologic agents, psychoeducation, Assertive Community Treatment (ACT), supportive employment/education, skills training, behavioral modification, and cognitive behavioral therapy (Dixon et al., 2010). Many of these interventions are intended to serve complementary goals, and children and adolescents diagnosed with EOS are likely to benefit most from a variety of supports incorporated within a multi-modal treatment plan, with psychotherapy playing an important role.

Staging Interventions by Illness Phase

Schizophrenia typically follows a chronic-recurrent course, with peak onset during adolescence and young adulthood. First-episode psychosis (FEP) often represents a time of crisis. Treatment initiation may be triggered by some crisis event such as aggressive behavior, a suicide attempt, or grossly disorganized behavior. At this stage, primary treatment goals include addressing safety concerns, connecting families with resources, establishing a diagnosis, and initiating appropriate medication treatment. Once medications take effect, however, most people with schizophrenia are unfortunately not symptom-free.

"Residual" stages of psychotic illness may involve some persistent low-level hallucinations or delusions, as well as many negative symptoms, which are less effectively targeted by existing medications (Arango, Garibaldi, & Marder, 2013). Youth whose primary psychotic symptoms are in remission are likely to continue to struggle with characteristic negative symptoms such as apathy and social skill deficits. Further, young clients may be wrestling with feelings of stigma or shame surrounding their diagnosis, and may have at least temporarily missed milestones or lost friendships as a result of their illness. Parents, too, may require help processing illness stigma or managing children's apathetic or oppositional attitudes and behaviors.

Over time, most clients (in one recent cohort study, about 65% over the three years following initial treatment; Caseiro et al., 2012) typically experience an exacerbation of symptoms requiring re-engagement with services, and possibly hospitalization/re-hospitalization, during which safety concerns and medication adjustments may reassert themselves as primary concerns. Thus, different interventions will be appropriate during different stages of the client's illness.

Evidence-Based Practice for First-Episode Psychosis (FEP) and Acute Illness Establishing Safety

Establishing safety and stabilization during acute illness should be the primary goal during initial engagement with services (McClellan et al., 2001). Psychotherapists encountering children and adolescents with acute or recent-onset psychosis should be aware that suicidal gestures and other dangerous behaviors constitute a major concern for this population. Within a 282-person incidence sample of patients with first-episode psychosis (mean age at illness onset of 21 years), 61 patients (22%) experienced at least one suicide attempt during the seven years following diagnosis; of these patients, 12 (4% of the total sample) completed suicide (Robinson et al., 2010). Although the vast majority of people with psychosis do not commit violent crimes, the first episode of psychosis is associated with increased risk for aggression and violence. Fortunately, engagement with treatment appears to substantially reduce the likelihood of dangerous behaviors (Large & Nielssen, 2011).

To assess for safety concerns, clinicians should ask both clients and caregivers directly about suicidal thoughts, suicidal actions or plans, and children's access to potentially lethal means (e.g., firearms in the home). For children who demonstrate suicidal behavior and express intention to follow through on a plan to harm themselves, close and constant observation, as well as removal of all access to means, may be the best way to manage immediate safety concerns. Counseling parents on reducing children's access to firearms is also vital to establishing safety for children with suicidal intention. Although any method of self-harm is cause for serious concern, 85% of suicidal gestures with a firearm prove fatal, compared to less than 2% of attempts using pills, poisoning, or sharp objects (Miller, Azrael, & Barber, 2012). Thus, speaking directly with parents about eliminating children's access to guns within their homes can make a difference between life and death.

Families with concerns about suicide or aggression should also be equipped with 24-hour safety plans that detail how they will deal with emergent safety issues. After discussing and defining possible crises, parents and children may be able to identify triggers or warning signs that may indicate an escalating situation.

Psychotherapists can model open communication about maintaining a safety plan, help children to identify trusted adults in whom they can confide, and help parents decide how they will manage concerns. Many cities and counties have 24-hour crisis hotlines or "warm-lines" that provide a preferable alternative to police or emergency services involvement (Walter, Petr, & Davis, 2006; Watson & Fulambarkar, 2012). Some research suggests that phone- and home-based crisis intervention services help to curtail need for inpatient hospitalizations (e.g., Brimblecombe, O'Sullivan, & Parkinson, 2003).

Supporting Medication Adherence

For children experiencing a first episode of psychotic illness or an acute exacerbation of psychotic symptoms, pharmacological intervention with antipsychotic medication (APM) is advised as a first-line evidence-based treatment. Children should receive a thorough assessment from a child psychiatrist familiar with the guidelines for pediatric prescribing. Unfortunately, APMs are associated with several adverse side effects, most commonly weight gain and increased risk for developing type-2 diabetes (Bobo et al., 2013). Side effects commonly associated with APMs should be carefully monitored, since there is evidence to suggest that teens may be particularly vulnerable to adverse medication effects (Bobo et al., 2013; Correll, 2008). Prescribers should regularly measure children's height and weight; check fasting blood levels of insulin, glucose, and triglycerides; and monitor children for other possible side effects such as extrapyramidal symptoms (i.e., involuntary movements or anomalies in motor coordination) (Mitchell, Delaffon, Vancampfort, Correll, & De Hert, 2012). Monitoring these side effects is deemed so important that some states require a pre-authorization for the prescription of APMs to youth under 18 receiving Medicaid, whereby authorization is contingent upon ongoing clinical review (e.g., Maryland Department of Health and Mental Hygiene, 2013). Psychotherapists can play a key role in referring young clients to a psychiatric prescriber, helping to monitor side effects, and coordinating follow-up to monitor medication effectiveness and safety.

Beyond initial prescribing, medication adherence may present a challenge for children with schizophrenia and other psychotic disorders. Studies suggest that 33% to 90% of clients receiving mental health services after receiving a psychotic disorder diagnosis are expected to discontinue use of prescribed medications within one year of treatment initiation (Conus et al., 2010; Gearing & Charach, 2009; Mullins, Obeidat, Cuffel, Naradzay, & Loebel, 2008). This figure may be even higher among younger consumers, who are known to struggle with adherence to both medical and behavioral interventions across medical and psychiatric diagnoses (Salema, Elliott, & Glazebrook, 2011). Faithful adherence to a medication regimen is an important predictor of illness prognosis, since individuals with psychosis who discontinue antipsychotic medications are 5 times more likely to experience symptomatic relapse or rehospitalization during the three years following initial treatment engagement. One large cohort study found that 94% of first-episode patients who discontinued their medications experienced a substantially impairing relapse of symptoms, compared to 51% of patients who reported good adherence to prescribed medications (Caseiro et al., 2012). Psychotherapists can help to improve medication adherence by creating a nonjudgmental space to discuss medication issues with clients and offering targeted interventions to address clients' medication concerns.

Families may struggle with medication adherence for a variety of reasons. Poor adherence may be driven by side effect concerns (e.g., weight gain, motor effects, fatigue, sedation), feelings of stigma about mental health treatment, difficulty organizing a daily medication regimen, and normal developmental concerns about wanting to avoid being different from peers. In some cases, reluctance to take medication may be tied to delusional symptoms. For example, a child who is paranoid may be suspicious that the medication is poisonous or worry that mental health practitioners intend to cause harm. Asking open-ended questions about medication concerns and reviewing clients' and families' understanding of the medication effects may elicit misinformation or distorted thoughts about treatment that may be impacting adherence.

Depending on which of these issues are present, psychotherapists can utilize several evidence-based approaches to assist clients in improving medication adherence. "Pragmatic" strategies that emphasize problem-solving and building medications into daily routines have the greatest support in the literature on adherence-supporting interventions (Barkhof, Meijer, de Sonneville, Linszen, & de Haan, 2012). Modeling effective problem-solving skills and connecting families with low-cost community resources can help with resolving logistical issues such as difficulty with accessing a qualified prescriber and navigating pharmacy refills, insurance coverage, and copays. Behavioral interventions can help to organize families who struggle with forgetting or children's refusal to take medications. For example, setting a cell phone alarm or pairing medication with a routine daily behavior (e.g., brushing teeth or checking homework) can help with reminding families to administer medications at the same time every day. Having everyone in the family take medications (or vitamins) together can help to normalize and support medication adherence. Parents might pair medications with a desired treat (e.g., a favorite juice or snack) or implement a point system to reinforce adherence for children who are reluctant to take medications as prescribed. Behavioral practice with swallowing pills may help to make the experience less aversive for children who have difficulty swallowing medications (Ghuman, Cataldo, Beck, & Slifer, 2004). Some youth may also benefit from arranging to have medications administered by a school nurse during the weekdays if parents have difficulty administering the medication consistently.

For children or families who are ambivalent about medication use, motivational strategies may be more useful for helping to support commitment to medication adherence. Although the evidence on motivational interviewing to support medication adherence among consumers with schizophrenia is mixed, some studies have found positive effects (Barkhof et al., 2012). Motivational interviewing emphasizes nonjudgmental listening, validating clients' ambivalence, encouraging clients to connect behaviors to their "bigger picture" goals and values, and setting small, attainable goals toward behavior change (Miller & Rollnick, 2012). Providing psychoeducation about how medications work and how adherence impacts prognosis may also be helpful. For families with concerns about side effects, validating those concerns and helping clients find compensatory strategies to combat troubling side effects may help to resolve ambivalence. For example, working with clients to improve diet and exercise may help to alleviate adherence issues stemming from concerns regarding antipsychotic-related weight gain.

Evidence-Based Practice for Ongoing, Recovery-Oriented Treatment Assertive Community Treatment (ACT)

Beyond supporting medication adherence, youth with schizophrenia and other psychotic disorders are likely to benefit from multi-component treatment "packages" that support both ongoing symptom remission as well as meaningful social, educational, and occupational recovery goals. Psychotherapists may find themselves coordinating care alongside other supports including psychiatrists, regular and special education teachers, school social workers, primary care pediatricians, and vocational counselors. "Systems of care" that are poorly coordinated can cause frustration for patients and families. Assertive Community Treatment (ACT) is an empirically supported service model that emphasizes coordination of care between professionals and frequent outreach to clients within their community (Dixon et al., 2010). ACT aims to organize efforts within an interdisciplinary treatment team so that all providers are working to advance the same treatment goals. Practitioners working within the ACT model emphasize consumer choice and community integration. ACT case managers may meet multiple times per week with clients at various settings, including home, school, work, and clinic. Within the ACT model, care is driven by consumers' long-term recovery goals (e.g., living independently, getting a job) rather than goals that are more narrowly focused on mental illness management (e.g., symptom reduction). Among patients with schizophrenia, ACT has been found to significantly reduce homelessness and hospitalizations (for review see Coldwell & Bender, 2007). Some evidence suggests that ACT also contributes to meaningful improvements in employment outcomes relative to standard care or other treatment packages (McFarlane et al., 2000).

Implementation of the ACT model for early onset psychosis has received minimal empirical attention; one pilot study did find that ACT was effective for engaging and treating adolescents with severe mental illness who initially refused treatment (Baier et al., 2013). The "wraparound" model offers a similar integrative approach to multi-disciplinary care that is more targeted to the needs of younger consumers. Similar to ACT, wraparound emphasizes consumer choice, community-based care, and a team approach that recognizes families' strengths, preferences, and areas of expertise (Bruns, Sather, Pullman, & Stambaugh, 2011). Some longitudinal evidence suggests that families engaged in wraparound care experience clinically significant improvements with regard to symptom reduction, positive behaviors, and caregiver wellbeing (Painter, 2012). Although wraparound has not been studied in randomized controlled trials, it offers a promising, child-focused model that has demonstrated positive results in preliminary research efforts.

Supporting Educational and Occupational Goals

Children with schizophrenia and related mental illnesses are likely to fall behind in school and may require special educational services to successfully pursue educational goals (Frazier et al., 2007). Consistent with the Individuals with Disabilities Education Act (IDEA) enacted as federal law in 1990 (and revised in 2004), students may be eligible for an Individualized Education Program (IEP), which specifies services that will help to ensure children's success within an appropriate educational setting. IDEA stipulates that schools are required to provide the necessary supports, which may include accommodations such as school-based counseling, a quiet space or extra time to complete work, or a one-to-one educational aide within a larger classroom. Psychotherapists can help parents to advocate for children within the school system by providing written recommendations for IEP accommodations and attending IEP meetings. Psychotherapists can also work with children to improve study skills, and communicate with teachers regarding IEP implementation (Nuechterlein et al., 2008).

Older teens may be interested in preparing for employment and independent living once they complete their education. Because many people with schizophrenia have significant social- and life-skill deficits (Röpcke & Eggers, 2005), explicit training on steps for successful social interactions, self-care, household tasks, and relevant job skills may be tremendously important for teens with these recovery goals. Several vocational support programs have been shown to improve employment outcomes for people with schizophrenia (Lehman et al., 2002). With regard to vocational goals, the "supported employment" model has the best empirical support for people with schizophrenia (Dixon et al., 2010). This model emphasizes obtaining competitive (not disability-focused) community positions, and eschews "readiness criteria" that may hamper job seeking. The best outcomes are observed for supported employment programs that provide assistance with job-seeking, involve mental health providers in supporting vocational goals, allow clients to choose which jobs they would like to pursue, and provide indefinite (not time limited) support (Killackey, Jackson, & McGorry, 2008; Nuechterlein et al., 2008).

Evidence-Based Psychotherapy

Although the interventions described in the preceding paragraphs provide a useful framework for approaching treatment for young clients with schizophrenia and other psychotic disorders, more "traditional" office-based psychotherapy is also important for maintaining progress toward recovery goals. Few controlled studies, however, have examined the impact of psychotherapy specifically for childhood psychosis. Below, we review family-based and individual psychotherapy approaches that have good empirical support for adults with schizophrenia, and/or for youth with behavioral difficulties that may have idiographic overlap for individuals seeking treatment for early onset psychotic disorders. These include family psychoeducation, parent skills training, behavior modification, social skills training, and cognitive behavior therapy.

Family Psychoeducation

Although we have highlighted the importance of psychoeducation with regard to medication adherence, many families will have more basic questions about what a diagnosis "means," how it has been ascertained, and whether it is liable to change over time. Information about the causes and symptoms of psychosis, as well as about effective treatment options, can help alleviate anxiety among both adolescents and their families. Although "too much/too fast" can be overwhelming for some consumers, effective psychoeducation can build a strong therapeutic relationship between consumers and providers, empower consumers to advocate for high-quality services, and reduce stigma and distress for identified patients and their families (Green, Wisdom, Wolfe, & Firemark, 2012).

Further, a substantial body of research supports the finding that family conflict may influence the course of schizophrenia over time. Individuals with schizophrenia whose families demonstrate high levels of "expressed emotion," characterized by critical attitudes toward the family member with schizophrenia, are more likely to experience re-hospitalization following initial engagement with mental health services (Hooley, 1985). This may be particularly true for children with schizophrenia, who are more likely to reside with and depend on adult caregivers. Caregivers of children with schizophrenia describe substantial stressors relating to raising adolescents with schizophrenia, ensuring their safety, and obtaining appropriate mental health services (Knock et al., 2011). Effective psychoeducation can help to reduce family stress by providing caregivers with information about the causes of children's behaviors and effective options for helping to manage their illness (Dixon et al., 2011). Psychoeducation can be delivered as a part of office-based family therapy, but may be particularly effective in a multifamily group setting such as the National Alliance on Mental Illness's "Family to Family" or "Basics" programs (Brister et al., 2012; Dixon et al., 2011; McFarlane, Dixon, Lukens, & Lucksted, 2003).

Behavior Modification

Behavior modification plans rely on operant learning principles to encourage the performance of desired behaviors. Behavior plans use reinforcement (in the form of praise, privileges, tangible rewards, or points or tokens that can be used toward future rewards) to encourage children to engage in appropriate and productive behavior. Although behavior modification has more extensive empirical support for treating youth with oppositional or disruptive behavior (Michelson, Davenport, Dretzke, Barlow, & Day, 2013), children with psychosis may benefit from behavior plans, daily report cards, or other forms of token economies designed to shape behavior. Working with parents to target specific behaviors may help to improve clients' overall functioning and resolve family conflicts despite the recurrence or chronicity of symptoms. For example, children might be reinforced with prizes or special activities for demonstrating desired behaviors such as completing chores and doing homework, and miss opportunities to earn rewards if they engage in disruptive behaviors such as refusing to follow parents' directives or throwing tantrums. Other non-desired behaviors can be discouraged through loss of rewards or privileges. Token economies and other programs of behavior modification have been widely used in adults with schizophrenia, as well as among youth with diverse mental health and behavioral concerns (Dickerson, Tenhula, & Green-Paden, 2005). Similar to children with other mental health diagnoses, clients with psychosis are likely to benefit from well-designed, individualized behavioral interventions.

Behavioral approaches might also involve role-playing and behavioral practice of specific social and vocational skills to compensate for specific skill deficits. Among adults with schizophrenia, social skill deficits predict poor occupational function (Dickinson, Bellack, & Gold, 2007); for youth, poor social skills may lead to frustration in school and problems with making friends or dealing with bullies. Young clients may benefit from role-playing to practice skills such as introducing themselves, using friendly body language, and participating appropriately in class. Older teens might wish to practice vocationally oriented skills such as greeting customers or practicing job interviews. Using rewards for practice may be helpful for engaging children who are reluctant to try new skills. The use of behavior modification principles to shape socially competent behavior has been explored in depth, with excellent empirical support, for children with autism and developmental delays (e.g., Nuernberger, Ringdahl, Vargo, Crumpecker, & Gunnarsson, 2013).

Cognitive Behavioral Therapy

Cognitive behavioral therapy (CBT) combines principles of behavioral modification with therapeutic interventions that help patients to identify and challenge distorted or unhelpful patterns of thinking. CBT has been widely applied to many disorders of adolescence and adulthood (especially the "internalizing" disorders such as depression and anxiety), and there is good evidence to suggest that CBT for psychosis (CBTp) is more effective than "treatment as usual" for reducing positive, negative, and general symptoms among people with schizophrenia (Sarin, Wallin, & Widerlöv, 2011).

CBT typically utilizes a "problem-oriented" framework to identify and structure treatment around specific goals. Unlike supportive or psychodynamic sessions, CBT sessions are usually somewhat structured and may follow a specific agenda that is more like an "educational" than traditionally therapeutic model. CBT therapists engage clients with an attitude of collaborative empiricism; that is, a focus on working together to "figure out" a client's goals and problem-solve barriers to achieving them (Tarrier, 2008). Clinicians play a Socratic role, using questions to help clients identify distorted thoughts and maladaptive behaviors (see Box 1 for an example of how a therapist might use a Socratic CBT approach to address a young client's concerns).

Although there has been limited research on using CBT to treat psychotic disorders in children and adolescents, studies of mostly-young cohorts receiving CBT during a first episode of psychosis indicate some benefit with regard to improvements in quality of life and functioning (Morrison, 2009). Reviews on the topic of CBT during first-episode psychosis emphasize the importance of "phasing" interventions to fit clients' needs; in other words, CBT may be most likely to have maximal effect once safety, medication, and case management concerns have been fully addressed (Addington & Gleeson, 2005; Marshall & Rathbone, 2011; Morrison, 2009).

Cognitive-behavioral approaches may also be effective for treating anxieties and behavioral concerns that arise secondary to psychotic symptoms. Nakamura et al. (2006) describe the successful treatment of water phobia in an adolescent with schizophrenia who had the delusion that monsters in the water threatened to swim into his ears. Clinicians helped the child to construct a fear hierarchy involving "mildly," "moderately," and "very" anxiety-provoking activities involving water, then collected daily fear ratings as they conducted gradual exposure to the identified activities. Psychotherapists may find it helpful to target treatment to specific behaviors (in this case, refusal to touch water), with more limited attention paid to the psychotic aspects of the refusal. This approach may be helpful for young clients with a variety of defiant and/or phobic behaviors that arise secondary to psychotic experiences.

Example CBT Session with Adolescent with Psychosis

"Joey" is a 17-year-old client with a diagnosis of schizophrenia. He began experiencing psychotic symptoms two years ago; since that time, he has been taking medications to help manage his symptoms and working with the IEP coordinator and counselor at his school. Now he is seeing a psychotherapist to address ongoing issues including odd and disruptive behaviors at school and difficulties getting along with other teens. During this check-in, the therapist encourages Joey to identify and challenge his unhelpful thoughts.

THERAPIST: How is school going this week, Joey?

JOEY: Bad. I hate school; I can't wait until I don't have to go anymore.

THERAPIST: What makes you say that?

JOEY: The other kids are rude. They all stare at me on the bus and in the hallway. They steal things from my locker.

THERAPIST: Someone stole from your locker?

JOEY: Yeah. I told you, they are rude.

THERAPIST: When did that happen?

JOEY: Well, if they had the chance, they would steal from me every day. I can tell they are planning something. I have different locks, so I switch between them.

THERAPIST: You feel like you need to be careful.

JOEY: I do need to be careful! Everyone is against me.

THERAPIST: It must be tough to get through the day with thoughts like that in your mind. Tell me, when was the last time an item disappeared from your locker?

JOEY: Last fall someone stole my iPod. I told my teacher but no one ever got caught.

THERAPIST: Your iPod? That's terrible! I'm really sorry that happened to you. Has anything like that happened since then?

JOEY: No, because I use the locks. But that's why I can't be friends with anyone.

THERAPIST: Well, it sounds like a smart decision to keep your things safely locked. That's a really bad experience to have. But I'm wondering why you feel like all the kids are "against you"—I'm not sure I understand your train of thinking.

JOEY (exasperated): I told you! They stole my stuff!

THERAPIST: Who stole your stuff?

JOEY: I don't know! Someone did!

THERAPIST: Someone? You mean, you think the thief acted alone?

JOEY: Well, yeah, probably. I guess he acted alone, because nobody saw him.

THERAPIST: So there was one kid—maybe two—who did something really mean and nasty.

JOEY: Yes.

THERAPIST: What about all the other kids in the class? Did they ever have things stolen from their lockers?

JOEY: Yeah, this girl Mariah, her phone got stolen. She is really popular; she probably hates me too.

THERAPIST: I want to focus on the theft issue right now, Joey. So, Mariah, who is popular, her phone was stolen. Does that mean that everyone is against Mariah? That Mariah can't be friendly to anyone at school?

JOEY (rolling his eyes): Of course not—I told you, she's popular!

THERAPIST: Oh, okay, right. You did tell me that. So wait, you're saying that even popular kids have to be careful to lock their lockers. Even though pretty much everyone in school thinks they are cool and wants to be their friend.

JOEY: Yeah, I guess.

THERAPIST: Huh. I wonder . . . even though it was very unlucky that someone stole your iPod . . . could it be that the other kids are not really "against" you? You just had some bad luck, like Mariah?

JOEY: Ummm. I don't know. Maybe. Yeah, maybe.

THERAPIST: Interesting. Let's take a minute to look at the thoughts-feelings-actions triangle we've been using. "Everyone's against me"—is that a thought, a feeling, or an action?

JOEY: It's a thought.

THERAPIST: That's right! And when you have that thought, how does it make you feel?

JOEY: Bad, I guess.

THERAPIST: Can you be more specific?

JOEY: Worried, and also angry.

THERAPIST: Good. Does that thought, and those feelings, do they affect your behavior?

JOEY: I don't know.

THERAPIST: Well sometimes if I feel worried and angry, I just want to go off somewhere by myself.

JOEY: Yeah, I want to be alone.

THERAPIST: Yeah, I would, too. So that thought—"everyone's against me"—is that a helpful thought or a hurtful thought, for you?

JOEY: Hurtful.

THERAPIST: Is it realistic?

JOEY: Well, maybe sometimes. But like I said, even Mariah got her phone stolen.

THERAPIST: That's a really good point. I wonder if there is a more helpful thought you could have in that situation.

JOEY: I could think about . . . how it could happen to anyone, not just me?

THERAPIST: Nice! I like it. So at school tomorrow, if you have the thought, "everyone's against me"—try following that up with your more helpful thought, "bad things can happen to anyone." And see if you notice a difference in the way you feel, or even the way you behave. I'll be very curious to hear how that goes.

Cognitive Rehabilitation

Although cognitive deficits are not criteria for diagnosis within the psychosis spectrum, many individuals with schizophrenia and related disorders demonstrate neuropsychological impairment across several domains of cognitive functioning relative to individuals unaffected by psychosis (Green, Kern, & Heaton, 2004; Kurtz, 2005). Deficits in areas such as processing speed and verbal memory are associated with poor social and occupational functioning, and have proven largely resistant to antipsychotic medications (Ueland et al., 2004; Wykes & Spaulding, 2011). For youth struggling with psychosis, greater cognitive deficits may predict poorer social development, reduced educational attainment, and more long-term disability (Bachman, Niendam, & Jalbrzikowski, 2011; Brewer et al., 2005; Lencz et al., 2006; Niendam et al., 2007; Wykes et al., 2007). Given such findings, researchers have recently begun to focus on whether psychotherapeutic interventions that explicitly target cognitive deficits might be able to positively influence cognitive abilities and functional outcomes among young people with psychosis.

In the last decade, cognitive rehabilitation (CR) approaches have been tested among adults with psychosis in clinical and vocational settings (McGurk, Mueser, Feldman, Wolfe, & Pascaris, 2007; McGurk, Twamley, Sitzer, McHugo, & Mueser, 2007; Silverstein et al., 2005). Trials involving CR have yielded improvements for patients on both cognitive tasks and daily functioning (Bell, Fiszdon, Greig, Wexler, & Bryson, 2007; Eack, Hogarty, Greenwald, Hogarty, & Keshavan, 2011). Since CR has been somewhat effective in improving cognition even in adult patients with chronic psychosis, researchers have set out to determine whether CR may be helpful to younger patients, who may have more neuroplasticity and who are earlier in the course of illness progression (Frazier et al., 2012).

Three studies have investigated the effectiveness of CR for improving cognitive and adaptive functioning among youth with psychosis (Ueland & Rund, 2004; Wykes et al., 2007; Urban et al., 2012). Although the studies were relative small (none involved more than 40 participants), all three suggested that CR packages involving a variety of tasks exercising cognitive domains (e.g., working and long-term memory, sustained attention, social perception, processing speed, and problem solving) may be effective for strengthening cognitive skills. Further, results from the three trials suggest that clients' cognitive improvement may translate to reduced symptom severity and improved social functioning. To determine if social outcome can be enhanced, current trials are underway to tailor CR for different age groups in adolescence, and create tablet- and phone-based CR game packages to keep the youth engaged in treatment. Further studies are needed, however, to understand the "active ingredients" in CR protocols and whether change in cognitive skills can reliably predict improvements in everyday functioning for youth with psychosis.

Evidence-Based Practice for Youth with Affective Psychosis

A thorough diagnostic assessment using validated instruments such as the Kiddie Schedule for Affective Disorders and Schizophrenia (KSADS; Kaufman et al., 1997) or the Children's Interview for Psychiatric Syndromes (ChIPS; E. B. Weller, Weller, Fristad, Rooney, & Schecter,, 2000) can help clinicians to tease apart whether clients' experiences meet criteria for schizophrenia, another primary psychotic disorder, or are better conceptualized within an alternative diagnostic category. Clinicians may note psychotic "features"—that is, delusional ideas, paranoid thinking, auditory or visual hallucinations, dissociative experiences—that fit several different clinical conceptualizations. For example, a child with post-traumatic stress disorder may have intense concerns about safety with little provocation; individuals suffering from panic attacks may report feeling like they are having "out of body" or "unreal" experiences.

More commonly, individuals with major depressive disorder (MDD) and bipolar I disorder (BID) may experience psychotic features accompanying major mood episodes. One multi-site study estimated the prevalence of psychosis within adults with MDD to be around 6% (Goes et al., 2007), and prevalence of psychosis within BID is estimated to be far higher, around 68% (Keck et al., 2003). Clinicians can distinguish between MDD or BID and schizophrenia-spectrum diagnoses by obtaining a thorough history with regard to the timing of symptoms, and whether the child has ever experienced psychosis in the absence of mood disturbances (American Psychiatric Association, 2013). Assessment tools such as the KSADS contain prompts that help clinicians to differentiate mood disorders from schizophrenia-spectrum diagnoses.

The prevalence of psychotic symptoms occurring in conjunction with mood disorders among children has not been conclusively determined. Most of the existing literature suggests that presence of psychotic symptoms among children and adolescents with mood disorders is relatively rare. For youth experiencing psychosis within the context of a primary mood disorder, clinicians are advised to consult the evidence base for addressing mood episodes. Following is a brief review of the evidence-based psychological and psychosocial treatments recommended for the treatment of childhood-onset MDD and BID.

Major Depressive Disorder

MDD is a mood disorder typified by one or more prolonged periods of sadness and disinterest in, or an inability to experience pleasure from, the activities a person normally enjoys, that affects physical health and daily functioning. Some, but not all, persons with MDD also experience psychotic symptoms. When they do, such symptoms tend to occur only when mood symptoms are also present. According to the *DSM 5*, psychotic features associated with MDD may be either mood congruent or mood incongruent. Mood congruent psychotic features often include typical depressive themes, such as "personal inadequacy, guilt, disease, death, nihilism, or deserved punishment" (American Psychiatric Association, 2013).

The efficacy of cognitive behavior therapy (CBT) in the treatment of mood disorders, including MDD, affecting children and adolescents is well established. Though CBT interventions for children and adolescents with MDD were initially derived from cognitive therapy for adults, CBT protocols have been adapted to provide a developmentally appropriate format for children (Fongay, Target, Cottrell, Phillips, & Kurtz, 2002). One of the most widely cited studies in this area, the National Institute of Mental Health (NIMH) Treatment for Adolescents with Depression Study (TADS), has widely informed practice guidelines for the treatment of MDD in youth (March et al., 2004). Using a randomized controlled design in which participants received 36 weeks of treatment, TADS demonstrated a combination of CBT and fluoxetine treatment was the superior treatment for the moderately to severely depressed adolescents participating in the study, as compared to either CBT or fluoxetine treatment alone (March et al., 2004).

The CBT portion of the TADS intervention is a manual-based treatment administered predominately in individual therapy, but also including some parent sessions, over three phases: acute treatment, continuation, and maintenance (Rohde, Feeny, & Robins, 2005). Throughout, it utilizes established cognitive and behavioral strategies such as treatment rationale, mood monitoring, goal setting, increasing pleasant activities, problem solving, identifying automatic thoughts and cognitive disturbances, and replacing cognitive distortions with realistic counter thoughts. Although the TADS study was not explicit about treating youth who had psychotic symptoms with depression, the strategies employed in the TADS study are consistent with many of the principles of treatment for psychosis described above.

Bipolar I Disorder

Bipolar I Disorder (BID), the more severe form of bipolar disorder, is characterized by the occurrence of one or more of manic or mixed manic-depressive episodes. Though the typical age of onset for BID is late adolescence or early adulthood, symptoms of BID with psychotic features can manifest during childhood or adolescence. Some of the more common psychotic symptoms associated with manic mood states include hallucinations or delusions consistent with themes of grandiosity, invulnerability, suspiciousness, or paranoia. Given that psychotic features associated with manic episodes can present very similarly to symptoms of schizophrenia and schizoaffective disorders (e.g., hallucinations, delusions, irritability, and agitation are symptoms associated with both BID and schizophrenia spectrum disorders), it can be challenging for clinicians to formulate a diagnosis based solely on the occurrence of such symptoms. Inquiring about or observing symptoms more specific to BID, including decreased need for sleep, hyperactivity, euphoric mood, or hypersexuality, can help clinicians to differentiate BID from schizophrenia spectrum disorders. For youth with BID, pharmacological treatments are considered the standard of care (McClellan, Kowatch, Findling, & Work Group on Quality Issues, 2007). Psychotherapeutic approaches including CBT and family-focused therapy and psychoeducation also have evidence for efficacy for managing BID (Fristad, Gavazzi, & Soldano, 1998; Miklowitz et al., 2008; Miklowitz, George, Richards, Simoneau, & Suddath, 2003; Pavuluri et al., 2004).

Ongoing Assessment

Throughout treatment, ongoing assessment of both clinical symptoms and daily functioning are important to ensure that symptom remission is maintained and that clients are progressing toward their goals. Clinicians can periodically assess psychotic symptoms along dimensions of frequency (*How often are you hearing the voices?*), intensity (*How real do they seem to you?*), distress (*How much does that bother you?*), and effect on functioning (*Can you ignore them? Do you do anything differently because of the voices?*). Standardized assessment tools, such as the Brief Psychiatric Rating Scale (BPRS; Overall & Gorham, 1962) and the Positive and Negative Syndrome Scale (PANSS; Kay, Fiszbein, & Opler, 1987) can be useful for this purpose; however, these clinician-administered tools require specialized training to establish reliable use. Self-report tools such as the Behavioral Assessment System for Children, second edition (BASC-2; Reynolds & Kamphaus, 2002) are easier to administer and solicit useful information about symptoms and functioning from children, parents, and teachers. Thompson, Kline, Reeves, Pitts, & Schiffman (2013) found that the "atypicality" scale embedded within the BASC-2 adolescent self-report form correctly identified 77% of youth meeting "psychosis risk" criteria according to a standardized clinician interview, suggesting that the BASC-2 may be useful for assessing emerging symptoms among young clients. Further, given its heterogeneous subscales (including information on mood, anxiety, disruptive behaviors, school problems, and adaptive skills) and age-normed standard scoring system, the BASC-2 is particularly relevant for children with comorbid concerns or primary mood disorder diagnoses. To assess changes in specific behaviors over time, clinicians can also use behavior charts that record frequencies of desired and non-desired activities as part of a behavior modification plan.

Conclusion

Despite the lack of a well-defined evidence base for treating children and adolescents with schizophrenia and other primary psychoses, clinicians can "borrow" elements of evidence-based treatments from the adult and child treatment literature. During initial and exacerbation stages of illness, psychotherapists play a key role in establishing and maintaining rapport, ensuring safety, and supporting medication adherence. Many clients with psychosis will require ongoing psychosocial supports; depending on the child, providers may work together to establish a combination of family, school, and individual interventions to help children meet their goals. Given the lack of manualized evidence-based treatment packages, clinicians working with youth with psychosis are advised to adopt a flexible, research-informed idiographic approach to treatment planning that recognizes clients' strengths and long-term recovery goals.

Notes

1 For the sake of illustration and protecting confidentiality, all cases presented in this chapter are conglomerations of actual patients treated by the authors. All identifying information has been removed.
2 Psychosis occurring within the context of a primary mood disorder is covered later in the chapter.

References

Addington, J., & Gleeson, J. (2005). Implementing cognitive–behavioural therapy for first-episode psychosis. *The British Journal of Psychiatry, 187*(48), s72–s76.

American Psychiatric Association. (2013). *Diagnostic and statistical manual of mental disorders* (5th ed.). Arlington, VA: Author.

Arango, C., Garibaldi, G., & Marder, S. R. (2013). Pharmacological approaches to treating negative symptoms: A review of clinical trials. *Schizophrenia Research, 150*(2–3), 346–352.

Asarnow, J. R., Tompson, M. C., & Goldstein, M. J. (1994). Childhood-onset schizophrenia: A follow-up study. *Schizophrenia Bulletin, 20*(4), 599–617.

Bachman, P., Niendam, T. A., & Jalbrzikowski, M. (2011). Processing speed and neurodevelopment in adolescent-onset psychosis: Cognitive slowing predicts social function. *Journal of Abnormal Child Psychology, 40*(4), 645–654.

Barber, M. E. (2012). Recovery as the new medical model for psychiatry. *Psychiatric Services, 63*(3), 277–279.

Barkhof, E., Meijer, C. J., de Sonneville, L. M. J., Linszen, D. H., & de Haan, L. (2012). Interventions to improve adherence to antipsychotic medication in patients with schizophrenia–A review of the past decade. *European Psychiatry,27*(1), 9–18.

Bell, M., Fiszdon, J., Greig, T., Wexler, B., & Bryson, G. (2007). Neurocognitive enhancement therapy with work therapy in schizophrenia: 6-month follow-up of neuropsychological performance. *Journal of Rehabilitation Research & Development, 44*(5), 761–770.

Brewer, W. J., Francey, S. M., Wood, S. J., Jackson, H. J., Pantelis, C., McGorry, P. D. (2005). Memory impairments identified in people at ultra-high risk for psychosis who later develop first-episode psychosis. *American Journal of Psychiatry, 162*(1), 71–78.

Brister, T., Cavaleri, M. A., Olin, S. S., Shen, S., Burns, B. J., & Hoagwood, K. E. (2012). An Evaluation of the NAMI Basics Program. *Journal of Child and Family Studies, 21*(3), 439–442.

Bobo, W. V., Cooper, W. O., Stein, C. M., Olfson, M., Graham, D., Daugherty, J., . . . & Ray, W. A. (2013,). Antipsychotics and the Risk of Type 2 Diabetes Mellitus in Children and Youth. *JAMA Psychiatry, 70*(10), 1067–1075.

Brimblecombe, N., O'Sullivan, G., & Parkinson, B. (2003). Home treatment as an alternative to inpatient admission: characteristics of those treated and factors predicting hospitalization. *Journal of Psychiatric and Mental Health Nursing, 10*(6), 683–687.

Bruns, E. J., Sather, A., Pullmann, M. D., & Stambaugh, L. F. (2011). National trends in implementing wraparound: Results from the State Wraparound Survey. *Journal of Child and Family Studies, 20*(6), 726–735.

Caseiro, O., Pérez-Iglesias, R., Mata, I., Martínez-Garcia, O., Pelayo-Terán, J. M., Tabares-Seisdedos, R., . . . & Crespo-Facorro, B. (2012). Predicting relapse after a first episode of non-affective psychosis: a three-year follow-up study. *Journal of Psychiatric Research, 46*(8), 1099–1105.

Coldwell, C. M., & Bender, W. S. (2007). The effectiveness of assertive community treatment for homeless populations with severe mental illness: A meta-analysis. *The American Journal of Psychiatry, 164*(3), 393–399. doi:10.1176/appi.ajp.164.3.393

Conus, P., Lambert, M., Cotton, S., Bonsack, C., McGorry, P. D., & Schimmelmann, B. G. (2010). Rate and predictors of service disengagement in an epidemiological first-episode psychosis cohort. *Schizophrenia research, 118*(1), 256–263.

Deakin, J., & Lennox, B. (2013). Psychotic symptoms in young people warrant ugent referral. *Practitioner, 257,* 25–28.

Dickerson, F. B., Tenhula, W. N., & Green-Paden, L. D. (2005). The token economy for schizophrenia: Review of the literature and recommendations for future research. *Schizophrenia Research, 75*(2–3), 405–416.

Dickinson, D., Bellack, A. S., & Gold, J. M. (2007). Social/communication skills, cognition, and vocational functioning in schizophrenia. *Schizophrenia Bulletin, 33*(5), 1213–1220.

Dixon, L. B., Dickerson, F., Bellack, A. S., Bennett, M., Dickinson, D., Goldberg, R. W., . . . & Kreyenbuhl, J. (2010). The 2009 schizophrenia PORT psychosocial treatment recommendations and summary statements. *Schizophrenia Bulletin, 36*(1), 48–70.

Dixon, L. B., Lucksted, A., Medoff, D. R., Burland, J., Stewart, B., Lehman, A. F., . . . & Murray-Swank, A. (2011). Outcomes of a randomized study of a peer-taught family-to- family education program for mental illness. *Psychiatric Services, 62*(6), 591–597.

Dyer, J. T. (1998). Treatment in the community in the absence of consent. *Psychiatric Bulletin, 22*(2), 73–76. doi:10.1192/pb.22.2.73.

Eack, S. M., Hogarty, G. E., Greenwald, D. P., Hogarty, S. S., & Keshavan, M. S. (2011). Effects of cognitive enhancement therapy on employment outcomes in early schizophrenia: Results from a 2-year randomized trial. *Research on Social Work Practice, 21*(1), 32–42.

Fleischhaker, C., Schulz, E., Tepper, K., Martin, M., Hennighausen, K., & Remschmidt, H. (2005). Long-term course of adolescent schizophrenia. *Schizophrenia Bulletin, 31*(3), 769–780.

Fongay, P., Target, M., Cottrell, D., Phillips, J., & Kurtz, Z. (2002). *What works for whom? A critical review of treatments for children and adolescents.* New York, NY: Guilford Press.

Frazier, J. A., Giuliano, A. J., Johnson, J. L., Yakutis, L., Youngstrom, E. A., Breiger, D., . . . & Hooper, S. R. (2012). Neurocognitive outcomes in the treatment of early-onset schizophrenia spectrum disorders study. *Journal of the American Academy of Child & Adolescent Psychiatry, 51*(5), 496–505.

Frazier, J. A., McClellan, J., Findling, R. L., Vitiello, B., Anderson, R., Zablotsky, B., . . . & Sikich, L. (2007). Treatment of early onset schizophrenia spectrum disorders (TEOSS):

Demographic and clinical characteristics. *Journal of the American Academy of Child & Adolescent Psychiatry, 46*(8), 979–988.

Fristad, M. A., Gavazzi, S. M., & Soldano, K. W. (1998). Multi-family psychoeducation groups for childhood mood disorders: Program description & preliminary efficacy data. *Contemporary Family Therapy,* 20, 385–402.

Gearing, R. E., & Charach, A. (2009). Medication adherence for children and adolescents with first-episode psychosis following hospitalization. *European Child & Adolescent Psychiatry, 18*(10), 587–595.

Ghuman, J. K., Cataldo, M. D., Beck, M. H., & Slifer, K. J. (2004). Behavioral training for pill-swallowing difficulties in young children with autistic disorder. *Journal of Child & Adolescent Psychopharmacology, 14*(4), 601–611.

Gillberg, I. C., Hellgren, L., & Gillberg, C. (1993). Psychotic disorders diagnosed in adolescence. Outcomes at age 30 years. *Journal of Child Psychology and Psychiatry, 34*(7) 1173–1185.

Goes, F. S., Sadler, B., Toolan, J., Zamoiski, R. D., Mondimore, F. M., MacKinnon, D. F., & Potash, J. B. (2007). Psychotic features in bipolar and unipolar depression. *Bipolar Disorders, 9*(8), 901–906.

Green, C. A., Wisdom, J. P., Wolfe, L., & Firemark, A. (2012). Engaging youths with serious mental illnesses in treatment: STARS study consumer recommendations. *Psychiatric Rehabilitation Journal, 35*(5), 360–368. doi:10.1037/h0094494.

Green, M. F., Kern, R. S., & Heaton, R. K. (2004). Longitudinal studies of cognition and functional outcome in schizophrenia: implications for MATRICS. *Schizophrenia Research, 72*(1), 41–51.

Hooley, J. M. (1985). Expressed emotion: A review of the critical literature. *Clinical Psychology Review, 5*(2), 119–139.

Kaufman, J., Birmaher, B., Brent, D., Rao, U. M. A., Flynn, C., Moreci, P., . . . & Ryan, N. (1997). Schedule for affective disorders and schizophrenia for school-age children-present and lifetime version (K-SADS-PL): initial reliability and validity data. *Journal of the American Academy of Child & Adolescent Psychiatry, 36*(7), 980–988.

Kay, S. R., Fiszbein, A., & Opler, L. A. (1987). The Positive and Negative Syndrome Scale (PANSS) for schizophrenia. *Schizophrenia Bulletin, 13*(2), 261–276.

Keck, P. E., McElroy, S. L., Havens, J. R., Altshuler, L. L., Nolen, W. A., Frye, M. A., . . . & Post, R. M. (2003). Psychosis in bipolar disorder: phenomenology and impact on morbidity and course of illness. *Comprehensive Psychiatry, 44*(4), 263–269.

Killackey, E., Jackson, H. J., & McGorry, P. D. (2008). Vocational intervention in first-episode psychosis: Individual placement and support v. treatment as usual. *The British Journal of Psychiatry, 193*(2), 114–120.

Knapp, M., Mangalore, R., & Simon, J. (2004). The global costs of schizophrenia. *Schizophrenia Bulletin, 30*(2), 279–293.

Knock, J., Kline, E., Schiffman, J., Maynard, A., & Reeves, G. (2011). Burdens and difficulties experienced by caregivers of children and adolescents with schizophrenia-spectrum disorders: A qualitative study. *Early Intervention in Psychiatry, 5*(4), 349–354.

Kurtz, M. M. (2005). Neurocognitive impairment across the lifespan in schizophrenia: An update. *Schizophrenia Research, 74*(1), 15–26.

Large, M. M., & Nielssen, O. (2011). Violence in first-episode psychosis: A systematic review and meta-analysis. *Schizophrenia Research, 125*(2), 209–220.

Lay, B., Blanz, B., Hartmann, M., & Schmidt, M. H. (2000). The psychosocial outcome of adolescent-onset schizophrenia: A 12-year followup. *Schizophrenia Bulletin, 26*(4), 801–816.

Lehman, A. F., Goldberg, R., Dixon, L. B., McNary, S., Postrado, L., Hackman, A., & McDonnell, K. (2002). Improving employment outcomes for persons with severe mental illnesses. *Archives of General Psychiatry, 59*(2), 165–172.

Lencz, T.S., Christopher W., McLaughlin, D., Auther, A., Nakayama, E., Hovey, L., & Cornblatt, B. A. (2006). Generalized and specific neurocognitive deficits in prodromal schizophrenia. *Biological Psychiatry, 59*(9), 863–871.

Liberman, R. P. (2012). Phase-specific recovery from schizophrenia. *Psychiatric Annals, 42*(6), 211–217.

Maryland Department of Health and Mental Hygiene (2013). Clinical criteria: Peer review program for antipsychotic use in children and adolescents less than eighteen years of age. Retrieved from https://mmcp.dhmh.maryland.gov/pap/docs/P2P_Review_criteria_1.pdf

Marshall, M., & Rathbone, J. (2011). Early intervention for psychosis. *Schizophrenia Bulletin, 37*(6), 1111–1114.

Maziade, M., Bouchard, S., Gingras, N., Charron, L., Cardinal, A., Roy, M. A., . . . & Martinez, M. (1996). Long-term stability of diagnosis and symptom dimensions in a systematic sample of patients with onset of schizophrenia in childhood and early adolescence. II: Postitive/negative distinction and childhood predictors of adult outcome. *British Journal of Psychiatry, 169*(3), 371–378.

McClellan, J., Kowatch, R., Findling, R.L., & Work Group on Quality Issues. (2007). Practice parameter for the assessment and treatment of children and adolescents with bipolar disorder. *Journal of the American Academy of Child and Adolescent Psychiatry, 46*(1), 107–125.

McClellan, J., Werry, J., Bernet, W., Arnold, V., Beitchman, J., Benson, S., . . . & Shaw, J. (2001). Practice parameter for the assessment and treatment of children and adolescents with schizophrenia. *Journal of the American Academy of Child & Adolescent Psychiatry, 40*(Suppl7), 4S-23S. doi:10.1097/00004583–200107001–00002.

McFarlane, W. R., Dixon, L., Lukens, E., & Lucksted, A. (2003). Family psychoeducation and schizophrenia: A review of the literature. *Journal of Marital and Family Therapy, 29*(2), 223–245.

McFarlane, W. R., Dushay, R. A., Deakins, S. M., Stastny, P., Lukens, E. P., Toran, J., & Link, B. (2000). Employment outcomes in family-aided assertive community treatment. *American Journal of Orthopsychiatry, 70*(2), 203–214.

McGurk, S. R., Mueser, K. T., Feldman, K., Wolfe, R., & Pascaris, A. (2007). Cognitive training for supported employment: 2–3 year outcomes of a randomized controlled trial. *American Journal of Psychiatry, 164*(3), 437–441.

McGurk, S. R., Twamley, E. W., Sitzer, D. I., McHugo, G. J., & Mueser, K. T. (2007). A meta-analysis of cognitive remediation in schizophrenia. *American Journal of Psychiatry, 164*(12), 1791–1802.

Michelson, D., Davenport, C., Dretzke, J., Barlow, J., & Day, C. (2013). Do evidence-based interventions work when tested in the "real world?" A systematic review and meta- analysis of parent management training for the treatment of child disruptive behavior. *Clinical Child and Family Psychology Review 16*(1), 18–34.

Miklowitz, D. J, Axelson, D.A., Birmaher, B., George, E.L., Taylor, D.O., Schneck, C.D., . . . & Brent, D. A. (2008). Family-focused treatment for adolescents with bipolar disorder results of a 2-year randomized trial. *Archives of General Psychiatry, 65*(9), 1053–1061.

Miklowitz, D. J., George, E.L., Richards, J. A., Simoneau, T.L., & Suddath, R.L. (2003). A randomized study of family-focused psychoeducation and pharmacotherapy in the outpatient management of bipolar disorder. *Archives of General Psychiatry, 60*(9), 904–912.

Miller, M., Azrael, D., & Barber, C. (2012). Suicide mortality in the United States: the importance of attending to method in understanding population-level disparities in the burden of suicide. *Annual Review of Public Health, 33,* 393–408.

Miller, W. R., & Rollnick, S. (2002). *Motivational interviewing: Preparing people for change.* New York, NY: Guilford Press.

Mitchell, A. J., Delaffon, V., Vancampfort, D., Correll, C. U., & De Hert, M. (2012). Guideline concordant monitoring of metabolic risk in people treated with antipsychotic medication: systematic review and meta-analysis of screening practices. *Psychological Medicine, 42*(1), 125.

Morrison, A. P. (2009). Cognitive behaviour therapy for first episode psychosis: Good for nothing or fit for purpose? *Psychosis, 1*(2), 103–112.

Mullins, C. D., Obeidat, N. A., Cuffel, B. J., Naradzay, J., & Loebel, A. D. (2008). Risk of discontinuation of atypical antipsychotic agents in the treatment of schizophrenia. *Schizophrenia Research, 98*(1), 8–15.

Nakamura, B. J., Schiffman, J., Lam, C. W., Becker, K. D., & Chorpita, B. F. (2006). A modularized cognitive-behavioral intervention for water phobia in an adolescent with childhood-onset schizophrenia. *Child & Family Behavior Therapy, 28*(3), 29–41.

Niendam, T. A., Bearden, C. E., Zinberg, J., Johnson, J. K., O'Brien, M., & Cannon, T. D. (2007). The course of neurocognition and social functioning in individuals at ultra high risk for psychosis. *Schizophrenia Bulletin, 33*(3), 772–781.

Nuechterlein, K. H., Subotnik, K. L., Turner, L. R., Ventura, J., Becker, D. R., & Drake, R. E. (2008). Individual placement and support for individuals with recent-onset schizophrenia: Integrating supported education and supported employment. *Psychiatric Rehabilitation Journal, 31*(4), 340–349.

Nuernberger, J. E., Ringdahl, J. E., Vargo, K. K., Crumpecker, A. C., & Gunnarsson, K. F. (2013). Using a behavioral skills training package to teach conversation skills to young adults with autism spectrum disorders. *Research in Autism Spectrum Disorders, 7*(2), 411–417.

Overall, J. E., & Gorham, D. R. (1962). The Brief Psychiatric Rating Scale. *Psychological Reports, 10*(3), 799–812.

Painter, K. (2012). Outcomes for youth with severe emotional disturbance: A repeated measures longitudinal study of a wraparound approach of service delivery in systems of care. *Child & Youth Care Forum, 41*(4), 407–425.

Pavuluri, M. N., Graczyk, P. A., Henry, D. B., Carbray, J. A., Heidenreich, J., & Miklowitz, D. J. (2004). Child- and family-focused cognitive behavioral therapy for pediatric bipolar disorder: Development and preliminary results. *Journal of the American Academy of Child and Adolescent Psychiatry, 43*(5), 528–537.

Reynolds, C. R., & Kamphaus, R. W. (2002). *The clinician's guide to the Behavior Assessment System for Children (BASC).* New York, NY: Guilford Press.

Robinson, J., Harris, M. G., Harrigan, S. M., Henry, L. P., Farrelly, S., Prosser, A., . . . & McGorry, P. D. (2010). Suicide attempt in first-episode psychosis: A 7.4 year follow-up study. *Schizophrenia Research, 116*(1), 1–8.

Rohde, P., Feeny, N., & Robins, M. (2005). Characteristics and components of the TADS CBT approach. *Cognitive and Behavioral Practice, 12*(2), 186–197.

Röpcke, B., & Eggers, C. (2005). Early onset schizophrenia: A 15-year follow-up. *European Child & Adolescent Psychiatry, 14*(6), 341–350.

Salema, N. E. M., Elliott, R. A., & Glazebrook, C. (2011). A systematic review of adherence- enhancing interventions in adolescents taking long-term medicines. *Journal of Adolescent Health, 49*(5), 455–466.

Schiffman, J., Chorpita, B. F., Daleiden, E. L., Maeda, J. A., & Nakamura, B. J. (2008). Service profile of youths with schizophrenia-spectrum diagnoses. *Children and Youth Services Review, 30*(4), 427–436. doi:10.1016/j.childyouth.2007.10.013.

Schiffman, J., & Dixon, L. (2011). Treatment issues and challenges facing young adults with chronic mental illness. *The Maryland Psychologist, 56,* 19–21.

Salema, N. E. M., Elliott, R. A., & Glazebrook, C. (2011). A systematic review of adherence-enhancing interventions in adolescents taking long-term medicines. *Journal of Adolescent Health, 49*(5), 455–466.

Sarin, F., Wallin, L., & Widerlöv, B. (2011). Cognitive behavior therapy for schizophrenia: A meta-analytical review of randomized controlled trials. *Nordic Journal of Psychiatry, 65*(3), 162–174.

Silverstein, S. M., Hatashita-Wong, M., Solak, B. A., Uhlhaas, P., Landa, Y., Wilkniss, S. M., . . . Smith, T. E. (2005). Effectiveness of a two-phase cognitive rehabilitation intervention for severely impaired schizophrenia patients. *Psychological Medicine, 35*(6), 829–837.

Tarrier, N. (2008). Schizophrenia and other psychotic disorders. . In D. H. Barlow (Ed.), *Clinical handbook of psychological disorders: A step-by-step treatment manual,* (pp. 463–491). New York, NY: Guilford Press.

Thompson, E., Kline, E., Reeves, G., Pitts, S. C., & Schiffman, J. (2013). Identifying youth at risk for psychosis using the BASC-2. *Schizophrenia Research, 151*(1–3), 238–244.

Ueland, T., Rishovd Rund, B., Borg, N. E., Newton, E., Purvis, R., & Wykes, T. (2004). Modification of performance on the span of apprehension task in a group of young people with early onset psychosis. *Scandinavian Journal of Psychology, 45*(1), 55–60.

Ueland, T., & Rund, B. (2004). A controlled randomized treatment study: The effects of a cognitive remediation program on adolescents with early onset psychosis. *Acta Psychiatrica Scandinavica, 109*(1), 70–74.

Walter, U. M., Petr, C. G., & Davis, S. (2006). Informing best practices for children in psychiatric crises: Perspectives and insights from families. *Families in Society: The Journal of Contemporary Social Services, 87*(4), 612–620.

Watson, A. C., & Fulambarker, A. J. (2012). The crisis intervention team model of police response to mental health crises: A primer for mental health practitioners. *Best Practices in Mental Health, 8*(2), 71–71.

Weller, E. B., Weller, R. A., Fristad, M. A., Rooney, M. T., & Schecter, J. (2000). Children's interview for psychiatric syndromes (ChIPS). *Journal of the American Academy of Child & Adolescent Psychiatry, 39*(1), 76–84.

Werry, J. S., McClellan, J. M., & Chard, L. (1991). Childhood and adolescent schizophrenic, bipolar, and schizoaffective disorders: A clinical and outcome study. *Journal of the American Academy of Child & Adolescent Psychiatry, 30*(3), 457–465.

Wykes, T., Newton, E., Landau, S., Rice, C., Thompson, N., & Frangou, S. (2007). Cognitive remediation therapy (CRT) for young early onset patients with schizophrenia: An exploratory randomized controlled trial. *Schizophrenia Research, 94*(1–3), 221–230.

Wykes, T., & Spaulding, W. D. (2011). Thinking about the future cognitive remediation therapy—What works and could we do better? *Schizophrenia Bulletin, 37*(suppl 2), S80-S90.

10

FORENSIC ISSUES WITH PSYCHOSIS AND YOUTH VIOLENCE

Maria G. Master, Littal Melnik, and Shelby Inouye

Recent years have seen an increasing focus on the risk that mentally ill patients will commit violent crimes. The media drumbeat highlights unprovoked shootings and mass acts of violence—often by young men or teenage boys—that fortify the impression that the mentally ill among us are dangerous or potentially lethal offenders. How do clinicians parse the facts from the feelings of unease and assess both the needs and rights of patients and the safety of society at large?

In this chapter, we argue that patients, clinicians, and society bear a shared burden of violence. In section 1, we examine the correlation between violence and psychosis in youth, as compared to adults, and offer a differentiated interpretation of violence committed by juveniles. In section 2, we consider forensic issues in delinquency and adjudicative competence and explore the tension between a societal ethic of crime deterrence/punishment and aspirations for rehabilitation/recovery of violent youth. Finally, in section 3, we briefly comment on the implications of gun control and the clinician's role in violence risk reduction.

Overview: The Burden of Violence

Case One

Wayne S. Fenton, MD, age 53, was a devoted physician and an associate director at the National Institute of Mental Health (NIMH). He was recognized as a national expert on the treatment of schizophrenia. On Saturday, September 2, 2006, Labor Day weekend, Dr. Fenton saw Vitali Davydov, aged 19, in consultation for treatment of severe psychosis. Vitali's father was present. At the conclusion of the consultation, an appointment for treatment was made for later in the week.

The next day, Sunday, September 3, the patient's father called Dr. Fenton, pleading with him to see his son immediately. He reported that Vitali was agitated and angry about taking his medications. At 4 p.m., Dr. Fenton saw the patient in a small, private office behind a locked door. The father left to run an errand.

Dr. Fenton encouraged Vitali to take an intramuscular long-acting antipsychotic. When the father returned, he found his son wandering about with blood on his hands. Dr. Fenton was discovered beaten to death. The patient later told police that he had feared a sexual assault, among other fears (Simon, 2011).

Case Two

Kyle, a 21-year-old man with schizophrenia, lived with his family, in an environment that was knowledgeable about and sensitive to the vulnerabilities associated with psychotic illness. Cheryl, his mother, became concerned about her son's disorganized behavior in June 2013. She brought Kyle to an emergency mental health clinic in order to have him evaluated for hospitalization. However, the staff declined to admit him, stating that Kyle was not an imminent danger to himself.

Two weeks later, Kyle became agitated at home and his brother, Alex, called 911 for help. As recorded, Alex told the dispatcher, "My brother is having a breakdown, a meltdown." His mother could be heard on the recording screaming in the background as Alex told the dispatcher his brother tried to cut himself with a pocketknife and also had an Airsoft gun, an imitation gun that shoots plastic pellets. Alex told the police that his brother had run from the house and down the street, carrying the toy gun in his hand. Alex told the dispatcher about the gun, "It's not real."

The dispatcher responded, "I know. I understand. Well, listen, the officers are trained in this type of thing. They're not going to go around shooting people, OK? And they understand the situation here. So, um, we just want to keep everybody safe." The dispatcher later said, "The first thing they're going to do is get Kyle under control so that he's safe and everybody else is safe . . ."

A short time later, the police caught up with Kyle, and shot him multiple times. He allegedly had pointed the toy gun at the officers (Eng, 2012; Goode & Healy, 2013).

Psychiatrists and other mental health clinicians bear a burden of violence unique to the populations we serve, as spotlighted by too many high-profile cases. Even highly seasoned clinicians, such as Dr. Fenton, can be vulnerable to unpredictable, life-altering violence. According to the Department of Justice in the National Crime Victimization Survey (NCVS) (1993–1999), the annual rate of being a victim of a nonfatal, job-related violent crime was 68.2 per 1,000 psychiatrists and 69.0 per 1,000 mental health workers. This compares with 16.2 per 1,000 physicians generally and 21.9 per 1,000 nurses. And, this rate can be considered against a background annual rate of job-related violent crime of 12.6 per 1,000 workers in all surveyed occupations (Friedman, 2006). Concerns about safety are one factor compelling a closer look at forensic issues in adolescent psychosis.

In certain cases, the treating clinician also carries a specific duty to outside parties whom a patient has indicated he may harm. The 1976 case of *Tarasoff v Regents* established that a therapist has a duty to protect third parties who are foreseeably endangered by their patients ("Tarasoff v. Regents of the University of California, 551 P.2d 334," 1976). The Supreme Court of California noted, "Protective privilege ends where the public peril begins." The *Tarasoff* case triggered passage of "duty to warn" or "duty to protect" statutes in almost every state (Herbert & Young, 2002; Widgery & Winterfield, 2013). Expanding on *Tarasoff*, for example, California statute now requires clinicians to warn the potential victim and to contact a law enforcement agency (*Cal. Civ. Code §43.92,* 2007).

Other legal precedent focuses on the degree of danger posed by a patient, rather than the identification of a potential victim, as in *Tarasoff*. In *Hammon v County of Maricopa,* the Supreme Court of Arizona (1989) did not require a specific threat by a patient as a prerequisite to doctor liability ("Hamman v. County of Maricopa, 161 Ariz 58, 775 P.2d 1122," 1989). In that case, the parents of John Carter brought him to the Maricopa County Hospital's emergency room because he had been exhibiting strange behavior. The psychiatrist interviewed Carter for about five minutes, noted signs of psychosis but did not review the medical record, which would have revealed that Carter had been previously hospitalized and secluded and restrained for assaultive behavior. The family reported to the doctor that their son had exhibited violence toward animals and that they were afraid of him. The doctor, however, denied hospital admission and returned Carter home with a prescription for antipsychotic medication. Shortly thereafter, Carter was home with his stepfather, who was working on a construction project. Carter became delusionally convinced his stepfather was going to harm his mother with the electric drill, and beat him until he had severe brain damage and died of a heart attack. The Court ruled that the psychiatrist had a duty to third parties when the psychiatrist could reasonably foresee that the patient's condition could endanger others who are in an "obvious zone of danger," even without a specific articulated threat. This potential liability thus raises apprehension about the clinician's ability to accurately assess a patient's risk of violence.

Yet, there are important competing concerns in discussing the topic of violence in the mentally ill. Questioning the correlation raises issues about unjustly stigmatizing the vast majority of the mentally ill population who are not violent. Casual characterizations increase the risk of perpetuating the well-documented discrimination observed in accessing housing options, employment opportunities, and other aspects of social integration (Corrigan & Watson, 2002). Moreover, the evidence suggests that the violent mentally ill themselves are also more likely to be victimized (Fitzgerald et al., 2005; Hiday, Swartz, Swanson, Borum, & Wagner, 1999; Hughes et al., 2012); to decline in social status (S. Aro, Aro, & Keskim, 1995); to have impaired social relationships (Swanson et al., 1998); and to be at risk of homelessness (Folsom et al., 2005) or to endure poor living conditions (Silver, Mulvey, & Monahan, 1999), as compared to nonviolent psychotic individuals (Khalid, Ford, & Maughan, 2012). According to Teplin, McClelland, Abram, & Weiner (2005), more than one-quarter of persons with severe mental illness had been victims of a violent crime in the year prior to their study, a rate more than 11 times higher than the general population rates, even after controlling for demographic differences. As illustrated by Kyle's tragic death, misinterpreting the disorganized behavior of a schizophrenic can make that adolescent exceptionally vulnerable. The burden of violence is in many respects shared among patient, clinician, and the larger community. Thus, better understanding the risk that the mentally ill might commit and also be affected by violence provides opportunities for both targeted treatment and crime prevention. In the case of children and adolescents, to whom we owe a particular duty to protect, this is a critical issue.

Section 1 Violence and Mental Illness: A Question of Correlation

To what extent are children and adolescents, generally, involved in violence? The rates have fluctuated over time. The juvenile proportion of violent crimes cleared by arrest or exceptional means grew from between 9% and 10% in the 1980s to 14% in 1994; after 1994, the proportion fell somewhat, remaining near 12% between 1997 and 2005 (Snyder, 2008). By 2002, 1,300 murders, or 1 in 12 murders (approximately 8%), involved a juvenile offender. The juvenile acted alone in 52% of these murders, acted with one or more juveniles in 9%, and acted with at least one adult offender in 39% (Snyder & Sickmund, 2006). The extent to which serious mental illness is a contributing factor is uncertain. There is a paucity of studies gathering data on violence in psychotic children and adolescents on a longitudinal basis. What we can glean is derived from studies looking primarily at other factors and age groups.

The evidence suggests that there is some increased risk that a psychotic adult will commit violence, as compared to an adult without mental illness. The NIMH's Epidemiologic Catchment Area (ECA) study examined the rates of psychiatric disorders in a representative sample of 17,803 subjects in five U.S. communities and obtained data on violence for about 7,000 of the subjects. The ECA study defines violence as having used a weapon such as a knife or gun in a fight and having become involved, with a person other than a partner or spouse, in more than one fight that came to blows. The study found that the presence of serious mental illness—i.e., schizophrenia, major depression, or bipolar disorder—was associated with a 2 to 3 times increased risk of violence, as compared to individuals without illness. The lifetime prevalence for violence among people with these serious mental illnesses was 16%, as compared to 7% among people without mental illness (Swanson, 1994).

The prison population certainly includes a significant population of individuals with serious mental illness (Kristof, 2014). One national survey demonstrated that the lifetime risk of schizophrenia was 5% among people convicted of homicide (Shaw et al., 2006). This is about 5 times higher than the 1.1% prevalence of schizophrenia in the general population ("Schizophrenia," n.d.). The Bureau of Justice Statistics (BJS) reports that as of midyear 2005, more than half of all prison and jail inmates had mental illness, including 61% of all state prison inmates who had a history of current or past violent offenses. According to the BJS report, 15% of state prisoners, and 10% of federal prisoners reported at least one symptom of psychotic disorder (James & Glaze, 2006). This suggests a significant need for mental health services in this population, although it does not necessarily demonstrate that schizophrenia per se leads to violence.

A diagnosis of schizophrenia, while relevant, appears to be only one factor in predicting violence. Comorbid substance abuse and active psychotic symptoms in the mentally ill additively increase the potential for violence (Walsh, Buchanan, & Fahy, 2002). The ECA study revealed that the prevalence of violence was 7.3% among perpetrators without mental illness, 16.1% in the case of major affective disorders or schizophrenia spectrum disorders, and then jumps to 35% where substance abuse is involved, and 43.6% where both substance abuse and major mental disorders coincide (Swanson, 1994). Other studies also find that rates of violence are higher in individuals with both substance abuse and schizophrenia (Elbogen and Johnson, 2009; Swanson et al., 2006). Moreover, even after discharge from treatment, the persistence of substance abuse disorders correlates with increased rates of violence by the mentally ill (Steadman et al., 1998).

Within the schizophrenic population, certain dynamic factors also appear to increase risk of violence. A systematic review and meta-analysis by Witt, van Dorn, and Fazel (2013) examined 110 studies, covering 45,533 adults, of which 8,439 were violent, and examined 146 individual risk and protective factors. The results indicated that multiple risk factors are strongly associated with increased risk of violence in individuals with psychosis. These risk factors, also confirmed by other studies (Torrey, 1994), include history of hostile behavior, recent drug misuse, and non-adherence with psychological or medical therapies. In addition, Witt and colleagues found criminal history was more strongly associated with violence than either substance use or demographic factors. Comparatively, at least one study found a *lower* rate of violence among individuals diagnosed with a major mental illness, including schizophrenia, who have no other compounding risk factors (Palijan, Radeljak, Kovac, & Kovacević, 2010). The presence of multiple psychosocial factors appears to compound the risk of violence in the psychotically mentally ill.

Youth are a distinct subset of violent offenders, due to their developmental status as well as their social and legal position in society. The presence of psychotic symptoms may be a risk factor for youth who commit violence (Lewis et al., 1998; Myers, Scott, A. W. Burgess, & Burgess, 1995). Interestingly, as compared to adults, the correlation between psychosis and violence is much less robust. In part, this may be explained by the lower rate of psychotic illness in younger children. In addition, violence may serve a distinct role in the mental life of an adolescent struggling with the developmental tasks of individuation, establishing gender identity, and negotiating inclusion into social peer groups. A violent solution to bullying, social rejection, or rebellion against authority may be less a product of psychosis than a maladaptive compromise among competing desires in a vulnerable individual.

In evaluating the risk of violence committed by youth, it is particularly important to consider factors other than frank psychosis. For example, juveniles are significantly more likely than adults to have killed out of desperation or terror, killed to protect themselves or others, and to have had a long-standing history of abuse, according to one study (Heide & Boots, 2007). Consistently high premorbid delinquency from childhood onward appears to directly increase the risk for violent behavior, independent of psychosis-related risk factors (Winsper et al., 2013). Clare, Bailey, and Clark (2000) found no significant link between symptoms of psychopathology and a propensity for criminally violent behavior in adolescents (as distinguished from violence in the context of a specific psychotic episode). They also note that violent behavior in adolescent psychosis is associated more closely with social factors than with specific symptoms of the psychotic illness. Overall, studies call into question the strength of the correlation between psychosis and violence in children and adolescents.

Mental illness other than psychosis appears to be more prevalent among adolescent and young adult criminal offenders as compared to adult offenders. The largest cohort study of 3,058 offenders undergoing forensic psychiatric inpatient assessment in Sweden over a five-year period (1997–2001) considered whether the rates of psychopathology among adolescents (15–17 years) and young adults (18–21 years) were similar to older offenders. The most striking difference was the raised prevalence of depression in younger offenders, as well as higher rates of attention deficit, disruptive, and autism spectrum disorders. Compared with the adult forensic psychiatric examinees, those aged 15–17 years and 18–21 years had higher rates of depression and childhood and developmental disorders but lower rates of psychosis, bipolar disorder, and substance use disorders. Compared with general psychiatric inpatients, offenders aged 15–17 years had a higher prevalence of depression and attention-deficit or disruptive disorders and lower prevalence of alcohol and drug misuse disorders. Of note, the prevalence of psychosis was increased in the older age groups. Adults, relative to juveniles, were significantly more likely to have histories of severe mental illness; to have reported delusions, hallucinations, and bizarre behavior; and to appear to be driven to kill to a larger extent by mental illness (M. Fazel, Langstrom, Grann, & Fazel, 2008).

In light of these findings, a risk assessment for youth should include a careful multifactorial analysis of the child's psychosocial history. Past incidents of violence toward self or others, including toward animals or property, should be noted. The severity, frequency, and chronicity of violence provides further context. Signs of antisocial or predatory behavior should be distinguished from highly charged affective responses to perceived threat. The degree of victimization and violence witnessed by the child may provide insights into vulnerability. And comorbid risk factors such as ADHD, conduct disorder, oppositional defiant disorder, impulse dysregulation, or substance abuse should be assessed in addition to mood and thought disorders.

Section 2 Crime and Punishment/Rehabilitation and Recovery

Case Three

At 15 years old, Alyssa faced adult criminal court for the murder of her 9-year-old neighbor. Following her arrest, she told officers that she had lured the younger girl in order to experience what it felt like to kill someone. In a journal entry read to the court, she wrote, "I strangled them and slit their throat and stabbed them now they're dead. I don't know how to feel . . . it was ahmazing [*sic*]. As soon as you get over the 'ohmygawd I can't do this' feeling, it's pretty enjoyable." She was remanded to a psychiatric institution to undergo evaluation, and received immediate psychiatric treatment.

Born to a teenage mother and a father incarcerated for assault, her lawyers argued that Alyssa was severely emotionally disturbed, with a history of self-injury, substance abuse, and suicide attempts. Her plea on lesser charges prevented a first-degree murder trial with the potential for a life sentence without parole. Before her sentencing, at age 18 years, Alyssa apologized to her victim's family, saying, "If I could give my life to bring her back I would—I'm sorry" (Rosa, 2012).

Increasing attention has been given to the role of mental health services, rather than punitive responses, in the management of youth offenders given the complex developmental and psychosocial contributors to youth violence. Over the past century, as clinicians and researchers have better understood the importance of brain and behavioral development, the climate has shifted from retribution to the rehabilitation of young criminal offenders. The Juvenile Justice and Delinquency Act of 1974 codified protections by shielding juveniles committing status offenses (age-dependent actions such as truancy or running away from home) from incarceration in juvenile correctional facilities. Moreover, the law was instrumental in supporting the establishment of community-based treatment programs and child mental healthcare.

Within the juvenile justice system, a child is delinquent if he has been found guilty of at least one crime that, if committed by an adult, would be punishable by law. Juvenile delinquents may be directed to correctional facilities or may receive probation with treatment mandated in the community. Community treatment programs include a broad range of approaches, such as individual therapy, family-based interventions, group homes, drug rehabilitation models, or even "boot camp" scenarios. Where serious mental illness has been identified, medication may be a significant factor in addressing mood or thought disorders. In this sense, to the extent psychosis played a significant contributing role to the violence, it may predict a more positive outcome than where other, less-readily treatable factors are a material backdrop to violence.

Since the early twentieth century, most states have established juvenile courts to consider youth crime with a view toward rehabilitation. The "best interests of the child" became the standard for adjudication of delinquency, rather than criminality. In a series of transformative cases between 1966 and 1975, the U.S. Supreme Court introduced aspects of criminal procedure designed to protect the liberties of youth while maintaining aspects of the protective relationship with the judge. These cases include *Kent v United States* (requiring due process for juveniles); *Breed v Jones* (preventing double jeopardy); *In re Gault* (expanding due process for juveniles to include notice of charges, right to counsel, right of confrontation/cross examination, and privilege against self-incrimination); *In re Winship* (raising standards for evidence to "beyond a reasonable doubt"); and *McKeiver v Pennsylvania* (rejecting a mandate for a jury trial) (Malmquist, 2002). Although the U.S. Supreme Court never explicitly required a minor to be competent to proceed with adjudication in juvenile court, most states now also require adjudicative competence for youth. Although the *Dusky* standard, discussed below, remains the norm, there is considerable variability and some states explicitly remove the question of immaturity as a factor in juvenile court (Mossman et al., 2007).

With the rise in violent crime by youth offenders in the 1980s through early 1990s, many states have revised the age at which juvenile offenders may stand trial in an adult criminal court. A trial in adult court may occur through several mechanisms. In the case of mandatory waiver, a state statue may require youth of a specified minimal age who commit a particular offense to be transferred to adult court. In many states, a statutory exclusion waiver removes certain age, offense, and prior record categories from juvenile jurisdiction. Thus, a child who commits a particular offense may begin proceedings directly in the adult court system. Other waivers permit prosecutor discretion or require a minor to bear the burden of proving that she should not be sent to adult court. Ultimately, the minor may be sent to adult court. Accordingly, the question of competency to stand criminal trial now reaches increasing numbers of adolescent offenders.

Competency to stand trial first developed in the case of adult offenders. The modern standard for competency to stand trial was articulated in the 1960 U.S. Supreme Court decision in *Dusky v United States.* The Court defined the test for competency as "whether a defendant has sufficient present ability to consult with his lawyer with a reasonable degree of rational understanding and whether he has a rational as well as factual understanding of the proceedings against him" ("Dusky v. United States, 362 US 402," 1960). Most jurisdictions define competence as "the defendant must have an understanding of the nature of the charges against him and the nature and purpose of court proceedings, and he must be able to cooperate with an attorney in his own defense" (Appelbaum & Gutheil, 2007). States have generally not altered the standard of competency to exempt juvenile defendants who may be too immature to understand the proceedings, despite robust research suggesting that developmental factors, emotional maturity, and younger age (under age 14) may be strong indictors of incompetence (Mossman et al., 2007; Savitsky & Karras, 1984). Although some states set a minimum age for jurisdiction, once a juvenile defendant achieves that age and is before the adult court, the same *Dusky* standard applies (Fortunati, Morgan, Temporini, & Southwick, 2006).

American courts typically require a court appointed clinician to examine the defendant, and generally the trial judge will determine competency. In cases where a jury makes this determination, the clinician's report is also an important basis for deliberation. A number of screening tools are used by clinicians to aid in assessing whether a defendant is competent to stand trial. These tests include: the Competency to Stand Trial Screening Test (CST); the Georgia Court Competency Test (GCCT); the Competency Checklist; the Competency to Stand Trial Assessment Interview (CAI); the Interdisciplinary Fitness Interview (IFI); the Computer Assisted Determination of Competency to Stand Trial (CADCOMP); the McArthur Competence Assessment Tool—Criminal Adjudication Tool (Mac CAT-CA); the Evaluation of Competency to Stand Trial—Revised (ECST-R); and the Competency Assessment for Standing Trial for Defendants with Mental Retardation (CAST-MR) (Melton, Petrila, Poythress, & Slobogin, 1997; Mossman et al., 2007). Of note, these tests are designed for adult offenders. The extent to which they can be reliably adapted for use with a child or young adolescent has been questioned (Oberlander, Goldstein, & Ho, 2001).

The skill and experience of the evaluator plays a critical role in a forensic assessment of a child or adolescent. Each child must be carefully evaluated as to his or her ability to meet the competency standard. School records, Individualized Education Plans (IEPs), and pediatrician and psychiatric treatment records are also critical collateral sources of information.

Assessments of knowledge, reasoning ability, and mental illness each may be a factor in a competency decision. We know that rational decision-making can be impaired by mental illness. Psychotic patients do not necessarily lack competence to stand trial, however, particularly where treatment can reconstitute an individual's ability to understand his circumstances and participate in court. Moreover, an intellectually or developmentally compromised child—whether or not psychotic—may be less capable of "rational" understanding than another child of the same age. *Jackson v Indiana*, 406 U.S. 715 (1972) permits the state to hold a defendant for a "reasonable time" to allow him to become competent.

Juveniles who are deemed incompetent due to knowledge deficit may be "remedied" through education or (less frequently) held until they mature to an age of competence. Distinguishing a knowledge deficit from one of reasoning ability, however, is a critical question that cannot be separated from a child's developmental status. While knowledge can be taught, reasoning ability is arguably not a learned faculty (Fortunati et al., 2006).

Section 3 Policy Considerations—Gun Control

Case Four

An engaging, outspoken 14-year-old boy enrolled in a New York City District 75 School (a special education school) was in psychiatric treatment for a long history of mood and behavioral dysregulation. He reported to his therapist that he would like to "get a gun" to "kill the guy who shot my friend." The therapist investigated to corroborate the patient's story, learning that the child's adolescent neighbor had been shot in the chest a few blocks from school, allegedly after refusing to hand over his new sports jacket to the perpetrator. The patient had notable interpersonal strengths, was adherent to treatment, and was under parental supervision, but lived in a community struggling with significant gang violence. How should the therapist respond to his threats?

The debate on gun violence has a particular resonance in child psychiatry, and a clinician may have additional duties in the case of the potentially violent, mentally ill adolescent. A gun was used in nearly 69% of murders by youth, according to data from 2002 (Snyder & Sickmund, 2006). Between 1997 and 2001, the Bureau of Labor Statistics collected the National Longitudinal Survey of Youth (NLSY97), asking a sample of nearly 9,000 youth who were ages 12–16 years on December 31, 1996, about aspects of their life, including law-violating behaviors. This study found that 16% of all youth carried a handgun, including 25% of males, by age 17 (Snyder and Sickmund, 2006).

At this time, reducing the risk posed by gun use remains primarily focused on an individual assessment, rather than mitigated by overarching societal protections. The federal Youth Handgun Safety Act (1996) made it unlawful for any person to provide a handgun to a juvenile under 18 years of age. Most states have similar statutes restricting handgun ownership by minors. However, rifles for hunting or target shooting are generally excluded from state and federal restrictions, and other weapons are less uniformly restricted across states. Moreover, only a few states make gun owners criminally liable for failing to store guns safely, out of the reach of children (Ash, 2001). Overall, risk reduction is not robust.

New York State has led the nation in linking mental illness to gun licensing, by requiring clinicians to report patients who are likely to engage in serious harm. A question now arises in New York State as to whether a risk assessment of an older adolescent may trigger a duty to report under statute. On

January 15, 2013, the New York legislature passed and the governor signed into law the New York Secure Ammunition and Firearms Enforcement Act of 2013 (NY SAFE Act). Among its provisions is one requiring mental health professionals to report patients who are "likely to engage in conduct that would result in serious harm to self or others," codified as Sec. 9.46 of the Mental Hygiene Law. The statue imposes a reporting obligation on every "mental health professional," defined as a "physician, psychologist, registered nurse, or licensed clinical social worker," who is "currently providing treatment services to a person" whose behavior meets the statute's requirements. All physicians and nurses, not only psychiatrists or psychiatric nurses, appear to be covered by the statute. A reporting obligation exists when a mental health professional "determines, in the exercise of reasonable professional judgment, that such person is likely to engage in conduct that would result in serious harm to self or others." Information about people reported under the statute will be contained in a State database that will be maintained for five years. The statute does not specifically exclude or include minors. Although minors are not eligible for gun licensing, an adolescent may become eligible within five years of a reporting date. Accordingly, it would seem reasonable to use the patient's age as one of the factors in making a determination as to whether that patient is "likely to engage in conduct that would result in serious harm."

In navigating reporting mandates and duties to warn, therapeutic content needs to be considered in the context of an integrated psychiatric formulation. Adolescents in particular bring complicated fantasies to treatment discussions, which should be interpreted against a history of actual violence, risk factors for violence such as delineated above, or severe psychotic disturbance. Since *Tarasoff* opened the door to liability, clinicians have repeatedly countered that predicting future dangerousness is beyond their expertise and simply is not possible (Gellerman & Suddath, 2005). Repeatedly, studies suggest that clinicians have limited tools and a poor track record for making long-term predictions of violence (Dolan & Doyle, 2000; Mossman, 1994). Moreover, patients have sued mental health providers alleging that confidentiality was breached when the providers made what they believed was a required "Tarasoff warning" (Peralta, 2002; Renaud, 2000). Linking violence to mental illness, as the New York SAFE Act has essentially codified, further runs the risk of stigmatizing and discouraging the mentally ill from seeking or being brought by family members for treatment. It remains to be seen whether the results will be the disabling of the most dangerous potential offenders.

Conclusions

Dangerousness is not a diagnostic judgment as much as a comprehensive psychosocial assessment. This complexity plays out in assessing which patients are at highest risk of committing violence, when an adolescence lacks competence to stand trial for his or her actions, as well as when a clinician must report on a potentially violent patient. The difficulty of assessing likely harm as well as competence is compounded in the case of adolescent patients, for whom we have substantially adapted adult screening tools not directly applicable to the underdeveloped brain of the child and adolescent. At the same time, reports of adolescent violence continue to be headline news, with public outcry at the lack of screening or intervention that contributed to the tragedies. While the impression that youth violence is occurring because of mental illness is likely overly simplistic, the fact remains we have a dire lack of mental health services for youth at risk.

References

Appelbaum, P. S., & Gutheil, T. G. (2007). *Clinical Handbook of Psychiatry and the Law* (4th ed., pp. 216–259). Philadelphia, PA: Lippincott Williams & Wilkins.

Aro, S., Aro, H., & Keskim, I. (1995). Socio-economic mobility among patients with schizophrenia of major affective disorder: A 17-year retrospective follow-up. *The British Journal of Psychiatry, 166*(6), 759–767.

Ash, P. (2001). Children's access to weapons. In D. Schetky & E. Benedek (Eds.), *Comprehensive Textbook of Child and Adolescent Forensic Psychiatry* (pp. 225–230). Washington, DC: American Psychiatric Press.

Cal. Civ. Code §43.92 (2007).

Clare, P., Bailey, S., & Clark, A. (2000). Relationship between psychotic disorders in adolescence and criminally violent behaviour: A retrospective examination. *The British Journal of Psychiatry, 177*(3), 275–279. doi:10.1192/bjp.177.3.275

Corrigan, P. W., & Watson, A. C. (2002). Understanding the impact of stigma on people with mental illness. *World Psychiatry, 1*(1), 16–20.

Dolan, M., & Doyle, M. (2000). Violence risk prediction: Clinical and actuarial measures and the role of the Psychopathy Checklist. *The British Journal of Psychiatry, 177*(4), 303–311. doi:10.1192/bjp.177.4.303

Dusky v. United States, 362 US 402. (1960).

Elbogen, E. B., & Johnson, S. C. (2009). The intricate link between violence and mental disorder. *Archives of General Psychiatry, 66*(2), 152–161.

Eng, J. (2012, June 9). Man shot to death by police even though family told 911 his gun was fake. *NBC News.* Retrieved from http://usnews.nbcnews.com/_news/2012/07/09/12643465-man-shot-to-death-by-police-even-though-family-told-911-his-gun-was-fake?lite

Fazel, M., Langstrom, N., Grann, M., & Fazel, S. (2008). Psychopathology in adolescent and young adult criminal offenders (15–21years) in Sweden. *Social Psychiatry and Psychiatric Epidemiology, 43*(4), 319–324.

Fitzgerald, P. B., De Castella, A., Filia, K., Filia, S., Benitez, J., & Kulkarni, J. (2005). Victimization of patients with schizophrenia and related disorders. *Australian and New Zealand Journal of Psychiatry, 39*(3), 169–174.

Folsom, D. P., Hawthorne, W., Lindamer, L., Gilmer, T., Bailey, A., Golshan, S., . . . Jeste, D. V. (2005). Prevalence and risk factors for homelessness and utilization of mental health services among 10,340 patients with serious mental illness in a large public mental health system. *The American Journal of Psychiatry, 162*(2), 370–6. doi:10.1176/appi.ajp.162.2.370

Fortunati, F., Morgan, C. A., Temporini, H., & Southwick, S. (2006). Juveniles and Competency to Stand Trial. *Psychiatry (Edgmont), 3*(3), 35–38.

Friedman, R. A. (2006). Violence and mental illness—how strong is the link? *The New England Journal of Medicine, 355*(20), 2064–6. doi:10.1056/NEJMp068229

Gellerman, D. M., & Suddath, R. (2005). Violent fantasy, dangerousness, and the duty to warn and protect. *The Journal of the American Academy of Psychiatry and the Law, 33*(4), 484–95. Retrieved from http://www.ncbi.nlm.nih.gov/pubmed/16394225

Goode, E., & Healy, J. (2013, January 31). Focus on mental health laws to curb violence is unfair, some say. *The New York Times.* New York. Retrieved from http://www.nytimes.com/2013/02/01/us/focus-on-mental-health-laws-to-curb-violence-is-unfair-some-say.html?pagewanted=all&_r=0

Hamman v. County of Maricopa, 161 Ariz 58, 775 P.2d 1122. (1989).

Heide, K. M., & Boots, D. P. (2007). A comparative analysis of media reports of U.S. parricide cases with officially reported national crime data and the psychiatric and psychological literature. *International Journal of Offender Therapy and Comparative Criminology, 51*(6), 646–75. doi:10.1177/0306624X07302053

Herbert, P. B., & Young, K. A. (2002). Tarasoff at twenty-five. *The Journal of the American Academy of Psychiatry and the Law, 30*(2), 275–81. Retrieved from http://www.ncbi.nlm.nih.gov/pubmed/12108565

Hiday, V. A., Swartz, M. S., Swanson, J. W., Borum, R., & Wagner, H. R. (1999). Criminal victimization of persons with severe mental illness. *Psychiatric Services, 50*(1), 62–68.

Hughes, K., Bellis, M. A., Jones, L., Wood, S., Bates, G., Eckley, L., . . . Officer, A. (2012). Prevalence and risk of violence against children with disabilities: a systematic review and meta-analysis of observational studies. *The Lancet, 379*(9826), 1621–1629.

James, D. J., & Glaze, L. E. (2006). Mental health problems of prison and jail inmates. *Bureau of Justice Statistics, NCJ 213600.*

Khalid, F. N., Ford, T., & Maughan, B. (2012). Aggressive behavior and psychosis in a clinically referred child and adolescent sample. *Social Psychiatry and Psychiatric Epidemiology, 47*(11), 1795–1806.

Kristof, N. (2014, February 8). Inside a mental hospital called jail. *The New York Times.* New York. Retrieved from http://www.nytimes.com/2014/02/09/opinion/sunday/inside-a-mental-hospital-called-jail.html?_r=0

Lewis, D., Pincus, J., Bard, B., Richardson, E., Prichep, L., Feldman, M., & Yeager, C. (1998). Neuropsychiatric, psychoeducational, and family characteristics of 14 juveniles condemned to death in the United States. *American Journal of Psychiatry, 145*(5), 584–589.

Malmquist, C. P. (2002). Overview of juvenile law. In D. H. Schetky & E. P. Benedek (Eds.), *Principles and Practice of Child and Adolescent Forensic Psychiatry* (pp. 259–266). Washington, DC: American Psychiatric Publishing.

Melton, G. B., Petrila, J., Poythress, N. G., & Slobogin, C. (1997). Competency to stand trial. In *Psychological Evaluations for the Courts: A Handbook for Mental Health Professionals and Lawyers* (2nd ed., pp. 119–155). New York, NY: Guilford.

Mossman, D. (1994). Assessing predictions of violence: being accurate about accuracy. *Journal of Consulting and Clinical Psychology, 62*(4), 783–792.

Mossman, D., Noffsinger, S. G., Ash, P., Frierson, R. L., Gerbasi, J., Hackett, M., . . . Zonana, H. V. (2007). AAPL practice guideline for the forensic psychiatric evaluation of competence to stand trial. *The Journal of the American Academy of Psychiatry and the Law, 35*(4). Retrieved from http://www.ncbi.nlm.nih.gov/pubmed/18398958

Myers, W. C., Scott, K., Burgess, A. W., & Burgess, A. G. (1995). Psychopathology, biopsychosocial factors, crime characteristics and classification of 25 homicidal youths.

Journal of the American Academy of Child and Adolescent Psychiatry, 34(11), 1483–1489.

Oberlander, L., Goldstein, N., & Ho, C. (2001). Preadolescent adjudicative competence: methodological considerations and recommendations for practice standards. *Behavioral Sciences & the Law, 19*(4), 545–563.

Palijan, T. Z., Radeljak, S., Kovac, M., & Kovacević, D. (2010). Relationship between comorbidity and violence risk assessment in forensic psychiatry—The implication of neuroimaging studies. *Psychiatria Danubina, 22*(2), 253–6. Retrieved from http://www.ncbi.nlm.nih.gov/pubmed/20562756

Peralta, J. (2002, April 18). Teacher files suit against hospital. *Orange County Register,* Santa Ana, p. 1.

Renaud, T. (2000, January 17). Ex-cop in Ga. wins rare confidentiality case. *National Law Journal,* p. A13.

Rosa, P. (2012, February 8). US teen killer in "amazing" murder sentenced to life. *The Telegraph.* New York. Retrieved from http://www.telegraph.co.uk/news/worldnews/northamerica/usa/9069456/US-teen-killer-in-amazing-murder-sentenced-to-life.html

Savitsky, J. C., & Karras, D. (1984). Competency to stand trial among adolescents. *Adolescence, 19*(74), 349–358.

Schizophrenia. (n.d.). Retrieved from http://www.nimh.nih.gov/statistics/1schiz.shtml

Shaw, J., Hunt, I. M., Flynn, S., Meehan, J., Robinson, J., Bickley, H., . . . Appleby, L. (2006). Rates of mental disorder in people convicted of homicide. National clinical survey. *The British Journal of Psychiatry, 188*(2), 143–147. doi:10.1192/bjp.188.2.143

Silver, E., Mulvey, E. P., & Monahan, J. (1999). Assessing violence risk among discharged psychiatric patients: towards an ecological approach. *Law and Human Behavior, 23*(2), 237–255.

Simon, R. I. (2011, March 3). Patient violence against health care professionals. *Psychiatric Times.* Retrieved from http://pro.psychcentral.com/2012/patient-violence-against-health-care-professionals/00775.html

Snyder, H. N. (2008). Juvenile arrests 2005. *Juvenile Justice Bulletin. US Department of Justice Office of Juvenile Justice and Delinquency Prevention.* National Juvenile Court Data Archive.

Snyder, H. N., & Sickmund, M. (2006). Juvenile offenders and victims: 2006 National Report. *Juvenile Justice Bulletin. US Department of Justice Office of Juvenile Justice and Delinquency Prevention.* National Juvenile Court Data Archive.

Steadman, H. J., Mulvey, E. P., Monahan, J., Robbins, P. C., Appelbaum, P. S., Grisso, T., . . . Silver, E. (1998). Violence by people discharged from acute psychiatric inpatient facilities and by others in the same neighborhoods. *Archives of General Psychiatry, 55*(5), 393–401. Retrieved from http://www.ncbi.nlm.nih.gov/pubmed/9596041

Swanson, J. (1994). Mental disorder, substance abuse, and community violence: an epidemiological approach. In J. Monahan & H. Steadman (Eds.), *Violence and Mental Disorder: Developments in Risk Assessment* (pp. 101–136). Chicago, IL: University of Chicago Press.

Swanson, J., Swartz, M., Estroff, S., Borum, R., Wagner, R., & Hiday, V. (1998). Psychiatric impairment, social contact, and violent behavior: evidence form a study of outpatient committed persons with severe mental behavior. *Social Psychiatry and Psychiatric Epidemiology, 33*(1), S86–S94.

Swanson, J. W., Swartz, M. S., Van Dorn, R. a, Elbogen, E. B., Wagner, H. R., Rosenheck, R. A, . . . Lieberman, J. A. (2006). A national study of violent behavior in persons with schizophrenia. *Archives of General Psychiatry, 63*(5), 490–9. doi:10.1001/archpsyc.63.5.490

Tarasoff v. Regents of the University of California, 551 P.2d 334. (1976).

Teplin, L. A., McClelland, G. M., Abram, K. M., & Weiner, D. A. (2005). Crime victimization in adults with severe mental illness. *Archives of General Psychiatry, 62*(8), 911–921.

Torrey, E. F. (1994). Violent behavior by individuals with serious mental illness. *Psychiatric Services, 45*(7), 653–62.

Walsh, E., Buchanan, A., & Fahy, T. (2002). Violence and schizophrenia: Examining the evidence. *The British Journal of Psychiatry, 180,* 490–495.

Widgery, A., & Winterfield, A. (2013). Mental health professionals' duty to warn. *National Conference of State Legislatures Legisbrief, 21*(1). Retrieved from http://www.ncsl.org/research/health/mental-health-professionals-duty-to-warn.aspx

Winsper, C., Singh, S. P., Marwaha, S., Amos, T., Lester, H., Everard, L., . . . Birchwood, M. (2013). Pathways to violent behavior during first-episode psychosis: A report from the UK National EDEN Study. *Journal of the American Medical Association Psychiatry, 70*(12), 1287–1293.

Witt, K., van Dorn, R., & Fazel, S. (2013). Risk factors for violence in psychosis: Systematic review and meta-regression analysis of 110 studies. *PloS One, 8*(2), e55942. doi:10.1371/journal.pone.0055942

INDEX